This book of original scope and methodolog..
ary essays on the 'high' political culture of ....
Through the exploitation of new manuscript material, or hitherto ....
artistic sources – the plates reproduce over sixty contemporary images – the
authors open up new perspectives on the ideas, institutions, and rituals of
political society.

Drawing on the evidence of art and literature, and using the latest techniques
for the discovery of lost mentalities, key aspects of Tudor political culture are
explored, including royal iconography, funereal symbolism, parliamentary elections, political vocabularies, kinship and family at court and in the country, and
the architecture of urban authority. In his Introduction the editor uses the
example of Henry VIII's historical break with Rome to suggest the seamless
links between politics and political culture, how and why the revolution of the
1530s needs to be seen against the backdrop of early-Tudor memories of Henry
V, the cult of chivalry and the invasion of France (1513), and the pre-
Reformation imagery of 'imperial' kingship.

TUDOR POLITICAL CULTURE

TUDOR POLITICAL CULTURE

Edited by

DALE HOAK

College of William and Mary

CAMBRIDGE
UNIVERSITY PRESS

PUBLISHED BY THE PRESS SYNDICATE OF THE UNIVERSITY OF CAMBRIDGE
The Pitt Building, Trumpington Street, Cambridge, United Kingdom

CAMBRIDGE UNIVERSITY PRESS
The Edinburgh Building, Cambridge CB2 2RU, UK
40 West 20th Street, New York NY 10011–4211, USA
477 Williamstown Road, Port Melbourne, VIC 3207, Australia
Ruiz de Alarcón 13, 28014 Madrid, Spain
Dock House, The Waterfront, Cape Town 8001, South Africa

http://www.cambridge.org

First published 1995
First paperback edition 2002

A catalogue record for this book is available from the British Library

Library of Congress Cataloguing in Publication data
Tudor political culture / edited by Dale Hoak.
      p.   cm.
ISBN 0 521 40494 0
1. Great Britain – Politics and government – 1485–1603.   I. Hoak, Dale.
DA315.T76 1995
942.05–dc20 94-760 CIP

ISBN 0 521 40494 0 hardback
ISBN 0 521 52014 2 paperback

To Megan and Brady

Contents

Illustrations

FIGURES

Contributors

J. F. R. DAY, Assistant Professor of English at Troy State University, read history at Regent's Park College, Oxford, before taking a Ph D in English literature at Duke University. His study of seventeenth-century character books and the sale of honour has been serialised in *The Coat of Arms*, the journal of the Heraldry Society.

DAVID DEAN, a member of the department of history at Carleton University, is the author of numerous articles on Elizabethan parliamentary history. He has co-edited *The Parliaments of Elizabethan England* (Oxford, 1990) and *Interest Groups and Legislation in Elizabethan Parliaments* (1989) and is completing a book on the legislation of the later Elizabethan parliaments.

JOHN GUY is Professor of Modern History and Head of the School of History and International Relations at the University of St Andrews. He is the author of *Tudor England* (Oxford, 1988), a co-editor of the *Cambridge Studies in Early Modern British History* series, and is currently writing the *New Oxford History of England, 1461–1547* for Oxford University Press.

PETER C. HERMAN (Ph D, Columbia University) teaches English at Georgia State University. He has edited *Rethinking the Henrician Era: Essays on Early Tudor Texts and Contexts* (Champaign, IL, 1994) and is presently at work on two projects, a study of Shakespeare's Elizabethan plays and another on the effects of antipoetic sentiment on Renaissance literature.

DALE HOAK, Professor of History at the College of William and Mary, has co-edited and contributed to *The World of William III and Mary II: Anglo-Dutch Perspectives on the Revolution of 1688–89* (Stanford, CA, 1995). He is presently writing a book on war, reformation, and rebellion in England, 1540–53, for the Cambridge Studies in Early Modern British History series.

NORMAN JONES, Professor of History at Utah State University, is the author of *Faith by Statute: Parliament and the Settlement of Religion, 1559* (1982) and

God and the Moneylenders: Usury and Law in Early-Modern England (Oxford, 1989), and co-editor of *The Parliaments of Elizabethan England* (Oxford, 1990) and *Interest Groups and Legislation in Elizabethan Parliaments* (1989).

JOHN N. KING is Professor of English at The Ohio State University. He has written three books published by Princeton University Press: *English Reformation Literature: The Tudor Origins of the Protestant Tradition* (1982), *Tudor Royal Iconography: Literature and Art in an Age of Religious Crisis* (1989), and *Spenser's Poetry and the Reformation Tradition* (1990).

THOMAS F. MAYER (Ph D, University of Minnesota) teaches history at Augustana College. The author of *Thomas Starkey and the Commonweal* (Cambridge, 1989), he has also edited Starkey's *Dialogue between Pole and Lupset* (Camden Society, 1989) and *Political Thought and the Tudor Commonwealth* (1992). He was a Mellon Fellow at Harvard and in 1992–3, a Fellow at Villa I Tatti, Florence.

DAVID HARRIS SACKS (Ph D, Harvard) is Associate Professor of History and Humanities at Reed College. The author of *Trade Society, and Politics in Bristol, 1500–1640* (2 vols., New York, 1985) and *The Widening Gate: Bristol and the Atlantic Economy, 1450–1700* (Berkeley, CA, 1991), he is working on monopoly and liberty in late Elizabethan and early Stuart England.

W. J. TIGHE, Assistant Professor of History at Muhlenberg College, received the Ph D degree from the University of Cambridge in 1984 for his dissertation on the gentelmen pensioners in the reign of Elizabeth I. The author of numerous articles on Elizabethan politics, government, religion, and society, he is currently engaged in a study of the Elizabethan court and privy chamber.

ROBERT TITTLER, who was trained at Oberlin College and New York University, lives and teaches in Montreal. His most recent work is *Architecture and Power, the Town Hall and the English Urban Community, 1500–1640* (Oxford, 1991). He is presently investigating the impact of the Reformation on English urban society.

RETHA M. WARNICKE (Ph D, Harvard), a Professor of History at Arizona State University, has published numerous articles on the Tudor period. Her most recent books are *Women of the English Renaissance and Reformation* (Westport, CT, 1983) and *The Rise and Fall of Anne Boleyn: Family Politics at the Court of Henry VIII* (Cambridge, 1989).

Preface

The contributors to this book were asked to explore new aspects of the Tudor polity or re-examine familiar topics in new ways. While all of the papers touch on big themes, together they hardly pretend to define even the central aspects of 'high' political culture. Religion and the law, for example, are not directly treated here; these would obviously have to be included in any sort of comprehensive assessment. As yet there exists no book-length survey of Tudor political culture; the multiple facets of so vast a subject, which necessarily include the symbols, rituals, and mentalities of popular political culture and the relevant intersections of literature and the arts, have so far exceeded the grasp of a single author. If such a book comes into being, it is hoped that the contributors to the present volume will have influenced both the 'look' of the subject and methodological approaches to it. In the 'Introduction' I have tried to suggest why a few of these approaches must now command the full attention of historians. By exploiting either new manuscript material or heretofore untapped visual sources, the contributors to *Tudor Political Culture* have been able to open up new perspectives on some of the most important problems in sixteenth-century English history.

An editor's debts can only be acknowledged, never fully repaid. At Cambridge University Press William Davies proved, in more ways than he can know, to be a model of patience and support. For their advice and assistance in identifying artistic sources and obtaining photographs I wish especially to thank Michael Archer, Deputy Keeper, Department of Ceramics, Victoria and Albert Museum; Melanie Barber, Deputy Librarian and Archivist at Lambeth Palace Library; A. Bavin and Angelo Hornak, London; Henry Button, Fellow Commoner, Christ's College, Cambridge; Thomas Lange, Rare Books Department, The Henry E. Huntington Library; Janet Larkin, Department of Coins, British Museum; Richard Mortimer, Keeper of the Muniments, and Mrs Enid Nixon, Assistant Librarian, Westminster Abbey Library; Rear-Admiral D. E. Macey, Receiver-General for the Dean and Chapter of Canterbury Cathedral; John D. Savage, Warden, St Catherine's Church, Ludham, Norfolk; James R. Sewell, City Archivist, Corporation of London Record Office; John Tuck, Head of

Publications, The John Rylands University Library of Manchester; and Robert C. Yorke, Archivist, The College of Arms. Invariably cheerful help was given by the staffs of the Reading Room and Students' Manuscript Room at the British Library; Bodleian Library; University Library, Cambridge; Institute of Historical Research and University of London Library; and the National Art Library, Victoria and Albert Museum. At the word processor Cindy Lemke transferred dozens of pages to disc and at the laser printer Theresa Cruz and Doris Emerson printed out numerous drafts of all parts of the manuscript.

Williamsburg, Virginia   DALE HOAK

Foreword

by GEOFFREY ELTON

History and our knowledge of it never stand still, and historians would therefore be ill-advised to turn immobile. And though the Tudor age has of late been treated as essentially worked through, there is a lot still to be done both by way of elaboration and by way of re-thinking: as this volume proves. Thus we have long regarded the sixteenth-century monarchy as the main and visible embodiment of the nation-state, but the work of Tom Mayer and especially of Dale Hoak provides a new and vastly extended background for the imperial claims derived from Constantine and brought forward by experiences in the wars with France. Especially interesting is the learned working out of the visible manifestations of power that made kingship and its instruments so real to the generality (John King and David Dean). We have always respected the functions of kin relationships, but Retha Warnicke's demonstration of the part played in court politics by family structures, or Bill Tighe's demonstration of the way a family used local influence to exert claims at court, both add important substance to generalization. One welcomes the evidence that the growth of effective power was not confined to royal persons but manifested itself in areas as diverse as town government (Robert Tittler) and the king's own parliament (Norman Jones). One especially welcomes informed insights into the role of heraldry and glory (J. F. R. Day) and the searching analysis which discerns the beginning of the oncoming attack on the kind of monarchy that Henry VIII thought God's gift to himself in the debates about monopolies (David Sacks) and about the proper role of counsel (John Guy). There should be, and no doubt there will be, much argument about these explorations of Tudor political culture. I hope that two, more or less ideological, themes too little regarded here will receive attention: both religion and the law in effect operated to limit the extremes of monarchism. From my point of view the most gratifying impression derives from the fact that of the twelve authors five were my graduate students and two more have been in frequent learned discourse with me. Yet not one of them – absolutely rightly – bothers to argue about my views, and Thomas Cromwell hardly appears! *Vivant libertas mentis et progressus historiae.*

Abbreviations

APC	*Acts of the Privy Council of England*, ed. J. R. Dasent, 32 vols., 1890–1907
BIHR	*Bulletin of the Institute of Historical Research*
BL	British Library
CPR	*Calendar of Patent Rolls, Elizabeth I*
CSP Dom.	*Calendar of State Papers, Domestic Series*
CSP Span.	*Calendar of Letters, Despatches, and State Papers, relating to the negotiations between England and Spain*, eds. G. A. Bergenroth, P. de Gayangos, M. A. S. Hume and R. Tyler (11 vols., 1862–1906)
DNB	*Dictionary of National Biography*
EHR	*English Historical Review*
Hall	Edward Hall, *Hall's Chronicle* (London, 1809)
Hartley	T. E. Hartley (ed.), *Proceedings in the Parliaments of Elizabeth I, 1558–1581* (Leicester, 1981)
HJ	*Historical Journal*
HMC	Historical Manuscripts Commission
Interest Groups	Norman Jones and David Deans (eds.), *Interest Groups and Legislation in Elizabethan Parliaments: Essays Presented to Sir Geoffrey Elton, Parliamentary History*, 8, 2 (1989)
JEH	*Journal of Ecclesiastical History*
LP	*Letters and Papers, Foreign and Domestic of the Reign of Henry VIII*, ed. J. F. Brewer *et al.*, 22 vols. in 35 (London, 1862–1932)
PRO	Public Record Office, Chancery Lane
REED	*Records of Early English Drama*
STC	*A Short Title Catalogue of Books Printed in England, Scotland, & Ireland and of English Books Printed Abroad, 1475–1640*, first compiled by A. W. Pollard and G. R. Redgrave; second edn, revised and enlarged, W. A.

Jackson, F. S. Ferguson, and Katherine Pantzer (3 vols.,
London, 1976–91)

Townshend   Heywood Townshend, *Historical Collections: An Exact
Account of the last four Parliaments of Elizabeth* (1680)

Unless otherwise indicated, the place of publication is London in the notes.

Introduction

The difference between politics and political culture is essentially the difference between political action and the codes of conduct, formal and informal, governing those actions. A history of the former treats the players of the game, a history of the latter, what the players presume the nature and limits of their game to be. Ideally, the two histories should be written as one: political 'reality' is by definition a compound of both.

If the reconstruction of lost political 'realities' comprehends the recovery of political cultures, the challenge for the historian lies in discovering the relevant cultural contexts. The subject matter of 'high culture' provides some obvious avenues of approach: political theory, whether the product of court propagandists or aspirants to office, a body of writing encompassing in particular words of advice and counsel offered to princes; chronicles, tracts and histories embodying social, religious, economic and political commentary, witting and unwitting; evidence of literacy, the dissemination of printed materials and the contents of educational curricula; poetry, prose and dramatic literature; artistic images, architectural programmes and decorative schemes in the fine arts; coronations, civic processions and entertainments of all types, including especially tournaments, masques, pageants, entries, past-times, disguisings and other 'revels' of the royal court.[1]

Of course the foregoing list hardly exhausts the range of possible approaches to the political cultures of the Tudor élite. Public and private ceremonies for the dead offer a potentially rich vein of material, since royal and aristocratic funerals were in a certain sense rituals of socio-political power and status.[2] The trick lies in how to 'read' the extant evidence of the rites and symbols of heraldic funerals, how to understand what contemporaries meant by the form and performance of their obsequies. A case in point is the problem of interpreting the funeral (29 June 1537) of Henry Percy, sixth earl of Northumberland, a peer

---

[1] John Guy has usefully surveyed numerous aspects of these fields in a chapter on 'Political Culture' in his *Tudor England* (Oxford, 1988), ch. 15, pp. 408–36.

[2] For an introductory survey (with a select bibliography) by an art historian, see Nigel Llewellyn, *The Art of Death: Visual Culture in the English Death Ritual c. 1500 – c. 1800* (1991).

best remembered for the sale and granting away of much of his property and the disinheritance of his brother, his only heir, in favour of Henry VIII at the time of the Pilgrimage of Grace. Using the heralds' account of the rite, Gerald Broce and Richard Wunderli thought that Percy's seemingly impromptu internment away from his family's ancestral lands and in the absence of his household officials reflected the triumph of Tudor centralism over the Percys' regional family interests, and so was 'a performance in changed political relations' between Crown and nobility.[3] R. W. Hoyle questioned this by noting that Broce and Wunderli had failed to consider whether the form of the funeral fulfilled the deceased's wishes, for there remains the possibility that, consistent with the pattern of Percy's life, a life of debt, illness, and attempts to provide lands to an affinity who were not his kin, his respectful, arguably well-ordered burial represented 'a definitive rejection of family and status'. A peer's funeral marked 'the occasion at which the estate passed from generation to generation. With a corpse but no heir and little family, a full funeral would have lacked its most vital actor.' Percy was not the victim of Tudor centralism or intimidation; the Crown actually tried to keep his estate together. His funeral logically punctuated Percy's self-effacing, tragic career.[4]

Percy's quiet, obscurely staged obsequies were clearly the exception to a funereal tradition of heraldic display, an aristocratic tradition designed to glorify an individual's knightly status in a society of formally recognized order, rank, and degree. Did Sir Philip Sidney's costly, magnificently mounted funeral procession in the streets of London symbolically subvert the natural order of Elizabethan society? A New Historicist's notion that it did is attacked below (chapter 7) by James Day. Day's argument, which properly situates Sidney's rites in the only context which could be considered relevant, that of heraldic funereal symbolism, makes fresh use of contemporary visual and literary sources as well as the official records of the heralds who organized Sidney's procession.

Day's methodology, which aims at an historically accurate reading of the iconography of honour, shows by how much the history of political culture is an exercise in reconstructing a particular mentality. Historians of the institutions of Tudor central government are not usually given to writing such history. David Dean shows (in chapter 10), however, that if they are to understand the nature of those institutions most fully they must learn to 'see' parliament, for example, as contemporaries would have done, and that the way to this end is the study of parliament as both image and ritual. Although the study of sixteenth-century English institutional rituals is hardly new, it is a study still in its infancy. Thus, while books and articles abound on the making of bills and acts, Dean's contribution is the first to consider how and why the ceremonies of the opening

---

[3] Gerald Broce and Richard M. Wunderli, 'The Funeral of Henry Percy, sixth earl of Northumberland', *Albion*, 22 (1990): 215.

[4] R. W. Hoyle, 'Henry Percy, sixth earl of Northumberland, and the fall of the House of Percy, 1527–1537', in G. W. Bernard (ed.), *The Tudor Nobility* (Manchester, 1992), p. 200.

and closing of a parliament were integral to the business done there, and what visual representations of parliamentary sessions tell us about the institutional mentalities of MPs. This is a new type of parliamentary history, one which makes use of some rare, previously unpublished contemporary images of parliamentary sessions (plate 56, for example).

Although they were non-ceremonial, parliamentary elections may also be classified as political rituals of the Tudor nation. By asking what both electors and the men elected understood those rituals of election (or, following Mark Kishlansky, 'selection') to mean in the reign of Elizabeth I, Norman Jones (in chapter 9) has opened up another window into the political 'mind' of the age. Sir Geoffrey Elton has said that the constitutional revolution of the 1530s transformed 'a community of partly independent orders within one country' into 'a unitary realm where one law ruled both monarch and subjects ...' If the result was the triumph of parliamentary law, i.e. the sovereignty of the king-in-parliament, 'it was in the parliaments of Elizabeth I that the problems now raised and the opportunities now offered first came to be a major concern in political life'.[5] This being so, it should be important to know what Elizabethan MPs thought they were doing in parliament, how, as Jones has said, they conceived of the nature of their representation and the place of parliament in their political culture. On whose behalf did MPs speak? Sixteenth-century political speech had so thoroughly absorbed the language of religion that on important matters of debate appeals to God might be supposed to have informed the wisdom of those who were speaking. But 'the departure of divinity from government', in Jones's apt phrase, left the way open to appeals to individual conscience, and so undermined traditional assumptions about the social basis of government, assumptions which presumed that in a divinely ordained social order of rank and degree, only the well-born enjoyed a natural right of counsel to the queen. Here was a revolution in political mentalities, in attitudes towards the authority for the making of statute, a revolution under-scoring the importance of the study of Elizabethan parliaments and the political vocabulary of Elizabethan parliamentary speeches.

If the law-making roles of Elizabethan MPs had been immeasurably enhanced by the Reformation, and if in the making of law parliament-men looked less to God than to their own consciences for a basis of right, there arose in practice a potential conflict between a queen of divinely ordained office possessed of real prerogatives and powers, including the power to summon and control parliaments, and a parliament representing free men, a community whose consent in parliament was required for the laws which embodied supreme authority. The conflict, as David Harris Sacks shows (in chapter 11) was made manifest in the parliamentary debates over royal patents of monopoly. The language of those

---

[5] G. R. Elton, '*Lex Terrae Victrix*: The Triumph of Parliamentary Law in the Sixteenth Century', in D. M. Dean and N. L. Jones (eds.), *The Parliaments of Elizabethan England* (Oxford, 1990), pp. 35, 36.

debates, and the bodily gestures of those who participated, including Queen Elizabeth's gestures in her famous 'Golden Speech' of 30 November 1601, need to be understood as part of what Sacks calls the accepted rituals of parliamentary accommodation. In the case of monopolies, the political culture of parliamentary debate employed, in Sacks's words, a distinctive 'language of benefits', the content, tone, and form of delivery of which explain why those who spoke it could accept by its terms a resolution of the apparent conflict between the royal prerogative and the interests of those who had not given their consent in a matter (they said) touching the livelihoods and property of the queen's free-born subjects.

Some members of parliament reckoned that on great matters of state theirs was a *right* of counsel, a mode of thinking, for example, that underlay Peter and Paul Wentworth's demand for full freedom of parliamentary speech. But as John Guy so tellingly argues (in chapter 12), none of the languages of political discourse in early modern England recognized parliament as a council in which members enjoyed such a right, and even if the queen had accepted such a view, she still might have rejected the Wentworths' logic on the grounds (as Guy says) 'that counselling was a duty not a right', even in the privy council. No one denied that princes needed good counsel. The question was by whom and on what terms, a question that the Reformation made more insistent, since, as Guy notes, it was the view of some common lawyers that the royal supremacy could only be exercised in parliament, that the queen's *imperium* was limited by parliamentary consent. Debates about whether parliament was the natural locus of *consilium* turned on the meanings of such words, meanings derived from their usage in different rhetorical traditions, the feudal-baronial and the humanist-classical. By clarifying the metaphors of 'counsel' in use under the Tudors and early Stuarts, Guy is able to show why the political rituals of linguistic accommodation discussed by Sacks broke down by 1642, why the vocabulary of 'counsel' failed to provide words sufficient 'for the orderly conduct of politics'.

Parliamentary rituals of accommodation, based fundamentally on an acceptable rhetoric of 'counsel', were designed to produce the harmony that ideally was supposed to characterize the relations of king, lords, and commons. In practice, of course, the exercise of power at the top reveals patterns of control, deference, and manipulation, not to mention the possibilities for exploitation always inherent in social and political hierarchies. Similar patterns of power were to be found in local politics. In chapter 5 Bob Tittler reminds us that after the 1540s, urban governments were becoming more oligarchic and structurally hierarchical. The men who enjoyed this power were often political newcomers, merchants, and master craftsmen without hereditary status, court ties or great regional patrons. Their new secular civic ceremonies were designed to create deference and respect, and their new buildings, especially their town halls, became centres for the display of their newly assumed dignity and authority. Architecturally and decoratively, they fabricated, in Tittler's words, an 'environment of civic hegemony': here was a new material culture of urban power. The breadth and depth of Tittler's researches in the architectural and written remains of this world leave no doubt about the nature of a changed political outlook among the governors of England's towns in the century after the Henrician Reformation.

One aspect of that changed outlook had to do with the social basis of a town's representation in parliament. As Norman Jones notes below, new urban leaders eagerly sought parliamentary franchises for reasons of political prestige, prestige sometimes gained not by sending resident townsmen to parliament, but by securing a great landed patron whose choice of an outside client for the town's seat in parliament would in turn secure for the mayor and aldermen access to regional networks of patronage among the gentry. This is a story of the penetration of the country by the town and *vice versa*, but one aspect of a political culture linking town and country to the court. Such linkage is illuminated in Bill Tighe's discussion (in chapter 6) of the official career of John Scudamore, a Herefordshire country gentleman who was active in his county's affairs in the 1570s and 1580s and who simultaneously held the offices of steward of Hereford city and gentleman pensioner at the court of Elizabeth I. Basing his account on Scudamore's heretofore untapped letters, Tighe builds up a picture of 'the great web' of patronage that connected Scudamore, via men like Sir James Croft, his father-in-law, and Croft's patron, the earl of Leicester, to the mayor and aldermen of Hereford, on the one hand and, on the other, Elizabeth I's privy chamber where his wife, the queen's kinswoman, served as chamberer. Scudamore's dual career as countryman and courtier reveals (in Tighe's words) the 'compenetration' of court influence and country authority, the dynamic basis of what Tighe calls 'the reciprocal nature of the relationship between courtiership and country status'. Within and between the circles of Scudamore's patrons and clients one sees in microcosm nearly the full extent of the social basis of high political culture in the Elizabethan era.

Scudamore's kin provided the keys to his access to offices in local and central government; the greater one's kinfolk or the closer their proximity to the person of the monarch, the better were one's chances of advancement. In aristocratic court society, family connections, and not ideology or faction, arguably define the best context for an appreciation of political action: this is the essence of Retha Warnicke's challenging analysis (in chapter 2) of the circumstances of the rise and fall of Anne Boleyn. Rejecting views which rely on the operations of 'Aragonese' or 'evangelical' factional interests, Warnicke shows that the history of the ties between the Boleyn and Howard families framed Anne's fortunes. However one interprets the evidence used to explain Anne's execution, it is clear that Warnicke's explication of the Boleyn-Howard affinity, which is properly set against the background of histories of English landed families, must serve as the starting point of all future accounts of one of the most sensational episodes in Tudor court politics.

In the coronation pageants staged for her on the occasion of her entry into London (29 May 1533), Anne Boleyn was repeatedly likened to St Anne and her daughter, the Virgin Mary, scenarios based on the late-medieval tradition of praising queens consort as types of holy women. In politics as in officially sponsored spectacles, the Tudors were users and makers of tradition. If in the dramatic literature of the pageant Anne was invested with the familiar religious attributes of a succession of great queens, in politics she none the less embodied a revolutionary break with the past. In his penetrating study of royal icon-ography generated after that break, John King (in chapter 4) shows how printed and painted images of the Tudor sovereigns, some officially sanctioned, others privately commissioned, reflected the ecclesiastical and doctrinal changes wrought successively by the Henrician Reformation, Edwardian protestantism, the Marian reaction, and the accession of Elizabeth I. King's study, which exploits title-page illustrations in the editions of three Bibles, selected woodcuts in John Foxe's *Actes and Monumentes* (the editions of 1563 and 1570), and illustrative material in Elizabethan devotional literature (among other visual sources), is the first systematically to reveal the surprising thematic continuities as well as changes in the new visual media of sixteenth-century politico-religious propaganda.

It has been said that the woodcuts and engravings in the frontispieces of the earliest Bishops' Bibles (1568, 1569) discussed by King constituted 'one of the most influential of all portrait forms of expression', the assumption being that since such Bibles were placed in every parish church, 'they must have been seen by almost every subject'.[6] Whether this is true in fact cannot be known; more certain is the existence of 'an almost universal cult of the royal image in Elizabethan England', a cult the popular relics of which could be seen around many necks. In Queen Elizabeth's day these were the cheap metallic medals 'with rings for suspension [which] were the lower-class equivalent of the cameos and miniatures worn by the upper orders'.[7]

Of course Elizabeth I did not invent this cult. If anyone did it was her grandfather, Henry VII,[8] who, as I have tried to show (in chapter 3), developed a new programme for the visual representation of the royal person. It is surely of psychological interest that the profile he ordered stamped on some of his coins is the first artistic likeness of an English king in that medium (plate 7c). Of greater interest are the images of him in 'majesty', for these appear for the first time in a variety of artistic media and almost invariably show him wearing the arched 'imperial' crown of England. Much has been written about the intellectual

---

[6] Roy Strong, *Portraits of Queen Elizabeth I* (Oxford, 1963), p. 30.   [7] *Ibid.*, p. 32.
[8] The best introduction to the ritualistic and symbolic settings for the projection of the royal image is Sydney Anglo, *Images of Tudor Kingship* (1992).

origins of English imperial kingship, a type of sovereignty first defined in law in 1533–34. The burden of my argument in chapter 3 is that those origins must be made to comprehend the history of the iconography of the closed crown, a royally sponsored artistic tradition dating from the reign of Henry V. Henry VIII made powerful use of this tradition from the very moment of his coronation; it should be clear now to whom he owed his 'vision' of the majestic symbolism of 'imperial' kingship.

At eighteen, when he came to the throne, Henry VIII wanted nothing so much as to be known as one who could match the valour of his namesake at Agincourt, and so in France in 1513 an English King Henry once again would lay siege to French walls and towns. There can be no doubt about how Henry VIII viewed Henry V's legacy in France. But, as Tom Mayer demonstrates (in chapter 1) in a powerful reappraisal of the jurisdictional implications of Henry VIII's first French war, the English occupation of Tournai, though short-lived (1513–17), anticipated the revolution of 1533–34, not a revived Lancastrian *imperium*. Mayer's analysis, which draws heavily on continental jurisprudential sources, should forever change the way we think about the theory and practice of early Tudor kingship.

Mayer's discussion of the legal ramifications of Henry VIII's administration of Tournai frames one of the great problems of early Tudor statecraft, why the king launched three strategically myopic and financially disastrous wars against France (1513, 1522–23, and 1544). Exclusively political explanations of the origins of these conflicts – that in 1513 a factious war party in the king's council pushed Henry into hostilities, that the balance within a new European state 'system' dictated England's role *vis-à-vis* France, etc. – fail to recognize how Henry conceived of the need for war in the first place. Honour, not reasons of state, informed his thinking about the proper conduct of kings, and the king whose conduct was most worthy of study in this context was Henry V.[9]

Henry VIII's self-conscious, self-promoting efforts to emulate the behaviour of Henry V has allowed students of this subject the convenience of discounting the seriousness of the Tudor claim to the French throne, a claim which, because it appears to us to have been anachronistic, seemingly renders irrational Henry VIII's aim of recovering France upon his accession. The political culture of English chivalry explains this seeming unreason. 'Chivalry' describes not only the ethics of knightly conduct – an 'honourable' sensibility institutionalized, for example, in the Order of the Garter – but also feats of arms, and both, it is clear, directly influenced politics at the courts of Henry VII and Henry VIII.[10] Because fifteenth-century kings, including Henry VII, had nationalized the cult of chivalry, Henry VIII felt compelled to equal or surpass the most virtuous deeds

---

[9] Steven Gunn, 'The French Wars of Henry VIII', in J. Black (ed.), *The Origins of War in Early Modern Europe* (Edinburgh, 1987), pp. 28–51.

[10] Steven Gunn, 'Chivalry and the Politics of the Early Tudor Court', in Sidney Anglo (ed.), *Renaissance Chivalry* (Woodbridge, Suffolk, 1990), pp. 107–28.

of the Lancastrians and Yorkists. Knightly glory required that he choose war in 1513; he must become a warrior in the mould of Henry V in order to recover his inheritance, the French crown worn by Henry VI at St Denis. His ability to do so became 'a test of his place in national history'.[11]

In the hands of early-Tudor propagandists, English national history could be written as Tudor dynastic history with a purpose, and in the making of the myth of Tudor legitimacy, both Henry V and his son, Henry VI, were given providential parts. Shakespeare's use of the myth created another kind of history, one so powerful that in the popular imagination his history plays, all of which he wrote in the 1590s, could be read in places as patriotic expressions of the spirit of the nation. *Henry V* (1599), the last of the cycle, has certainly been read and performed as such. Thus the 'history' of the history plays, the product of a surpassingly brilliant Elizabethan imagination, conveys the essence of the Tudors' political genius, their ability to identify their kingship with their subjects' sense of nationhood and national purpose. Or so it would seem. In chapter 8, Peter Herman advances the provocative thesis that *Henry V* disproves this, that the play really attempts a 'deconstruction of Tudor legitimacy', that it subtly undercuts the legend of Henry V by giving voice to the undeniable socio-political tensions of the 1590s, to the recorded hostility of some Elizabethans to Elizabeth I and her government. Herman's argument obviously underscores the importance of reading the play in context. In his 'Introduction' to The New Cambridge Shakespeare edition of *King Henry V*, Andrew Gurr draws attention to one of the indisputable facts of English public life in the 1590s, the national preoccupation with war and the morality of war. Military manoeuvres overseas, war-weariness (as the decade progressed), fear of invasion, the presence of large numbers of troops in London, the unprecedented, enormous outpouring of published military propaganda, and books about strategy and tactics: these and the popular memory of Henry V and his victories (which was peaking in the 1590s) together form part of the essential background of the play.[12]

A systematic study of the political culture of Tudor warfare has yet to be written. In concluding this introduction, I should like to suggest how, for the reign of Henry VIII, such a study might treat the seamless links between politics and political culture, how it might reveal the interconnectedness of seemingly disparate phenomena, in this case Henrician chivalry, overseas war, 'imperial' iconography, and the Reformation of the 1530s. We have already seen how the culture of knightly honour explains the motivation of Henry's war policy in 1513. The martial aspects of that culture also explain the king's intensely personal interest in the waging of war. Henry's early, very lavish court tournaments (1509–11), jousts in which the athletic young king himself played the central part, were more than symbolic war-games; in a certain sense they were

---

[11] Gunn, 'The French Wars of Henry VIII', p. 39.
[12] *King Henry V*, ed. Andrew Gurr (Cambridge, 1992), pp. 1–2, 17, 23–5, 28.

dress rehearsals for the invasion of 1513. The tourneys of the period prior to 1513 also can be seen as links to later, more momentous events. Although the break with Rome in 1533, for example, is usually framed against the backdrop of royal dynastic policy, the policy that propelled Anne Boleyn to prominence by 1526 does not alone explain Henry's attack on the English Church in 1530–31. The famous *praemunire* manoeuvres of 1530–31 were also spurred by a financial crisis. Henry needed to claim a superior jurisdiction over English clerics in order to gain full access to ecclesiastical revenues. At a time when the Church was relatively rich, the crown was sliding towards bankruptcy, a slide precipitated by the cost of Henry's first two wars against France. It is not, I think, unreasonable to suggest that early-Tudor war-making, and the tourneys which were a prelude to it, were forceful engines of the events propelling Henry towards the revolution of the 1530s.

Another dimension of early-Tudor warfare suggestively connects the culture of Henrician chivalry to the papacy and via the papacy, to the inflated image of Henry VIII as a king of the greatest stature. This connection is revealed by contemporary Anglo-papal conceptions of the *religious* nature of the first French war, a war which in 1512 both London and Rome were projecting as a crusade to defend Pope Julius II against Louis XII, the schismatic king of France. It was agreed that if in the course of the crusade Henry defeated Louis, Julius himself would crown Henry king of France, transferring to him all of Louis's lands and titles: so much Julius had promised Henry in a brief of 1512. This unique promise, which Henry would never forget, died with Julius in 1513, but in 1521 when Julius's successor, Leo X, was reminded of it, he twice gave Henry reason enough to believe that Rome had accepted him as the most worthy of Christian kings, a crusader and conqueror. This acceptance first took the form of the papally conferred title *Defensor Fidei*. Although specifically chosen in October 1521 in reward for Henry's *Assertio Septem Sacramentorum* against Luther, the title also effectively embodied the pope's gratitude for Henry's repeated pronouncements of loyalty, the most spectacular expression of which had been Henry's self-dedicated, very detailed offer of about August 1519 personally to lead a crusade against the Infidel.[13] (Henry had been reading in manuscript an English history of the crusades compiled especially for him.)

A second, now-forgotten gesture of thanks in 1521 was Pope Leo's own extraordinary proposal for an enormous funerary monument for Henry, the completed wooden model of which, by Baccio Bandinelli, was described by Leonardo Sellaio in a letter of 14 December 1521 to Michelangelo. Bandinelli's never-realized scheme, which resembles some of Leonardo da Vinci's designs for the Trivulzio monument, would have rivalled in cost and scale Michelangelo's tomb for Julius II; indeed, it probably would have been the most grandiose tomb ever built for any person in Christian history. The design called for an

[13] J. J. Scarisbrick, *Henry VIII* (1968), p. 105.

equestrian statue of the king atop a triumphal arch modelled on that of Septimius Severus in Rome; 142 life-size bronze statues of prophets, apostles, etc. were to be placed about the arch. Although we do not know just how Bandinelli intended to portray his mounted subject – as *imperator* or conquering crusader? – it has been remarked that the combination of arch and equestrian ensemble is clearly imperial in character.[14] In this the architect was probably following imperial Roman models, though the combination would have been unique for the representation of a contemporary European king. Since from the moment of his accession Henry had wanted the world to know that he was the equal of an emperor – he so presented himself on the international stage in 1513 in the presence of Emperor Maximilian I (see chapter 3) – the intriguing question is, had the papacy, in the person of Leo X, accepted the Tudors' by then well-known assertion of an English king's 'imperial' dignity? Bandinelli's design for Leo X's projected monument for Henry VIII suggests an affirmative answer, though one doubts that in 1521 anyone in Rome quite understood the importance Henry had attached to the iconography of early-Tudor 'imperialism'. Just how much importance is suggested by his government of French laity and clergy in English Tournai, the subject of the first chapter.

[14] Margaret Mitchell, 'Works of Art from Rome for Henry VIII: a study of Anglo–papal relations as reflected in papal gifts to the English king', *Journal of the Warburg and Courtauld Institutes*, 34 (1971): 178–203, especially 178–96. There is no evidence of Henry's knowledge of either the model or the intended gift. A monumental effigy of him on horseback probably would have pleased him greatly, for he was an exceptionally able rider capable of some remarkable, if showy, feats of horsemanship. At the tournament of February 1511 at Westminster, he had deftly guided his mount through some extraordinary leaps and turns, and in a final display, caused it to rear and pound the barrier, the noise of hooves on wood resounding like the 'shott of Gunnys'; cited in Sydney Anglo, *The Great Tournament Roll of Westminster* (Oxford, 1968), p. 53.

1 On the road to 1534: the occupation of Tournai and Henry VIII's theory of sovereignty

THOMAS F. MAYER

It is commonly thought that Henry VIII gained possession of Tournai in 1513 in much the way his Victorian successors created their empire. Having had little idea what he intended in the first place, Henry proceeded to waste a good deal of effort and resources over the next six years trying to accomplish he knew not what in his new territory.[1] This view contains a large element of truth, but it is not entirely fair to Henry. The king found himself caught on the cusp of a complicated process of linguistic and conceptual change as ideas of feudal government unravelled and were slowly replaced by something new. Although this development would carry yet further into the future, by the mid 1510s Henry had already formed a very high view of his kingship. At first glance much of Henry's behaviour seems identical to that of his medieval predecessors from Edward III on, but subtle differences often reinforce the conclusion, derived from Henry's bolder claims, that something new was emerging. This process of transformation has not received much attention, but it must if contingency is to be restored to the study of Tudor history.[2] Henry's chivalric honour, which dictated the capture of Tournai as well as heroic efforts to hold it (but which did not provide much more help on the score of what to do with his conquest) gradually gave way to new notions of sovereignty which went a long way in the direction of those deployed in the 1530s.[3] A concept of the state as monopolist of violence and ultimate repository of all claims on allegiance was slowly

My thanks to A. J. Slavin, G. R. Elton, and S. E. Lehmberg for their comments on this chapter, and to the American Council of Learned Societies, University House at the University of Iowa (especially its director, Jay Semel) and the Augustana Research Foundation, which provided financial assistance for a study of early Tudor political vocabulary, of which this is a part.

[1] For more or less this position, see especially C. G. Cruickshank, *The English Occupation of Tournai 1513-1519* (Oxford, 1971) and G. R. Elton, *Reform and Reformation: England 1509-1558* (Cambridge, MA, 1977), pp. 38-9.

[2] See David Starkey's conclusion to Christopher Coleman and David Starkey (eds.), *Revolution Reassessed: revisions in the history of Tudor government and administration* (Oxford, 1986), p. 201.

[3] S. J. Gunn presents chivalry as a powerful motive behind Henry's continental wars in 'The French wars of Henry VIII', in J. Black (ed.), *The Origins of War in Early Modern Europe* (Edinburgh, 1987), pp. 35-7.

displacing a culture of honour which had sanctioned a 'politics of violence' and therefore left little room for sovereignty or unconditional demands for loyalty. This process, in so far as it was conscious, depended partly on Henry's manipulation of chivalry to give him complete control of lordship, but, as becomes clear in the case of Tournai, imitation of French models also led him to develop a new idea of kingship.[4]

A difficulty in interpreting Henry's claim to exercise sovereignty over his new territory immediately arises in that Henry, in common with his fifteenth-century predecessors, saw no need to sort out the amalgam of *auctoritas* and *potestas* which had gone into that concept. In addition, much of his language embodies a highly unstable mix of feudal terms with assertions which go beyond mere suzerainty.[5] The king began with the standard late medieval definition of sovereignty according to which he had final political authority over Tournai and was entitled to exercise his jurisdiction without interference from outside authorities.[6] But at the same time Henry groped after more. In the secular sphere, the king asserted that he had inherited the same measure of authority over Tournai as had belonged to the French kings, which automatically meant a large increment to his power. If Henry had been at all sincere about emulating his French predecessors, that would have also given him a much greater measure of control over the Church, and Henry undoubtedly proposed to restrict the pope's authority in Tournai within narrower limits than those current in England. The king sometimes failed to press his superiority over the spirituality

[4] Mervyn James analyses the culture of honour and Henry's attempts to control it in *English Politics and the Concept of Honour 1485–1642*, *Past and Present Supplement*, iii (1978), pp. 1, 6, 17–18, 31. For Henry's Francophilia as a source of models for conduct and institutions, see David Starkey, *The Reign of Henry VIII: Personalities and Politics* (1985), p. 77, and John Guy, 'The French King's Council', in R. A. Griffiths and J. Sherborne (eds.), *Kings and Nobles in the Later Middle Ages. A tribute to Charles Ross* (Gloucester, 1986), p. 278. R. J. Knecht emphasizes the importance of cultural borrowings from France in the sixteenth century, although he discusses only the impact of Huguenot political thought; *The Lily and the Rose: French Influences on Tudor England* (Birmingham, 1987). I am grateful to Professor Knecht for sending me a copy of his inaugural lecture in the University of Birmingham.
[5] According to A. J. Slavin, '*Craw v. Ramsey*: new light on an old debate', in Stephen B. Baxter (ed.), *England's Rise to Greatness 1660–1763*, (Berkeley, CA, 1983), pp. 31, 48, such hybrid language should be expected at least as late as the Restoration.
[6] Marcel David, *La souveraineté et les limites juridiques du pouvoir monarchique du IXe au XVe siècle* (Paris, 1954), pp. 67–8. This book deserves to be better known amongst historians of England. It is much superior on this problem to S. B. Chrimes, for example, who in *English Constitutional Ideas in the Fifteenth Century* (Cambridge, 1936) did not spell out what Henry or his subjects meant by sovereignty but merely offered statements of the following sort: '"prerogative" does not mean merely "feudal rights" but means something very much akin to "sovereignty"' (p. 42). It is undoubtedly difficult to define sovereignty; this is not the place to revive the old debate between medievalists and students of early modern Europe over it. Suffice it to say that there is a distinct change in language in the sixteenth century, like that undergone by the closely related term 'state', which deserves more careful attention than it has had thus far. Even Bernard Guénee, one of the most stimulating historians of state-building, seriously obscures the conceptual issue when he argues that 'it is . . . reasonable to admit the existence of a State once the population of a limited area is subject to government', whatever that 'state' might be called; *States and Rulers in Later Medieval Europe* (Oxford, 1985), p. 6. For some helpful (but not entirely trustworthy) observations on the transformation of the idea of 'state' in this period see Quentin Skinner, *Foundations of Modern Political Thought* (2 vols., Cambridge, 1978), ii, pp. 352–8.

of Tournai, but his own agents thought he was encroaching on its rights in unprecedented and dangerous ways. The prince who declared resoundingly in 1515 that 'by the ordinance and sufferance of God we are king of England, and the kings of England in time past have never had any superior but God alone', and used that claim to restrict papal jurisdiction in England, pressed the same highly significant point even further in the *tabula rasa* of the conquered territory of Tournai.[7] Henry and his then chief agent, Thomas Wolsey, met little success implementing his design, but Henry did not need to wait until 1533 to trumpet his 'imperial' conception of kingship.[8]

From the standpoint of language, even when conceived as utterances which must necessarily be performed by individuals, it does not matter a great deal who conceived the new twist. As John Guy and Graham Nicholson have shown, a whole congeries of thinkers held similar ideas about empire and royal power before the 1530s. In fact, Guy has recently suggested a fundamental reorientation of the debate about the intellectual origins of the Tudor Revolution away from the badly posed question of who bore responsibility, Henry or Thomas Cromwell, toward an analysis something like Carl Becker's 'climate of opinion'.[9] Never the less, in the case of Tournai, the question of primacy may not pose quite such a conundrum. Henry himself most likely hit on the sweeping claim to sovereignty over it.[10] This conclusion emerges in part by a process of

[7] Guy has conclusively demonstrated both that Henry's claim was indeed made in 1515 and not later, and that Henry meant to maintain that he could 'monitor the reception of canon law' and thereby prevent the pope from trenching on 'his territorial sovereignty on the basis of the Petrine commission'; 'Henry VIII and the *praemunire* manoeuvres of 1530–1531', *EHR*, 97 (1982): 498, and Thomas Cromwell and the Intellectual Origins of the Henrician Revolution', in Alistair Fox and John Guy, *Reassessing the Henrician Age: Humanism, Politics and Reform 1500–1550* (Oxford, 1986), pp. 166–7. Guy reduces the significance of Henry's 'oracular pronouncement' somewhat in his latest consideration of it, claiming that Henry had no idea of its theoretical implications and was only after 'money and power' in making it; John Guy, *Tudor England* (Oxford, 1988), p. 110.

[8] Walter Ullmann, '"This Realm of England is an Empire"', *JEH*, 30 (1979): 184. Paul Sawada offers more on Henry's 'Byzantine' notion of kingship in 'Das Imperium Heinrichs VIII und die erste Phase seiner Konzilspolitik', in Erwin Iserloh and Konrad Repgen, eds., *Reformata reformanda: Festgabe für Hubert Jedin*, Reformationsgeschichtliche Studien und Texte, Supplementband 1:1 (1965), pp. 476–507. Cruickshank is strong on the difficulties in Henry's way, although he may overemphasize some of them in order to support the thesis that the entire operation was a silly adventure.

[9] Guy, 'Cromwell and the Henrician Revolution', especially p. 178; Carl Becker, *The Heavenly City of the Eighteenth-Century Philosophers* (New Haven, CT, 1932), ch. 1; Graham Nicholson, 'The Nature and Function of Historical Argument in the Henrician Reformation', unpublished Ph D dissertation, University of Cambridge, 1977. See also Richard Koebner, '"The Imperial Crown of this Realm": Henry VIII, Constantine the Great, and Polydore Vergil', *BIHR*, 26 (1953): 29–52.

[10] If truth be told, Henry must have had the help of at least one civil lawyer for his most important claims, as we shall see. But who he (or they) may have been remains an unanswered question. A canonist like Richard Sampson could have filled the bill, but any lawyer who had supplemented a training in the civil law by becoming a canonist as well would have been disinclined to volunteer reasons for greater royal power, except perhaps under pressure. It does not appear that such was yet applied. I have been unable to establish whether Henry's partisan in Tournai, Jean le Sellier, was a civilian, and Sampson's helpful 'doctor of Bruges' has not been identified. He may have been among the members of the imperial delegation with whom Sampson helped to negotiate a new commercial treaty during the occupation. If so, Phillipe Wielant is perhaps the most likely candidate, as the most serious civil lawyer of the five or six possibilities. See Edward Surtz, 'Saint Thomas More and his Utopian Embassy of 1515', *Catholic Historical Review*, 39 (1953): 274–5, 280, and especially 284–6.

elimination. Wolsey and his representative, Richard Sampson, confined themselves to defending Wolsey's title to the bishopric by the rules which their opponents laid down, staying strictly within the canonist language of administration and injunction as well as that of homage and fealty. Someone finally cut through this protracted dispute with the French bishop-elect by asserting royal sovereignty over *all* the inhabitants of Tournai, both lay and clerical, even against the pope. In light of Wolsey's and Sampson's caution, it makes sense to conclude that Henry not merely signed but also authored the letter to Leo X which laid out this position in great detail. Other royal officers in Tournai were at least as equally unlikely to have hit on this solution as Wolsey or Sampson. They couched a long series of complaints in familiar begging or chivalric terms. Again, someone responded by telling them not to worry because the king was fully in control. This sort of 'cost-cutting' measure would very likely have appealed to a king always interested in finding ways to reduce expenditure on Tournai.

The king's case appeared immediately in the treaty of capitulation. It demanded not only that all residents of Tournai equally, both spiritual and temporal, take Henry as their 'natural et souverain Seigneur' (a phrase repeated frequently), but it also insisted that he had 'tous et quelzconques droitz et souveraineté, dignitez, prerogatives, preheminences regalles et jurisdiction aussi amplement et en telle et semblable forme et manière' as Louis XII had. All the officers of the city were therefore to deliver its keys 'en signe et recognoissance de souveraineté'. The inhabitants were further commanded to swear an oath of allegiance, and any who would not had twenty days to leave the *banlieue* of Tournai.[11] A draft of this oath may give us an idea of what was intended. It demanded a fairly standard 'iuramentum fidelitatis' of all the citizens, who were to swear that 'we will be true, undoubted and faithful subjects of our king'. Henry was also called 'supremus rex'.[12] Thus from the beginning Henry claimed that all the inhabitants of the territory of Tournai, both clerical and lay, were equally subordinate to him as the ultimate authority and enforced his claim by an oath in exactly the way he would drive home his new title in 1534.

This oath, of course, could be purely feudal, but a comparison of the language of the treaty demanding it with that of the famous Treaty of Brétigny suggests that both the oath and Henry's idea of sovereignty were more than feudal. Although it has been customary to emphasize the concern with sovereignty in Edward III's treaty, in fact it ranks low on his list of explicit demands and probably stands as shorthand for the whole range of feudal obligations.[13]

---

[11] Adolphe Hocquet, *Tournai et l'occupation anglaise* (Tournai, 1901), p. 104, treaty of capitulation, 23 September 1513. Summarized in Cruickshank, *English Occupation*, pp. 5–6, 37–9, but without this precise claim. *Cf.* PRO, PRO 31/8/144, fos. 268–9.

[12] PRO, SP 1/230, fo. 65 (*LP*, i, no. 2319). The oath is summarized in Cruickshank, *English Occupation*, p. 40.

[13] Maurice Keen continues a long tradition in his commentary on Brétigny in 'Diplomacy', in G. L. Harriss (ed.), *Henry V: The Practice of Kingship* (Oxford, 1985), pp. 181–91. All the references he

For example, in article seven it comes dead last in a long list of things King Jean was to surrender, all of them feudal. Other articles never mentioned the word. It figures somewhat more prominently in the separate letters of renunciation which Edward and Jean were to promulgate after the treaty took effect, but once again in a strictly feudal sense, and at least twice in the plural.[14] Similarly, the term sovereignty appears neither in the description (or title) of the 'supreme court' which Edward established for Guyenne, nor, even more significantly, in the opinions of the doctors of Bologna on Edward's claims to the duchy.[15] By contrast, in Henry's treaty sovereignty was second in his list of demands, frequently repeated, and never plural. The meaning of this difference is not entirely clear, but it may mark the distance between sovereignty as suzerainty and sovereignty as full political authority.

In the treaty of surrender Henry did not elaborate on the important point that he had inherited the same powers over Tournai as had belonged to Louis XII. Three years later, in a reply to articles delivered by a delegation from Tournai, he did. The Tournaisiens' protest that poverty made it impossible for them to pay for their own defence was ruled out by a historical argument, which led into a justification of a complete overhaul of Tournai's government based on Charles VII's similar review sixty years earlier. The poor economic condition which Tournai alleged arose not from the conquest, Henry sternly told the town, but from long-standing misgovernment and corruption. Therefore he intended to hold a 'visitation of the state of the said town, as well upon the finances as upon the privileges franchises statutes and ordinances of the same'. Sounding the authentic note of reform, Henry promised that he would preserve whatever was good

as well for the conservation of the said sovereignty of the king, as for the weal and utility of the said town & of the common weal of the same, and moreover correct or reform, revoke and annul all that by good & sufficient informations shall be found to the contrary.

Basing himself on documents in the town archives, Henry went on to recount how Charles had sent three members of his privy council with a full mandate to act in his person

offers in addition to those in the treaty employ similarly feudal language, e.g. some of the articles which went into the treaty of Troyes (T. Rymer (ed.), *Foedera, . . .* (20 vols., 1704–35), ix, pp. 762–3, 788–90): 'Diplomacy', p. 189. See also W. M. Ormrod, 'Edward III and his Family', *JBS*, 26 (1987): especially 412, where suzerainty, sovereignty, and 'rights of a superior lord' are used interchangeably.

14 Rymer (ed.), *Foedera*, vi, p. 221. David, *Souveraineté*, p. 78, argues that the plural stood as shorthand for lists of attributes. This is also the sense in which M. G. A. Vale uses the word in the singular, which may therefore be anachronistic; *English Gascony, 1399–1453: a Study of War, Government and Politics During the Later Stages of the Hundred Years' War* (Oxford, 1970), pp. 3–4.

15 Pierre Chaplais, 'Some Documents Regarding the Fulfillment and Interpretation of the Treaty of Brétigny (1361–1369)', *Camden Miscellany*, 19 (third ser., LXXX, 1952), pp. 53–4, 61, 70.

to the intent to take & visit all their books & estates of finances & also all their letters or registers of all their privileges statutes & ordinances franchises & liberties. And those foresaid to set or suspend & to deprive them (if need be) of all their privileges, as of all jurisdictions & governance. And to put all into the hands of the said king, & for generally & specially to do their business in all matters that they shall find need to be done.

Once they had completed their investigation, Charles's commissioners 'did institute and ordain diverse statutes and ordinances' to which the Tournaisiens were entirely bound. Charles himself had confirmed these new laws in the following year, and all three of his successors had done the same later.[16]

Henry then asserted that his confirmations, which he had issued with great liberality almost from the moment of conquest, were of the same force as those made by Charles and his successors.[17] Therefore 'it appeareth clearly by the said reduction, that the king our said sovereign lord is abiden in the same estate and in such power & authority as those French kings were before the said reduction'. Furthermore, Henry had a right equal to theirs to 'cause due visitation upon all the estate of the said town and upon their privileges statutes ordinances franchises and liberties of the same, for to augment or diminish them, change, alter, or to revoke in all or in part'. All this he could do 'as well for the conservation of his sovereignty, as for the weal and profit of the common weal of the said town'. The only explicit standard Henry offered by which to measure his new legislation was reason.[18] Thus the king claimed legislative sovereignty over Tournai, justifying himself by an appeal to history in the name of the commonwealth. It need not be emphasized that the tactics of the 1530s followed these lines exactly.[19] It should also be observed that Henry here claimed broader powers than he had over any similarly large and important English borough, more even than his French models customarily enjoyed.[20] No English king would attempt to exercise this degree of control over any English towns, not

[16] For the original visitation, see Gaston du Fresne de Beaucourt, *Histoire de Charles VII*, v, *Le roi victorieux (1449–1453)* (Paris, 1890), pp. 335–6. The royal orders issuing from the investigation were incorporated in the 'Traité de Saint-Pourçain', which I have not been able to see.

[17] Although Henry has been faulted from that day to this for being too generous in these confirmations, he was only following the precedent set by French monarchs who granted large privileges (or confirmed those of their ancestors) at their accessions. Bernard Chevalier, 'The *Bonnes villes* and the King's Council in Fifteenth-Century France', in J. R. L. Highfield and Robin Jeffs (eds.), *The Crown and Local Communities in England and France in the Fifteenth Century* (Gloucester, 1981), pp. 113–16.

[18] PRO, SP 1/113, fos. 242r–44r.

[19] Nor did it take Henry very long to adopt the argument from the common weal to justify financial impositions; PRO, SP 1/15, fo. 36r, Henry VIII to Jerningham, 26 Mar., s.a. (*LP*, ii, no. 3055). It is of great interest, too, that when Henry's officers reported problems in Tournai which required money to remedy, they did not realize the importance of appealing to the common weal.

[20] Chevalier asserts against Henry See that Charles VII and Louis XI either had no coherent urban policy, or at least certainly did not intend to keep the *Bonnes villes* under their thumb; '*Bonnes villes*', pp. 110, 118–24, and see Chevalier, *Les bonnes villes de France du XIVe au XVIe siècle* (Paris, 1982), pp. 101–2, for an even stronger claim that the kings were pursuing an 'operation de séduction' for the sole benefit of the towns.

even in the *quo warranto* enquiries of Charles II's reign.[21] Interestingly enough, Henry could once again have found his nearest precedent in the reign of Edward III, but, like Edward's claims to sovereignty, it was again put forward in a much less sweeping form. A statute of 1354 regulating complaints against city governments provided that a borough would lose its charter on a third offence.[22]

Henry also turned to some of the same tools to enforce his sovereignty as would play integral parts in the Tudor revolution, parliament and the common law. Almost as soon as Tournai fell, Henry called upon it to send representatives to a parliament scheduled for early 1514.[23] This was, of course, twenty years before Calais received parliamentary representation at the very end of the Reformation Parliament. The first statute of the parliament of 1514 concerned the administration of justice in Tournai, and mandated the partial integration of Tournai into the English legal system.[24] Chancery received oversight of contracts made in Tournai and judgments on actions of debt undertaken in English courts were to be enforced by the chancellor's order to the officers of Tournai.[25] This was another point at which Henry went further than his medieval predecessors; chancery had no role in Edward III's Guyenne.[26] Part of the problem of justice in Tournai lay in the practical problem of exercising royal authority at a distance. In February 1514, during the parliament, a court of five was established at Tournai to handle appeals formerly made to the *parlement* of Paris which was described as 'en souveraineté'. The new court was to exercise all the authority of its predecessor, 'tout ainsi et par la manière que par avant la réduction'.[27] More than a year later, Henry explained that he had set up such a court because 'es matiéres d'appellacions et ressort de souveraineté [non] convenoit passer la mer' and he had therefore ordained 'une court souveraine en laquelle on porroit avoir toutes provisions comme on feroit en sa court souver-

[21] G. R. Elton, *Reform and Renewal: Thomas Cromwell and the Commonweal* (Cambridge, 1973), pp. 106–9, and Robert Tittler, 'The emergence of urban policy, 1536–58', in Robert Tittler and Jennifer Loach (eds.), *The Mid-Tudor Polity c. 1540–1560* (1980), pp. 74–93, recount the much more supportive attitude of the Crown towards the towns beginning during Cromwell's regime. Freedom to make ordinances without royal interference and handle finances was not usually spelled out in borough charters, which suggests that neither presented problems to either crown or borough, at least not on the scale of Tournai. See the table in Maurice Beresford, *New Towns of the Middle Ages: Town Plantation in England, Wales, and Gascony* (Oxford, 1976), p. 126. John Miller rebuts the traditional interpretation that Charles II was after quasi-absolutist power over the boroughs, arguing instead that the king merely intended to insure that loyal men ran them. At no time in his reign did the crown go any further than to claim the power to remove elected officials, and Miller found only one case where the initiative behind a new charter came from the king: 'The Crown and the Borough Charters in the Reign of Charles II', *EHR*, 100 (1985): 25–52. My thanks to Prof Tittler for much help with the problem of the constitutional position of the towns.
[22] *The Statutes of the Realm* (11 vols., 1817), i, pp. 346–7. This legislation was in part a reaction to Edward's much more high-handed dealing with Southampton fifteen years earlier, which Susan Reynolds argues 'probably seemed less fitting as autonomous government became more established': *An Introduction to the History of English Medieval Towns* (Oxford, 1977), pp. 112–13.
[23] Hocquet, *Tournai*, no. 27, 18 November 1513; *LP*, i, no. 2450.   [24] *LP*, i, no. 2590.
[25] *Statutes of the Realm*, iii, pp. 92–3.
[26] Vale, *English Gascony*, p. 5.
[27] Hocquet, *Tournai*, pp. 119–20, Westminster, 26 February 1514; PRO, C82/401; PRO 31/8/144, fo. 237; *LP*, i, no. 2684.107; and see Cruickshank, *English Occupation*, pp. 192–3.

aine et de adviser premièrement gens notable pour excerser ladite souveraineté'.[28] It is not clear what law this court was to administer, but the fact that it
stood in for Henry's court suggests that it may have been common – or at least
some kind of English – law. This is another difference from Edward's treatment
of Guyenne, where it was explicitly spelled out that the *curia superioritatis*
would *not* administer the common law.[29] In any case, Henry's plan encountered
resistance; in 1516 he still had to insist that the Tournaisiens get on with it and
hold the court.[30]

The handling of the lieutenancy of Tournai reveals further dimensions of the
sovereignty Henry claimed. Much of the form and content of the patent
appointing William Lord Mountjoy lieutenant was identical to the standard
model developed in the fifteenth century, but again there are subtle differences.[31] Henry granted Mountjoy 'merum et mixtum imperium ac jurisdiction-
em omnimodam in cives, incolas et pro tempore inhabitantes quoscumque ...
ad nos regaliam et coronam nostras Franciae ratione quacumque pertinentem et
spectantem seu pertinere et spectare consultam et solitam'. It will be noted that
Henry here treated all the 'cives ... quoscumque' of Tournai as equally his
subjects, even if he had apparently learned a lesson from Henry VI and did not
intend to amalgamate his French and English crowns.[32] All the citizens were to
obey Mountjoy 'sicuti nobis ipsis, si in persona nostra praesentes essemus'.[33]
'Merum et mixtum imperium' had long been standard code amongst civil
lawyers for legislative sovereignty, but *regalia* (the English 'regalie', or regality
which will return below) had served in fifteenth-century England with majesty
as an equivocation designed to avoid openly attributing supreme authority to
the crown.[34] Palsgrave would define 'regality' as the sovereignty of a king.[35] Its
combination in this patent with civil law seems to mean that Henry had begun
to stretch its definition into expanded authority for himself. However that may

[28] Hocquet, *Tournai*, p. 130, Henry VIII to Tournai, 20 July 1514, from the now destroyed Archives
Communales.
[29] Vale, *English Gascony*, p. 5.   [30] PRO, SP 1/113, fo. 238r.
[31] Vale describes the medieval patents in *English Gascony*, p. 7.
[32] Hocquet, *Tournai*, p. 113, Mountjoy's nomination as lieutenant, 20 January 1515; PRO C76/196,
m. 6; Rymer (ed.), *Foedera*, xiii, p. 387; *LP*, i, no. 2617 (22). See Cruickshank, *English Occupation*,
pp. 44–5, 189.
[33] Hocquet, *Tournai*, p. 135. For more on the notion of representation expressed here, see D. Starkey,
'Representation through Intimacy: a study in the symbolism of monarchy and court office in early
modern England', in I. M. Lewis (ed.), *Symbols and Sentiments: Cross-cultural Studies in Symbolism*
(1977), pp. 187–224.
[34] David, *Souveraineté*, p. 75. For *merum et mixtum imperium* see especially the indispensable work of
C. N. S. Woolf, *Bartolus of Sassoferrato: His Position in the History of Political Thought* (Cambridge, 1913), pp. 143–60, and on the extension of Bartolo's thought about *merum et mixtum
imperium* into a broader theory of sovereignty, Francesco Ercole, 'Impero universale e stati
particolari: la "civitas sibi princeps" e lo stato moderno', in his *Da Bartolo all'Althusio. Saggi sulla
storia del pensiero pubblicistico del Rinascimento italiano* (Florence, 1932), pp. 49–156. According
to Ercole, p. 81, *merum et mixtum imperium* was itself originally a hybrid term which embraced even
feudal rights and jurisdiction.
[35] *Oxford English Dictionary*, s.v. 'regality'.

be, it is clear that his sovereignty was closely attached to himself, but none the more limited for that.

The lieutenant's responsibility for appointing and discharging office holders clarified just how far the authority of Henry's 'person' stretched or would stoop. During one of the periodic runnings down of the garrison, Mountjoy's successor, Sir Richard Jerningham, balked at dismissing some of the soldiers without royal letters authorizing such action, but he was told

that the same should not stand with his [Henry's] honour, but inasmuch as ye be the king's lieutenant and chief officer there, it is judged most convenient that ye should by the virtue of the king's commandment lately directed unto you … discharge them without any such letters, and in case that any of them be obstinate, repugning against your doing, that then ye should punish them for their disobedience and contempt accordingly, for by too much favour and mild dealing many things had been done there to the derogation of the king's honour.[36]

Jerningham's patent apparently does not survive, so that it is impossible to say whether he too had 'merum et mixtum imperium', but the blending of the language of honour with the exercise of sovereignty in this letter is of greater interest.[37]

The conflicting claims to loyalty which made Tournai such a good place to raise issues of sovereignty show up most clearly in the battle over the bishopric between Wolsey and Louis Guillard, the French bishop-elect. Here Henry took decisive action. At one point after Leo X had given the see back to the Frenchman, Henry reared up in all his royal dignity and demanded that the bishopric be returned to Wolsey because the pope's action had offended royal sovereignty.[38] This broke with Wolsey's and Sampson's much more cautious campaign to dislodge Guillard with the available tools. Wolsey first tried a tactic which Sampson had suggested, and appealed to Francis I to settle the matter. He also asked for letters from Margaret of Savoy, regent in the Low Countries, ordering Guillard to surrender the bishopric.[39] The earl of Worcester assured Wolsey that Francis would 'do that in him is to do you honour & profit'. To that end the French king had written a letter 'by the counsel and advice of the *parlement* [of Paris] for maintaining of his right of sovereignty in Flanders'.[40] This may well have been the wrong thing to say, since it conflicted not only with the exalted claims Henry would shortly make but also with the already recorded transfer of the sovereignty once exercised by the *parlement* of Paris to Henry's new court in Tournai.

However this appeal to his enemy Francis may have consorted with Henry's notions of his honour, the administration of the see and the affront to Wolsey's

[36] PRO, SP 1/16, fos. 110v–111r, Wolsey to Jerningham, 16 January, s.a. (*LP*, ii, no. 3886).
[37] Cruickshank, *English Occupation*, p. 45, also could not locate Jerningham's patent.
[38] For the diplomatic manoeuvrings, see Cruickshank, *English Occupation*, pp. 145–85.
[39] PRO, SP 1/9, fo. 121r, Sampson to Wolsey, Bruges, 23 September 1514; fo. 149r, Wolsey to Worcester, draft (*LP*, i, no. 3378); fo. 151r, Wolsey to Worcester, 22 October [1514] (*LP*, i, no. 3379).
[40] BL. Cotton MS., Caligula D. vi, fo. 202r, Abbeville, 3 October [1514] (*LP*, i, no. 3331).

honour and therefore the language of canon law and chivalry most interested Wolsey, as Sampson also repeatedly pointed out.[41] Wolsey also insisted that the only reason he wanted the see was because Henry had given it to him.[42] Thus his honour and Henry's were intimately intertwined right from the beginning. Of course, everyone realized that if Wolsey held the see, that would reinforce Henry's authority in Tournai.[43] Probably in mid-1515 Sampson again invoked his master Wolsey's honour in recommending continued adherence to strictly legal remedies, but Sampson noted at the end of this letter that two other courses of action existed: giving up (which would 'not be for the king's honour & profit') or trying Francis once more.[44] Neither Sampson nor Wolsey ever got beyond this strategy.

It may be significant that some Tournaisiens wanted them to go much further, in particular the chief 'collaborator', Jean le Sellier. He had been one of the deputies to the parliament of early 1514, and may have played an even more important role.[45] In December 1516 he began a letter of advice by arguing tamely enough that Henry held the temporalities of the see by conquest. More than that, Guillard's attempt to have his case transferred to Bruges was an offence to Henry's dignity as was Guillard's attempt to establish the episcopal court outside Tournai in 'foreign jurisdiction'. The matter therefore required Henry's personal attention.[46]

Le Sellier's intervention may have helped to bring the affair to a crisis in late 1516 and early 1517. The immediate trigger was Guillard's success persuading Leo to revoke Wolsey's administration and give the see and its temporalities to him. In a fascinating blend of chivalric-cum-legal language with unequivocal complaints about infringed sovereignty, Henry blasted his ambassador in Rome, Silvestro de Gigli, for having let that happen and provided de Gigli with an arsenal of arguments with which to attack the pope.[47] The letter began with the fairly bland protest that Leo's action was 'derogatory to our dignity royal' and 'contrary to all law and justice redounding greatly to our dishonour, [and] the defeating and derogation of our right and prerogative royal within the regalie of our city of Tournai'.[48] Henry continued by reprimanding the pope for

---

[41] See especially PRO, SP 1/10, fos. 174r ff., instructions from Wolsey to Sir William Sidney for negotiations with Francis I (*LP*, ii, no. 468), and e.g., Sampson's letter of 16 November 1514, BL, Cotton MS., Caligula D. vi, fo. 288 (*LP*, i, no. 3445) or of 20 May 1515, *ibid.*, fo. 294v (*LP*, ii, no. 480).

[42] *LP*, ii, no. 468.

[43] PRO, SP 1/10, fo. 194r, Sir Thomas Spinelli to Wolsey, Bruges, 28 May [1515?] (*LP*, ii, no. 521), and SP 1/13, fo. 2r, Sampson to Wolsey, Bruges, 12 February [1516?] (*LP*, ii, no. 1530).

[44] BL, Cotton MS., Galba B. iii, fo. 373v., Sampson to Wolsey, n. p., n. d., unsigned (*LP*, ii, no. 769).

[45] BL, Cotton MS., Galba B. v, fo. 365vr, Sampson to Wolsey, Tournai, 15 December 1514 (*LP*, i, no. 3545).

[46] *LP*, ii, no. 2695, Jean le Sellier to Edward Ponynges, 22 December [1516?].

[47] The letter is summarized with insufficient attention to its language in Cruickshank, *English Occupation*, pp. 179–81.

[48] There are alternate versions of this letter in PRO, SP 1/13 and BL, Cotton MS., Vittellius B. iii (*LP*, ii, no. 2871). The former is partly in Brian Tuke's hand. The quotation here comes from SP 1/13, fo. 247r and fo. 122r of Vit. B. iii. The latter omits 'the regalie' in the last phrase.

having proceeded in a matter 'wherein princes and other have right and interest' without giving him notification and allowing him to respond, a purely legal point. After suggesting that Leo may have been the victim of subterfuge, Henry raised the level of discourse [*words in italics* in BL, Cotton MS., Vitellius B. iii, fo. 122v]

Truth it is that we having the supreme power as lord and king in the regalie of Tournai without recognition [*recognizance*] of any superior owe [*ought*] of right to have the homage fealty and oath of fidelity as well of the said pretended bishop by reason of his temporalities which he holdeth of us as of other within the precincts of the same territory.[49]

That Guillard do homage and fealty may have been a narrowly feudal demand, but the *supremus rex in regno suo* was now putting it. This is a critically important point, for the kings of France had in large part built their revived monarchy in the fifteenth century on the juristic basis that they had all the powers of the emperor. How Henry might have come upon this idea that the *rex in regno suo est imperator* (to employ one of the innumerable variants of phrasing) is as yet unknown. The English civilian Alanus had apparently invented the idea in the early thirteenth century, and it had thereafter migrated first to Sicily and the court of Frederick II and then to France and the partisans of Philip the Fair.[50] The great Italian jurist Bartolus of Sassoferrato extended it to argue that any *civitas* which did not recognize a superior was *sibi princeps* and therefore had all the jurisdiction of the emperor.[51] The phrase recurred frequently in pleadings before the *parlement* of Paris in the fifteenth century, but its later history is otherwise not well known.[52] Italian civilians in the fifteenth and sixteenth century kept alive both the original form of this idea and also Bartolus's cognate, applying them variously to such lesser princes as the duke of Milan or non-Tuscan *civitates* like Venice; some of these legists were certainly known in England.[53] Many English students passed through Italian law schools,

[49] PRO, SP 1/13, fo. 247v; BL, Cotton MS., Vit. B. iii, fo. 122v.
[50] Richard Koebner summarized this development in *Empire* (Cambridge, 1961), p. 36.
[51] Woolf, *Bartolus*, p. 109; Ercole, 'Impero universale e stati particolari', pp. 81–146. See also Julius Kirshner, 'Civitas sibi faciat civem: Bartolus of Sassoferrato's Doctrine on the Making of a Citizen', *Speculum*, 48 (1973): 706, and Maurice Keen, 'The Political Thought of the Fourteenth-Century Civilians', in Beryl Smalley (ed.), *Trends in Medieval Political Thought* (Oxford, 1965), pp. 116–24.
[52] André Bossuat, 'La formule "le roi est empereur en son royaume". Son emploi au XVe siècle devant le parlement de Paris', *Revue historique de droit français et étranger*, fourth ser., 39 (1961): 371–81.
[53] Paulus de Castro took the lead in putting these arguments; see especially his *Consiliorum sive responsorum* (Venice, 1581), ii, no. 34, fo. 17r. Other Italian jurists who made either or both cases included: Pietro Paolo Parisio, one of the most important of early sixteenth-century Italian canonists, *Consiliorum* (4 vols., Venice, 1593), i, no. 1, fo. 3v and no. 69, fo. 134r; Mariano Socini the Elder, *Consiliorum* (Louvain, 1551), iii, no. 3, fo. 6v; Carlo Ruini, *Responsorum sive consiliorum* (5 vols., Venice, 1571), ii, no. 22, fo. 262r; Aimone Cravetta *Consiliorum sive responsorum* (5 vols., Venice, 1568–92), i, no. 135, fo. 122v; Francesco Curzio (or di Corte) the Younger, the greatest luminary of the law school of Padua in the first part of the sixteenth century (when it was probably the most prominent in Europe), *Consiliorum* (2 vols., Venice, 1571), i, no. 61, fo. 93r; Alessandro Tartagni, *Consiliorum seu responsorum* (9 vols., Venice, 1597), i, fo. 4r; Giason del Maino, the foremost Italian jurist of the last quarter of the fifteenth century, *Consiliorum* (4 vols., Lyon, 1544), iv, no. 101, fo. 10r and ii, no. 227, fo. 99r. It appears especially prominently in the important *consilia* of

especially Padua and Bologna, but it is too early even to suggest that they could have imported this idea.[54] It is much more likely that Henry learned it from a French source, perhaps directly from the *parlement* of Paris, which had continued to defend the sovereignty of the Crown even when its wearer was Henry VI. That king's regent, the duke of Bedford, attended some sessions of the court during which the rights of the French crown were stated in no uncertain terms, and the *parlement* continued to do that throughout the English occupation.[55]

To return to Henry's argument. The king went on to fulminate against the clause in Leo's bull allowing Guillard to invoke the *brachium secularis* (which would mean war), but Leo's threat to excommunicate 'all and singular the persons spiritual and temporal of our said regalie' who refused to admit Guillard posed a more serious threat yet, since according to Henry it implied 'as much as to discharge our subjects there from their fidelities and allegiances towards us'. Returning to the language of law and chivalry, the letter glossed this as 'so exorbitant and contrary to the laws of God and man justice and reason, that it is the greatest dishonour that ever came to the pope'.[56] Later Henry reiterated this point, adding that 'our subjects spiritual and temporal' would therefore have to 'maintain our rebel against us to our dishonour and unsurety'.[57]

Much of the rest of this letter employed similarly chivalric language, but the nature of some of the claims Henry put forward once more belied his old-fashioned words. Expanding his early objection to Leo's failure to notify him of the case, Henry maintained that the pope [*words in italics* in BL, Cotton MS., Vitellius B. iii, fo. 124v]

Mariano Socini the Younger, one of the mainstays of both the Paduan and Bolognese legal faculties in the first half of the sixteenth century, and perhaps once a partisan of Henry's divorce; see e.g. his *Consiliorum sive malis responsorum* (4 vols., Venice, 1580), i, no. 69, fos. 103r and 104r (a case of 1526); ii, no. 100, fo. 139v; iii, no. 98, fo. 158v (a general statement of the principle, relying mainly on Paulus de Castro; a case of 1547); no. 126, fo. 198r (1548); iv, no. 82, fo. 135r; no. 92, fo. 151r (appealing to the examples of the *doge* of Venice and the king of France, 1555); etc. Marco Mantova Benavides, who dominated the faculty of Pauda almost throughout the sixteenth century, also adverted to the concept in his *Consiliorum sive responsorum*, (2 vols., Venice, 1559), ii, fos. 66v–69v; Mantova certainly delivered an opinion favourable to Henry's divorce. For their *consilia*, see Edward Surtz, *Henry VIII's Great Matter in Italy: An Introduction to Representative Italians in the King's Divorce, mainly 1527–1535* (Ann Arbor, MI, 1978), i, pp. 272 (Socini) and 298ff. (Mantova). My thanks to Professor Antonio Padoa Schioppa for his hospitality at the Istituto per la storia di diritto italiano, Università di Milano, which greatly facilitated my researches on this point.

54 On the fifteenth-century students, see Rosamond J. Mitchell, 'English Law Students at Bologna in the Fifteenth Century', *EHR*, 51 (1936): 279–87, and 'English Students at Padua, 1460–1475', *Transactions of the Royal Historical Society*, fourth ser., 19 (1936): 101–17. Some of their successors can be identified in E. Martellozzo Forin (ed.), *Acta graduum academicorum gymnasii patavini* (Padua, 1969–71), but the record is very defective. See also G. A. Andrich, *De natione anglica et scota iuristarum universitatis patavinae ab anno 1222 usque ad annum 1738* (Padua, 1892).

55 André Bossuat, 'Le parlement de Paris pendant l'occupation anglaise', *Revue Historique*, 229 (1963): 19–40. Bossuat asserts in his conclusion (pp. 39–40) that the court was drawing on Roman law and putting forward the idea of *rex imperator*, but none of the texts he cites makes this explicit.

56 PRO, SP 1/13, fo. 248r; BL, Cotton MS., Vit. B. iii, fo. 123r.

57 PRO, SP 1/13, fo. 248r; BL, Cotton MS., Vit. B. iii, fo. 124r.

attempteth to take from us the superiority regalie preeminence jurisdiction and authority that we have in the region and dominion of Tournai in that he in our absence and without our knowledge hath in this great matter so much touching our honour fulminate[d] the censures and by his delegates called and adjourned us and our subjects [*delegates*] out of the regalie and territory to places unsure under the obedience of other princes in derogation of our honour and contrary to justice whereas all causes be determined [*determinable*] within the same and no appeal or resort either to the court of Paris or elsewhere can have place there.[58]

This last point had already been given effect almost three years earlier in the establishment of the sovereign court in Tournai, but now Henry asserted directly to the pope and as a general principle that appeals could go no further. It does not require emphasis that the case in question was an ecclesiastical one. Henry here put forward the tenet enshrined in the enacting clauses of the Act in Restraint of Appeals, even if he did not couch his point in that statute's imperial language. Never the less, both provincial self-determination and empire appear together in his highly important letter to the pope, even if they were not yet linked.

Perhaps equal significance attaches to Henry's willingness to threaten Leo. The king began by reminding the pope of 'all the benefits we have done to him and the church of Rome', fighting the schismatic Louis XII, paying Swiss troops and entering into alliances 'more for his surety than for our own', and Henry then noted that he would 'have good cause to think our benevolence labour costs and charges full ill employed and bestowed in that behalf', a fairly meek threat.[59] But as Henry revolved in his mind the injury Leo had done him, so his resolve to be revenged if need be increased. Complaining once more that he and Wolsey had received no notice of the case, Henry obliquely threatened withdrawal of obedience.[60] Finally, Henry made what sounds like a personal threat against Leo, warning him that 'if he in his person would thus rigorously without ground of justice proceed against us we would not suffer it'. In case Leo missed the point, Henry repeated it, writing that

if his holiness take regard to his honour and surety he will not only forthwith revoke the said bull and extinct the disordered process made by authority thereof but also be well ware how he grant semblable bulls against the sovereignty of princes hereafter remembering the danger that may ensue unto him by the same.

Fully aroused, Henry went for the strongest attack and most powerful defence he could muster. The pope's position (and perhaps life) would be at risk if he should continue to interfere with 'the sovereignty of princes'. Perhaps not by coincidence, Henry had used the doubly hybrid phrase 'the sovereignty of our regalie' to underline his determination to prevent any outside authority from

---

[58] PRO, SP 1/13, fo. 249r; BL, Cotton MS., Vit. B. iii, fo. 124v.
[59] PRO, SP 1/13, fo. 248v; BL, Cotton MS., Vit. B. iii, fo. 123v.
[60] PRO, SP 1/13, fo. 249r; BL, Cotton MS., Vit. B. iii, fo. 124v.

interfering in Tournai immediately before issuing this thunderous denunciation.[61]

The highly interesting terms in which Henry referred to Guillard's status grow out of the treaty of 1513. After originally labelling the bishop-elect 'our disobedient and untrue vassal and subject', Henry dropped 'vassal' on the dorse of that folio, even though the 'subject' still owed homage and fealty.[62] Sampson also called Guillard merely 'subject'.[63] Thus it would appear that Henry was attempting the same manoeuvre against Guillard as Louis XI had pioneered against the duke of Brittany, converting him from vassal to subject and thereby substituting for a feudal hierarchy a more modern notion of a congeries of equal subjects. This move, of course, was a necessary precondition for the expansion of royal sovereignty into absolutism, even if its history may not be quite as clear as has been suggested.[64] The evolution of the concept of subject in England is more obscure yet, but it still appears that Henry was probably following in Louis's footsteps.[65]

Henry's strong language against the pope took almost immediate effect. The pope replied to the king in an abject letter, protesting that he had never intended to encroach on Henry's 'maiestate et amplitudine' nor to slight the king's efforts to help. Leo assured Henry that the clause about the invocation of the secular arm, to which Henry had particularly objected, was common form and certainly not aimed 'ad tuum statum quod absit perturbandum'. This the pope would never do. Not only would he always study peace, he had not meant to appeal to military power anyway.[66] Two days later Cardinal Guilio de Medici wrote

[61] *Ibid.*   [62] PRO, SP 1/13, fo. 248.

[63] BL, Cotton MS., Galba B. iii, fo. 362r (*LP*, ii, no. 553), Sampson to Wolsey, Bruges, 3 June [1515]. *LP* gives the date as 1 June.

[64] Barthélemy-Amédée Pocquet du Haut-Jussé, 'A political concept of Louis XI: Subjection instead of Vassalage', in P. S. Lewis, *The Recovery of France in the Fifteenth Century* (New York, 1971), pp. 196–215. This idea may not have originated with Louis XI. Peter Lewis, 'Jean Jouvenel des Ursins and the Common Literary Attitude to Tyranny in Fifteenth-century France', in *Essays in Later Medieval French History* (1985), p. 172n, claims that the jurist Jean de Terre-Vermeille had developed Louis's position in the early fifteenth century, but the idea was even older. Lewis may be correct about de Terre-Vermeille, but the evidence he cites for this notion's antiquity does not seem to support his case. None of the texts cited in Lewis's source, Pierre Chaplais, 'La souveraineté du roi de France et le pouvoir législatif en Guyenne au début du xive siècle', *Le Moyen Age*, 69 (1963): 450–2, makes this exact point, although Chaplais, too, apparently meant to say that they did. The treaty of 1294 between Philip the Fair and Guyenne perhaps comes closest in the assertion that Philip was sovereign over all the peers and their subjects, but this is not the same thing as saying that those peers and subjects were *equally* subject to the king, as Louis was to insist. Ralph Giesey offers the most extended treatment of de Terre-Vermeille in 'The French Estates and the Corpus Mysticum Regni', in *Album Helen Maud Cam* (Études présentées à la commission internationale pour l'histoire des assemblées d'Etats, xxiii) (Louvain, 1960), especially 164–5. I have been unable to see the very rare 1526 edition of de Terre-Vermeille's work, which contains his discussion of the distinction between vassals and subjects.

[65] The best available discussion is in W. S. Holdsworth, *A History of English Law* (1963), ix, pp. 72–9, which skips from an unclear treatment of the gradual extension of the strictly feudal idea of the faith between king and subject to Calvin's case in 1609. The distinction between aliens and subjects interested Holdsworth much more than the idea of a subject *per se*, and this remains true of more recent scholarship, e.g. Slavin, '*Craw vs. Ramsey*'.

[66] PRO, SP 1/13, between fos. 253 and 254, Leo X to Henry VIII, 5 February 1517 (*LP*, ii, no. 2873).

again to explain what had transpired, and the day after that de Gigli wrote a begging letter to Henry, as if nothing had happened. The ambassador at least thought the king should have been fully mollified that quickly.[67] After only another two weeks, Leo wrote Wolsey exonerating the man who had caused all the trouble, Cardinal Adriano Castellesi, who had fully realized his error in failing to notify Wolsey of the revocation.[68] In late March Wolsey replied to de Gigli reassuring him that all was well and emphasizing that he had taken so much interest only because the matter touched 'regiae majestatis et meum honorem' so closely.[69] It will be noted that Wolsey confined himself to chivalric language.

Thus Henry successfully asserted his claim to territorial sovereignty over Tournai, even against the pope. However far Wolsey may have been willing to go to support Henry, some of the king's and Wolsey's actions made Sampson intensely uncomfortable, especially the idea that the secular power could interfere in spiritual matters. Sampson surely thought that Henry meant to expand his authority at the expense of the Church, which he considered a very dangerous move. As Sampson reported, the English had intruded themselves into a situation of severe tension between lay and spiritual Tournaisiens. No doubt Sampson was mindful of the close resemblance between that state of affairs and the Hunne and Standish cases at home, which had also motivated Henry to an unequivocal claim to sovereignty. Part of the problem according to Sampson stemmed from the 'sedition' among the common people of Flanders, which he noted early meant 'if it were the greatest lord of their own land, they would do him displeasure'.[70] Three months later Sampson reported that he was loath to execute process against Guillard's officials lest that harm the whole of the clergy 'because the temporalty in these parts be so minded against the spirituality so that if there should be any scisma, there should immediately many thing be taken from the spiritual jurisdiction, which was hard ever to recover', especially the bishop's financial advantages.[71] Sampson stayed within a narrowly legal definition of Wolsey's position throughout, especially when he wrote in May 1515 that he would rely on the spiritual sword and then ask help from the temporal. He meant to proceed with extreme care, begging Wolsey to find 'a more clear and faithful title' for his officers, even though he was prepared to exercise spiritual authority 'moderately' in the meantime.[72] When Wolsey tried to persuade Sampson that the archbishop of Rheims had no power as

67 PRO, SP 1/13, fo. 256, Rome, 7 February 1517 (*LP*, ii, no. 2879) and fo. 258r, Rome, 8 February (*LP*, ii, no. 2886).
68 PRO, SP 1/13, fo. 263r, Leo X to Wolsey, Rome, 21 February 1517 (*LP*, ii, no. 2947).
69 Edmund Martène and Ursin Durand (eds.), *Veterum scriptorum et monumentorum . . . amplissima collectio*, iii (Paris, 1724), col. 1275B–C, Wolsey to de Gigli, London, 24 March 1517 (*LP*, ii, no. 3045).
70 PRO, SP 1/9, fo. 107r, Sampson to Wolsey, Brussels, 6 September 1514 (*LP*, i, no. 3246).
71 BL, Cotton MS., Galba B. v, fo. 365r, Sampson to Wolsey, Tournai, 15 December 1514 (*LP*, i, no. 3545).
72 BL, Cotton MS., Caligula D. vi, fo. 294, Sampson to Wolsey, Tournai, 20 May 1515 (*LP*, ii, no. 480).

metropolitan to interfere in the case, Sampson wrote back the strictly legal answer that Wolsey was wrong and that his only option was to countersue the archbishop.[73]

Wolsey also apparently suggested to Sampson that Henry's claim to sovereignty could solve his problems. Sampson reacted with horror. He informed Wolsey bluntly that 'though [the] temporal sword divideth or taketh away temporal power or jurisdiction, yet hath it no such power nor strength canonice in spiritual jurisdiction'. Worse, Wolsey was asking him to endanger his soul. Sampson launched into a long passage in Latin explaining just how much he feared spiritual jurisdiction and concluded 'My lord I write thus to your grace for that mine opinion and conscience thus leadeth me. And more largely I think my conscience not informed with no saint's scrupulosity, but directed with plain truth.'[74] Sampson may not have been a Thomas More, but he seems to have felt himself in danger of being forced into much the same position. Sampson had, it is true, urged Wolsey to get Henry to stake a claim to the same complete control of ecclesiastical patronage in Tournai as he enjoyed in England and Calais, but that had come originally by papal privilege.[75] Sampson, whatever the extent of his legal learning, was not up to the task of suggesting any radical solution to Wolsey's problem. Judging from Wolsey's acquiescence in Sampson's objections, neither was he. Whatever Sampson's legal and conscientious scruples, his almost casual proposal that one of the chief ecclesiastical trouble makers in Tournai could be assassinated reveals the limits of his thinking.[76]

Although this suggestion must remain speculative for the moment, it seems plausible to argue that Henry's new claims against the Church, like his attempts to expand his secular authority, also rested on French precedent. Henry might have fulminated violently against Louis XII's council of Pisa, and joined the pope to suppress that embodiment of Gallicanism, but his policy toward the spirituality of Tournai amounted to very nearly the same thing as Louis's towards the French Church.[77] When Henry conquered Tournai, the French king enjoyed almost as much control over his Church as Henry would have after the supreme headship. By the anti-papal pragmatic sanction of Bourges, annates and appeals to Rome had been abolished, and the crown had received almost unrestricted control of clerical elections, at least in practice. The pragmatic also enshrined the principle of the superiority of council to pope. During the English occupation of Tournai, the extent of royal control of the French Church became a serious issue as Francis negotiated a new concordat with Leo at Bologna, an

[73] BL, Cotton MS., Caligula D. vi, fo. 296r, Sampson to Wolsey, Bruges, 26 May (month endorsed) 1515 (*LP*, ii, no. 512); Cotton MS., Galba B. iii, fo. 363v, Sampson to Wolsey, Bruges, 8 June 1515 (*LP*, ii, no. 566).
[74] BL, Cotton MS., Galba B. iii, fo. 363v, Sampson to Wolsey, Bruges, 8 June 1515 (*LP*, ii, no. 566).
[75] BL, Cotton MS., Caligula D. vi, fo. 291r (*LP*, ii, no. 1707).   [76] *LP*, ii, no. 2274.
[77] For Henry's pious outrage over Pisa see J. J. Scarisbrick, *Henry VIII* (Berkeley, CA, 1968), pp. 26, 28–9. Guy notes that Henry 'envied' Francis's ability to control the French Church under the terms of the Concordat of Bologna, but does not notice how the situation had changed from that obtaining under the earlier concordat; *Tudor England*, p. 114.

agreement which encountered strenuous resistance from both the *parlement* and the university of Paris stoutly reasserting Gallican claims.[78] Even if the English had been ignorant of the pragmatic before then, they certainly learned of its provisions during this extended controversy.[79] Castellesi mentioned it to Wolsey in 1515 in his report on what had happened at Bologna.[80] De Gigli referred to it during Sampson's campaign to get Henry to exercise control over the appointment to benefices in Tournai, warning Wolsey that the pope claimed the pragmatic had never applied there.[81] This would seem to have been a red rag to a bull. Of greater importance, a series of now unfortunately anonymous reports from France beginning in April 1515 kept the English informed in detail about the progress of negotiations and the heated opposition to the concordat.[82] The most intriguing of these dispatches included a copy of a book, allegedly printed by royal order, recounting 'ensemble les dolleances . . . dommagez et destruyement, que peult avoir le royaulme [de] France à cause de la cassastion et abolition de la Pragmati[que San]cio et du Concordat du Pappe et du Roy'.[83] As the last clauses make clear, this information was hopelessly garbled, nor can this alleged book be identified. Naturally, the only book printed by command of Francis – who passionately wanted the concordat to be accepted officially and applied relentless pressure to his opponents – was the concordat itself.[84] Nevertheless, had the book referred to in the dispatch existed it could have sowed seeds in Henry's mind, and the whole of the controversy certainly emphasized that his great rival had more power over the Church than he.

Competitors or no, Henry did not hestitate to imitate French kings. He made his dependence on fifteenth-century French kings explicit in his claim to as much legislative sovereignty over Tournai as Charles VII had enjoyed. In addition and still as his French models had done, Henry supported his idea by both an appeal to the common weal and to history. But above all, when he turned to the same civil law maxims as the French kings had employed in the course of the fifteenth century in order to make themselves emperors in their realm, it appears that he

---

[78] But as Édouard Maugis pointed out, the traditional emphasis on the Gallicanism of the *parlement* should not be overdone; *Histoire du parlement de Paris de l'avènement des rois Valois à la mort d'Henri VI* (3 vols., Paris, 1913–16), i, p. 729. See also Roger Doucet, *Étude sur le gouvernement de François Ier dans ses rapports avec le parlement de Paris* (Paris, 1921), pp. 38ff. The best treatment of the concordat of 1516 and its relation to its predecessor is R. J. Knecht, 'The Concordat of 1516: a Reassessment', in H. J. Cohn (ed.), *Government in Reformation Europe, 1520–1560* (New York, 1971), pp. 91–112. Knecht stresses that the concordat neither much augmented the already extensive powers of the crown, as the traditional interpretation had it, nor cost Francis much.

[79] The best, if strongly biased, treatment of the reception of the concordat of Bologna is Jules Thomas, *Le concordat de 1516* (3 vols., Paris, 1516), ii, pp. 235–312, and iii, pp. 59–85.

[80] *LP*, ii, no. 1284, 14 February 1515.   [81] *Ibid.*, App. no. 35 (April 1517).

[82] *Ibid.*, no. 1835, 30 April 1515; no. 3550, 28 July [1517]; no. 3703, 28 September [1517]; no. 3818, 1 December [1517].

[83] Quoting *ibid.*, no. 3702, 28 September [1517].

[84] *Catalogue des actes de François le Ier* (Paris, 1887–1910), v, no. 16683 and viii, no. 32302 (both 12 April 1518). See also Thomas, *Le concordat*, iii, p. 84, for yet another edict commanding the printing of the concordat. The university's judicial appeal to the *parlement* was printed, but this would seem unlikely to have been the book mentioned here; J. K. Farge, *Orthodoxy and Reform in Early Reformation France* (Leiden, 1985), p. 226.

meant to replicate their success. Although still sometimes cloaking himself in feudal language, Henry, like Louis XI, had gone beyond a feudal monarchy.[85] As Walter Ullmann argued, much enlarged claims flowed as a necessary consequence once the king was identified with the Roman emperor, including an enhanced measure of control over the clergy in their capacity as public persons. Similarly, and again as Ullmann suggested, Henry's personal sovereignty was grafted onto the 'territorial-national elements' in the Roman law to produce the same 'reification' of Henry's personal sovereignty. Ullmann long maintained that all this lurked in the background in 1534, but he did not suggest a mechanism by which this arsenal of arguments became available to Henry and Cromwell.[86] It now appears that the conflict over Tournai played a major role in its transmission.

Henry's *imitatio* of Philip the Fair and his agents on the score of *rex imperator* may have been unconscious at this time, but it began a process which led to deliberate borrowing by the time of the publication of both the original Latin version and an English translation of the *Dialogus inter militem et clericum* in 1531. This book is another little-studied place where the theory of empire and imperial kingship cropped up, in this case reinforced by Old Testament models.[87] The *Dialogus* (or 'Disputatio' as it was first called) grew out of the same circle of radical reformers around Philip as produced Marsilio of Padua, long alleged to be the patron saint of the Henrician Reformation.[88] However that may be, the *Dialogus* still fitted Henry's circumstances perfectly more than two hundred years after it was written, and its idea of *rex imperator* remained every bit as radical in England. Wherever Henry found it in the first place, his new claim flew in the face of Sir John Fortescue's celebrated contrast between the *dominum regale* of the king of France, expressed by *rex in regno suo*, and the *dominium regale et politicum*, or limited monarchy of the kings of

---

[85] Bossuat, 'Le roi est empereur', especially pp. 380–1. P. S. Lewis outlines the fifteenth-century French idea of unlimited royal sovereignty in 'France in the Fifteenth Century: Society and Sovereignty', in *Essays in Later Medieval French History*, especially pp. 5–6 and 187, and *Later Medieval France: The Polity* (1968), pp. 84–7. For Charles VII's at least theoretically 'absolute' monarchy, see M. G. A. Vale, *Charles VII* (Berkeley, 1974), pp. 230–2. For a sketch of a similar argument, see Guy, *Tudor England*, p. 81.

[86] Walter Ullmann, *Medieval Foundations of Renaissance Humanism* (1977), pp. 49–50, 119.

[87] A. J. Perry (ed.), *Dialogus inter militem et clericum*, Early English Text Society, old ser., vol. 167 (1925), p. xliv, for the authorship, and pp. 36–7, for monarchy and imperial powers. It has been argued that Cromwell was responsible both for unearthing the *Dialogus* and for having the translation altered to further emphasize *royal* sovereignty: Steven W. Haas, 'The *Disputatio inter clericum et militem*: Was Berthelet's 1531 Edition the First Henrician Polemic of Thomas Cromwell?', *Moreana*, 14 (1977): 65–72.

[88] In fact Georges de Lagarde as much as accused Marsilio of plagiarizing his cohorts' ideas. On the original circumstances of the *Dialogus* see de Lagarde, *La naissance de l'esprit laique au déclin du moyen age*, III, *Le Defensor Pacis* (Louvain, 1970), pp. 294–8, and Richard Scholz, *Die Publizistik zur Zeit Philipps des Schönen und Bonifaz VIII. Ein Beitrag zur Geschichte der politischen Anschauungen des Mittelalters* (Stuttgart, 1903), pp. 345–8. I offer some further reasons for caution in continuing to appeal to Marsilio as icon of reform in 'Thomas Starkey, an Unknown Conciliarist at the Court of Henry VIII', *Journal of the History of Ideas*, 49 (1988): 207–27. See most recently Shelley Lockwood, 'Marsilius of Padua and the Case for the Royal Ecclesiastical Supremacy', *Transactions of the Royal Historical Society*, 6th ser., 1 (1991): 89–119, which deals with William Marshall.

England. As Peter Lewis put it, 'the practice of arbitrary rule in France ... terrified' Fortescue.[89] Henry must have made a deliberate choice thus to break with tradition.

Meaning to criticize Henry at the conclusion of his thorough study of the occupation of Tournai, C. G. Cruickshank wondered whether the king thought that his outpost 'was the beginning of a new English empire on the continent'.[90] It would seem that Henry had just that in mind. Such large assertions about Henry's vision of his kingship are less surprising now than they would have been even ten years ago, in light of the work of Nicholson, Guy, Virginia Murphy, and George Bernard.[91] Henry might not yet have been able to maintain that 'this realm of England is an empire', but he had taken a long step in that direction. And in light of Henry's addition of 'Imperial' to the names of two ships in 1513 or 1514, together with the issue of coins for Tournai bearing the closed imperial crown, it may not be true that the king had long 'cherished the idea [or empire] as a conviction in which he *secretly* gloried'.[92] Likewise, the inchoate notion of sovereignty which Henry had developed by the time of Tournai fulfills most of the criteria laid down by Sir Geoffrey Elton, even if it did not amount to the two-fold modern idea of sovereignty, both internal and *erga omnes*.[93] It had territorial extension and embraced all the residents of Tournai, both clerical and lay, all of whom had to take an oath of obedience to the king, and all of whom, even Guillard, were equally subjects. It was exercised in part through parliament and the English legal system. It ran against, perhaps even especially against, the pope, whom Henry forced to back down almost completely, even if once again the king's practical success fell a little short of his theoretical accomplishments. He had yet to push that attitude into the spiritual supremacy which Guy identifies as the second of the three basic principles of national sovereignty current by 1530, but Henry embraced the other two – secular *imperium* and provincial self-determination – in his dealings with Tournai.[94] Elton long ago predicted how a theory like Henry's could have

[89] Lewis, 'France in the Fifteenth Century', p. 27.   [90] Cruickshank, *English Occupation*, p. 267.

[91] V. M. Murphy, 'The debate over Henry VIII's first divorce: an analysis of the contemporary treatises', unpublished Ph. D. dissertation, University of Cambridge (1984), shows that Henry had a coherent policy on his divorce from at least 1527. Bernard, following Ullmann and drawing on the same evidence he used of Henry's revision of the coronation oath (BL, Cotton MS., Tiberius E. viii, fo. 89r), argues that Henry meant to control the privileges of the church from the moment of his accession: 'The Pardon of the Clergy Reconsidered', *JEH*, 37 (1986): 262. Although Guy now agrees with Bernard ('Cromwell and the Henrician Revolution', p. 173), Dr S. G. Lockwood's discovery that Henry worked from the version of the oath in *The Statutes. Prohemium Johannis Rastell* (London, J. Rastell, 1527; *STC* 9518) means the odds are against Henry having expressed the precise imperial pretensions embodied in it before the late 1520s. I have confirmed that the same oath did not appear in either the 1517 or 1519 version of this work, although it might still have circulated in some other form before that.

[92] Koebner, '"Imperial Crown of this Realm"', p. 31 [emphasis added]. He notes the two ships on p. 30. For the coins, see C. E. Challis, *The Tudor Coinage* (Manchester, 1978), pp. 65–6.

[93] G. R. Elton, *England under the Tudors* (second edn, 1974), p. 161. For similar definitions see David, *Souveraineté*, p. 82, and F. H. Hinsley, *Sovereignty* (second edn, Cambridge, 1986), p. 26.

[94] Guy, 'Cromwell and the Henrician Revolution', pp. 159, 161. Guy has more recently redrawn the distinction between what Henry claimed in 1515 and the Act of Supremacy and Appeals, calling the

arisen out of a conflict over secular authority like Henry's with Francis, engendering national sovereignty emphasizing kingship rather than supreme headship.[95] Thus the case of Tournai led Henry to take a long step toward the 1530s. But this is to get things backwards. We know where Henry and others were going, but he could not have, at least not to the same degree. The conflation of feudal language with that of civil law and the hybrid terminology which resulted took a long time to sort out. The process of revolution was a more gradual, less conscious one than we have thought.[96]

Given the strength of Henry's position in the mid 1510s, it might almost be asked why he waited so long to proceed to the break with Rome and achieve the full sovereignty defined by Elton and Guy. A partial answer arises from the fact that two of the elements to which Henry clung most doggedly in his first marital crisis also cropped up in the struggle over Tournai, the certainty of his conscience and the equally strong conviction that kings were entitled to special treatment in matrimonial causes. During the negotiations for princess Mary's marriage to the dauphin which was to form part of the settlement of Tournai, Henry opined to Richard Pace that the canon law which prevented a betrothal 'ante annos nubiles' 'is otherwise used in matrimoniis principum quam hominum privatorum'. Pace did not believe the king, but Wolsey was none the less ordered to investigate.[97] Likewise, at about the same time Jerningham was ordered to tell Francis I that Henry would see to it that King Charles's agent was admonished 'to take special regard to the saving of his master's conscience and conservation of his honour whereupon dependeth his salvation before God and estimation in the world', since Henry 'expressly showed that like as above all other earthly things he doth specially regard the observation of his promise for discharge of his conscience'.[98] These two points together with Henry's success in bullying Leo X suggest that the king simply could not believe that he could not achieve the same result with Leo's successor. This, of course, did not happen. Since it did not, the process by which Henry's and others' ideas solidified and became the empire of England demands further attention.

---

former 'territorial' and the latter 'magisterial'. The first affected only Henry's exercise of his regalian rights within England, but the latter was a claim like Constantine's to control all dimensions of 'the church's external life': Guy, *Tudor England*, p. 111.

[95] Elton, *England under the Tudors*, p. 162.

[96] Guy, 'The Privy Council: Revolution or Evolution?' and J. D. Alsop, 'The Structure of Early Tudor Finance, c. 1509–1558', in Coleman and Starkey (eds.), *Revolution Reassessed*, make similar arguments. See also Donald Logan, 'Thomas Cromwell and the Vicegerency in Spirituals: a Revisitation', *EHR*, 103 (1988): 658–67, which offers a study emphasizing contingent process in another phase of the creation and implementation of Henry's supremacy. Logan modifies S. E. Lehmberg's view that Cromwell deliberately set out to control all ecclesiastical jurisdiction, but this does not fundamentally affect Lehmberg's interpretation of the significance of the position which Cromwell assumed: 'Supremacy and Vicegerency: a Re-examination', *EHR*, 81 (1966): 225–35.

[97] PRO, SP 1/16, fo. 316r, 30 June [1518?] (*LP*, ii, no. 4275).

[98] PRO, SP 1/21, fo. 23. This phrase could be partly formulaic, since it occurs in other diplomatic documents, for example in article thirty of the Treaty of Brétigny, but it is never wise to underestimate Henry's self-righteousness.

2   *Family and kinship relations at the Henrician court: the Boleyns and Howards*

RETHA M. WARNICKE

Fearing that the death of his second young child was a sign that he was being punished by God for a fundamental sin, Richard, earl of Cornwall, the future king of the Romans and the brother of Henry III, king of England, dispatched a letter to Pope Gregory IX, enquiring about the validity of his marriage to Isabella Marshall, who was some nine years older than he. About 300 years later, his brother's descendant, Henry VIII, with a similar motivation, asked Clement VII to convene a tribunal to determine the legality of his union with Catharine of Aragon. In both cases the marriages were upheld but with two very different outcomes. In 1235, shortly after receiving his papal reply, Cornwall's wife gave birth to a healthy male child.[1] By contrast, Henry's enquiry produced the decisions which precipitated the English Reformation.

Given this historical perspective, the Tudor king's fears that the death of his infants was linked to disobedience to divine law appear far from unusual. From the earliest recorded papal decree concerning royal marriages to well beyond the English Reformation, childlessness was regularly ascribed to the sinfulness of would-be parents.[2] Protestants similarly harped on the refrain that God closed and opened wombs to punish and reward his worshippers. Viewing healthy children as 'Gods gifts', they warned that parents' sins, especially lechery, brought 'judgments upon their children'. Richard Greenham specified that when married people 'raging with boyling lusts meete together as brute beasts . . . it is the just judgement of God to send them monsters, untimely births or disfigured children . . .'.[3] Even doctors treating infertility in the 1570s comforted

I wish especially to thank G. R. Elton, Regius Professor Emeritus, University of Cambridge, for reading several drafts of this chapter and making many helpful suggestions. My thanks also to Mary Robertson, archivist, Huntington Library, and Dale Hoak, College of William and Mary, for their assistance.

[1] T. W. E. Roche, *The King of Almayne, a Thirteenth-Century Englishman in Europe* (1966), pp. 45–52.

[2] C. E. Smith, *Papal Enforcement of Some Medieval Marriage Laws* (Port Washington, NY, reprint, 1972), pp. 70, 123.

[3] F. Dillingham, *Christian oeconomy* (1609), p. 37, for 'gifts'; T. Gataker, *Jeroboams sonnes decease* (1627), p. 41, for 'judgments'; J. Cleland, . . . *the institution of a young noble man* (Oxford, 1607), p. 208; P. Boaistuau, *A most excellent hystorie, of the institution of christian princes*, tr. J. Chillester (1571), pp. 179–82, where it is pointed out that 'incontinence' made Solomon lose his son; Richard

their patients with the claim that 'Children are given to men. It's God that giveth them.'[4] Satan's agents, chiefly witches, were also blamed for impotency and infant mortality.[5]

Marginalizing these family issues, scholars have customarily explained Henrician court politics with a factional theory that is either bereft of ideology or is based on the competing religious views of the participants. Presiding over these actors, the king, upon whom the title, Defender of the Faith, was bestowed, is said to have been manipulated by the factions' leading ladies and their allies. This theory holds the implicit assumption that the court was divided into two deadly parties or factions, the members of which were linked together by mutual personal or ideological goals, one composed of favourites generally in charge of the king's actions and the other of disgruntled, powerless courtiers who were seeking to dislodge them. Court commentators warned against permitting the presence of this kind of divisiveness, for it held within it the seeds of dissension and rebellion, as was to occur in the Elizabethan court of the 1590s. As early as 1509, John, bishop of Rochester, had referred to the general royal concern about this potentially dangerous political arrangement in praising the ability of Margaret, countess of Richmond, in preventing the growth of 'factions' in her household.[6]

A more promising method of studying court politics is to frame the discourse within two family themes. The first is the on-going papal effort to enforce strict marital rules upon princes whose family ambitions required a system that enabled them to replace infertile spouses. Childless leaders seeking divorce often resorted to claims that their marriages had violated the canonical impediments of consanguinity, affinity, public honesty, or spiritual matters. The second theme, the major subject of this chapter, is the attempt of aristocratic families at court to gain royal favour and patronage for the advancement of their houses. Court commentators did sometimes, but not usually, refer to their followings as 'factions', for such groupings were actually loose associations formed around royal favourites, groups that quickly vanished when those favoured lost the king's friendship. The rise of the Boleyns and the Howards should be seen from this perspective since the success of both families greatly depended upon their

Greenham, 'Seven godlie and fruitefull sermons upon sundrie portions of holie scripture,' in *The Workes*, (third edn, 1601), p. 89.
[4] J. Smith of Nibley, *The Lives of the Berkeleys*, ed. J. Maclean (3 vols., Gloucester, 1883–85), ii, p. 385.
[5] R. M. Warnicke, *The Rise and Fall of Anne Boleyn: Family Politics at the Court of Henry VIII* (Cambridge, 1989), pp. 195, 231.
[6] E. E. Ives, *Anne Boleyn* (Oxford, 1986), pp. 121–7, and *Faction in Tudor England* (1979); M. Dowling, 'Anne Boleyn and Reform', *JEH*, 35 (1984): 31–46; for contemporary definitions, see A. de Guevara, *The Diall of Princes*, tr. T. North (1568), pp. 109, 118; and L. Ducci, *Ars aulica or the courtiers arte*, tr. E. Blount (1607), p. 260. For a discussion of Elizabethan factions, see Simon Adams, 'Favorites and Faction at the Elizabethan Court', in R. H. Asch and A. M. Burke (eds.), *Princes, Patronage and the Nobility: The Court at the Beginning of the Modern Age* (New York, 1991), pp. 265–88; J. R. B. Mayer (ed.), *The English Works of John Fisher*, Early English Text Society, extra series, 27 (1876), p. 188. For Fisher and other early references to factions, see the relevant entry in *Oxford English Dictionary*.

activities at court where family relationships, it will be argued, were at the heart of political competition. Spreading out from this vital centre were the mutual give-and-take of client and affinity rights and duties. That the Reformation began in the 1530s means also that religious debate played an important role at court, but family connections still offer the best method of understanding aristocratic court society.[7]

The history of the English family is a complex subject that cannot be adequately covered in a chapter of this length, but some attributes must be examined before turning to court politics. The household, which was composed of the nuclear family plus servants, had a mean size of about four members, a number that varied greatly among the social orders: lower-class families might have no servants while some nobility might have hundreds.[8] Numerous genealogies provide evidence that the landed élite placed great value on identifying their male ancestry and perpetuating their patrilineage. One strategy of the aristocracy for safeguarding their patrimony was to pass estates on to heirs by the rules of primogeniture. Long viewed as a method that left the siblings of male heirs without support, scholars have recently established that fathers regularly provided estates and annuities for younger sons and dowries for daughters. The popular legal device of enfeoffment to uses actually demonstrated parental desire to gain some liberty of disposal in the interests of daughters and younger sons as well as to avoid death duties. By naming a male heir as caretaker of the inheritance, the primogeniture system, furthermore, seems to have caused more family solidarity and less violence than did the practice of partible division,[9] although when relatives disputed among themselves, it was still usually over inheritance rights rather than ideological differences.[10]

Judith Hurwich has established that the kinship structure of the English landed élite was both patrilineal and bilateral. Although their estates descended by primogeniture, the aristocracy relied upon a kindred of maternal and paternal relatives to define marriage partners and to establish obligation for aiding one another.[11] Individuals called upon even their remotest kin for aid

---

[7] For these factions, see G. B. Harrison (ed.), *Advice to his son by Henry Percy, ninth Earl of Northumberland* (1930), p. 108; A. Stafford, *The guide of honour, or the ballance wherin they may weigh her actions* (1634), p. 95; D. Balmori, 'Family and Politics: Three Generations (1790–1890)', *Journal of Family History*, 10 (1985): 247–57, argues that even in some modern societies, politics is best studied through family alliances.

[8] P. Laslett, 'Mean household size in England since the Sixteenth Century', in P. Laslett and R. Wall (eds.), *Household and Family in Past Time* (Cambridge, 1972), pp. 125–59.

[9] L. Pollock, 'Younger Sons in Tudor and Stuart England', *History Today*, 39 (1989): 23–9.

[10] M. James, *Family, Lineage, and Civil Society: A Study of Society, Politics, and Mentality in the Durham Region, 1500–1640* (Oxford, 1974), pp. 26–7; M. Slater, *Family Life in the Seventeenth Century: the Verneys of Claydon House* (Boston, MA, 1984), p. 29.

[11] J. J. Hurwich, 'Lineage and Kin in the Sixteenth-Century Aristocracy: Some Comparative Evidence on England and Germany', in A. L. Beier, D. Cannadine, and J. M. Rosenheim (eds.), *The First Modern Society: Essays in English History in Honour of Lawrence Stone* (Cambridge, 1989), pp. 35–41; D. Cressy, 'Kinship and Kin Interaction in Early Modern England', *Past and Present*, 113 (1986): 38–69, for the dispute about the existence of kinship ties.

seemingly unhindered by incompatible religious views. In 1574, for example, Sir Thomas Copley, a Catholic exile, who, like Mildred, Lady Burghley, was a descendant of Sir Henry Belknap, wrote for support to her husband, who responded that he was the 'more inclyned' to help Copley because he was 'of blood and kyndred' to Lady Burghley. Explaining that he had 'allwaies taken confort in lovying hir kynred' and showing to them 'good friendship', Burghley admitted that he had several times challenged Copley's protestant enemy, William, Lord Howard of Effingham, in council meetings 'and otherwise' when he had tried to exploit the exile's recusancy status for personal gain. In 1582, Copley was still soliciting help from his kin, among them Sir Francis Walsingham whose wife was also a distant cousin. Perhaps hoping to diminish the queen's preference for her Howard cousins, Copley revealed to Walsingham his 'bond of nature' with Elizabeth who, through the Boleyns, was, like him, a descendant of the fifteenth-century Thomas, Lord Hoo and Hastings.[12]

From the medieval Clares to the late-seventeenth-century Hamiltons, co-operations and solidarity dominated family life, for many peers remained interested in the welfare of their offspring after they had reached adulthood. Although, for example, the children of Richard Boyle, earl of Cork, resided at home only between the ages of three and nine, the earl made the decisions concerning their education and interfered in their lives after their marriages. When any child resisted his authority, the other family members joined with him in isolating the erring offspring and forcing a reconciliation.[13] Younger sons or daughters gained religious office, won royal posts, found homes, or married well by exploiting their kindreds. Evidence abounds that maternal uncles aided their nephews and nieces, that fathers-in-law assisted their sons-in-law, and that widows sought support from their male relatives.[14] Michael Altschul has pointed out about the Clares that 'The promotion of family interests was of concern not only to the earls themselves but also to their brothers and sisters, wives and in-laws.'[15]

Some qualifications must be made. This solidarity may have prevailed only among the top 2 or 3 per cent of the population with wealth, property, and influence. Second, the longevity of heads of households and other members of the older generation may have been crucial to the enforcement of these obligations. Third, at court, commentators warned, favourites should be careful not to trust their kinfolk 'too much', not even their brothers, for they, too, would be

---

[12] *Letters of Sir Thomas Copley of Gatton, Surrey, and Roughey, Sussex, Knight and Baron in France to Queen Elizabeth and her Ministers*, ed. R. C. Christie (New York, reprint, 1970), pp. 35–6, 133–4, 145.

[13] M. Altschul, *A Baronial Family in Medieval England: The Clares 1217–1314* (Baltimore, MD, 1965), p. 48; R. K. Hamilton, *The Days of Duchess of Anne: Life in the Household of the Duchess of Hamilton, 1656–1716* (New York, 1973), pp. 31–3; N. Canny, *The Upstart Earl: A Study of the Social and Mental World of Richard Boyle, First Earl of Cork* (Cambridge, 1982), pp. 104–8.

[14] K. Mertes, *The English Noble Household, 1250–1600, Good Governance and Politic Rule* (Oxford, 1988), p. 55, argues that the less immediate family members in the household were children.

[15] Altschul, *Clares*, pp. 46, 48.

competing for greater favour from the monarch.[16] Finally, while aristocratic goals remained somewhat constant to the end of this period, changes did occur: the number of servants became smaller; the machinery of domestic government became more sophisticated; reliance upon the court increased, and new methods, such as the strict settlement, were adopted for preserving the patrimony.[17]

Studies of Anne Boleyn naturally begin with her paternal ancestry, but it must be noted that her bilateral heritage was more esteemed than that of any other English consort of Henry VIII. Her great-grandfather Geoffrey Boleyn, a mercer, was in 1457 elected lord mayor of London, an office that bestowed great honour upon him.[18] In ceremonial processions and banquets, lords mayor were situated with barons, mitred abbots, and the three chief justices and, until the 1530s, were sworn of the royal council.[19] In 1454 Geoffrey's brother, Thomas, became master of Gonville Hall, Cambridge, and, at his death, bequeathed a window to the college library.[20] That he served as master and that his grandnephew, William Boleyn, chose to attend Gonville Hall, earning a B.A. and an M.A. and becoming its Preacher in 1512, may explain why Anne Boleyn seems to have favoured graduates of that college. Her uncle, William, surely benefited from her relationship with the king, for in 1529 he became prebendary of St Paul's and archdeacon of Winchester.[21]

The Gonville Hall master, as a cleric, had, of course, remained unmarried, but his brother Geoffrey had enhanced the family's lineage by wedding Anne, the elder daughter of Lord Hoo and Hastings. In turn, Geoffrey's heir, William, and his grandson, Thomas, also married noble ladies the daughters of Thomas Butler, earl of Ormond, and of Thomas Howard, earl of Surrey (second duke of Norfolk), respectively. It was through these latter two peers that Anne could trace her ancestry back to Edward I.[22] To place the Boleyns' accomplishments in perspective, only about 14 per cent of the heraldic Norfolk families in the

---

[16] A. de Guevara, *The Diall of Princes*, p. 138; R. A. Houlbrooke, *The English Family, 1450–1700* (1984), pp. 43–4, 52, 58, deemphasizes kinship but admits when the elders survived, more opportunity for contacts existed.

[17] Eileen Spring, 'The Family, Strict Settlement, and Historians', *Canadian Journal of History*, 18 (1983): 379–98; Mertes, *The English Noble Household*.

[18] Warnicke, *Anne Boleyn*, pp. 1–47; W. L. E. Parsons, 'Some Notes on the Boleyn Family', *Norfolk Archaeology*, 25 (1935): 386–407.

[19] F. J. Furnivall (ed.), *Early English Meals and Manners*, Early English Text Society, old ser., 32 (1868), pp. 70–2; J. A. Guy, 'The Privy Council: Revolution or Evolution', in C. Coleman and D. Starkey (eds.), *Revolution Reassessed: Revisions in the History of Tudor Government and Administration*, (Oxford, 1986), p. 74.

[20] J. Venn, *Caius College* (Cambridge, reprint, 1923), p. 18.

[21] Parsons, 'Boleyn Family', p. 404; Dowling's claim ('Anne Boleyn and Reform', pp. 31–46) that her interest in Gonville Hall depended upon an alliance with William Butts, the physician of the third duke as well as of Henry VIII, is further eroded when it is learned that Butts had no degrees from Gonville Hall and his tenure there is problematic. See F. W. Steer, 'The Butts Family of Norfolk', *Norfolk Archaeology*, 29 (1946): 181–200, and J. Venn, *Biographical History of Gonville and Caius College, 1349–1897* (Cambridge, 1897), i, p. 17. For Norfolk and Butts see A. Borde, *A compendyous regyment or a dyetary of healthe* (1567) (dedication dated 5 May 1547).

[22] Warnicke, *Anne Boleyn*, pp. 6–28.

early-modern period could claim fifteenth-century gentry forbears while at least one in five families was connected with trade. In fact, when Anne's grandfather, William, was made a knight of the bath at the succession of Richard III, he joined the top ranks of a prestigious order of only about 500 men.[23] An important figure in Norfolk, he became increasingly associated with royal employment and with service to the Howards, holding a commission from John, first duke of Norfolk, in his capacity as admiral. At Henry VII's accession, the Boleyns, unlike the Howards, whose duke had died fighting against the Tudors at Bosworth Field, had remained in favour: the king visited their Blickling home in 1498 and appointed William the third baron of the exchequer in 1502, by which time a Boleyn marriage with the Howards had been effected.[24]

Anne's maternal ancestors were even more distinguished. Celebrating the bilateral tradition, Thomas Milles wrote in 1610 that it was not unheard of for sons to take the names of their mothers who were of greater nobility than their fathers.[25] Anne retained her birth name until 1529 when she exchanged it for Rochford at her father's elevation to the earldom of Ormond, a title he claimed through his maternal heritage, but by then she and the Boleyns had long been taking advantage of their Howard kindred. Later generations, would, like Abraham Darcie, praise her daughter Elizabeth as a Howard:

> Nay, which is more that Royall Branch of Fame,
> Elizabeth, by the Mother Anne Bouline,
> of th' Howards Blood, is borne a famous Queene . . .[26]

Surrey, of course, had fought with his father at Bosworth Field, and after release from the Tower he was sent to Yorkshire as lieutenant of the North Parts. By 1501, the year his daughter, Elizabeth, married Thomas Boleyn, he had become a royal councillor and the lord high treasurer of England. Thomas, his heir and namesake, and Edward, his second son and lord high admiral, who were the children of his first wife, Elizabeth Tylney, also served the Tudors as faithful warriors and were, like him, well rewarded. In 1512 Thomas, the husband of Anne of York, sister of the late queen, remained loyal in the face of an army mutiny in Spain, and in 1513 succeeded his brother as admiral upon the latter's death at Brest.[27]

[23] M. J. Sayer, 'Norfolk Visitation Families: A Short Social Structure', *Norfolk Archaeology*, 36 (1975): 176, 178; Parsons, 'Boleyn Family', p. 399.
[24] Warnicke, *Anne Boleyn*, pp. 6–28; F. Blomefield, *An Essay Towards a Topographical History of Norfolk* (second edn, 11 vols., 1805–10), iv, pp. 33–4; G. Temperley, *Henry VII* (Westport, CT, reprint, 1971), p. 416.
[25] T. Milles, *The catalogue of honor or treasury of true nobility peculiar to Great Britain* (1610), p. 14; see also A. Crawford, 'The Private Life of John Howard: A Study of a Yorkist Lord. His Family and Household', P. W. Hammond (ed.), *Richard III: Loyalty, Lordship and Law* (1986), pp. 5–24; M. J. Tucker, *The Life of Thomas Howard, Earl of Surrey and second Duke of Norfolk, 1443–1524* (1964), and D. Head, 'The Life and Career of Thomas Howard, Third Duke of Norfolk: The Anatomy of Tudor Politics', unpublished Ph.D. dissertation, Florida State University, 1978.
[26] A. Darcie, *Honors true arbor, or the princely nobilitie of the Howards* (1625), p. 3.
[27] H. Ellis (ed.), *Original Letters Illustrative of English History* (11 vols. in 3 series, 1825–46), second ser., i, p. 196; third ser., i, p. 154; E. Cartwright, *The Parochial Topography of the Rape of Bramber*,

Their septuagenarian father's victory over the Scots at Flodden Field in 1513 – at a time when their kinswoman, the future Queen Anne, was about six years old[28] – not only caused a grateful king to restore the family's dukedom and many of their ancestral lands but also led Alexander Barclay to praise the glorious deeds of the duke, whose title bestowed upon him the right to be styled 'prince'.[29]

During his lifetime, he was to share this high status with only two others: Charles Brandon, duke of Suffolk, and Edward, third duke of Buckingham, whose daughter in 1513 became the second wife of his heir, Thomas Howard. The honour Norfolk had won was a source of pride for all his kin. Norfolk's son, Edmund, wrote to Wolsey seeking his mediation with the king. In the letter he lamented:

I maye repent that evyr I was noble mans sone borne ledying the sorafull lyffe that I leyff, and if I were a poore mans sone I myght . . . delve for my levyng . . .: and so maye I not doo nowe but to gret reproche and shame to me and all my blood.[30]

About a century later, John Smyth reminisced about the pride of Katherine, Lady Berkeley, grandchild of the third duke, and daughter of the poet, Henry, earl of Surrey:

Of pace the most stately and upright all times of her age that ever I beheld; of stomacke great and haughty, no way diminishing the greatness of birth and marriage by omission of any ceremony, at diet or publike prayers; whose book I have usually observed presented to her with the lowest curtesies that might bee . . .

And when she went walking:

not permitting either her gentleman usher, gentlewoman, or any other of her house to come nearer to her than the appointed distance . . .

He also remembered the morning he was hurrying to deliver breakfast to her son and, seeing her from a distance, gave her 'a running legge or curtesy'. She made him repeat the bow one hundred times but only after she had personally demonstrated it.[31]

During most of Henry VIII's reign, the proud Howards remained a strong presence in the kingdom. Partly because they were warriors, attention has focused on their political competition with that great clerical administrator, Thomas, Cardinal Wolsey. Although the Howards competed with Wolsey and his patron, the aged Richard Fox, bishop of Winchester, for royal favour, the

---

in the *Western Division of the County of Sussex*, (2 vols. in 3, 1815–32), ii, pt. ii, pp. 195–7; H. Miller, *Henry VIII and the English Nobility* (Oxford, 1986), pp. 212–14, for how well Henry treated the Howards.
[28] A study of the actual manuscript Anne sent her father from Malines supports the conclusions of Hugh Paget, 'The Youth of Anne Boleyn', *BIHR*, 54 (1981): 163–7, about the letter's erratic spelling and penmanship; Warnicke, *Anne Boleyn*, pp. 12–13.
[29] *The Eclogues of Alexander Barclay From the Original Edition by John Cawood*, ed. B. White, Early English Text Society, old ser., 175 (1928), pp. xxxviii–xl.
[30] Ellis (ed.), *Original Letters*, third ser., i, p. 160.   [31] Smyth, *Berkeleys*, ii, pp. 382, 384–6.

depth of the Wolsey-Howard animosity has been overstated and does not agree with how contemporary court reporters believed princes' favourites operated. Greg Walker has recently downplayed the mutual hostility between the two, establishing, for example, that the motivation behind John Skelton's attacks on Wolsey in the 1520s has been misunderstood. So far from being a political agent of the Howards, the poet was acting on his own in an attempt to obtain the cardinal's patronage. Like other ministers, Norfolk and Wolsey disagreed about public policy and the third duke was gratified to see the cardinal lose power in 1529. Nevertheless, the Howard family, who were often away on the battlefield, frequently asked for personal assistance from Wolsey, the king's minister at Westminster who had a knack for getting things done – surely the reason he remained in Henry's good graces for so long. For the smooth running of his government, the king expected his ministers generally to cooperate with each other, and evidence exists that he encouraged reconciliations among them after they had engaged in public disputes.[32]

They, as well as other councillors, sometimes conferred with Henry at his court, the core of which was his household, for all those who served him privately were comprehended in it, and even the households of his relatives were referred to as courts. His was where, for his convenience, all kinds of public and private business could take place. Although a distinction was made between the two kinds of activities, speculation has persisted that early-modern people did not differentiate between public and private, that the concepts were blended together in customs that defy definition.[33] Contemporaries used 'public' and 'private' too frequently for historians to assert so confidently that the speakers or writers were confused about the definitions of the words. William Vaughan's comments in 1600 offer a starting point for discovering how 'public' and 'private' were viewed. He identified four functional parts of the 'private' family, the first three being the interaction between spouses, parents, and children, and masters, and servants. The fourth or 'acquisitive' part was the 'private' family's acceptable economic activity, as, for example, a trade.[34] In his colloquy, 'The

---

[32] Edward, Lord Herbert of Cherbury, *The life and raigne of King Henry the Eighth* (1649), p. 8; G. Walker, *John Skelton and the Politics of the 1520s* (Cambridge, 1988), pp. 6–7, 53; Ellis (ed.), *Original Letters*, third ser., i, pp. 150, 157, and T. Wright (ed.), *Three Chapters of Letters Relating to the Suppression of Monasteries*, Camden Society, 26 (1843): 248, for cooperation; J. G. Nichols (ed.), *Narratives of the Days of the Reformation*, Camden Society, 77 (1859): 258, prints a document which has a bystander claiming that in 1539 the king forced the council to reconcile with Cranmer; see also de Guevara, *The Diall of Princes*, pp. 110, 122, 123.

[33] *The Acts and Monuments of John Foxe*, ed. G. Townsend (8 vols., New York, reprint, 1965), iv, p. 65, refers to Catherine's household as a court; B. J. Harris, 'Women and Politics in Early Tudor England', *HJ*, 33 (1990): 260, has the most recent claim that private and public were conflated.

[34] W. Vaughan, *The golden-grove moralized in three books: necessary for all such, as would know how to governe themselves, their houses or their countrey* (1600), sig. M7–8; J. Cleland, *Institution of a young noble man*, p. 181, said 'a private person is bound to honour those who are publike and in office'. See also R. Horne, *The Christian governour, in the common-wealth and private families* (1614), sig. Giii; and Ducci, *Ars aulica*, p. 12; D. A. L. Morgan, 'The King's Affinity in the Polity of Yorkist England', *Transactions of the Royal Historical Society*, fifth ser., 23 (1973): 2, points out that Yorkist kings had twice as many household officials as 'public' servants.

Poetic Feast', Erasmus had also emphasized this distinction when he had one character ask another: 'Are you a private citizen or do you hold public office?' The response was:

I have a public office. Bigger ones were available, but I chose one that would have sufficient dignity to assure respect and be the least troublesome . . . and what's more, I have means of assisting my friends occasionally.[35]

Anomalies did exist. Some members of the privy chamber were councillors and thus held both private and public offices. Henry could at his convenience call upon private servants who were members of aristocratic families to perform public duties. Then, too, some officials, caught up in the continuing process of agencies moving out of the court, from household to public status, might hold a post that dealt with public business but had not yet entirely separated from the household.[36]

Also complicating matters is the fact that the words 'private' and 'public' have a second meaning: they can define what kind of audience, open or secret, may participate in an event or occurrence. A good example of the Tudor definition of 'private' as secret is the attachment of this word to royal agencies. When the council became a well-defined and more focused body, it was named 'privy', and when the king and some servants of his chamber removed into a more isolated space, that portion of the chamber and its staff were referred to as 'privy'.[37] In its 'secret' meaning, 'private' can describe either public or family business.

One significant difference from modern practices, as Miriam Slater has pointed out and as the above statement by Erasmus highlights, was the lack of bureaucratic professionalism. Individuals went to court to obtain both public and household offices as well as other favours for their relatives and friends, friends referring in this sense to the client/patron relationship.[38] In a letter to Thomas Cromwell, for example, Sir William Parr requested help for his nephew in obtaining a position in the privy chamber in return for which Parr promised Cromwell the young man's loyalty and clientage next only to that which was owed the king. What Parr did not promise was that his nephew was the best man for the job or that he held certain ideals about court life. From Sir Peter Carew, a gentleman of the privy chamber to Henry VIII, to Endymion Porter, a courtier of Charles I, the lives of courtiers provide evidence that relatives often

[35] *The Colloquies of Erasmus*, ed. C. R. Thompson (Chicago, IL, 1965), p. 193; see also J. Ferne, *The Blazon of Gentrie* (1586), pp. 58–9.
[36] G. R. Elton, *The Tudor Revolution in Government* (Cambridge, reprint, 1960), p. 375; D. Starkey, 'Intimacy and Innovation: the Rise of the Privy Chamber, 1485–1547', in D. Starkey (ed.), *The English Court: from the Wars of the Roses to the Civil War* (New York, 1987), pp. 71–118.
[37] Elton, *Tudor Revolution*, pp. 316–69; Starkey, *The English Court*, pp. 71–118.
[38] M. Slater, 'The Weightiest Business: Marriage in an Upper-Gentry Family in Seventeenth-Century England', *Past and Present*, 72 (1976): 27.

set their young kin on the path to successful careers in this way.[39] Another sign of pre-professionalism is that many officials retained public papers in their own private libraries after retirement from royal service.

All court treatises, whether written in the Tudor or Stuart period and whether about Italian, Spanish, French, Flemish, or English courts, agree that courtiers seeking offices, lands, and profits, formed groups around royal favourites.[40] No author identified an ideological connection, and Don Antonio de Guevara, whose treatise was translated by Francis Bryan in 1548, even stated: '. . . in princes courtes the custome and use is to speake of God and live after the worlde'.[41] Most authors criticized courtiers' pursuit of pleasure and profit at the expense of ideals. Some warned their readers to seek other professions and recommended that they stay in their 'country'; others offered suggestions for success: flattering the monarch and maintaining as many friends as possible were high on their lists.[42] Patronage was, in fact, dispensed through a complex system of relationships, and writers emphasized that although a courtier should select one favourite as his major patron, he needed to become the client of others. Monarchs bestowed their largess capriciously, and if one patron lost favour or was absent from court, another one could be called upon. Some issues also might be better raised with one favourite than another. Above all, it was agreed that success depended upon the ability to compromise and to dissimulate.[43]

Royal favourites, such as Norfolk, could necessarily count in their following their household members, other relatives, retainers, and any clients who looked to them for support. Unless they were of the same kindred or unless they had

[39] D. Starkey, 'The Age of the Household: politics, society and the arts *c*. 1550–*c*. 1600', in S. Medcalf (ed.), *The Later Middle Ages* (New York, 1981), p. 252, for the Parr reference; Ellis, *Original Letters*, third ser., iii, p. 16, also has an offer made to Cromwell by Henry, Lord Stafford; J. Vowell alias Hooker, *The Life and Times of Sir Peter Carew, Kt.*, ed. J. Maclean (1857), pp. 9–10; G. Huxley, *Endymion Porter: The Life of a Courtier, 1587–1649* (1959), p. 24.

[40] A. Chartier, *Here foloweth the copye of a lettre whyche maistre Alayne Charetier wrote to hys brother*, tr. W. Caxton (Westminster, 1483); Erasmus, *The Education of a Christian Prince*, tr. L. K. Born (Morningside Heights, NY, 1936), pp. 153–5; *The Eclogues of Alexander Barclay*, p. 36, warns that competition to become a royal favourite could set relatives against each other but points out (p. 118) that the kindred of those who were in favour were advanced; T. Wyatt, 'Epistolary Satires', in *The Complete Poems*, ed. R. A. Rebholz, (New Haven, CT, 1981), pp. 186–94; A. de Guevara, *A dispraise of the life of a courtier*, tr. from the French by F. Bryan (1548); James I, *The Political Works of James I*, ed. C. H. McIlwain (Cambridge, 1913), pp. 30–6; H. Romei, *The courtiers academie, comprehending severall dayes discourses*, tr. J. K. (1598); Cleland, *Institution of a noble man*, pp. 173–245; N. Breton, *The court and country or a briefe discourse betweene the courtier and country-man* (1618); E. Du Refuge, *A treatise of the court or instructions for courtiers*, tr. J. Reynolds (1622); Stafford, *The guide of honour*, p. 95; P. M. Smith, *The Anti-Courtier Trend in Sixteenth-Century French Literature* (Geneva, 1966), pp. 26–7, points out that even Castiglione's courtier put great weight on appearance or image at court and the pursuit of personal glory.

[41] Guevara, *Dispraise of a courtier*, sig. Fvii.

[42] R. Virgoe, 'Aspects of the County Community in the Fifteenth Century', in Michael Hicks (ed.), *Profit, Piety and the Professions in Later Medieval England* (Wafleboro Falls, NH, 1990), p. 5, points out that 'country' almost never meant the whole kingdom.

[43] Guevarra, *Dispraise of a courtier*, sig. Gvii; Cleland, *Institution of a noble man*, p. 175; see K. B. Neuschel, *Word of Honour: Interpreting Noble Culture in Sixteenth-Century France* (Ithaca, NY, 1989), p. 19, for more about the complex relationships of the early-modern nobility.

come to court under the sponsorship of a more powerful courtier, favourites did not usually combine together in long-term factions or parties, although on certain public issues some of them might from time to time work with each other. Too much was at stake for them in maintaining their own followings to brand themselves publicly and selectively with a particular programme of action, unless it was one that the king was aggressively pursuing, such as the marriage with Anne Boleyn. It was crucial for control of their 'countries' that favourites like the duke of Norfolk have independence of action and at the same time access to the king's patronage. Of the writs issued for the parliament of 1529, for example, several were dispatched to Norfolk, who selected his servants and those who had been employed by his deceased father. His grandson, the fourth duke, later explained to William Cecil that it would be insupportable if the queen's service in Norfolk or Suffolk were committed to any one other than himself.[44]

Without a formal relationship such as kinship or that which could be proved by one's livery, contemporaries were surely unable to identify all members of a following. Besides the difficulty in associating people with particular favourites, a group could potentially emerge around anyone at court. All with royal favour, even the lowliest cook, theoretically could win a share of courtly largess.[45]

Another interesting aspect of this problem is that most people at court were male, a gender difference that also characterized the members of the queen's household, excepting her immediate attendants. This fact did not, as Lois Schwoerer has discovered, prevent the few women residing at court or others from attending court to seek favour for their kin or for themselves or, indeed, from joining or leading family networks.[46] With possibly one or two exceptions, Tudor women did not hold public office,[47] but they could influence public affairs indirectly by helping male relatives obtain public posts or by suing on behalf of private family concerns that might have public consequences, as, for example, attempting to maintain a family's weir against community opposition.[48]

Most of the evidence that court politics formed a one-dimensional process, with factions led by Wolsey or Cromwell or Anne Boleyn taking turns in manipulating royal actions, depends upon the reports of Eustace Chapuys, the Imperial ambassador, whose English residency will be discussed later. Considering the speed with which Wolsey, Cromwell, and the queen were dispatched

[44] J. M. W. Bean, *From Lord to Patron: Lordship in Late Medieval England* (Manchester, 1989), p. 236; James, *Family, Lineage and Civil Society*, p. 35; R. J. W. Swales, 'The Howard Interest in Sussex Elections, 1529 to 1558', *Sussex Archaeological Collections*, 114 (1976): 52; for the fourth duke, see A. H. Smith, *County and Court: Government and Politics in Norfolk, 1558–1603* (Oxford, 1974), p. 27. For a discussion of religious patronage, see below.

[45] *The Eclogues of Barclay*, p. 114.

[46] L. G. Schwoerer, *Lady Rachel Russell, 'One of the Best of Women'* (Baltimore, MD, 1988), pp. xv–xxviii; Harris, 'Women and Politics', pp. 259–82; see also S. H. Mendelson, *The Mental World of Stuart Women: Three Studies* (Amherst, MA, 1987), p. 11.

[47] Ellis (ed.), *Original Letters*, third ser., iii, p. 142, for example.   [48] *LP*, ix, nos. 850, 892.

after they lost royal favour, the suggestion that they and their affinity had been powerful enough to manipulate the king into committing himself to political causes that he considered repugnant to his conscience must be dismissed as somewhat unrealistic. Henry VIII's persistence in obtaining the divorce from Catherine and his unrelenting hold on the royal supremacy, for example, demonstrate that on some issues he could not be dissuaded. Ultimately, the court was his household and the favourites who held power in it, while on occasion successfully persuading or even forcing him to adopt their proposals, necessarily had to operate within certain boundaries. Complex political manoeuvering existed. Greg Walker has recently determined, for example, that it was Henry, not an all-powerful Wolsey, as has long been thought, who expelled four members of the privy chamber in 1519.[49] The king raised and destroyed favourites and their followings and his ability to do so formed part of the criteria for judging his governing skills. As Henry Percy, ninth earl of Northumberland, was later to remark, even 'factions' in a noble household were 'not amiss' if well managed.[50]

The Boleyns' rise to prominence was in association with the Howards. One of the keys to political power, wealth, and influence was family connections, and abundant evidence indicate that the second and third dukes actively assisted their adult children, siblings, and in-laws. Besides serving on several local commissions with the second duke and his two elder sons, Thomas Boleyn probably benefited from his father-in-law's appointments to escort Margaret and Mary Tudor to meet their bridegrooms in 1503 and in 1514, respectively, for he was one of the gentlemen attendants of both princesses.[51]

Leaving aside, for the moment, how the Howards befriended Boleyn's daughter, it will be helpful to review some of their actions on behalf of their other kin. Among his married children, the second duke is known to have aided both the impoverished Edmund and Anne, countess of Oxford. In 1516, and perhaps at other dates, Edmund and his wife, Joyce Culpepper, resided at his father's London home in Church Street, Lambeth.[52] In 1523 the duke agreed to provide housing for his daughter, Anne, and her husband John, fourteenth earl of Oxford; the two continued to reside with her brother, Surrey, when he succeeded as third duke.[53] After her husband's death in 1536, Mary, duchess of Richmond, also lived with her father.[54]

---

[49] G. Walker, 'The "Expulsion of the Minions" of 1519 Reconsidered', *HJ*, 32 (1989): 1–16; E. Hall, *Henry VIII*, ed. Charles Whibley (2 vols., 1904), ii, p. 154, pointed out the widespread desertion of Wolsey when he lost the king's favour; see also D. Loades, *The Tudor Court* (1986), p. 134, about the insecurity of royal favourites at court.

[50] Herbert, *King Henry*, p. 1; G. B. Harrison (ed.), *Advice to his son by Henry Percy*, p. 108.

[51] Warnicke, *Anne Boleyn*, pp. 6–28.

[52] G. Brenan, *The House of Howard* (2 vols., New York, 1907), i, p. 79, n. 1; H. Howard, *Indications of Memorials, Monuments, Printings, and Engravings of Persons of the Howard Family* (n.p., 1834), p. 13.

[53] H. Ellis, 'Copy of an Order made by Cardinal Wolsey as Lord Chancellor, respecting the Management of the Affairs of the young Earl of Oxford', *Archaeologia* 19 (1821): 62–5; E. M. Richardson, *The Lion and the Rose: The Great Howard Story* (1922), p. 70.

[54] *LP*, xxi, no. 548.

Other actions of this duke prove that he was concerned about the well-being of his kinfolk. On 1 July 1531, Antonio de Pulleo, baron de Burgo, papal nuncio in England, wrote a letter to Clement VII revealing that Norfolk had asked him to intercede with the pope for a dispensation concerning a benefice for an unnamed sister's son who was then almost five years old. The legate recommended that Clement grant the dispensation, even though it was an extraordinary favour, because he needed a friend at court and Norfolk was extremely powerful.[55]

Both Agnes, dowager duchess of Norfolk, the widow of the second duke, and her stepson, the third duke, supervised the education of their grandchildren. Her custody of Catherine, the future queen, is well known, but it is less well known that the duke also oversaw in his home the education of his grandchildren, the offspring of his son, Surrey, and Frances, daughter of John, sixteenth earl of Oxford. In 1546, when the duke was imprisoned for treason, his daughter Mary, Lady Richmond, gained custody of the children, but upon his release from the Tower in 1553, he resumed control of them[56] and, the next year, from his bed where he lay dying, having 'grown weake with age and sicknes', gave his grandchild, Katherine, in marriage to Henry, Lord Berkeley, and Katherine and her husband continued to live with him until his death shortly thereafter.[57]

Although no direct evidence substantiates the involvement of either the second or third duke in the intermarriage of aristocratic Norfolk families, the Howards, for example, had long had close contacts with the Sheltons and the Parkers. Sir John Shelton, a frequent visitor to Framlingham, a Howard castle in Norfolk, married Anne Boleyn, an aunt of Queen Anne and the governess of Mary Tudor, the king's daughter. In addition, Jane Parker, the wife of George Boleyn, Lord Rochford, was a granddaughter of Lady Alice Morley, whose second husband was Edward Howard, the admiral who died in 1513. Jane Parker's sister Margaret also wed Shelton's heir.[58]

Anne Boleyn was surely invited to live at the Burgundian and French courts because she was the granddaughter of Norfolk, who had been involved in the marriage negotiations between Mary Tudor and Charles V as well as Louis XII. That Anne's father was an experienced diplomat was helpful, but she would still have been identified abroad as the duke's grandchild. In the spring of 1520, when he was assuming some of the duties of his aged father, Surrey attempted to arrange a match between his niece, still living in France, and James, heir of Sir Piers, earl of Ormond, the disputed Irish heir of her great-grandfather. The successful conclusion of this match would have benefited not only Anne, for

[55] M. J. Haren, 'A Suit of the Duke of Norfolk for Papal Favour, July 1531', *BIHR*, 60 (1987): 107–8. My thanks to Carla Ferrara, Arizona State University, for assistance in translating the Italian.

[56] R. M. Warnicke, *Women of the English Renaissance and Reformation* (Westport, CT, 1983), p. 101.

[57] Smyth, *Berkeleys*, ii, pp. 284, 376, 381.

[58] Ellis (ed.), *Original Letters*, third ser., i, p. 376; M. J. Tucker, 'The Ladies in Skelton's Garland of Laurel', *Renaissance Quarterly*, 22 (1969): 344–5; Brig Gen Bulwer (ed.), *The Visitation of Norfolk in the Year 1563, Taken by William Harvey, Clarenceaux King of Arms* (2 vols., Norwich, 1878–95), ii, 345.

whom the title of countess of Ormond would have been almost guaranteed, but also her father and his mother and aunt, who had hoped to retain the Irish title and estates of the deceased Ormond for the lineage of themselves, his English descendants. The king and Wolsey supported these efforts of Surrey, who served for less than two years in Ireland as the king's lieutenant.[59]

From 1527, when the validity of Henry's marriage to Catherine was brought into question, neither Surrey (then the third duke), nor his stepmother balked at the royal plans. Every one of Anne's steps on the path to her wedding was supported by her uncle, most of the other Howards, her parents, and her Boleyn kin, all of whom benefited from her relationship with the king. Catherine's only Howard ally was the duke's wife, estranged from him because of his affair with Elizabeth Holland, whose father and brother served in the ducal household. Norfolk subscribed to the letter sent to the pope favouring the divorce and gave testimony against Catherine at Blackfriars. In 1532 he escorted Anne and Henry to Calais where he was elected to the Order of St Michael, the French equivalent of the Order of the Garter. His heir, the companion of Henry's illegitimate son, Henry Fitzroy, duke of Richmond, accompanied the young man on a visit to the French court.[60] In 1533, while Anne was being crowned, Norfolk was in Paris,[61] smoothing diplomatic acceptance of her succession.[62] Later that year, his daughter Mary wed Richmond, the premier duke in England. Even the rumours, probably false, that Anne blamed her miscarriage in 1536 on Norfolk's revelation to her of the king's riding accident indicates a public awareness of their close relationship.[63] By her fall, her uncle, who had been building on his father's acquisition of lands, had become the chief property owner in Norfolk, partly as a result of their family's success at court.[64]

During the years Anne was in royal favour, scattered evidence suggests that Sir Thomas Boleyn (who became the earl of Wiltshire and Ormond in 1529) and his wife, Elizabeth Howard, approved of their daughter's marital plans. Anne's mother attended her at court in 1528 and personally visited York Palace with her and the king after Henry had confiscated it from Wolsey in 1529. That the

---

[59] Warnicke, *Anne Boleyn*, pp. 32–4; Lambeth Palace Library, Lambeth MS. 602, fos. 71–8; *LP*, iii, nos. 972, 1004, 1011.

[60] Ellis (ed.), *Original Letters*, first ser., ii, p. 27; David Head, 'Norfolk', pp. 215–60; B. J. Harris, 'Marriage Sixteenth Century Style: Elizabeth Stafford and the Third Duke of Norfolk', *Journal of Social History*, 15 (1982): 371–82; G. F. Nott (ed.), *The Works of Henry Howard, Earl of Surrey, and of Thomas Wyatt the Elder* (2 vols., 1815), i, p. xcv, n. 2.

[61] W. Thomas, *The Pilgrim: A Dialogue on the Life and Actions of King Henry the Eighth*, ed. J. A. Froude (1861), 92.

[62] C. A. Mayer, 'Anne Boleyn et la version originale du "Sermon du bon pasteur" d'Almanque Papillon', *Bulletin de la Société de L'Histoire du Protestantisme Français*, 132 (1986): 337–46, points out that the 'Sermon', which was a wedding present for Anne and Henry, was written by Papillon rather than Clement Marot. My thanks to John Currin, University of Minnesota, for bringing this article to my attention.

[63] *CSP Span.*, v, pt.-2, no. 21; Warnicke, *Anne Boleyn*, pp. 196–200.

[64] R. Virgoe, 'The Recovery of the Howards in East Anglia, 1435–1529', in E. W. Ives, R. J. Knecht, and J. J. Scarisbrick (eds.), *Wealth and Power in Tudor England: Essays Presented to S. T. Bindoff*, (1978), pp. 1–20.

countess remained close to her Howard kin is suggested by the decision at her death in 1538 to bury her in their Lambeth chapel where her mother Elizabeth, countess of Surrey, had been buried in 1507.[65]

Speculation persists that Norfolk resisted the elevation of his niece to the queenship, a puzzling assertion given his indisputable support for the Crown and his efforts to win the queenship for another niece, Catherine, in 1540. Family honour, as well as the prospect of material reward, should have compelled him to promote a union that made him the king's uncle. The major source for the statement that he was opposed to his niece's elevation is to be found in the letters of Chapuys.[66]

The diplomat's comments about Norfolk must be disputed for several reasons. First, they are incompatible with the duke's actions before the spring of 1536 when Anne fell from power. No conceivable motive can explain why this proud man of high noble standing should have confided such a personal matter in the way alleged to a foreigner of inferior social status – a diplomat sprung from the lesser aristocracy of Savoy. Other valid reasons for challenging Chapuys's word arise from the nature of diplomacy and from his personal characteristics. By the sixteenth century, major powers were maintaining two kinds of ambassadors, resident and extraordinary. The resident ambassador seldom had the authority to negotiate treaties, a role that belonged to the special envoy who was usually of higher social and political status and who had the advantage of more immediate governmental intelligence. The resident diplomat's most important function was to gather news, which, however incredible, was to be reported to his government, for it was not his function to act as censor.[67]

As Charles V also explained, an ambassador often resorted to bribery to obtain information, operating thereby, as was widely known, as an inexpert spy. Those who were bribed were recognized as special friends and had the task of leaking information to the diplomat about their master's policies. When Henry's councillors 'leaked' information to Chapuys, they either fed him the official line or revealed alleged secrets that he wished to hear: some, such as the claim that Cromwell was opposed to the dissolution of the monasteries, bordered on the ridiculous.[68] The English knew that they had to be careful in their dealings with the clever Chapuys; Stephen Vaughan, who had been assigned to monitor the envoy's visit with Catherine of Aragon in late 1535, for example, reassured Cromwell after a meeting with Chapuys in 1540 that he, Vaughan, had been 'wyly ynough' for the sly diplomat. Word had earlier reached John Hackett in Flanders that Chapuys's predecessor in England had

---

[65] Warnicke, *Anne Boleyn*, pp. 82, 91, 112; G. Brenan, *Howard*, i, pp. 78–9; Ellis (ed.), *Original Letters*, third ser., ii, p. 133.
[66] Ives, *Anne Boleyn*, p. 193; *CSP Span.*, iv, pt. 2-1, no. 1048.
[67] D. Queller, *The Office of Ambassador in the Middle Ages* (Princeton, NJ, 1967), pp. 88–94.
[68] Queller, *Ambassador*, p. 94; *CSP Span.*, v, pt. 2, nos. 43, 130.

been so closely watched 'no man can speke with hym without ther be oon with hym'.[69]

Chapuys had taken up Catherine's cause upon his arrival in London after the recess of the court at Blackfriars. Until Anne's succession, her uncle often communicated with Chapuys, ingratiating himself with the diplomat in the hope that he might learn secret information concerning Charles V. In this context, the duke's statement that both Anne's father and he were opposed to the king's decision to marry her was significant because this information enabled the hostile ambassador to assume that Anne, presumably acting without family support, had bewitched Henry into divorcing Catherine. Following this assumption to its logical conclusion, Chapuys could then blame Anne instead of the king for the European crisis that the marital dispute had created. Far from being a valid private account of the royal household, Chapuys's dispatches provide an intriguing history of what he thought, and of what others wanted him to think, about court politics. The fact is that after 1531, when Catherine of Aragon was rusticated, no major courtier was willing to plead with the king on her behalf and, with the break-up of her household, her support at court ceased to exist. Even Thomas More's continuation as lord chancellor rested on the assumption that the king and parliament could decide the succession, and when he resigned it was to defend a Church whose unity was under attack. In 1533, the king's councillors, including William, Lord Mountjoy, Catherine's own chamberlain, attempted to persuade her to accept the title of princess dowager.[70]

Chapuys was at court only once during the spring of 1536 and thus dependent upon information that Cromwell and others chose to provide. Nevertheless, Professor E. W. Ives has argued that, on 18 April, Cromwell deserted the Boleyns, took over leadership of a presumed 'Aragonese faction', gained the aid of Jane Seymour, and persuaded Henry to agree to the execution of Anne. Manipulated by this alleged faction, Henry thus became the first and ultimately the only English king ever publicly to execute his consort, a wife, furthermore, whom he believed absolutely innocent of the charges of incest and adultery against her. Surely, the momentous decision to arrest his innocent queen, a niece of the duke of Norfolk, required more consideration and thought on Henry's part than the few days that fell between 18 April and 1 May. Even the heralds needed more time than this to stage an ennoblement! As an ironic twist, the

[69] *State Papers of Henry VIII* (11 vols., 1830–52), viii, p. 197; W. C. Richardson, *Stephen Vaughan: Financial Agent of Henry VIII* (Baton Rouge, LA, 1953), p. 19; E. F. Rogers (ed.), *The Letters of Sir John Hackett, 1526–1534* (Morgantown, WV, 1971), pp. 128, 331. In R. Merriman (ed.), *Life and Letters of Thomas Cromwell*, (2 vols., Oxford, 1902), ii, pp. 192–5, 207–8, Cromwell refers to Chapuys's actions in a perplexed manner.

[70] G. Mattingly, 'A Humanist Ambassador', *Journal of Modern History*, 4 (1932): 175–85; *CSP Span.*, iv, pt. 2-2, no. 1161 (p. 884); Warnicke, *Anne Boleyn*, pp. 2–3, 122–3; Gertrude, countess of Exeter, a friend to Catherine, was used by the king's ministers to feed Chapuys's lies. See William R. Harwood, 'The Courtenay Family in the Politics of Region and Nation in the Later Fifteenth and Early Sixteenth Centuries', unpublished Ph.D. dissertation, University of Cambridge, 1978, p. 127.

hostile Chapuys was one of the few reporters who believed Anne was innocent, a fact that becomes even more interesting when it is noted that Cromwell later contradicted the story he had confided to Chapuys about manipulating Anne's death. He informed English ambassadors abroad that the queen's conduct had been so abominable the women of her privy chamber could not conceal it.[71]

According to Chapuys, Cromwell had set this conspiracy in motion because Anne, who resided at Greenwich that spring until her arrest on 1 May, had persuaded Henry to support the French alliance. Chapuys accepted the absurd charge that she had been directing royal diplomacy even though he knew the king was in residence at London from about 24 February, during the last days of festival, until Easter Sunday, which in 1536 fell on 16 April. The diplomat even commented about the royal couple's unusual separation. Anne was, further-more, not so pro-French as Chapuys was led to believe. From late 1534 when Francis I suggested her stepdaughter, Mary, instead of her daughter, Elizabeth, as a bride for one of his sons, Anne had displayed a cool, distant attitude toward the members of the French embassy. Regardless of her relationship with them, the significant evidence about Anglo-French relations is that as soon as Henry and Cromwell learned Catherine was dead, they began to downplay their friendship with Francis.[72]

The erroneous belief that Anne interfered in foreign policy decisions in an aggressive way recently has led two scholars to propose entirely different and diametrically opposed theories about her fall. While Professor Ives has accepted Chapuys's claim that Cromwell brought about the innocent queen's death because of this interference, Dr G. W. Bernard has argued that the French embassy had special knowledge about the goings-on in her lying-in chamber. Citing verses from a poem written by Lancelot de Carles, secretary to the French ambassador in London, Bernard has argued that she was actually guilty of the charges against her. Misunderstandings about the roles of early-modern diplo-mats and members of their staff are at the heart of these two mistaken scholarly versions of her fall. Documents, whether epistles or verses, which were written by diplomats must be (as detailed above), treated as evidence of gossip circulat-ing at court, information deliberately leaked, or of official releases and not as reliable evidence for intimate events occurring in the privy chamber. The poet,

---

[71] Ives, *Anne Boleyn*, pp. 335–57; *LP*, x, no. 873.

[72] *CSP Span.*, v, pt. 2, no. 29 (p. 59), no. 43 (p. 84); Warnicke, *Anne Boleyn*, p. 200; G. W. Bernard, 'The Fall of Anne Boleyn', *EHR*, 106 (1991): 588, claimed that we should not 'attach too much significance to Chapuys's report that Henry and Anne had not been seeing much of each other . . .', thus, completely ignoring Chapuys's comments that Henry was in London that spring. Bernard (*ibid.*, p. 606) also declared that the 'accusations' against Anne in 1536 were not 'indiscriminate' even though the government actually accused her of having had incestuous relations with her brother, for example, in a town and on a date that were physically impossible. In the indictment she was charged with putting sexual ideas into the minds of five men some days before actually having sexual relations with them, a practice of which witches were regularly accused; see Warnicke, *Anne Boleyn*, pp. 215, 301, n. 50. See also Dale Hoak, 'Art, Culture, and Mentality in Renaissance Society: The Meaning of Hans Baldung Grien's *Bewitched Groom* (1544)', *Renaissance Quarterly*, 28 (1985): 488, 505.

equally importantly, had got wrong some crucial public facts, such as the sequence in which the trials of Anne and her brother took place. He also treated the sorrow and despair of the Princess Mary, who was a proposed bride for his king's son, with great gentleness.[73]

The somewhat intriguing three-and-one-half-month delay between Anne's miscarriage and her arrest can be explained better by contemporary religious and legal customs than by Professor Ives's theory about Cromwell's diplomatic and factional manoeuvering or by Dr Bernard's claim that she was actually guilty of adultery and that the king only learned about that misbehaviour in April. From thirty to forty days after birth, women remained secluded in their lying-in chambers, returning to family and social life only after their churching. By the time Anne was able to leave her rooms, the Hilary term was ending and lenten season was fast approaching. Twice a year, towards the end of Hilary and Trinity term, the nine common-law judges met to select their assize circuits. With them on their lenten and summer circuits went almost the entire legal profession. Consequently, the government's usual procedure was to delay until the regular legal terms the Westminster and London trials of accused traitors, who were normally arrested about four to six weeks before their indictments.[74] Those of Anne and her alleged lovers were held, of course, during Easter term.

The reason for her death surely was her miscarriage of a child that was probably deformed, a tragedy that would have been interpreted as an especially evil omen for the king and his realm at a time when he had only recently assumed the royal supremacy. In 1510 he had earlier prevented the court and the rest of Christendom from learning of Catherine's simple miscarriage because he deemed it a bad omen. More recently, in 1534, when one of Anne's pregnancies ended mysteriously, a similar silence reigned over the circumstances. Besides declaring Anne guilty of adultery, as noted above, Dr Bernard has challenged this explanation of her fall, pointing out that there was 'strong contemporary evidence that the foetus was not deformed'; his contemporary evidence is nothing more than a statement by Chapuys that the foetus 'had the appearance of a male'. Indeed, since only women were admitted into the lying-in chamber, except for visits by the would-be mother's husband, Chapuys could only have been repeating what was told him by those at court, who had good reason to dissemble.[75] In 1536, then, Cromwell's mission was to prevent the diplomatic

---

[73] Ives, *Anne Boleyn*, pp. 355–88; Bernard, 'The Fall of Anne Boleyn', 584–610; Lancelot de Carles, *Epistre contenant le procès criminel faict à l'encontre de la royne Anne Boullant d'Angelterre* (Lyon, 1545), printed in G. Ascoli, *La Grande-Bretagne Devant L'Opinion Française* (Paris, 1927), pp. 231–73, lines 239–60, 679–1038.

[74] Surrey was indicted on 13 January 1547, just before the opening of Hilary term; the council may have speeded up his trial because of the illness of the king, who died later that month; J. S. Cockburn, *A History of English Assizes, 1558–1714* (Cambridge, 1972), pp. x–xii, 1–23, 49.

[75] Warnicke, *Anne Boleyn*, pp. 173–5, 200; John Ponet, *A Short Treatise of Politic Power, 1556* (Menton, England, 1970), sig. Kiiii, pointed out how monstrous births in Mary's reign were thought to be bad omens for her; Smith, *Papal Enforcement*, p. 82, reported that Robert, king of France (r. 996–1031) repudiated his wife probably because she gave birth to a deformed child; CSP Span., ii, p. 133; v, pt. ii, no. 21 (p. 39); Bernard ('The Fall of Anne Boleyn', p. 586) questioned whether

corps from learning the cause of Anne's disgrace. Chapuys readily accepted the fabrication about her manipulation of foreign policy because he already viewed her as an implacable enemy of the emperor and a bewitcher of the king. After 1534, when their relationship with Anne had become somewhat estranged, members of the French embassy would have had no reason to reject the official line about her guilt.

Even if a 'faction' had succeeded in bringing about her fall (the theory of Professor Ives that hitherto has had widespread acceptance), it must not be described as Aragonese, for Cromwell, its alleged leader, never acted on behalf of the deceased Catherine or her daughter. Following Anne's execution, Mary did return to court, but only after Cromwell had forced her to accept her father's supremacy and her own illegitimacy. It is important to emphasize that the secretary's presumed leaks of information to Chapuys that spring about Anne's fall had helped to ensure the diplomat's later support in this pressuring of Mary to submit to her father's will.[76] Far from disclosing the actions of a presumed 'faction', the events of 1536 reveal a movement aimed against Anne that involved all major courtiers. Once the king had withdrawn his favour, all her supporters, her kin, her household, and her clients deserted her. Her uncle, Norfolk, headed the commission that tried her. Even her aunt, Anne Shelton, became Princess Mary's friend although Chapuys at one time had suspected Lady Shelton of mistreating the princess when she was her governess. With her husband, Lady Shelton supported the succession of Mary to the throne in the crisis of 1553.[77] No one except Thomas Cranmer, archibishop of Canterbury, dared to speak out on Anne's behalf in 1536; he protested to the king that although he could not believe that Anne was an adultress, he knew that Henry would never have proceeded against her without valid reasons.[78]

The king's enquiry into his marriage with Catherine of Aragon coincided with religious debates of the Reformation era, debates that naturally played an important role at court but not, arguably, in the bifurcated, factional way often described. Recently, persuasive arguments have been made for greater diversity

witches actually had deformed children; for contemporary references to witches having deformed babies, see Thomas Cooper, *The mystery of witch-craft* (1617), pp. 121–4. See also *The Maleus Maleficarum of Heinrich Kramer and James Springer*, ed. M. Summers (New York, 1971), p. 113, for a discussion of how the devil infected babies of witches impregnated by their husbands; see also Jean Donnison, *Midwives and Medical men: A History of Inter-Professional Rivalries and Women's Rights* (New York, 1977) pp. 1–3. Bernard ('The Fall of Anne Boleyn', p. 587) also revealed how rooted he is in modern attitudes toward sexuality by his questioning whether having to admit to impotency would be 'any less humiliating for the king than the report of a deformed foetus'. Of course it would be, because impotence specific to one woman was thought to be caused by witchcraft, whereas the birth of a deformed foetus could possibly be blamed on the father's behaviour. If my theory is correct, Henry chose to blame Anne rather than himself. For impotency, see *Maleus Maleficarum*, pp. 4–5, 26, 56.

[76] D. Loades, *Mary Tudor* (Oxford, 1989), pp. 81–2, 101–3; *CSP Span.*, v, pt. ii, no. 70 (pp. 183–5).

[77] T. H. Swales, 'The Redistribution of the Monastic Lands in Norfolk at the Dissolution', *Norfolk Archaeology*, 34 (1966): 14–44; *CSP Span.*, v, pt. 2, no. 9 (p. 14).

[78] G. Burnet, *The History of the Reformation in the Church of England* (3 vols. in 6 parts, Oxford, 1816), vol. i, pt. i, pp. 364–7.

among reformers than the traditional protestant/Catholic division. J. F. Davis has suggested that Erasmian humanism combined with local reform in such a way as to give rise to a series of evangelical movements in Europe and that Thomas Bilney, who was martyred in 1531, was a leading spirit of such a movement in England, although Bilney's views have remained somewhat difficult to categorize.[79] So popular has the notion of these movements become that some scholars have begun to use the term evangelical as though it were synonymous with proto-protestantism.[80]

Anne Boleyn, it has been argued, was an evangelical who joined with Cromwell in a court 'faction' to manipulate the king into marriage and into religious reform.[81] That these two were interested in some kind of reform is true: she patronized Cranmer, who promoted Henry's divorce and who was in 1537 to praise Cromwell for doing 'more than all others together in whatever has hitherto been effected respecting the reformation of religion and of the clergy . . .'.[82] That Anne and Cromwell belonged to the same presumed 'faction', much less one that was held together by religious zeal, is, however, unlikely. Ennobled as the lady marquess of Pembroke in 1532, she did not require the assistance of a royal minister to win Henry over to marriage, an action to which he had been so committed in 1527 that he had requested a papal bull to validate the union. Four years later, Henry turned to Cromwell for assistance in finding a way to divorce Catherine legally, a path that by its very nature would result in a challenge to the legal jurisdiction of the papacy. In the meantime, Anne promoted the reading of the scriptures, interceding in 1528 with Wolsey on behalf of a cleric imprisoned on a charge of owning heretical books, and writing in 1534 to Cromwell, soon to be the vicegerent, on behalf of an individual condemned for printing the New Testament. From 1527 until 1536, her power and her following depended entirely upon Henry's favour. Evidence abounds that she used her influence on behalf of her Howard and Boleyn kin.[83]

How 'evangelical' was used in contemporary writings will be helpful to an understanding of Anne's role at court. In its purest form, the word refers to the first four gospels of the New Testament, but in the early Tudor period it often described reliance on the scriptures as the major religious authority. From the

---

[79] J. F. Davis, 'The Trials of Thomas Bilney and the English Reformation', *HJ*, 24 (1981): 775–90; G. Walker, 'Saint or Schemer? The Heresy Trials of Thomas Bilney, Reconsidered', *JEH*, 40 (1989): 219–30; see also G. R. Elton, 'Persecution and Toleration in the English Reformation', in *Persecution and Toleration: Studies in Church History*, vol. xxi (Oxford, 1984), pp. 163–87; G. H. Williams, *The Radical Reformation* (Philadelphia, PA, 1962), pp. 2–16.

[80] M. Dowling (ed.), 'William Laytmer's Cronickille of Anne Bulleyn', *Camden Miscellany, XXX*, fourth ser., vol. 39 (1990), pp. 30, 34–6, 39; S. Brigden (ed.), 'The Letters of Richard Scudamore to Sir Philip Hoby, September 1549–March 1555', in *Camden Miscellany XXX*, fourth ser., vol. 39 (1990), pp. 74–5.

[81] Dowling, 'Anne Boleyn and Reform', pp. 31–45.

[82] H. Robinson (ed.), *Original Letters Relative to the English Reformation*, Parker Society (2 vols., Cambridge, 1846), i, p. 15.

[83] Warnicke, *Anne Boleyn*, pp. 68–9, 110–11, 155.

mid-1530s Englishmen seem to have extended the name more selectively to those who denied the papal supremacy. In 1546 William Thomas, for example, explained that when Henry had enjoined his doctors to decide whether his action as king could be judged by a papal legate, they had questioned whether they should rely on the canon or the 'evangelical' law. Reportedly, 'smiling at the ignorance of so fond a question', he answered: 'the Gospel of Christ ought to be the absolute rule unto all others'. Their 'evangelical' conclusion was that popish authority over kings was a usurped authority.[84]

By contemporary standards, Henry was surely one of the most devoted of the English 'evangelicals', for he repeatedly favoured Biblical law over papal decrees. Interested in theology, a pastime that Erasmus had recommended to all kings in 1516, Henry also fostered religious debate at court.[85] Cranmer learned that when the king received a religious book, he requested at least two courtiers of different opinions to review it for him. After considering their reports, he declared his own judgments about any disputed points. Operating within these procedures, Cranmer and Wolsey, certainly, and Anne, probably, presented him with religious books.[86] Henry also placed limits on such debate. In May of 1531, after having given the king one of William Tyndale's works forwarded by Stephen Vaughan, Cromwell revealed to a friend Henry's displeasure with it, warning him thereafter not to show himself favourably inclined towards Tyndale.[87] Court favourites clearly were not committed to furthering religious views opposed by the king: in order to stay in power after 1527, they supported the divorce and after 1534, the royal supremacy. Most, like the English generally, were probably far less interested in this debate than was their monarch, for the finer points of theology would have had little meaning for their untrained minds.[88]

Given the way patronage was dispensed, royal favourites who wished to promote reform, with the important exception of Cranmer and possibly Hugh Latimer, seldom rewarded and attracted followings or factions of only like-minded people. Studies of patronage indicate that most positions in the Church

---

[84] Thomas, *Pilgrim*, pp. 20–1; in *Letters of Thomas Cromwell*, pp. ii, 202–4, 220–1, Cromwell seems to be using 'evangelical' in this sense; see also Jean de Valsergues d'Ablin, *A notable discourse plainlye and truely who are the right ministers of the catholic church* (1575), epistle to the reader, sig. 8, for the following English translator's comment: 'We must, I say beware, that we be not deluded, and under colour of Evangelical veritie, be made to receave pernitious and damnable heresies, as alas the more pitie, hath miserably chaunced to our noble Realm of Englande, under colour of bringing us to truth, leading us awaye from truth, to the utter decaye of all godliness, and setting up of counterfaite religion.'

[85] Erasmus, *Education of a Christian Prince*, p. 153.

[86] Robinson (ed.), *Original Letters*, i, p. 15; ii, pp. 611–12; Ellis (ed.), *Original Letters*, second ser., i, p. 286; Warnicke, *Anne Boleyn*, pp. 111–13.

[87] Merriman (ed.), *Letters of Thomas Cromwell*, i, p. 335.

[88] R. Whiting, *The Blind Devotion of the People: Popular Religion and the English Reformation* (Cambridge, 1989), pp. 23, 38, 266–8; M. Bowker, 'The Henrician Reformation and the Parish Clergy', *BIHR*, 50 (1977): 30–1; T. Fuller, *The Worthies of England*, ed. J. Freeman (1952), pp. 29, 207, 259, names many who served four or five Tudors despite the religious changes.

were granted for local or family reasons,[89] as Wolsey's statement to Cromwell shows:

And grete pitie it . . . that any strangers shulde have any preferrement by lease, copy, or otherwise afore any one my pore kynne, unto whom I am naturally and of charitie bounden to see in their necessities.[90]

An eighteenth-century civilian justified the actions of Matthew Hutton, the Elizabethan archbishop of York, in leasing his episcopal property by quoting from St Paul's first Epistle to Timothy: 'If any provide not for his own, and especially for those of his own house, he hath denied the faith, and is worse than an infidel.'[91]

As one who supported the reading of Scripture but who seems to have adhered to traditional beliefs concerning the sacraments and good works, Anne patronized family and friends who in future fell on both sides of the protestant/ Catholic divide. For example, Margaret Douglas, a later Catholic claimant to the throne, as well as Mary, duchess of Richmond, a patron of John Foxe, the martyrologist, served her. Lady Richmond's father, the third duke of Norfolk who actively supported the royal supremacy, is usually termed a conservative Catholic,[92] but in the 1540s his daughter became a protestant and his two sons were criticized for eating meat during Lent and disputing too much over the scriptures.[93] The queen's most devoted attendant may well have been Anne Savage, who witnessed Anne's marriage to the king in 1533. The future wife of Thomas, Lord Berkeley, she was to win notoriety for her strong Catholic stance.[94]

To describe Catherine of Aragon and her friends as conservative Catholics, furthermore, is misleading, although they necessarily were supportive of the papal supremacy. Catherine patronized Juan Luis Vives and Thomas Wyatt, as well as John Fisher, bishop of Rochester; the latter, of course, attempted to attract humanist scholars to Cambridge. David Loades has recently pointed out that the religious settlement of her daughter, Queen Mary I, though it restored the papal supremacy, can basically be associated with Christian humanism.[95] While balking at an evangelical heresy that was Lutheran or sacramentarian in nature – one that denied the sacramental system and doctrine of good works of

[89] R. O'Day and F. Heal, *Continuity and Change: Personnel and Administration of the Church in England, 1500–1642* (Leicester, 1976), pp. 68–9; F. Heal, *Of Prelates and Princes: A Study of the Economic and Social Position of the Tudor Episcopate* (Cambridge, 1980), pp. 163–4.
[90] Ellis (ed.), *Original Letters*, second ser., ii, p. 31.
[91] St Paul's epistle, quoted in G. D. Squibb, *Founders' Kin: Privilege and Pedigree* (Oxford, 1972), p. 1.
[92] Ellis (ed.), *Original Letters*, first ser., ii, p. 85; Nott, *Works of Henry Howard*, page c.
[93] Warnicke, *Women of the Renaissance*, p. 101; Miller, *Henry VIII*, p. 117.
[94] Smyth, *Berkeleys*, p. 253.
[95] Warnicke, *Women of the Renaissance*, pp. 31–7; T. Wyatt, *Of the quyete of mynde* (1528), dedication; B. Bradshaw, 'Bishop John Fisher, 1469–1535: the man and his works', in B. Bradshaw and E. Duffy (eds.), *Humanism, Reform and the Reformation: the Career of Bishop John Fisher* (Cambridge, 1989), pp. 6–7; Loades, *Mary Tudor*, pp. 244–5; D. Fenlon, *Heresy and Obedience in Tridentine Italy: Cardinal Pole and the Counter-Reformation* (Cambridge, 1972), pp. 4–19.

Catholicism – many Henrician churchmen and courtiers could accept without too much difficulty the distribution of the Bible in the vernacular, fewer holy days, and the abolition of the great shrines and pilgrimages, all of which were compatible with the humanism of Erasmus.[96] The major issue that split this intellectual community apart in the 1530s was the royal supremacy.

Ultimately, the best explanation for the rise and fall of Anne Boleyn draws upon family and kinship relations. In 1527 when the king decided to divorce Catherine, a queen whose infant sons had died in the nursery, he set in motion events that were encouraging to religious reform. At the same time, the Howards and their kin and affinity, including the Boleyns who were already in favour because of the second duke's victory over the Scots, won increased influence at court when the king chose Anne, a Catholic evangelical, as his bride. After, she, in turn, proved unable to provide Henry with the desired surviving male child and was probably delivered of a deformed foetus, loss of royal favour led to her downfall and the desertion of her household, kin, and clients. After her death, reform moved at a pace set by the king, the supreme head of the new Church of England, a king who continued to pray for the birth of a healthy male heir, the greatest sign of God's good will.

[96] *The Colloquies of Erasmus*, pp. 46–78, 285–312; C. M. N. Eire, *War Against the Idols: The Reformation of Worship from Erasmus to Calvin* (Cambridge, 1986), pp. 28–53.

3　*The iconography of the crown imperial*

DALE HOAK

At Leaden Hall in London on 29 May 1533 onlookers beheld an astonishing sight, a cloud so cleverly contrived that it parted on cue, releasing on wings a wondrous device, the heraldic white falcon of Anne Boleyn. Cloud and mechanical falcon were part of an elaborate tableau, but one of many staged for Anne on the occasion of her entry into London that day, a day of pageantry so spectacular, remembered Edward Hall, that 'he that saw it not would not believe it'. Anne and her party had stopped at Leaden Hall in order to witness the climax of her falcon's dynastic 'flight', and she was not disappointed in what she saw, for when the bird landed on a golden root in a bed of red and white roses an angel swooped down from the same cloud and to the sound of 'great melody' placed a crown on its head, all in obvious anticipation of Anne's own coronation two days later.[1]

The coronation pageants of May 1533, the greatest of the domestic public spectacles staged by the Tudors, allowed royal propagandists like Nicholas Udall and John Leland, the authors of the Leaden Hall script, the opportunity to advertise Anne's indispensable role in the promotion of Henry VIII's new 'imperial' authority, for the crown borne by the angel was, as Hall noticed, 'a close crowne of gold', or 'imperial' diadem. The message was clear: God had conferred imperial authority on Anne and Henry's issue by her, or as Udall's cruder verse put it, 'an Angel descending crowned the empire-worthy bird . . .'.[2]

---

[1] Hall, *Chronicle*, pp. 800–1.

[2] The verses written by Udall and Leland for Anne's coronation pageants were printed by F. J. Furnivall (ed.), *Ballads from Manuscripts: Ballads on the Condition of England in Henry VIII's and Edward VI's Reign* (2 vols., 1868–72; reprinted New York, 1968), i, pp. 373–404; the quotation is on p. 376. Leland's holograph draft of the script (BL, Royal MS. 18 A. lxiv, fos. 8–9) is cited and discussed by John N. King, *Tudor Royal Iconography: Literature and Art in an Age of Religious Crisis* (Princeton, NJ, 1989), pp. 50–2 and notes 56–9; King notes especially the way in which the tableau played upon the association of Anne and the Virgin Mary, an association reflected in numerous visual and verbal aspects of other coronation pageants. Hall's description is in Hall, *Chronicle*, p. 800–1. Recent accounts of Anne's entry into London include Retha M. Warnicke, *The Rise and Fall of Anne Boleyn: Family Politics at the Court of Henry VIII* (Cambridge, 1989), pp. 123–7; E. W. Ives, *Anne Boleyn* (Oxford, 1986), pp. 273–84; and Sydney Anglo, *Spectacle, Pageantry and Early Tudor Policy* (Oxford, 1969), pp. 252–4. The device of the falcon with sceptre, arched crown, and roses appears to have been invented for Anne on the occasion of her marriage, allowing Udall and Leland to exploit the symbolism of her new badge. For some references to artistic representations of Anne's imperial falcon, see Ives, *Anne Boleyn*, pp. 289–90, 294, 300 and plates 28 and 35.

The 'empire' of which Anne Boleyn was worthy had of course first been identified in law only one month earlier in the Act of Appeals, the statutory basis of the transformation of Henry's jurisdiction from 'royal' to 'imperial'.[3] The theory of 'imperial' monarchy articulated in the Act assumed that in his own realm, the empire that was England, the king functioned as an emperor – *rex in regno suo est imperator*, as the medieval formula ran[4] – and like Charlemagne and Charlemagne's successors, the medieval Christian emperors, Henry, when he was portrayed artistically in the conventional iconography of 'majesty', was typically shown enthroned, holding the symbolic instruments of imperial rule, the sceptre of state, a secular emblem of sovereignty, and the orb surmounted by a cross, a sign of world-wide Christian dominion. As an 'imperial' king, he was also depicted wearing an arched, or closed, crown.

The Carolingians introduced arched crowns into Western Europe, a style probably derived from the early Germanic helmet (whose wide, skull-hugging crossed bands afforded protection against blows to the head) or from the Byzantine's emperor's arched *stemma*, which was also originally a helmet.[5] Technically speaking, the only closed crown of authentically 'imperial' character was that of the Holy Roman Emperor. Originally of open design, it was modified in the eleventh century by Conrad II (1024–39), who gave it a jewelled crest, or arch, running from front to back, and again in the fifteenth century by the Habsburgs, who added two large mitre-like cusps on either side of the central arch.[6] This mitred, single-arched crown of the Empire was of unique

---

3 The text of the Act of Appeals of 1533 (24 Henry VIII, c. 12) is accessible in G. R. Elton (ed.), *The Tudor Constitution: Documents and Commentary* (second edn, Cambridge, 1982), pp. 353–8. In 1979 Professor Ullmann drew attention to Henry's concern with the transformation of his authority from royal to imperial, noting the changes Henry intended to make in promises kings of England since Edward II had sworn at their coronation. Henry himself redrafted the form of those regal promises: the 'jurysdiccion and dignite ryall' of the traditional oath became in Henry's new phrase a 'crown or imperial jurisdiction'; Walter Ullmann, '"This Realm of England is an Empire"', *Journal of Ecclesiastical History*, 30 (1979): 183, citing BL, Cotton MS. Tiberius E. viii, fo. 100. However, Professor Ullmann was wrong in dating Henry's redrafting to 1509. Shelley Lockwood, a research fellow at Christ's College, Cambridge, has established (in her as yet unpublished research) that a date in the late 1520s is more likely, a date coinciding with Henry's attempt to discover the historical basis of his presumed authority over the English Church, authority termed 'imperial' in the Act of Appeals. I wish to thank Miss Lockwood for her kindness in communicating to me by letter the essence of her findings.

4 For the thirteenth-century origins of the concept *rex in regno suo est imperator*, see Richard Koebner, *Empire* (Cambridge, 1961), p. 36. Tom Mayer has argued that Henry VIII may have discovered the formula in fifteenth-century French sources; for this and references to pre-Tudor French and Italian usages, as well as recent scholarship on the question, see Mayer's essay above, pp. 11–30, and T. F. Mayer, 'Tournai and Tyranny: Imperial Kingship and Critical Humanism', *HJ*, 34 (1991): 235, note 69.

5 Edward Francis Twining, *A History of the Crown Jewels of Europe* (1960), p. 106. The Metropolitan Museum of Art in New York City possesses a good example of a *Spangehelm*, a Frankish chieftain's arched helmet of about the seventh century; see the reproduction in Howard Hibbard, *The Metropolitan Museum of Art* (New York, 1986), p. 143. The comprehensive, definitive study of medieval crowns is Percy Ernst Schramm, *Herrschaftszeichen und Staatssymbolik. Beiträge zu ihrer Geschichte vom dritten zum sechzehnten Jahrhundert* (3 vols., Stuttgart, 1954–65), vols. ii and iii.

6 Twining, *Crown Jewels of Europe*, p. 329ff.; Philip Grierson, 'The Origins of the English Sovereign and the Symbolism of the Closed Crown', *British Numismatic Journal*, 38 (1964): 128.

design. The closed personal crowns of the emperors were of a different style, typically exhibiting two high, intersecting arches.[7] Other European crowns were also closed. The Hungarian crown of St Stephen and the Bohemian crown of St Wenceslas, for example, employed crossing bands of metal rising above a ridged circlet, the arches of the former being low and flat, those of the latter, higher and more pointed.[8]

In England, the images of kings on Anglo-Saxon and Norman coins and in illuminations appear to point to the early use of closed crowns of various shapes,[9] but such images, it has been noted, cannot necessarily be accepted as representations of reality, as they probably reflect the whims of artists and engravers.[10] In fact, during the thirteenth and fourteenth centuries, the earliest period for which the evidence is incontrovertible, the English royal crown was open, without arches, as was the Capetian crown. It is thought that kings of England eventually adopted a closed crown in order to distinguish the nature of their regality from that of their French counterparts. If so, when? And when did the closed English crown acquire an 'imperial' meaning?

Percy Ernst Schramm, the acknowledged authority on medieval *Staatsymbolik*, concluded that Henry VII introduced the closed crown into England, but Schramm's views, which appeared in 1954–56, were corrected in 1964 by the British numismatist, Philip Grierson. Citing historians of the regalia who knew that Henry V (1413–22) had worn a closed crown, Grierson speculated that this was the 'arched' crown of St Edward which Froissart said had been used at Henry IV's coronation in 1399, a crown perhaps first fashioned in the reign of Richard II.[11] Controversy over the date of origin of this crown is irrelevant, since (as will be seen) attention should have been directed to another arched crown in use in Henry V's reign, one sometimes confused with St Edward's. In any case, Grierson emphatically rejected the notion that the closed crown acquired an 'imperial' meaning in Henry V's reign; Henry VII, he argued, was the instigator of such a change.[12] It is certainly true that by the late fifteenth century, in England as on the continent, virtually any type of closed crown was designated 'imperial', 'a natural consequence', it has been said, of the spread of the notion *rex in regno suo est imperator*. Thus Charles VIII was the first king of

---

[7] Thus the crowns of the Emperor Sigismund, as shown on his seals in contemporary portraits; Twining, *Crown Jewels of Europe*, p. 127.

[8] Grierson, 'Origins of the English Sovereign', 127.

[9] Twining, *Crown Jewels of Europe*, pp. 106, 111, 133.

[10] Grierson, 'Origins of the English Sovereign', 128.

[11] Schramm, *Herrschaftszeichen und Staatsymbolik*, iii, pp. 1041–3; Grierson, 'Origins of the English Sovereign', 129–30. In his later notes, published posthumously, Schramm credited Grierson's work: *Herrschaftszeichen und Staatsymbolik: Nachträge aus dem Nachlass* (Munich, 1978), pp. 58–9.

[12] '... there is no evidence of any ideological reason behind the form of the English crown at so early a date'; Grierson, 'Origins of the English Sovereign', 130, note 1; '... by the 16th century it had come to be very generally accepted that the closed crown was specifically "imperial" in character'; *ibid.*, 132.

France to wear the closed imperial crown ('une riche couronne d'or à l'impér-aille'), apparently not later than 1494.[13]

In what follows, I shall endeavour to establish, if only in outline, the iconography of the English crown imperial from its beginnings to the mid-1570s. This history, I shall argue, shows that Henry V established the practice of wearing a closed royal crown, and that this crown (which was not mentioned by Froissart) acquired the designation 'imperial' during his reign. It will be seen that Henry VI, Edward IV and Richard III successively advanced the symbolism of the crown imperial; that Henry VII and Henry VIII (before the Reformation) exploited this symbolism in heretofore unnoticed ways; and that protestants at the courts of Edward VI and Elizabeth I invested the Tudors' crown imperial with new meaning.

The earliest reliable visual evidence for the use of the closed crown in England is in stone at Westminster Abbey and dates from about 1438–52; it consists of two sculpted representations of Henry V. In his will of 1415, Henry V made provision for the construction of a chantry over his tomb in the Abbey. For the external facings of this raised chapel, John Thirsk, Henry VI's master mason, designed a series of narrative reliefs, or panels, illustrating great events in the life of the king; those decorating the sides of the bridge spanning the ambulatory dramatize the two principal moments of his coronation on 9 April 1413. The first, on the south side of the bridge, records the actual moment of crowning; two prelates are shown placing a crown on the head of the seated king. The second, reproduced here from the north side of the bridge (plate 1), records the moment when, in the course of the ceremony, the peers rendered fealty to their already-crowned sovereign.[14] These panels are of the utmost importance for students of royalist symbolism, as the artist has represented *two* arched crowns of different size and shape. The crown in the coronation scene on the south side of the chantry appears to be a small, tight-fitting, helmet-like diadem with low, flattened arches. The larger, more ornate crown in the panel on the north side, the one shown here (plate 1), exhibits two prominent arches which rise higher above the king's head; at the point of the crossing there is a sizeable finial in the shape of a cross.[15]

[13] Ralph E. Giesey, *The Royal Funeral Ceremony in Renaissance France* (Geneva, 1960), p. 118, note 60. At the funeral of Louis XII the king's effigy wore a 'couronne d'or entière en façon d'empire'; *ibid.* Giesey said 'the closed crown [was] called the *couronne impériale* because of its similarity to the imperial crown, and to distinguish it from the open crown used in France during the middle ages . . .'; *ibid.*, p. 19.

[14] See W. H. St John Hope, 'The Funeral, Monument, and Chantry Chapel of King Henry the Fifth', *Archaeologia*, 65 (1930): 172–5 (and the plates opposite p. 173); Royal Commission on Historical Monuments, *An Inventory of the Historical Monuments in London* (5 vols., 1924–30), i, p. 71 and plates 138 (showing the south face) and 135 and 136 (the north side); Lawrence Stone, *Sculpture in Britain. The Middle Ages* (The Pelican History of Art: Harmondsworth, Middlesex 1955), pp. 204–5.

[15] Martin Holmes noticed this difference between the two crowns; 'New Light on St Edward's Crown', *Archaeologia*, 97 (1959): 217 and pl. lxxx.

Plate 1. The coronation of Henry V, a detail of a sculpted stone panel on the north side of the bridge of Henry V's chantry at Westminster Abbey, executed 1438–52 by John Thirsk, Henry VI's master mason. Thirsk has portrayed not the actual crowning, but the rendering of fealty by the lords to an already-crowned king. Henry is enthroned in majesty in his parliament robes. His right hand is broken off; his left holds the remains of a rod or sceptre. He is surrounded by standing and kneeling peers, including, on the right, the mitred figures of Thomas Arundel, archbishop of Canterbury, and on the left, the abbot of Westminster, William of Colchester, both of whom are using their hands to support the king's arms and his heavy (partially restored) arched crown.

As the panel on the south side of the chantry illustrates Henry V's crowning, the smaller arched crown depicted there must be St Edward's crown, i.e. the crown which by tradition was reserved exclusively for the actual coronation. In his description of the coronation of Henry IV in 1399, a description presumably based on an eye-witness's account, Froissart said that St Edward's crown was indeed 'arched over',[16] but he said nothing of a second crown, also arched. Now St Edward's crown was considered to be a holy relic – it was kept and revered as such with other relics at St Edward's shrine at the Abbey – and so was not associated with the dignity royal. Another crown, the king's own crown of estate, 'our great crown', as King John called it, symbolized the powers of kingship, and, as already noted, from the beginning of the thirteenth century at the latest, this crown, like the French royal crown, had been open, not closed. As there exists no trace before 1413 of the use of any sort of arched crown other than St Edward's, the evidence of the sculpted panel on the north side of Henry V's chantry (plate 1) suggests that Henry V added arches to the heretofore open 'great crown', giving it a distinctive new shape, that of a crown whose pronounced upward-sloping crossed bands were topped by a cross-shaped finial. Strictly speaking, of course, Thirsk's sculpture is evidence not of the existence of such a crown in April 1413, but of the fact that an artist in the employ of Henry VI associated such a crown with Henry V at the time of his coronation. The association is credible, as Thirsk was first appointed by Henry V in 1420. In any case, the crown Thirsk pictured here is almost certainly the re-fashioned 'great crown' of England, what a later age would call the imperial state crown.[17]

More to the point is the probable association of this new closed crown with the theory of the 'imperial' dignity of the English king. This theory, so well developed in the writings of thirteenth- and fourteenth-century 'legists' at the

[16] Froissart, *Chronique*, vol. xvi of *Oeuvres de Froissart*, ed. Kervyn de Lettenhove (Brussels, 1872), p. 207. Froissart's wording – 'Et puis fut apportée la couronne saint Édouard, et estoit laditte couronne archie en trois . . .' – should read '. . . archie en *croix* . . .', as Grierson persuasively pointed out: Grierson, 'Origins of the English Sovereign', 129, note 2.

[17] See M. R. Holmes, 'The Crowns of England', *Archaeologia*, 86 (1937): 76–80, for the 'great crown', St Edward's crown and the implications of Froissart's description; and Holmes, 'New Light on St Edward's Crown', 216–18, for the distinctive nature and shape of St Edward's crown. As Holmes pointed out ('New Light on St Edward's Crown', 217–18), there exists independent visual evidence for the low, flat-arched shape of St Edward's crown, a crown with a small rounded finial very unlike the cross-shaped finial atop the imperial crown: see the crown worn by the effigy of St Edward the Confessor on Henry VII's tomb-screen at Westminster Abbey (reproduced in Holmes, 'New Light on St Edward's Crown', pl. lxxix, b) and the crowns of St Edward twice shown in the very expertly observed pen-and-ink drawings executed in 1532 (probably by an artist of Netherlandish origin) in the vellum 'Islip Roll' in the Library of the Society of Antiquaries, conveniently reproduced in large facsimile in W. H. St John Hope, 'The Obituary Roll of John Islip, Abbot of Westminster, 1500–1532', *Vestusta Monumenta*, vol. vii (1906), pp. 1–13. The drawing of Henry VIII's coronation on the third membrane of the 'Islip Roll' shows Archbishop William Warham placing St Edward's crown on the king's head (St John Hope, 'Obituary Roll', pl. xxiv and Holmes, 'New Light on St Edward's Crown', pl. lxxvi, d). In the 'Islip Roll', in the architectural border of the abbot's death chamber, St Edward the Confessor is portrayed standing, holding a sceptre and the ball and cross, and wearing his arched crown (St John Hope, 'Obituary Roll', pl. xxi; Holmes, 'New Light on St Edward's Crown', pl. lxxvi, b.).

French court,[18] found expression in some lines composed about 1420 by John Page, a soldier who fought with Henry at the siege of Rouen (July 1418–January 1419). Proclaiming the king obedient to no one but God, Page said that Henry was 'Within his own [realm] emperoure, / And also Kyng and conqueroure'.[19] Henry V's status as an emperor–king was recalled in the translation of Tito Livio Frulovisi's *Vita Henrici Quinti* (c. 1438), a translation commissioned in 1513 by Henry VIII on the eve of his own invasion of France and his meeting there with his ally, Emperor Maximilian I. The translation preserves the story of the dramatic, sword-in-hand reception staged by Henry V's brother, Humphrey, duke of Gloucester, for Emperor Sigismund on the occasion of Sigismund's visit to England in 1416. Gloucester greeted him in the surf off Dover, demanding that before Sigismund wade ashore, he foreswear exercising in England any authority as emperor. One suspects that Gloucester and Henry V had rehearsed this confrontation beforehand: it '. . . was thus deuised', said the 'Translator', 'for sauinge of the Kings Imperiall Maiestie, [who] is an Emperor within his Realme'.[20]

These words were written in 1513 or 1514, but the man who conveyed the story to Livio's 'Translator' was the seventh earl of Ormond (d. 1515) who had heard it from his father, the fourth earl (1392–1452), who had fought with Henry V at Agincourt.[21] From another eye-witness in the English camp at Agincourt, the Seigneur de St Rémy, we know that on the field of battle Henry V wore over his helmet 'a rich gold crown' with arches, one 'circled like the imperial crown'.[22] Artistically, the closest we can get to Henry V in action is the drawing of him reproduced here from a mid fifteenth-century English book of arms (plate 2); the artist, probably a herald, pictured him riding his charger in full armour and wearing a closed crown over his basinet, as at Agincourt.[23] The contemporary designation 'imperial' for this new crown is clear enough: Georges Chastellain saw the real thing in the king's funeral cortège in 1422, 'an

[18] Koebner, *Empire*, p. 36.
[19] Quoted in *The First English Life of King Henry the Fifth*, ed. C. L. Kingsford (Oxford, 1911), p. xxxiv.
[20] When Sigismund's boat dropped anchor off Dover, Gloucester and the English greeting party rode into the water 'with there swordes drawen . . .', warning Sigismund that 'if he would enter [England] as an Emperor, as into a realm as vnder his Empire, or any thinge of his Imperiall power therein to commaunde, they were ready to resist him in the Kings name'. When Sigismund assured the duke that he came 'as the Kings friend . . . and not as an Emperor of this Realme', Gloucester returned to the shore 'and receaued the Emperor' honourably; *ibid.*, pp. 67–8. See also C. S. Kingsford, 'A Legend of Sigismund's visit to England', *EHR*, 26 (1911): 750–1.
[21] Thomas Butler (d. 1515), the seventh earl of Ormond and the youngest son of James, the fourth earl, was about ninety years old when he related the story to Livio's 'Translator'; he was about thirty years old when his father, James, died; J. H. Wylie and W. T. Waugh, *The Reign of Henry V* (3 vols., Cambridge, 1914–29; reprinted New York, 1968), iii, pp. 445–8.
[22] '. . . une riche couronne d'or serquellée comme impérialle couronne': Jean le Févre, Seigneur de St Rémy, *Chronique*, ed. F. Moran (2 vols., Paris, 1876–81), i, p. 244, also quoted in Grierson, 'Origins of the English Sovereign', 130, note 5. A band of French gentlemen, vowing to knock this crown off Henry's head or die trying, succeeded in breaking it; St Rémy, *Chronique*, i, p. 250.
[23] BL, Harleian MS. 2169, fo. 2. For a brief note on this manuscript, see 'A Fifteenth-Century Book of Arms', *The Ancestor*, 3 (1902): 185–213.

Plate 2. A pen-and-ink drawing of Henry V in a mid-fifteenth-century book of arms (BL, Harleian MS. 2169, fo. 2). The artist, probably a herald, was perhaps remembering Henry in action at Agincourt (1415), where, according to an eye-witness, on the field the king actually wore an arched crown over his battle-helmet. The verse above extols the warrior-king as 'The fyfth Herrey of Knyghthode the lodesterre ... Gretly expert and marchall dyscyplyne. Worthy to stonde amonge the worthy ix ...'

Plate 3. In this pen-and-ink drawing of Henry VI in armour (BL, Harleian MS. 2169, fo. 3), a companion to the drawing of Henry V (plate 2), the herald/artist imagined the mounted king wearing on his basinet the closed English crown over his open French diadem.

Imperial diadem of gold and precious stones' set on the head of Henry's boiled-leather effigy.[24]

Nothing in the contemporary record, however, tells us what Henry V intended by the wearing of this new crown. Perhaps he really meant to project in a symbolic way the older notion that in England, English kings were emperors too. If Henry learned the theory *rex est imperator* from French sources, as was possible, he may have understood that such sources invariably were concerned to distinguish a king and his *imperium* from the Holy Roman Emperor and his *imperium* within the Empire: in fourteenth-century French legalistic usage, *rex est imperator* conveyed, not an abstract, generalized conception of royal powers or statehood, but the respect due to a king who was an independent, sovereign ruler, one whose standing rivalled that of the emperor.[25] However, if Henry V wished to emphasize his equality with Emperor Sigismund, Sigismund's visit cannot have been the occasion for the innovation of the English crown imperial, as some have assumed,[26] since Henry was wearing the new crown the year before Sigismund's coming.

As conqueror, king and emperor, Henry V laid claim to the crown of France. The 'imperial' character of his closed crown was not, however, based on a territorial conception of an Anglo-French 'empire'. Henry's son and successor, the infant Henry VI (b. 1421), simply fell heir to two thrones, and so was twice crowned, first with the closed English crown at Westminster Abbey on 6 November 1429 and afterwards, on 16 December 1431 at Saint-Denis, with the open crown of France.[27] The distinction between the physical shape of those two crowns was clearly remembered by the fifteenth-century artists who visually reconstructed the coronation scenes: witness the painting of the ceremony at Saint-Denis in the manuscript of Jean de Waurin's *Anchiennes croniques de l'Angletere*, now in the Bibliothèque Nationale, Paris,[28] and the pen-and-ink drawings of both ceremonies in the so-called 'Warwick MS.' in London, a roll illustrating 'pageants' in the life of Richard Beauchamp, earl of Warwick (1389–1439).[29] Although the images in the 'Warwick MS.' date from 1493, they

[24] Cited by Desmond Seward, *Henry V: The Scourge of God* (New York, 1988), p. 213, from the description in George Chastellain, *Oeuvres*, ed. Kervyn de Lettenhove (Brussels, 1863–66), i, pp. 339–40.

[25] Koebner, *Empire*, p. 37.

[26] Thus Twining's error (*Crown Jewels of Europe*, p. 127), which Grierson noted: 'Origins of the English Sovereign', 130, note 1.

[27] At his coronations, the boy-king received his crowns from his great-uncle, Henry Beaufort, the lord chancellor and cardinal-bishop of Winchester; R. A. Griffiths, *The Reign of King Henry VI* (1981), pp. 190, 193.

[28] See the monochrome reproduction of the illumination from Bibliothèque Nationale, Paris, MS. Fr. 83, in John Cannon and Ralph Griffiths, *The Oxford Illustrated History of the British Monarchy* (Oxford, 1988), p. 239.

[29] BL, Cotton MS. Julius E. iv, fo. 23v, for the drawing of the coronation of Henry VI at Westminster, and *ibid.*, fo. 24r, for the one showing the scene at Saint-Denis. As these images represent a late fifteenth-century view of events which occurred as early as 1389, they must be used with caution. The artist has all of the English kings portrayed here, including Richard II (*ibid.*, fo. 1v, at Beauchamp's

confirm what English heralds in the 1450s very well knew, that despite French rejections of his claim to a French kingdom, Henry VI 'By just tytyll' was born 'To were ij crownys of Ynglonde and of Fraunce', which is precisely the way the mid-century author–illustrator of the previously cited book of arms represented him, steed-borne and armed (like his father), wearing on his helm both crowns at once, the closed English crown surmounting the French open one (plate 3).[30]

We should not suppose, however, that in their representations of Henry VI as king of England, contemporary artists adhered to an exclusive iconographic formula; although he is the first English monarch for whom we possess official, contemporaneous visual evidence of the use of the closed crown – the miniature of him in the illuminated initial of the foundation charter of 1441 of King's College, Cambridge, is perhaps the earliest such evidence[31] – English court artists portrayed him in majesty with an open crown as late as 1460,[32] as did the artist, probably of the Flemish school, who imagined him receiving in 1471 a presentation copy of Cardinal Johannes Bessarion's published *Orationes* against the Turks.[33] Official routines have a way of extending the life of artistic traditions; the seal used for French affairs under Edward IV, which also employed the device of the open crown, served as the model for various seals in use as late as 1532.[34]

None the less, after 1461 the symbol of the closed imperial crown appears with greater frequency in a variety of contexts and media. Of the many examples in the reigns of Edward IV and Richard III, five ranging over a period of twenty-five years may be cited here for their artistic and historical sig-

baptism), Henry IV (*ibid.*, fo. 2r, shown knighting Beauchamp) and Henry V (*ibid.*, fo. 16v, creating him an earl) wearing arched crowns. Obviously his intent was to distinguish the English crown from the French one: he shows Henry V's contemporary, Charles VI, in France wearing the open crown (*ibid.*, fo. 21r). The drawings were reproduced in *Pageant of the birth, life and death of Richard Beauchamp, Earl of Warwick, K.G., 1389–1439*, eds. Viscount Dillon and W. H. St John Hope (1914). The date of the drawings was fixed by E. Maunde Thompson, 'The Pageants of Richard Beauchamp, Earl of Warwick, commonly called the Warwick MS.', *Burlington Magazine*, 1 (1903): 151–66.

30 BL, Harleian MS. 2169, fo. 3, originally reproduced in 'A Fifteenth-Century Book of Arms', *The Ancestor* 3 (1902): 188.

31 See the splendid colour reproduction in Cannon and Griffiths, *Oxford Illustrated History*, p. 212, where the source is cited (*ibid.*, p. 694) as King's College Library, Cambridge, MS. Mun. KC/18/NI. The crowned king and the lords of parliament are shown kneeling before the Virgin Mary; an enlarged, finely detailed version of Henry VI's arched crown surmounts a shield of his arms above the initial.

32 See the illuminated initials on the plea rolls in the court of king's bench for Easter and Michaelmas 1460 (PRO, KB 27/796 and KB 27/798, respectively) reproduced in Erna Auerbach, *Tudor Artists* (1954), plates 1a and 1b.

33 See the splendid colour reproduction of this miniature – the original painting is on parchment – in the Vatican Library copy of Bessarion's *Orationes et epistolae ad Christianos principes contra Turcos* (Paris, 1471), the copy exhibited at the Library of Congress in 1993: Anthony Grafton (ed.), *Rome Reborn. The Vatican Library and Renaissance Culture* (Washington, DC, 1993), pl. 57, p. 64. The scene, a fanciful one of Burgundian decorative motifs, shows the king sitting on a low platform beneath a canopied enclosure holding a sceptre in his right hand and receiving the *Orationes* from the author in his left hand. In fact Guillaume Fichet, the rector of the University of Paris, sent Edward IV this copy; *ibid.*

34 Grierson, 'Origins of the English Sovereign', 131, citing the relevant plates in A. B. and A. Wyon, *The Great Seals of England* (1887).

nificance: the painting of Edward IV in majesty, dated *c.* 1461, in the original manuscript of John Lydgate's *Troy Book*, a manuscript composed for Sir William Herbert and given by him to the king;[35] Edward IV's third Great Seal (in use 1471–80), the first Great Seal of England to bear the insignia of the crown imperial;[36] a miniature of 1477 showing Caxton presenting the first dated book printed in England to an enthroned Edward IV (plate 4);[37] the crowned head of Edward IV in stained glass, said to be a remarkable likeness dating from about 1482, in the great north (royal) window of the northwest transept of Canterbury Cathedral (plate 5);[38] and, from a contemporary transcription of the statutes of Richard III prepared for the mayor and aldermen of London, the illuminated initial showing the lords of parliament surrounding Richard III in majesty (plate 6).[39]

Henry's VII's attempts to establish the legitimacy of his authority are well-known; the artistic manifestations of this effort are to be seen in the proliferation of new images of the king as an 'imperial' monarch. A commission of 28 March 1489 for the coinage identifies the earliest datable source of the new emphasis; all of the coins were to be changed in order that they might bear more

35 BL, Royal MS. 18. D. ii, fo. 6. Lydgate's work, in five books of about 29,000 lines, is a paraphrase in verse of the prose 'Historia Toiana' of Guido della Colonne. It was written and illuminated for Sir William Herbert (earl of Pembroke, 1468) and his wife, Anne Devereux. Although the work may originally have been composed *c.* 1455–56 and intended as a gift to Henry VI (that is before Herbert went over to the Yorkist cause in 1457), it is now generally accepted that Edward IV is the king portrayed here, and since Herbert is not shown with the Garter, which he acquired in 1462, the date therefore must be 1461. Blanks for some of the miniatures were filled in later by an artist of the Flemish school, possibly as late as 1516–23; Sir George F. Warner and Julius P. Gilson, *Catalogue of Western Manuscripts in the Old Royal and King's Collections* (vol. ii, 1921), pp. 308–10.
36 Wyon, *Great Seals*, p. 60 and no. 87 (pl. xv); Francis Sandford, *A Genealogical History of the Kings of England, and Monarchs of Great Britain, &c, from the Conquest, Anno 1066. to the Year, 1677* (1677), p. 381. To appreciate the (reconstructed) detail of the original wax seal, one should consult the engraving in Sanford, *Genealogical History*, p. 353. The arched imperial crown can clearly be seen in the photograph of the Great Seal reproduced in Charles Ross, *Edward IV* (Berkeley and Los Angeles, CA, 1974), pl. 20a (facing p. 337).
37 Lambeth Palace Library, MS. 265, fo. vi. For the identification of the figures, see Charles Ross, *Richard III* (Berkeley and Los Angeles, CA, 1981), pl. 12a (facing p. 107).
38 The window was a gift of Edward IV, who was a frequent visitor to the Cathedral and to Becket's shrine at Canterbury in the period 1461–81. The original arrangement of the lights, or glass panels beneath the tracery – there are seven in each of three tiers dedicated to the Virgin Mary – is conjectural, as the whole was systematically smashed on 13 December 1642 by Richard Culmer, the iconoclastic pike-bearing puritan rector of Chartham, Kent. However, Edward IV's crowned head, said to be a faithful piece of portraiture from the workshop of William Neve (king's glazier, 1476–1505), survived Culmer's symbolic violence. For all of this, see the following: G.S. [*sic*], *Chronological History of Canterbury Cathedral* (Canterbury, 1883), pp. 176, 179, 189; Richard Culmer, *Cathedrall Newes from Canterbury* (1644), which is reprinted in G.S., *Chronological History*, pp. 283–316 (where Culmer's description of the window is found on pp. 312–13); N. H. J. Westlake, *A History of Design in Painted Glass* (4 vols., 1879–94), iii, p. 53; John D. Le Couteur, 'Notes on the Great North Window of Canterbury Cathedral', *Archaeologia Cantiana*, 29 (1911): 323–32; G. Eveleigh Woodruff and William Danks, *Memorials of the Cathedral & Priory of Christ in Canterbury* (1912), p. 206; Bernard Rackham, *The Ancient Glass of Canterbury Cathedral* (1949), pp. 156, 159, 174; Christopher Woodforde, *English Stained and Painted Glass* (Oxford, 1954), pp. 30, 35.
39 Corporation of London Record Office, *Cartae Antique*, Richard III: Cust 7.

Plate 4. Edward IV receiving from John Caxton a presentation copy of *The Dictes or Sayengis of the Philosophres,* the first dated book printed in England; a miniature of 1477 providing clear visual evidence of Edward IV's use of the arched crown (Lambeth Palace Library, MS. 265, fo. vi).

prominently both Henry's likeness and 'the King's arms of England and France'.[40] The new twenty-shilling double gold ryal of 1489, which Henry himself named the 'sovereign', was among the first English coins to display the insignia of the closed crown (plate 7a). Because of their far greater circulation, the new silver groats and shillings of 1504, which featured a crowned Henry VII in profile (plate 7c), brought the symbolism of the crown imperial before a far wider audience.[41] These profile coins, which were designed by a German artist, Alexander of Brugsal, were without precedent; the first to bear an artistic

[40] D. M. Metcalf, *Sylloge of Coins of the British Isles, 23: Ashmolean Museum, Oxford. III. Coins of Henry VII* (1976), p. xxvii.

[41] A commission of 3 July 1504 probably explains the origins of the new silver profile coins, first issued in substantial numbers in August 1504. Between Michaelmas 1504 and Michaelmas 1505, the first year of the new issue, £45,000 in silver was coined, almost double that of 1503–04 and triple that of 1502–03; Metcalf, *Coins of Henry VII,* pp. xxxii–xxxiii. The design of the groats had seen almost no change since the mid-fourteenth century; Grierson, 'Origins of the English Sovereign', 134.

Plate 5. Edward IV in stained glass, a detail of the great north window in the northwest ('Martyrdom') transept of Canterbury Cathedral. The window, which was dedicated to the Virgin, was Edward IV's gift in memory of Edward I and Marguerite of France. The original plan of the lights remains conjectural, for on 13 Dec. 1643 Richard Culmer, zealous iconoclast, systematically smashed most of the glass. However, Edward IV's head and arched crown, dating from *c.* 1482, survived Culmer's attack; the portrait, from the workshop of William Neve, king's glazier (1476–1505), is said by art historians to be a remarkably faithful likeness. It is known that in the original scheme, the kneeling king faced in the central light of this tier not the oversized crown imperial seen today, but the image of a shrine containing a crucifix.

Plate 6. A rare contemporary portrait of Richard III in majesty, showing the enthroned king with sceptre and crown imperial and surrounded by the lords of parliament; the illuminated initial capital ('R') of a copy of Richard's statutes transcribed for the mayor and aldermen of London (Corporation of London Record Office, *Cartae Antique* Richard III, Cust. 7).

(a)

(b)

(c)

Plate 7. (a) Henry VII's sovereign, a twenty-shilling double gold ryal minted in 1489, was one of the first English coins to bear the insignia of the closed crown. On the obverse Henry is shown seated in majesty on a Gothic throne facing forward; on the reverse the crown imperial surmounts a shield of the royal arms over a rose. Henry's sovereign closely resembled the design of (b) Maximilian I's *réal d'or*, or gold double noble struck at Bruges in 1487, suggesting that the Habsburg coin was the immediate model for the Tudor ryal. In fact Spanish *enriques*, the prestigious gold coins of Henry IV of Castile (1454–74), inspired both. (c) Henry VII's silver shilling, designed by Alexander of Brugsal and struck 1500–09, was the first coin to bear an artistic likeness of an English king. Such unprecedented profile coins brought the emblem of the crown imperial before a much wider domestic audience.

likeness of an English monarch, they set standards of unsurpassed 'dignity and beauty' for the English coinage.[42] By contrast, the pattern for the earlier gold sovereign closely resembled that of a Habsburg coin struck at Bruges in 1487, the gold double noble, or *réal d'or*, of Maximilian I (plate 7b). Since the resemblance could not have been accidental, it appeared to Grierson that Maximilian's coin provided Henry VII with the model for a crown that could be styled 'imperial'.[43] The earlier history of the closed crown in England renders this unlikely. In any case, as D. M. Metcalf has persuasively shown, there existed a more prestigious Spanish source for both the *réal* and the Tudor sovereign, the *enriques*, or large gold coins of Henry IV of Castile (1454–74). The choice of the Spanish model served a powerful political purpose. On the same day that Henry VII issued the commission for his new coins, King Ferdinand and Queen Isabella ratified the Treaty of Medina del Campo, the terms of which pledged their daughter, Catherine, in marriage to Henry's infant son, Arthur (b. 1486). For Henry VII, the treaty secured a dynastic alliance unmatched since the days when Henry V had married a French king's daughter; diplomatically, Medina del Campo brought the Tudors onto the European stage. The treaty implied (as Metcalf noted) that the Tudor arms and crown could stand comparison with those of Castile and Leon. In other words, Henry VII's dynastic policy in Spain, and not his presumed need to rival Maximilian's 'imperialism', explains his decision to mint new coins displaying the symbol of his crown imperial.[44]

Gold was a king's currency; fifteen tons of it cast in sovereigns was supposed to augment the magnificence of the house of Tudor in the eyes of princes overseas. Domestically, in important commissions for stained-glass windows, Henry VII sought not only to rival the magnificence of his Yorkist precedessors but also project an image of the Tudors as rightful wearers of the crown imperial. At Great Malvern Priory Church, for example, where Richard, duke of Gloucester, and Anne Neville had donated the west window, Henry approved, at sometime between May 1499 and April 1502, the installation of the great Magnificat window in the north transept. There, in some of the richest, most brilliantly coloured glass ever glazed and painted in England, was to be

---

[42] George C. Brooke, *English Coins from the Seventh Century to the Present Day* (third edn, revised, 1950), p. 163.

[43] Grierson, 'Origins of the English Sovereign', 118–22, 133–4. Grierson noted that when minted in small quantities, such Renaissance coins served less as a medium of exchange than a princely treasure-trove. Henry's large issue suggests that the coins not only advertised the king's augmented dignity, but were also a 'natural consequence' of inflated prices and, via Portugal, a more plentiful supply of African gold; *ibid.*, p. 119.

[44] Metcalf, *Coins of Henry VII*, pp. xxvii–xxviii. For the sake of comparison, Metcalf included drawings of Maximilian's *réal*, Enrique IV's ten-*enriques* coin, and Henry VII's sovereign (*ibid.*, fig. 4). Metcalf noted that the gold Spanish *enriques* 'were the prestige currency of a powerful state, whereas the *réal* was apparently a very limited issue'. Moreover, in 1489 Maximilian was not yet emperor, and as he was then being held captive, it was not clear that he would win the allegiance of even the German princes; *ibid.*, p. xxviii. On the new sovereign, see also C. E. Challis, *The Tudor Coinage* (Manchester, 1978), pp. 47–52.

seen '. . . a lively image of that wise and devout King Henry the Seaventh, prayeinge, all armed saveing his head, whereon he weareth his imperiall crowne . . .'.[45]

The gift of the Magnificat window at Great Malvern, nominally an act of commemorative piety, arguably marked the end of the Yorkists; in panels illustrating the 'joys' of the Virgin, it celebrated the triumph of the Tudors, new possessors of the crown imperial.[46] In chapels, halls, and churches elsewhere, other commissions for windows and painted screens reveal a further dimension of the new emphasis on the iconography of the crown imperial, Henry VII's desire to link himself and his kingship visually to those considered to be his most worthy progenitors, Edward the Confessor, Henry V and Henry VI, as well as the legendary Arthur and the first of the Christian Roman Emperors, Constantine. Of the importance to early Tudor propaganda of Constantine the Great and Arthur, little needs to be said. Via Geoffrey of Monmouth and various chronicles, including *The Brut*, politico-historical legend had fixed

[45] These were the words of Thomas Habington (1560–1647), that extraordinary surveyor of antiquities in Worcestershire, at sometime between 1588 and 1615; Thomas Habington, *A Survey of Worcestershire*, ed. John Amphlett (2 vols., Oxford, 1895, 1899), ii, p. 187. (Habington's father, John, was cofferer to Elizabeth I; his mother, Catherine, was a gentlewoman of the queen's privy chamber.) Habington saw the window, reportedly one of the most beautiful in England, before a thundrous wind blew it out on the night of 26–7 November 1703. First restored in 1860–61, it was re-leaded and reassembled in 1915–19 under the supervision of G. McN. Rushforth, whose *Medieval Christian Imagery as illustrated by the painted windows of Great Malvern Priory Church* (Oxford, 1936) is the definitive account; see especially pp. 268, 369, 373ff., 398ff., 411, and, among the plates, the reproductions of the window (fig. 171) and Henry VII (fig. 182). L. A. Hamand, *The Ancient Windows of Great Malvern Priory Church* (St Albans, 1947), is an instructive brief introduction; see especially pp. 1–7 and 69–81. Originally the window consisted of three tiers of seven lights illustrating the 'joys' of the Virgin. In the bottom tier of 'donor' panels are the figures of the king and queen, Prince Arthur and three knights of the body, Sir Reginald Bray, Sir John Savage, and Sir Thomas Lovell. The figure of the king in gold and white armour in the righthand corner panel – Henry is shown kneeling on a red cushion before a desk on which rests an open book, his gold sceptre lying on the book – is a mixture of original and modern glass; the glaziers probably were among the king's own. Henry's crowned head, with its shoulder-length yellow hair, survived the storm of 1703 intact. In 1913, before restoration, the disembodied head, probably thought to be that of an angel, occupied a place at the top of the Annunciation scene; Philip Nelson, *Ancient Painted Glass in England 1170–1500* (1913), p. 213. The youthful visage is artistically not a true portrait. The gold crown, however, is very carefully observed; it 'consists of a jewelled circlet from which rise alternate crosses paty and fleurs-de-lis separated by smaller knops, all ornamented and tipped with pearls. From the crosses and fleurs-de-lis spring crocketed arches, but their meeting place and finial is lost'; Rushforth, *Medieval Christian Imagery*, p. 399. At Great Malvern Mr Steve Erickson very kindly photographed Henry VII's image for me on an overcast day in July 1992.

[46] The Magnificat window 'answered' not only the Yorkists' gift of the west window at Great Malvern but also the dynastic imagery of Edward IV's great window at Canterbury Cathedral, a window whose compositional scheme it copied. At Canterbury one beheld, in the figure of Edward IV's son, Edward, the future of the Yorkist dynasty. At Great Malvern the image of Henry VII's son, Arthur, is central; the gift of the window coincided with Arthur's marriage to Catherine of Aragon, a marriage obviously embodying Henry VII's hopes for the Tudor succession. After Bosworth and before Arthur's birth, however, the legitimate heir to the throne was Edward, earl of Warwick, the son of Edward IV's deceased brother, George, duke of Clarence, and Malvern Chase, originally part of the Neville family estate, was part of Warwick's inheritance. It cannot be a coincidence that the installation of the Magnificat window followed immediately upon Warwick's attainder and execution on 28 November 1499, when Henry VII acquired the manor of Malvern Chase. See Rushforth, *Medieval Christian Imagery*, pp. 373–6, and S. B. Chrimes, *Henry VII* (Berkeley and Los Angeles, CA, 1972), p. 337.

Arthur's descent from Constantine, who, because his canonized mother, Helena, was thought to be English, had joined British kingship to the emperorship of Christian Rome.[47] In this scheme, if Emperor Constantine was a king of England, all kings of England after him stood in an 'imperial' line, and could be shown so crowned. Thus among the nine crowned figures in armour in the north ('royal') window at St Mary's Hall, Coventry, a window probably given by Henry VII *c.* 1500, are two reputed kings of England, 'Constantinus Anglicus, Imperator Christianissmus' and 'Rex Arthurus conquestor inclitus', and standing between them are the two kings from whom the donor traced his imperial descent, Henry V and Henry VI.[48]

Of particular interest are the uses which Henry VII made of images of Henry VI, his simple-minded step-uncle who, soon after his murder at the hands of the Yorkists (1471), had come to be regarded as both martyr and saint. The 'Woorship of Holy Kinge Henry (as they called him) . . .' became a national cult, and among the most sincerely worshipful was Henry VII, whose veneration of Henry VI, we are told, 'amounted almost to superstition'.[49] By pairing his own image with that of Henry VI and, for good measure, Edward the Confessor's, Henry VII strove to strengthen his claim to hold legitimate descent from England's holiest 'imperial' kings. In the windows on the north wall of the chapel at Christ's College, Cambridge, for example, Henry VI appears twice in glass crafted by Henry VII's glaziers, first with God Almighty and Edward the Confessor, and again with Henry VII and Elizabeth of York, and in each group the figures of the kings wear crowns imperial.[50]

[47] Richard Koebner, '"The Imperial Crown of this Realm": Henry VIII, Constantine the Great, and Polydore Vergil', *BIHR*, 26 (1953): 31.

[48] Nelson, *Ancient Painted Glass*, p. 200. The window is 'credibly conjectured' to have been given by Henry VII in commemoration of his visit to Coventry early in his reign; Rackham, *Ancient Glass*, p. 159. The glass has been attributed to William Neve, the king's glazier; Brian Coe, *Stained Glass in England: 1150–1550* (1981), pp. 20, 122, and Woodforde, *English Glass*, p. 30.

[49] W. St John Hope, *Windsor Castle. An Architectural History* (3 vols., 1913), ii, p. 478. Miracles and cures were said to have been worked in Henry VI's name; testators left alms in his blessed memory; lights were everywhere burned before his effigy; the pilgrimage to his grave-site at Windsor, where wax votive offerings were made, was so big as to rival that to Becket's shrine at Canterbury: Ronald Knox and Shane Leslie (eds.), *The Miracles of King Henry VI* (Cambridge,, 1923), pp. 3–7. Almost everything connected to Henry VI, including the dagger that killed him, became an object of religious devotion. Pilgrims at Windsor were 'perswaded that to put upon a Man's Heade an olde red Velvet Hatte of his (that laye theare) was a Sovereigne Medicine against the Head-ache'; even the 'small Chippe of his Bedsteade' which was kept at Windsor acquired the status of 'a precious Relique'. These references and that to the 'Woorship of Holy Kinge Henry' were written about 1577 by William Lambard, *Dictionarium Angliae Topographicum et Historicum* (1730), p. 422, and are quoted in St John Hope, *Windsor Castle*, ii, p. 415, who also details (*ibid.*, pp. 478–80) Henry VII's unsuccessful attempts to have his uncle canonized and his remains moved from Windsor to Westminster Abbey to be placed in Henry VII's new chapel, near Henry VII's intended tomb. On the cult of Henry VI, see also Bertram Wolffe, *Henry VI* (1981), pp. 351–8; Ralph A. Griffiths and Roger S. Thomas, *The Making of the Tudor Dynasty* (Gloucester, England, 1985), pp. 185, 187; and Sydney Anglo, *Images of Tudor Kingship* (1992), pp. 61–73.

[50] There are six figures in these windows at Christ's, three large and three small. The larger ones, which include (from west to east), standing figures of Henry VI, the Almighty, and Edward the Confessor, date from early in the reign of Henry VII. The three smaller kneeling figures of Henry VI, Henry VII, and Elizabeth of York belong to the period 1505–10; Bernard Rackham, 'The Ancient Windows of Christ's College Chapel, Cambridge', *Archaeological Journal*, 109 (1953): 132–42.

Plate 8. The apotheosis of Lancastrian 'imperial' kingship: Henry VI as a saint with nimbus and imperial crown; detail of a painted wooden screen of *c.* 1500 in St Catherine's Church, Ludham, Norfolk. By furthering the cult of 'Holy' King Henry, Henry VII sought not only to draw upon the sanctity of his step-uncle's name, but also promote the idea that in fulfillment of the saint-king's prophecy, the Tudor succession enjoyed divine ordination.

Plate 9. Wearing his imperial crown and holding a sceptre, Henry VII in majesty presents bound ordinances to a group of kneeling prelates, including William Warham, archbishop of Canterbury, Richard Fox, bishop of Winchester (whose mitres rest at Henry's feet), and John Islip, abbot of Westminster; the illuminated initial of the indenture of 16 July 1504 for the foundation of the king's chapel in Westminster Abbey (PRO, E. 33.2, fo. 1). Henry VII intended that his new chapel become *the* religio-political shrine of British 'imperial' monarchy. Believing himself to be the providentially designated successor to Henry V and 'Holy' King Henry VI, he would situate his tomb next to Henry V's chantry and transfer his step-uncle's remains from Windsor to the Abbey, a move which, had it succeeded, would have relocated the centre of the cult of Henry VI to a site adjacent to his own tomb.

The artistic promotion of the cult of Henry VI in local churches points to a deeper religio-political purpose. It was widely believed that Henry VI had possessed prophetic gifts of divine inspiration and that before his death he had foretold Henry Tudor's accession to the throne. If Henry VI were really a saint, such a prophecy carried a supremely potent political message, that God had willed the Tudor triumph.[51] This explains Henry VII's persistent efforts to

[51] Anglo, *Images of Tudor Kingship*, pp. 63–6, 71.

secure his uncle's canonization and the simultaneous appearance of pictures of Henry VI as a saint on the screens and in the windows of numerous parish churches. By sponsoring such images, did Henry VII hope to win the respect of the faithful and draw down upon his own crown the sanctified power of his uncle's name? Consider the image of *c.* 1500 of Henry VI with both halo and closed crown on the painted wooden screen at St Catherine's Church, Ludham, Norfolk: here is the Tudor apotheosis of Lancastrian 'imperial' kingship (plate 8). The wall painting of Henry VI with a nimbus at Alton Church, Hampshire, provides a similar example.[52]

The centre of the cult of Henry VI was at Windsor Castle, where Henry VI was buried within St George's Chapel. There, in a large wall painting executed about 1493–96 in Dr Oliver King's Chapel, Henry VII was portrayed standing alongside England's most recent 'imperial' kings.[53] But this ensemble included Yorkists, and as Henry VII had adopted Henry V and Henry VI as the kings from whom exclusively he traced his 'imperial' descent, he was determined that his own tomb be situated next to the tombs of Henry V and Henry VI in Westminster Abbey, which would require that Henry VI's remains be moved there from Windsor, to be re-interred near the monument intended for Henry VII in a new chapel adjacent to Henry V's tomb and chantry.[54] The re-burial never took place, but the indenture of 16 July 1504 for the foundation of the new chapel bears, as the chapel itself later would do, the symbolic impress of the crown which Henry would have the world believe had come to him from Henry V and Henry VI by providential means: the illuminated initial, which shows Henry VII in majesty presenting a book of ordinances to kneeling prelates, is surmounted by the device of the Tudor arms and crown imperial, the very crown the king is wearing in the miniature (plate 9).[55]

After 1489 artists working in England apparently understood that images of

[52] Paintings of Henry VI with crown and sceptre reportedly became quite common in parish churches during the early Tudor period. Knox and Leslie list eight surviving examples, including Alton Church, Hampshire , and St Catherine's, Ludham, where the figure also exhibits a nimbus; Knox and Leslie (eds.), *Miracles of King Henry VI*, p. 6. The following hymn to Henry VI was found on the fly-leaf of a primer of 1508 at St Cuthbert's College: '. . . O crownyd kyng with scepture in hand / Most nobyll conquerer I may theee call / For thou has conquered I undyrstand / A hevnynly kyng-dome most imperyall' (*ibid.*, p. 9). Was the composer thinking of such a painting of Henry VI?

[53] At Windsor Dr Oliver King (d. 1503) was a canon and registrar of the Order of the Garter after 1489. Bishop of Exeter from 1493, he was translated to the bishopric of Bath and Wells in 1496. The picture decorating the wall of the chapel where his tomb is located is eleven feet square and consists of four panels in each of which the figure stands on a pedestal bearing his name and arms. Henry VII is shown in his blue parliament gown, which is sewn with gold fleurs-de-lis, and a red, minever-tipped mantel. He holds the orb and sceptre and wears the arched imperial crown; St John Hope, *Windsor Castle*, ii, pp. 413–14 and plate lvii facing p. 414.

[54] See *ibid.*, ii, pp. 478–9, for the terms of the indenture of 26 July 1498 between Henry VII and the abbot and convent of Westminster for the removal of Henry VI's body from Windsor to the chapel at Westminster, 'the which chapell oure said souerain Lord entendith to make and bilde of new and in the same not ferre from his said Uncle to be buryd hymself'. For a recent discussion of these plans and a reproduction of the contemporary design for a monument intended for Henry VI, see also Anglo, *Images of Tudor Kingship*, pp. 67–8 and fig. 12, p. 69.

[55] PRO, E 33.2, fo. 1.

Plate 10. The most graphically forceful image of Tudor royal 'imperialism': Henry VII in majesty surrounded by six of his councillors, a woodcut on the title-page of *Leteltun teners newe correcte*, the 1510 edition of Sir Thomas Littleton's 'primer in the common law'. The strong diagonals and verticals of the composition, which frame the king's rigidly bold, face-forward pose, pull the viewer's eye inexorably to the disproportionately large crown, which the artist has set against a patterned background of lines representing the carved (raised) back of Henry's throne. The effect is to 'magnify' the crown even more, making it a radiant emblem, as it were, of Henry VII's 'imperial' majesty.

Henry VII crowned were always to exhibit the king wearing the now-distinctive arched diadem. The woodcut illustration of the king in majesty on the title page of Sir Thomas Littleton's *Tenures* (plate 10) would appear to be an unremarkable example, were it not for the extraordinary influence of Littleton's work. The *Tenures*, which was the first, and for many years the only, printed book on English law, was so much read after its first printing (1481 or 1482) that it came to possess, in the words of J. H. Baker, a 'unique authority' in shaping English legal culture: it became 'the primer of the common law'.[56] Three of the first five editions appeared during Henry VII's reign under the mark of Richard Pynson, king's printer; one of these, the edition of 1496, was apparently the first to carry the woodcut reproduced here from the title page of the 1510 edition, *Leteltun teners newe correcte* (plate 10).[57] Of all of the representations of Henry VII in majesty this is perhaps the most graphically forceful. If the search for the intellectual origins of the jurisdictional revolution of the 1530s is to be pushed back to the Inns of Court after 1485, to see 'how far juristic thought [there] mirrored royal policy . . .',[58] perhaps one place to begin is with the image of Henry VII's 'imperial' kingship beheld by generations of readers of Littleton, an image Pynson was still using in the seventh (1516) and eighth (1518?) editions of the *Tenures*.[59]

The range and variety of such imagery in so many different officially sponsored or royally generated media after 1489 appears to confirm the origins in Henry VII's reign of a royalist programme for the representation of the crown imperial. A unique example in cloth introduces us to the ceremonial settings for the contemporary display of such insignia. In his will Henry VII bequeathed to the abbot and monastery of Westminster a set of twenty-nine copes of cloth of gold and crimson silk, each one thrice emblazoned with the crown imperial over the Beaufort portcullis. Among the most splendid vestments then being woven in Europe, these costly copes, originally ordered *c.* 1498–99, were probably first worn at Henry VIII's coronation on 24 June 1509. Then and on subsequent occasions, such as the Field of the Cloth of Gold (1520), they advertised the splendour and supremacy of the Tudor crown.[60]

In 1509 John Wynattes carved a device of the 'Crowne Imperiall' for what were probably the decorative, heraldic trappings of the coronation.[61] The

---

56 *The Reports of Sir John Spelman*, ed. J. H. Baker, vol. ii (The Selden Society: vol. 94, 1978), p. 178. I wish to thank David Sacks for guiding me to Baker's 'Introduction' to *The Reports*.
57 The first six editions listed in *STC*, vol. ii (1976), are those of 1482 (*STC* 15719), 1483? (*STC* 15720), 1490 (*STC* 15721), 1496 (*STC* 15722), 1502? (*STC* 15722.5) and 1510? (*STC* 15723).
58 John Guy, 'Thomas Cromwell and the Intellectual Origins of the Henrician Revolution', in Alistair Fox and John Guy, *Reassessing the Henrician Age: Humanism, Politics and Reform 1500–1550* (Oxford, 1986), p. 177.
59 On the *recto* of the title page, or first leaf, of the 1516 edition (*STC* 15724) in the British Library (shelfmark C. 113. n. 2) is a full-page woodcut of the royal arms surmounted by the crown imperial; on the *verso* is the same woodcut of Henry VII adorning the *recto* of the title pages of the editions of 1496 and 1510. *The National Union Catalogue Pre-1956 Imprints*, vol. 336 (1974), p. 334, lists an edition of 1518? of *Leteltun tenuris newe correcte* by Pynson not included in *STC*. On the *recto* of the title page of this copy of 1518? is a woodcut of the king's arms surmounted by the Tudor rose and a scroll supported by angels; on the *verso* is the woodcut of Henry VII from the editions of 1496 and 1510.
60 Lisa Monnas, 'New Documents for the Vestments of Henry VII at Stonyhurst College', *Burlington Magazine*, 131 (1989): 345–9. Twenty-four were at the Abbey in 1563, but the eleven extant in 1608 were 'burned by Puritans in 1643'; *ibid.*, p. 346.
61 Cited by Pamela Tudor-Craig, 'Henry VIII and King David', in Daniel Williams (ed.), *Early Tudor England* (Woodbridge, Suffolk), p. 183, n. 1. At Greenwich on 8 July 1511 Wynattes was paid 20s 'for carvynge of the crowne Imp[er]iall and the lyon to the same', another wooden heraldic device

Plate 11. At Henry VIII's coronation, the hack humanist poet Stephen Hawes composed *A Joyfull medytacyon* on the event, published by Wynkyn de Worde in London in 1509. The woodcut on the title-page projects the emblematic image of prelates crowning Henry and Catherine of Aragon with imperial diadems. King and queen sit smilingly beneath oversized badges of identification, a rose and pomegranate, respectively.

emblematic woodcut illustration on the title page of Stephen Hawes's poetic 'medytacyon' on the coronation, published in London by Wynkyn de Worde in 1509, shows two prelates holding imperial crowns above the heads of Henry and Catherine of Aragon (plate 11).[62] The elaborate tourneys and jousts staged at Westminster on 25–26 June 1509 in celebration of the coronation featured a specially built tilt-galley in the form of a castle, and 'on the toppe thereof', said the chronicler Hall, '[was] a great Croune Emperiall . . .'.[63]

No contemporary images of the coronation jousts have survived, but for the even more lavish tourney mounted at Westminster on 12 and 13 February 1511 in celebration of the birth of Prince Arthur there is the extraordinary manuscript

which included a replica of the king's helm; 'for gyldnge of the crowne and of the lyon in fyne golde' John Broklne was paid 20s; PRO, LC 9/50, fo. 158b.

[62] Stephen Hawes, *A Joyfull medytacyon to all Englonde of the coronacyon of our moost naturall souerayne lorde kynge Henry the eyght*, printed by Wynkyn de Worde in London in 1509, the unique copy of which (in Cambridge University Library) has been republished in a facsimile edition by Scholars' Facsimiles and Reprints: *The Works of Stephen Hawes*, ed. Frank J. Spang (Delmar, NY, 1975).

[63] Hall, *Chronicle*, p. 510. On the coronation jousts of 25–6 June 1509, see Sydney Anglo, *The Great Tournament Roll of Westminster* (Oxford, 1968), pp. 46–9 (especially p. 46 for the castle-like tilt gallery).

at the College of Arms known as the Great Tournament Roll of Westminster, thirty-six painted membranes of vellum almost sixty feet long.[64] The illumination preserves a unique visual record of the politico-cultural purposes of the Tudor tournament-as-spectacle: here is the staged, chivalric magnificence of young Henry's court, an orchestrated magnificence meant to rival that of the Burgundian court from which the forms of such martial pageantry were derived. In serial fashion, the artist, probably a herald, portrayed three scenes from the two-day affair, portions of the opening and closing processions and a view of the twenty-year-old sovereign himself in action. Henry VIII's gorgeous pavilion of purple velvet and cloth of gold, a portable tent large enough to shade a fully-armoured king on horseback, serves as a focal point for a segment of the second scene showing the mounted combatants (plate 12). The 'imperial' nature of this royal magnificence is fixed visually by the golden device (probably of wood) atop Henry's pavilion, an enormous arched crown linking the initials of king and queen above a radiant sun. In the third scene from the closing ceremony on 13 February, one of the contestants, probably Thomas Howard, son of the earl of Surrey,[65] is shown riding in procession, bearing the king's great helmet on a staff, the helmet surmounted by the crown imperial (plate 13). That this is a picture of Henry's actual gem-studded gold crown is suggested by the presence of the king himself immediately behind Howard in the procession (plate 14).[66]

If the chivalric war-games at court in 1509 and 1511 were dress rehearsals for Henry's subsequent invasion of France, the English conquest of Tournai (1513) provided a grander, worldly stage for the display of Henry's 'imperial' stance. The painting which Henry probably commissioned as a formal record of his overseas campaign depicts his meeting on the field of battle with his ally, Maximilian I (plate 15). The artist, probably Flemish, has taken pains graphically to register the fact that in his new-won French domain, Henry VIII's standing, like that of Henry V's in 1416, was not inferior to that of the emperor: in size and prominence of place the device of the Tudor crown imperial on Henry's white field pavilion challenges that of the Habsburg crown on Maximilian's tent.[67] From the mint at Tournai Henry also issued new coins in 1513 bearing the impression of his imperial crown,[68] and in England his shipwrights

---

64 The roll measures approximately 14′ ¾″ × 59′ 6″. *The Great Tournament Roll of Westminster. A Collotype Reproduction of the Manuscript* (Oxford, 1968) consists of black-and-white and colour plates of the roll, each slightly larger than half size.

65 See Anglo (ed.), *The Great Tournament Roll*, p. 104, n. 1, for the identification.

66 The helmet-bearer is shown on membrane 34, the mounted king on membrane 35 of the illumination; College of Arms, MS. Great Tournament Roll of Westminster.

67 The panel, probably painted soon after the event by an unknown Flemish artist, may have been commissioned by Henry VIII as a formal record of his campaign and meeting with Maximilian I. For a full description, see Oliver Millar, *The Tudor, Stuart and Early Georgian Pictures in the Collection of Her Majesty the Queen* (2 vols., 1963), text vol., p. 54 (catalogue no. 22). On the campaign itself, see Charles Cruickshank, *Henry VIII and the Invasion of France* (New York, 1990) (a reprint of *Army Royal*, the British edition of 1969).

68 C. E. Challis, *The Tudor Coinage* (Manchester, 1978), pp. 65–6.

Plate 12. The portable royal pavilion of purple velvet and cloth of gold topped by the golden device of the crown imperial linking the initials 'H' and 'K' above a radiant sun; a detail of a herald's illumination of the jousts held at Westmister, 12–13 Feb. 1511, in celebration of the birth of Henry's short-lived son, Prince Arthur (College of Arms, MS. Great Tournament Roll of Westminster, membrane 24).

Plate 13. A herald's portrait of Henry VIII's helm-bearer, probably Thomas Howard, son of the earl of Surrey, carrying on a staff the king's great silver jousting helmet (labelled 'Le heaulme du Roy') and gold crown imperial; detail of a scene from the closing ceremony of the tourney at Westminster, 12–13 Feb. 1511 (College of Arms, MS. Great Tournament Roll of Westminster, membrane 34).

Plate 14. The royal procession passing by a tilt-gallery during the closing ceremony of the jousts of 12–13 Feb. 1511. Henry ('Le Roy desarmey') sits astride a grey charger, holding a broken tilting stave in his right hand; he wears a cape of sable and a huge sable-trimmed robe of cloth of gold, a gem-set gold chain and a crimson hat with gold badges. The blue horse bard is set with the queen's initial, 'K', in gold, and is bordered with 'LOYALL' in gold. Queen Catherine sits in the centre of the tilt-gallery beneath a gold canopy, her ladies-in-waiting on the right and various gentlemen on the left. Henry's footmen wear tunics of grey and yellow, gold chains, red hose and black caps and shoes; all carry batons striped in green and white, the Tudor livery colours. (Detail of College of Arms, MS. Great Tournament Roll of Westminster, membranes 34 and 35.)

launched (in February or March 1513) the great cannon-bearing *Henry Imperial*, 'the most powerful warship the world had ever seen'.[69]

The pre-Reformation pageants which advanced Henry's claims to an 'imperial' status identified Charlemagne as the historic source from whom the king was said to have inherited two of the symbols of imperial rule, the sword of

---

[69] David Loades, *The Tudor Navy* (Aldershot, Hants, 1992), pp. 62, 67. The flagship of the new Tudor standing navy, the *Henry Imperial* (later called the *Henry Grace à Dieu*) displaced 1,500 tons and cost £8,000 to build.

justice and the closed crown. The fact that the Habsburgs wore the crown of the empire founded by Charlemagne was easily explained; in the pageant of 6 June 1522 celebrating the entry of Charles V into London, an actor playing the role of Charlemagne presented a sword and imperial crown to both Henry and the emperor.[70] Henry would also have Charles V know that the Tudor *imperium* predated Charlemagne, that from Constantine the Great it derived through King Arthur. During Charles's stay in 1522 Henry escorted the emperor to Winchester Castle to see Arthur's Round Table, a gigantic wooden disc dating (we now know) from the reign of Edward I (1272–1307) but first painted *c.* 1516–17 with the figure of a robed and bearded king in majesty holding orb and sword and wearing an imperial crown. One can only imagine what Charles thought when he beheld this figure, for although it was labelled 'Kyng Arthur', the visage was that of Henry VIII.[71]

The identification with Arthur aside, there can be little doubt that in 1521, on the eve of Charles's visit, Henry VIII thought of himself as very like an emperor,

---

[70] King, *Tudor Royal Iconography*, p. 47.
[71] Martin Biddle and Beatrice Clayre, *Winchester Castle and the Great Hall* (Winchester, 1983), p. 40. I wish to thank Dennis J. O'Brien of Cumberland College (Kentucky) for providing me with this reference and a colour reproduction of the image of 'Kyng Arthur' at Winchester Castle.

as much the 'imperial' heir of Charlemagne as any wearer of the crown of the
Holy Roman Empire. Visual confirmation of this exists in the form of Henry's
gift of the magnificent painted windows installed in 1521 in the chapel of Sir
William Sandys's Hampshire house, The Vyne. In these windows a kneeling
Henry VIII appears next to a standing figure who, with sword and orb, assumes
the pose reserved for a patron-saint and supporter, in this unique case, Henry
VIII's namesake, the canonized Holy Roman Emperor, Henry II of Bavaria.
Emperor-saint and Tudor king both wear arched crowns, though Henry VIII's,
like his patron's, is of the Habsburg imperial style, doubtless explained by the
fact that the glass was designed and painted in Antwerp or Liège, both imperial
cities.[72]

[72] A former knight of the bedchamber and treasurer at Calais, Sandys had helped organize the
festivities at the Field of the Cloth of Gold. When he rebuilt The Vyne, Sandys incorporated in it an

Plate 15. *The Meeting of Henry VIII and Emperor Maximilian I*, a large
(39″ × 81″) panel at Hampton Court, probably by a Flemish artist. Oliver
Millar, former Keeper of the Queen's Pictures, speculated that it was painted
in 1513 for Henry VIII as a formal record of his French campaign and his
meeting with the emperor. The action is spread across three horizontal
zones. In the foreground Henry (on the right) and Maximilian (on the left),
in armour and on horseback, greet each other. In the middle, the two
sovereigns appear again on horseback between ranks of pike-bearing
footmen standing before their encampments. In both zones the size and
placement of horsemen, pikemen, cannon, and pavilions is designed to
establish visually an equality of power and prestige between Habsburg
emperor and Tudor king. The battle of the Spurs is in progress in the
background outside the towns of Tournai (left) and Thrérouanne (right).

older structure, a chapel which he moved from a site nearby. However, Henry VIII's gift of Flemish
glass, probably from designs by Dirik Vellert, was 'an offering by the king and his family to the

It is tempting to think that the Vyne windows, so 'imperial' in character, were installed in anticipation of Charles V's visit of 1522, for on the occasion of that visit Henry clearly meant for Charles to take cognizance of the history and magnificence of the Tudor crown. The earliest extant description of the imperial state crown of England dates from 1521,[73] and the crown described there, which is said to be 'a masterpiece of early Tudor jeweller's art',[74] quite possibly was first fashioned for Henry VIII. Although it is of a type worn by Henry V and his fifteenth-century successors, a type featuring alternating crosses and fleurs-de-lis of gold rising above the rim of the circlet, its four golden arches and border exhibit more stones and pearls than appear in earlier images of crowns imperial, and the centre petals of the five fleurs-de-lis bear distinctive medallions – small, finely worked gold-and-enamel figures of Christ, the Virgin and Child and St George.[75] This is the crown listed in all subsequent Tudor inventories of the royal plate and jewels (1532, 1550, 1574 and 1597), the crown painted in remarkable detail by Daniel Mytens in 1631 (plates 16 and 17), just eighteen years before parliament destroyed it and Charles I's monarchy.[76]

Henry VIII's assumption of the supreme headship of the new Church of England stimulated powerful revisions of the iconography of the king in majesty. For example, Henry could be shown holding the Book of God's Word instead of the orb; in Holbein's woodcut illustration for the title page of Coverdale's Bible (1535), the king hands the Book to prelates for distribution to his subjects (plate 23), thus fulfilling one of the chief planks of the reformists' religious pro-

ancient endowed chapel of the Virgin, and not a mere compliment to the owner of a private chapel'; G. McN. Rushforth, 'The Painted Windows in the Chapel of The Vyne in Hampshire', *The Walpole Society*, 15 (1927): 1–20 (the quotation is on p. 8) and plate II(b); G. McN. Rushforth, 'The Origin of the Windows in the Chapel of The Vyne in Hampshire: Additional Notes to the Painted Windows in the Chapel of the Vyne', *The Walpole Society*, 25 (1937): 167–9. A colour reproduction of Henry VIII's image at The Vyne appears in Antonia Fraser, *The Wives of Henry VIII* (New York, 1992), between pp. 50–2.

73 'King Henry VIII's Jewel Book', ed. by Edward, bishop suffragan of Nottingham, in *Reports and Papers of the Associated Architectural Societies*, 17 (1883–84): 155–229 (where the description of the crown is on pp. 158–9).

74 Sir Roy Strong, 'A Vanished Realm: The Lost Treasures of Britain', *The Sunday Times Magazine* (19 November 1989), p. 33.

75 Every jewel and feature of the crown was described in the inventory of 1521; 'King Henry VIII's Jewel Book', pp. 158–9. Although artistic representations of the crown imperial pre-dating the inventory of 1521 cannot be wholly trusted, it is clear that the finely observed ones depicted on Henry VII's head at Great Malvern (c. 1499–1500: see note 46 above) and (in 1511) in the Great Tournament Roll of Westminster (plate 13), though set with precious gems, are less ornate than the one described in the inventory. However, the crown of Henry VI at St Catherine's Church, Ludham, Norfolk (plate 8), painted in Henry VII's reign, exhibits arches etc. garnished with gems and pearls in the fashion of the one in the 1521 inventory, which counted twenty-eight pearls on the arches. Did Henry VII create the crown imperial described in 1521? A. Jefferies Collins hinted as much, without citing the visual evidence noticed here: A. Jefferies Collins (ed.), *Jewels and Plate of Queen Elizabeth I. The Inventory of 1574* (1955), 'Introduction' and pp. 264–6.

76 In August 1649 'the imperiall crowne of massy gold', weighing 7 lbs 6 oz, was taken from the Upper Jewel House in the Tower and 'totallie broken and defaced' by parliamentary trustees charged with the sale of Charles I's goods. The gold, worth £280, was sent to the mint to be coined; the sale of the stones and pearls between January 1650 and October 1651 yielded £1,001-10-6; Collins (ed.), *Jewels and Plate of Queen Elizabeth I*, pp. 264–6.

Plate 16. The Tudor imperial state crown as it appeared in 1631 (detail of plate 17, Daniel Mytens's state portrait of Charles I). First described in an inventory of the king's jewels and plate in 1521, it was perhaps first fashioned for Henry VIII. Five alternating crosses and fleurs-de-lis of gold rise above the rim of the gem-set border, or circlet. Set into the centre petals of three of the fleurs-de-lis were little gold-and-enamel medallions featuring full-length, exquisitely wrought figures of Christ; in a fourth was St George and in the fifth (seen here), the Virgin and Child. The circlet, arches and cross-shaped finial consisted of 7 lbs. 6 oz. of gold garnished with a multitude of pearls and precious stones. Henry VIII removed an unknown number of these gems; in 1649 the parliamentary agents charged with the destruction of the crown counted 58 rubies (37 balas and 21 small), 28 diamonds, 19 sapphires, 2 emeralds, and 168 pearls, the whole lot of which was sold in 1650–51 for £1,001-10-6.

gramme, the dissemination of the scriptures in English.[77] The scene bears the heavy impress of Henry's imperial authority: the prelates kneel in obedience to the supreme head who wears the imperial crown, the crown which in the emblem below surmounts the Garter encircling the royal arms. As will be seen, this device of the arched crown, Garter, and royal arms became the *impresa* of protestant imperialism in the reigns of Edward VI and Elizabeth I. Of course

[77] King, *Tudor Royal Iconography*, pp. 54–63, especially pp. 59–60; Roy Strong, *Holbein and Henry VIII* (1967), pp. 14, 16 and plate 8. And see below, pp. 104–8.

Plate 17.   Daniel Mytens, *Charles I* (oil, 1631); National Portrait Gallery, London.

Henry was not himself protestant; the theories of imperial kingship under-girding his break with Rome were designed to establish his judicial supremacy in the Church of England. Those theories need not be recited here; it will be enough to recall how useful for Henry's definition of imperial monarchy was the history of the Church under Constantine.

Frances Yates noted how, via Erasmus, protestant writers in the reigns of Edward VI and Elizabeth I adapted those historical arguments to the cause of religious reform. Erasmus had told Charles V that '. . . the Emperors are anoynted sacred for this very purpose, that they may eyther maynteyne or restore, or elles enlarge and spredde abrode the religion of the gospell'.[78] This charge Nicholas Udall, co-author of Anne Boleyn's coronation pageant, inserted as a preface to his 1548 English translation of Erasmus's *Paraphrases*, a book which Edward VI's councillors ordered placed in every parish church in England. By providing 'the Byble to bee sette forth in the Englishe tounge . . . in euerye churche', Udall argued, the 'fyre of Goddes woorde' had consumed papal authority in England in Henry VIII's reign. It was now left to your 'Emperiall Maiestie', Edward VI, heir to Henry's 'Emperiall crowne and sceptre', to 'consumate & finishe such regall enterpryses . . .' in religion.[79]

Among those who promoted Udall's prescription most zealously was the London printer, John Daye (or Day). In 1549 Daye developed a new colophon featuring the Garter, royal arms, and crown imperial between two columns (plate 18). As this colophon was based on Charles V's own columnar device, it was, I think, meant to 'answer' the mark of international Catholic (Habsburg) imperialism: for patriotic English reformists it became the protestant '*Plus Ultra*', so to speak, of Tudor imperialism, and was still being so used in 1570.[80]

At Edward VI's court Daye enjoyed the patronage of some very well-connected reformists, men like John Cheke, the king's tutor, and William Cecil, then personal secretary to Protector Somerset.[81] When Cecil returned to power as Queen Elizabeth's chief councillor, Daye became the conveyor, arguably the chief conveyor, of the graphic imagery of English protestantism, for it was Daye, the foremost publisher of illustrated books in Tudor England, who published the illustrated first two editions (1563 and 1570) of that bible of English protestant nationalism, the *Actes and Monumentes* of John Foxe. Daye himself

---

[78] From the preface to Erasmus's paraphrase on St Matthew in the 1548 English edition of his *Paraphrases*, quoted in Francis Yates, *Astraea: The Imperial Theme in the Sixteenth Century* (New York, 1977), p. 55.

[79] *The first tome or volume of the Paraphrase of Erasmus vpon the newe testamente*, tr. Nicholas Udall (London, 1549), fos. iiia, iiiia, and vi.

[80] Ronald B. McKerrow, *Printers' & Publishers' Devices in England and Scotland 1485–1640* (1949), p. 41 and no. 115; Earl Rosenthal, '*Plus Ultra, Non Plus Ultra*, and the Columnar Device of Emperor Charles V', *Journal of the Warburg and Courtauld Institutes*, 34 (1971): 204–28; Earl Rosenthal, 'The Invention of the Columnar Device of Emperor Charles V at the Court of Burgundy in Flanders in 1516', *Journal of the Warburg and Courtauld Institutes*, 36 (1973): 198–230. The 1570 edition of Foxe's *Actes and Monumentes* bore Daye's Elizabethan mark; Yates, *Astraea*, pp. 57–8 and pl. 6a.

[81] John King, *English Reformation Literature: The Tudor Origins of the Protestant Tradition* (Princeton, NJ, 1982), pp. 94–6.

Plate 18. For the design of his colophon of 1549, the London printer, John Daye, set the Garter and Edward VI's crown imperial and arms between a pair of columns, a composition based on the internationally recognizable personal device of Emperor Charles V. Charles's two-column device was inscribed with an invented Latin motto, '*Plus Ultra*', roughly 'Yet Beyond', possibly a reference to the extension of the Habsburg imperium overseas, i.e. 'Yet Beyond' the pillars of Hercules. For zealous reformists at the courts of Edward VI and Elizabeth I, Daye's mark became the patriotic emblem of protestant Tudor imperialism, a silent but assertive English response, as it were, to the mark and motto of international Catholic (Habsburg) imperialism. The woodcut reproduced here is from a leaf in the 1551 edition of Taverner's Bible. Daye's initials are set on shields on the bases supporting the columns.

almost certainly fixed the theme and composition of the images in those editions.[82]

The woodcuts in the *Actes and Monumentes* visually recast the story of Henry VIII's recovery of 'true', i.e. 'imperial', religion. Although Foxe did not approve of Henry VIII's conservative doctrinal settlement, he rejoiced at Henry's destruction of papal authority in England. For Foxe, medieval popes were anti-Christs who had taken from kings (the heirs, through Charlemagne, of Constantine) the symbols of imperial rule – crowns, thrones, robes, palaces, etc. Believing Constantine's mother to have been English, Foxe hailed the

---

[82] King, *Tudor Royal Iconography*, pp. 133–4.

reestablishment of an imperial kingdom of England, for him an event of millennial importance, as it marked the restoration of the 'true' Church of England after centuries of domination by the bishop of Rome.[83] If an English king, King John, had once surrendered his crown to Rome, as one of the woodcuts in the 1570 edition pictured John doing, Henry VIII had not only reclaimed it but also brought the papacy to heel, as seen in another woodcut from the same edition (plate 19).[84]

Foxe's book was placed in most parish churches where it was easy for parishioners to 'see' this story without actually having to read the text. Frances Yates observed that the transparent evangelism of Foxe's hagiographical text has distracted attention from the very different tone of the illustrations, a tone which reflected 'a return to Constantinian, imperial Christianity . . . the kind of religion which Foxe regards as alone pure'.[85] One of the woodcuts in Foxe actually portrayed Elizabeth I as a second Constantine, the object of the reverential admiration of three men, Foxe and Daye and their sponsor at court, Thomas Norton, another of Cecil's confidants from the days of Somerset's Protectorate (plate 20).[86]

For zealous protestants like Daye and Norton, the appearance of the second (1570) edition of Foxe was of great religio-political importance. The timing of the publication was probably coordinated politically with Cecil in response to recent Catholic attacks on the sovereignty and integrity of the queen and England, in particular the rebellion of the northern earls (1569) and the pope's excommunication of Elizabeth I (1570). In 1570 the queen, her Church, and her religion were under siege; Foxe, Daye's friend and close collaborator, answered this attack with the argument of imperial reform; of the restoration of true religion by the sacred English monarchy; of the re-founding of the true church under the protestant kings of the English Empire.

If Elizabeth I was an 'imperial' queen, as court artists so often represented her (plate 21), it was all the more important in the crisis of 1569–70 to commemorate the origins of her protestant imperial sovereignty with a suitable monument to her father and brother; to Henry VIII, the architect of anti-papal Anglican imperialism, and to his 'Imperial Majesty', Edward VI, that godly prince who had brought 'true religion' to England. Since Henry's tomb then lay but half completed in the 'tomb-house' at Windsor, it was proposed to finish his monument and design a new one there for Edward, whose remains lay in an

[83] Yates, *Astraea*, pp. 43–4; Strong, *Holbein and Henry VIII*, p. 7; King, *Tudor Royal Iconography*, p. 153.

[84] In John Foxe, *Actes and Monumentes of Thynges Passed in Every Kynges Tyme in this Realme* (2 vols., 1570); the image reproduced in plate 19 is from a copy of the third edn (p. 1028) at the Huntington Library, San Marino, CA.

[85] Yates, *Astraea*, p. 44.

[86] John King (*Tudor Royal Iconography*, pp. 156–7, n. 52) credits Professor Patrick Collinson with the suggestive identification of Norton. Parliamentarian and religious writer – Daye published many of his works – Norton also contributed material to Foxe's book. The woodcut initial capital 'C', which appeared in the first (1563) of *Actes and Monumentes*, is discussed most fully in King (*ibid.*, pp. 154–6) and Yates, *Astraea*, pp. 42–3.

1028.   K.Henry.8.   The Pope suppressed in England.

Writing against the pope,

Ex Edw. Halle.

The Byshop of Rochester, & syr Tho. More, sent to the Tower, & they bicause they refused to be sworne.

be sworne. During this Parliament tyme, euery Sonday preached at Paules crosse a bishop, which declared the pope not to be head of the church.

After this, Commissions were sent ouer all Englãd, to take the othe of all men and women, to the Act of succession. In which, few repined except D. John Fisher byshop of Rochester, syr Tho. More late lord Chauncellor, and D. Nicholas Wylson person of S. Thomas Apostles in London. Wherefore these 3. persons, after long exhortation to thē made by the bishop of Canterbury at Lambeth, refusing to be sworne, were sent to the tower, where they remayned, & were oftentymes motioned to be sworne: but the Byshop and syr Tho. More excused thē by their writings, in which they sayd, that they had written before the sayd Lady Katherine to be Queene, & therfore could not well goe frõ that which they had written. Likewise the Doctor excused, that

he in preaching had called her Queene, and therfore now could not withstay it againe: Howbeit at length he was wel contented to dissemble the matter, and so escaped: but the other two stoode agaynst all the realme in their opinion.

From the moneth of Marche this Parliament farthermore was proroged to the iij. day of Nouember abouesayd. At what tyme, amongest other diuers statutes, most graciously and by the blessed will of God it was enacted, that the Pope, and all his colledge of Cardinals, with his pardons & Indulgences, whiche so long had clogged this realme of England, to the miserable slaughter of so many good men, & which neuer could be remoued away before, was now abolished eradicate, & exploded out of this land, & sent home agayne to their owne countrey of Rome, from whence they came, God be euerlastingly praysed therfore. Amen.

¶ The Pope suppressed by K. Henry the eight.

1534.

The Pope inhorsed, but his chaplaines ready to holde the stirrup for hõ to get vp agayne.

The lamentable weeping & howling of all the religious route for the fall of their god the Pope.

An other prophecie of the fall of the Pope.

¶ Papa cito moritur, Cæsar regnabit vbiq̃,   Et subito vani cessabunt gaudia cleri.

¶ An Acte concerning the kinges highnes to be the supreme head of the Church of England, and to haue authoritie to reforme and redresse all errours, heresies, and abuses in the same. Cap. 1.

ALbeit the kings maiestie iustly and rightfully is & ought to be the supreme head of the church of England, and so is recognised by the Clergy of this realme in their Conuocations, yet neuerthelesse for corroboration and confirmation

◄ *Plate 19.* 'The Pope suppressed by K. Henry the eight', a woodcut which first appeared in the second (1570) edition of John Foxe's *Actes and Monumentes* published by John Daye. Daye determined the subject matter and composition of this and the other illustrations in Foxe, and for this edition he recycled the colophon he had designed in 1549 (plate 18); he is probably the bearded man seen in profile between Thomas Cromwell and Thomas Cranmer (left rear). For Foxe and Daye, Henry VIII had restored the 'true' Church of England, a church of which the king, not the pope, was supreme head. The woodcut, which heads Foxe's transcription of the 1534 act for the royal supremacy (26 Hen. VIII, c.1), shows Henry in majesty trampling Pope Clement VII; the king, who wears his arched imperial crown atop a feathered hat, hands the Book of God's Word to an obviously pleased Cranmer, an anachronistic gesture, since Henry conveyed Coverdale's Bible to his subjects in 1535, not 1534 (see plate 23). Although Clement has literally been 'unhorsed' by Henry's act (as the marginal note to the left of the pope's mount explains), he might yet recover; one of his chaplains (lower left) holds 'the stirrup for him to get vp agayne'. Papal supporters include bishop John Fisher, who is trying to assist Clement to his feet, and Reginald Pole, whose name adorns the brim of his anachronistic cardinal's hat; they and the others, all 'weeping & howling', lament 'the fall of their god the pope'. The dissemination of Scripture via English protestant imperial authority will ensure the suppression of Rome's authority.

unmarked grave in Henry VII's Chapel at Westminster Abbey.[87] Although unrealized, this Elizabethan royal funerary scheme, together with contemporary accounts of the funerals of both kings, preserve important, heretofore unnoticed evidence of the imperial theme in Tudor political culture.

The scheme was probably Cecil's.[88] Cecil, as already noted, first came to the fore politically in Protector Somerset's household (1547–49). Somerset was the

---

[87] On 8 August 1553 Edward VI was buried in a white marble vault beneath the altar made by Pietro Torrigiano in 1517–20 for Henry VII's tomb. Torrigiano's altar was destroyed by parliamentary radicals in 1644. Edward VI's gravesite, which is still unmarked, was viewed and described by Sir Christopher Wren on 11 February 1685, when he and others on command of James II undertook excavations in Henry VII's Chapel in search of a possible site for the burial of Charles II. Digging westward from a point about six feet east of Henry VII's tomb, they encountered in an underground chamber '. . . a verry noble, large entire stone of white marble of a cooped forme sloeping gently from the centre to its extremities whose corners, sides & edges were curiously wrought, carved and embossed with letters raised high there on all of the same marble . . . viz: EDWARDUS SEXTUS etc [*sic*]. The position of which stone exactly corresponds to the site of the stately and magnificent brazen Altar and canopie that stood over the same . . .'; Westminster Abbey Library, no. 67180, a typescript transcription of Cambridge University Library MS. Dd. viii. 39. A seventeenth-century engraving of the altar is reproduced in H. M. Colvin, D. R. Ransome, and John Summerson, *The History of the King's Works*, vol. iii [1485–1660], pt. 1 (1975), plate 17.

[88] Among Cecil's papers in the Lansdowne MSS. is 'A Calendar for kinge Henry Theightes Tombe', an undated survey addressed to Cecil probably *c.* 1558–62 of 'all thinges wrought and unwrought touching . . .' the project; BL, Lansdowne MS. 94, fos. 27–8. Lansdowne MS. 6, fo. 90 is the marquess of Winchester's letter of 12 September 1563 to Cecil (Burghley) detailing, apparently at Cecil's request, the progress of work on Henry VIII's tomb, together with an estimate of the changes necessary if a second tomb were also to be built. It is clear that the final decision was to be the queen's. Winchester's estimates were based on Lansdowne MS. 116, no. 13, what Howard Colvin has called 'a professional survey'; Colvin *et al.*, *King's Works*, iii, pt. 1, p. 321, note 1. On 27 July 1567 Winchester forwarded to Cecil a set of plans for the project: PRO, SP 12/43, fo. 73.

Plate 20. Elizabeth I as a second Constantine, a woodcut in the first (1563) edition of Foxe's *Actes and Monumentes*. Foxe dedicated his book to the queen, likening her rule to that of Constantine, for just as the first Christian Roman emperor had halted the persecution of the early Church, so Elizabeth's succession had put an end to the suffering of reformists under Mary I. Imperial rule brings peace and concord, symbolized here by the fruitful yield of the cornucopia which forms the upper part of the initial capital 'C' (for 'Constantine'). This bounty includes three Tudor roses which have grown from the union of the two roses of Lancaster and York (on the left). The Empress Elizabeth holds majestic sway over the fallen papacy: she sits enthroned with orb and sword above the pontiff – identified here by his tiara – whose body, entwined with serpents, forms the lower part of the 'C'. The queen's imperial stance has broken the 'keys' of papal dominion. It has been suggested that Elizabeth's three admirers are, from right to left, John Daye, John Foxe and their agent at court, Thomas Norton. If (as John King has said) their attitude resembles the Adoration of the Magi, the queen becomes suggestively linked to both Virgin and Child, and indeed, in the 1570 edition of his *Actes and Monumentes*, Foxe replaced his Constantinian dedication with one beginning with 'Christ', the initial 'C' of which enclosed this picture.

Plate 21. Elizabeth I in majesty, an illuminated initial capital at the head of the plea roll in the court of queen's bench, Easter 1572 (PRO, KB 27/1241).

patron of a number of protestant *émigré* artists, among them a sculptor, William Cure (d. 1579) of Amsterdam, the principal craftsman at Somerset House, the Protector's new London residence. Cure's workshop counted the most important sculptors and carvers in England, including Cornelius, his eldest son. In the 1560s and 1570s Cornelius Cure won a number of commissions in London for the design and carving of funerary monuments, all of them for court-connected protestant gentlemen who, like Cecil, had risen to prominence during Somerset's Protectorate; Cornelius was eventually awarded the commission for Cecil's own tomb.[89]

In 1573 Cornelius Cure was paid £4 by warrant of the exchequer for a ground plan and elevation for a tomb for Edward VI; for an additional £41 14s 8d Cure and his collaborator, Richard Rowlands, produced drawings and two highly detailed scale models of Henry's tomb, one possibly full-size.[90] Only the 'platt' for Edward's monument has survived, a large, coloured drawing almost certainly from Cure's hand (plate 22).[91] Cure's design mirrors the Franco-Italianate classical style of his smaller London tombs and the various building projects patronized by the Elizabethan members of the 'Somerset Circle' of protestant gentlemen.[92] Among the decorative tomb-motifs one notices the numerous crowns imperial – on the head of the effigy, atop the Tudor rose and fleur-de-lis, and surmounting the royal arms (plate 22).

No visual evidence survives to suggest the appearance of Henry VIII's tomb, but a conjectural reconstruction by Alfred Higgins in 1894, on which our drawings of side and end elevations are based (figures 1 and 2), gives some indication of the scale of a monument which would have been the costliest, most splendid tomb ever built in England, more than twice as grand as Henry VII's at Westminster Abbey, according to the architect, Benedetto da Rovezzano.[93] In

[89] Margaret Whinney, *Sculpture in Britain 1530–1830* (Harmondsworth, Middlesex, 1964), pp. 16–17; John Summerson, *Architecture in Britain 1530–1830* (Harmondsworth, Middlesex, 1953), pp. 10, 17.

[90] PRO, E 351/3209; Colvin *et al.*, *King's Works*, iii, pt. 1, p. 321.

[91] Bodleian Library, Gough Maps 45, no. 63; Colvin *et al.*, *King's Works*, iii, pt. 1, p. 321.

[92] Summerson, *Architecture in Britain*, p. 17 and p. 348, note 3; Nicholas Pevsner, 'Hill Hall', *Architecture Review* (May 1955), pp. 307–9. The designation 'Somerset Circle' is my own. In addition to Cecil, members of this group included, among others, Sir Richard Blount, Sir John Thynne, and Sir Thomas Smith. Hill Hall was Smith's Essex house, begun *c.* 1564.

[93] The fullest account of the making of Henry VIII's tomb is Alfred Higgins, 'On the Work of Florentine Sculptors in England in the early part of the sixteenth century; with special reference to the tombs of Cardinal Wolsey and Henry VIII', *Archaeological Journal*, 51 (1894): 129–220, especially pp. 164ff. See also Colvin *et al.*, *King's Works*, iii, pt. 1, pp. 320–1; St John Hope, *Windsor Castle*, ii, pp. 482–5; and P. G. Lindley, 'Playing check-mate with royal majesty? Wolsey's patronage of Italian Renaissance sculpture', in S. J. Gunn and P. G. Lindley (eds.), *Cardinal Wolsey: Church, state and art* (Cambridge, 1990), pp. 261–79. Construction began in a yard at Westminster in 1529, when the king seized materials for a tomb for Wolsey on which Benedetto had been working since 1524; Benedetto's remark is in his letter of 29 June 1529, in Latin, to Wolsey, printed in Higgins, 'Sculptors', pp. 201–2, and cited by Colvin *et al.*, *King's Works*, iii, pt. 1, p. 320. Benedetto's supervision ended in 1543, though payments for materials were still made in the period 25 December 1544–15 April 1545 (PRO, E 336/27, also Westmister Abbey Library no. 64299), when work fell under the supervision of Nicholas Bellin of Modena. Nicholas's work is last mentioned on 28 August 1551 (*APC*, iii, p. 347). In 1565 the tomb was dismantled and moved from Westminster to the

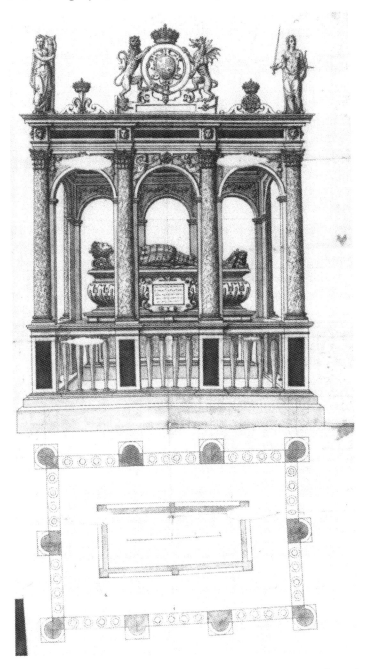

Plate 22. Cornelius Cure's 'platt' of *c.* 1573 for a tomb for Edward VI, a coloured drawing measuring 14″ × 24″ (Bodleian Library, Gough Maps 45, no. 63). The monument of marble and bronze was to have been built at Windsor next to Henry VIII's tomb, the capstone of an Elizabethan scheme to memorialize England's first protestant 'imperial' king.

addition to massive amounts of black and white marble for the platform, podium and base supporting the sarcophagus, the design called for more than seventeen and a half tons of gilded bronze for forty-eight statues, two friezes (each running almost fifty feet in length), ten ten-foot pillars, ten huge (nine foot) candlesticks, and a full-size effigy of the king (figure 1). Brass representations of the crown imperial were integrated emblematically in virtually all elements of the design; at both ends of the tomb pedastal *putti* supported shields of the king's arms (figure 2), each of which was surmounted by a large, superbly wrought replica of the crown, while the same device surmounted similar shields on the candlesticks, four of which survived and may be seen today flanking the high altar of the cathedral church of St Bavon, Ghent.[94]

The scheme of such tombs was derived from the columned, stationary great 'herses' of the royal funerals, elaborate domed structures of wood enclosing the coffin and holding banderoles and burning tapers.[95] Essentially the royal hearse (whether standing or wheeled) was a torch-lit, temporary pavilion for the display of the king's 'Arms of all his Dominions, titles, genealogies', etc., in the centre of which was a bier for the recumbent figure of the royal person, an effigy of plaster, wax or wood which lay atop the coffin.[96] Henry III was the first English king to be carried to his grave in a coffin, and his funeral (1272) was apparently the first to feature such an effigy.[97] By the time of Henry V's funeral, the effigy had come to be clothed realistically in the deceased's own crown and robes; Henry V's effigy was the first to be invested in repose with 'imperial'

'tomb-house' at Windsor (the present Prince Consort's Chapel), where, in a reassembled but unfinished state, it stood until 1645–46 when parliament ordered it 'defaced' and its marble and broken brass bits sold overseas. (The orders are reprinted in Higgins, 'Sculptors', pp. 217–18.) Only the sarcophagus and base survived in place, eventually becoming part of Lord Nelson's tomb at St Paul's. Paul Hentzner, who saw the tomb at Windsor in 1598, said that more than £60,000 had been spent on it (before work ceased, probably by 1553); his description in his *Itinerarium* (Breslau, 1617) is translated from the Latin and quoted in St John Hope, *Windsor Castle*, ii, p. 490, note 20. See also Colvin *et al.*, *King's Works*, iii, pt. 1, pp. 320–2; Lindley, 'Italian Renaissance sculpture', pp. 264, 267.

[94] Higgins, 'Sculptors', pp. 166–84, 189–90. Higgins printed a number of accounts and records of payments for work done on the tomb in the period from December 1530 to July 1536. Four and a half pounds of wax costing 2s 1d were used in August 1531 for making the two brass replicas of the crown imperial (*ibid.*, p. 209); in November 1531 8d was spent on soldering 'la chorona imperialie' and Robert the Englishman received £1 for polishing or finishing it (*ibid.*, p. 212). Anthony Triest, bishop of Ghent in 1622–53, bought the four candlesticks which are now at St Bavon. The local Flemish-language guide to the cathedral contains an excellent full-page monochrome reproduction of the device of the crown and shield supported by griffin and greyhound: R. van de Wielle, *De Sint-Baafskatedraal te Gent* (Ghent, 1978), p. 37.

[95] Higgins, 'Sculptors', p. 172. For Henry VIII's funeral in 1547 two enormous hearses were built at Windsor and Westminster; the great gilded, double-storied domed construction at Windsor, with its thirteen 'great pillers', rose thirty-five feet from the floor of the choir in St George's Chapel: John Strype, *Ecclesiastical Memorials* (Oxford, 1822), ii, pt. 2, pp. 294–5, the printed version of College of Arms MS. I. 11, fos. 91–106, a contemporary account by one of the heralds. A second herald's account is cited and quoted in W. St John Hope, 'On the Funeral Effigies of the Kings and Queens of England, with special reference to those in the Abbey Church of Westminster', *Archaeologia*, 40 (1906): 541 (College of Arms MS. I. 14, fo. 68b).

[96] From the description of the wheeled, horse-drawn hearse, or 'chayre', which carried Henry VII's funeral effigy from Richmond to St Paul's on 9 May 1509; quoted in St John Hope, 'Funeral Effigies', p. 539.

[97] St John Hope, 'Funeral Effigies', p. 542.

insignia. In 1547 'A fake coffyn' on the stationary hearse at Westminster[98] bore a 'representation' of Henry VIII so like the king 'in all points' that an eye-witness referred to it as if it were Henry, 'holding in his right hand a sceptre of gold; in his left hand the ball of the world with a cross [and] Upon his head a crown imperial of inestimable value'.[99]

This 'goodly image', or 'picture', of Henry lay in state until the royal funeral chariot was made ready to carry it to Windsor. Like earlier spectacles staged by the Tudors, Henry VIII's funeral procession was essentially theatrical, and it gave Edward VI's councillors an exceptionally good opportunity – 'the weather being very fair, and the people being very desirous to see the sights' – to convey in a solemn but grand way the Crown's 'imperial' dignity. Leading the procession were 250 torch-bearing mourners in long 'gowns and hoods with badges on their left shoulders, the red and white cross in a sun shining, crown imperial over that'.[100] To eyes not yet blinded by gas or electric lighting, photographic images and television screens, these bright, embroidered badges, made especially for the occasion, must have been very impressive indeed. Even more impressive to the multitude denied access to the hearse at Whitehall was the sight of the 'very long and large' domed four-columned chariot overlaid with cloth of gold, bearing on a gold-draped coffin what seemed to be Henry himself, a figure ablaze, head to toe, in crimson and scarlet clothes – satin doublet and hose and crimson velvet shoes – his crimson robe trimmed in miniver and gold, the Garter around his neck, a 'fayre armering sworde by his side', two pearl-studded bracelets on his wrists and on his hands 'a payer of new gloves with many ringes . . .', all of the rings set with flashing jewels; and on his head, which lay on two great pillows of blue and gold, 'The Crowne Emperiall of Englande of goulde sett with precious stones . . .'.[101]

In 1422, as already noted, the crown adorning the head of Henry V's funeral effigy was described as an 'Imperial diadem of gold and precious stones', a closed crown of the type the king had worn in triumph at Agincourt. From the victor at Agincourt Henry VIII inherited a dual legacy, the legacy of the king as conqueror, the king who *in regno suo est imperator*. At Tournai in 1513 he endeavoured to show by how much he embodied the meaning of Agincourt, the achievement of English 'imperial' kingship. With him were men whose grand-fathers had been with Henry V at Agincourt, men whose forebears were alive at the time when Henry V secured Emperor Sigismund's recognition of the inviol-

---

[98] Alnwick Castle, Syon MSS. (Northumberland Papers), no. 467, fo. 106b.
[99] Strype, *Ecclesiastical Memorials*, ii, pt. 2, p. 298. The modelling of the early Tudor funeral effigies was of the highest artistic standard. The extant plaster head of Henry VII's funeral effigy has been convincingly attributed to Pietro Torrigiano; Edward VI's now-lost effigy was fabricated and painted by Nicholas Bellin of Modena: Carol Galvin and Phillip Lindley, 'Pietro Torrigiano's portrait bust of King Henry VII', *Burlington Magazine*, 130 (1988): 892–902.
[100] Strype, *Ecclesiastical Memorials*, ii, pt. 2.
[101] St John Hope, 'Funeral Effigies', pp. 540–1 (quoting College of Arms MS. I. 14, fo. 67).

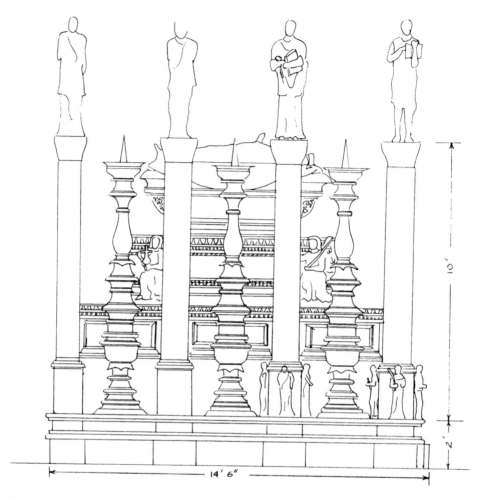

ability of an English king's *imperium*. Although that recognition had become the stuff of legend by 1513, there can be no doubt that in 1415, by wearing a new crown, one arched 'like the imperial crown', Henry V had changed English perceptions of the symbolism of the king's *imperium*, and his successors would make use of what appeared to be imperial acceptance of this new emphasis.[102] So in France in 1513, in the presence of another emperor, Henry VIII would pose as the conqueror who had reclaimed the basis of Henry V's true dignity: *rex est imperator* in English Tournai. Henry VIII was clearly thinking of the nature of that dignity four years later when he entertained the notion of his election to the crown of the Holy Roman Empire. He asked Cuthbert Tunstal how such an election would affect the dignity of the Tudor crown. Tunstal's reply is

[102] At Henry VI's coronation in 1429 the memory of Henry V's relations with Emperor Sigismund was extolled by royal propagandists precisely in order to convey to the foreign dignitaries present the distinctive nature of Henry VI's *imperium*; Griffiths, *Reign of King Henry VI*, p. 190.

◄   *Figure 1.* A side elevation of the bronze and marble tomb designed by
Benedetto da Rovezzano for Henry VIII (pen-and-ink drawing by Megan
Hoak, based on Higgins's conjectural reconstruction of 1894). When the
foreigner, Paul Hentzner, saw it in a half-completed state at Windsor in
1598, he reckoned that more than £60,000 had been lavished on a tomb
which Benedetto had said was meant to be the largest, most splendid
funerary monument ever built in England. In fact, work on it, first begun at
Westminster in 1524 (when Henry VIII confiscated materials for Wolsey's
tomb), had ceased before it was moved to Windsor in 1565. In the early
1570s Cecil and others unsuccessfully moved the queen to complete a project
which, like the plan for Edward VI's monument (plate 22), many former
Edwardians at court had come to identify with the origins of Elizabeth I's
'imperial' sovereignty. In Higgins's reconstruction, the ensemble of tomb
and altar sat on a platform of black marble measuring about thirteen by
twenty-six feet, the whole enclosed by a grill of brass and marble five feet
high. A life-size recumbent effigy of Henry in yellow bronze lay atop the
sarcophagus of polished black touchstone; the sarcophagus and its base of
white marble rested on a black marble podium fourteen and a half feet long,
ten feet wide and five feet high. The metallic elements consumed seventeen
and a half tons of gilded bronze: in addition to the effigy, there were ten
square pillars, each ten feet tall, spaced evenly about the perimeter of the
podium; the figures of ten apostles, each over four feet tall, atop the pillars;
thirty-four smaller statues, each about two feet in height, at the bases of the
pillars; ten enormous candlesticks, each nine feet high, between the pillars;
and two friezes running around the sides of the podium.

instructive: '. . . the crown of England is an Empire of itself . . . for which cause
your grace weareth a close crown . . .'.[103]

An understandable preoccupation with Henry VIII's later search for texts and
precedents which would justify in law his claim to an exclusive ('imperial')
jurisdiction over the English church quite possibly has distorted our view of
cause and effect in the thinking which produced the Henrician Revolution, for
like Tunstal's words, which are too often read in anticipation of the Act of
Appeals, that search should properly be understood against the background of
the history and use of the closed crown in England. As has been seen, the
pre-Reformation visual programme of royally sponsored 'imperial' symbolism
was very extensive; it clearly pre-dated Henry's coronation and self-
promotional adventure at Tournai. Henry VII was the true architect of the
symbolism of Tudor 'imperial' kingship, and his commissions for artistic
images of himself wearing an arched crown leave no doubt of his purpose: he
would show his subjects that his 'imperial' magnificence exceeded that of the
Yorkists and that his arms could stand comparison with those of any European
sovereign. Proof of his 'imperial' legitimacy he would trace back to two sources,
to Henry V, the father of his 'holy' step-uncle and the first to wear the crown
imperial; and to Constantine, who had supposedly bequeathed to kings of

[103] Tunstall to Henry VIII, from Mechlin, 2 February 1517: *LP*, ii, pt. 2, no. 2911.

Figure 2. End elevation of Henry VIII's tomb (pen-and-ink drawing by Megan Hoak, based on Higgins's conjectural reconstruction of 1894).

England a unique 'imperial' status. He took over the chief symbol of Lancastrian 'imperial' kingship, the closed crown, greatly magnifying its use in a variety of artistic media; iconographically, it is salutary to recall just how 'Constantinian' were certain aspects of this tradition.[104] Henry VIII absorbed

[104] Perhaps the best evidence is to be found in commissions for painted windows. At Ashton-under-Lyne, Lancashire, the figures of Henry VI and Edward the Confessor are depicted in the fifteenth-century glass of some tracery lights; glass panels on the south side of the nave dating from *c.* 1480 depict events in the life of St Helena and Constantine the Great. The fifteenth-century glass in the southwest windows of the ante-chapel at All Souls, Oxford, contain figures of kings, each with sceptre and orb, including Constantine and Henry V; St Helena appears in an eastern window and in a north window, Henry VI and King Arthur; Nelson, *Ancient Painted Glass*, pp. 130–2, 165. See note 48 above.

this artistic programme most fully at the outset of his reign, making powerful use of the symbolism of the crown imperial in numerous settings at court and abroad. This evidence points to the well-springs of his later quest for the origins of his own True Monarchy: he had been taught to 'see' the symbolic meaning of the closed crown of England long before he changed his 'jurysdiccion and dignite ryall' to a 'crown or imperial jurisdiction'. This being so, it is time that we assign to the visual aspects of pre-Reformation imperial ideology a prime place in shaping Reformation political culture, in fashioning the 'Empire' that England became in 1533.

Earlier versions of different parts of this paper were presented with slides at meetings of the American Historical Association (San Francisco, December 1989), the Mid-Atlantic Renaissance-Reformation Seminar (University of Virginia, March 1990), and the Sixteenth-Century Studies Conference (Atlanta, October 1992). For their invitation to present my findings in the form of a public lecture in the Sir Thomas Browne Institute, University of Leiden (April 1990), I am especially grateful to Professor Johannes van den Berg and Dr Ernestine van der Wall of the faculty of theology at Leiden. The research for the final version, for the most part undertaken in Cambridge, Oxford, and London, was generously supported in 1992 and 1993 by grants from the Committee on Faculty Research at the College of William & Mary.

4   *The royal image, 1535–1603*

JOHN N. KING

The onset of the Reformation in England entailed a fundamental transformation of the public image of the English monarch.[1] Until the completion of the breach with the Church of Rome, Henry VIII conformed to the policy of his predecessors by paying homage to the pope as the head of the Church universal and spiritual leader of all Christendom. However, when the Act in Restraint of Appeals of 1533 recognized in England Henry's supreme headship of ecclesiastical and secular affairs, his apologists were free to combine the regal symbol of the sword with the image of the book that artistic tradition had long associated with saints and clerics. The composite biblical symbol of the Sword and the Book would play a vital role in the campaign to establish an image of the Tudor monarch as a theocratic ruler capable of unifying ecclesiastical and secular authority. Long after Henry's death, variations of this motif infiltrated portrayals of Edward VI and Elizabeth I, his protestant offspring, as continuators of his separation from the papacy. In a rare instance, this figure even appeared in parodic form in pageantry designed to validate the effort of Mary I to turn back the Reformation and to restore adherence to the see of Rome. Through a host of inversions and variations, the Sword and the Book attained wide currency as a well-known symbol of Tudor royalism.

Hans Holbein the Younger established the definitive portrayal of Tudor protestant royalism when he fashioned the title-page border for the 1535 Coverdale Bible as a depiction of tacit royal consent to the publication of the scriptures in translation (plate 23). Restoration of the vernacular Bible as the source of spiritual understanding was a fundamental protestant concern inherited from humanists like Erasmus. Although the volume was not formally

---

[1] This subject is treated in John N. King, *Tudor Royal Iconography: Literature and Art in an Age of Religious Crisis* (Princeton, NJ, 1989). The present chapter incorporates the findings of that study in a revised form. A degree of overlap exists between the discussion of Henry VIII's image in the present chapter and my 'Henry VIII as David: The King's Image and Reformation Politics', in *Rethinking the Henrician Era: Essays on Early Tudor Texts and Contexts*, ed. Peter C. Herman (Champaign, IL, 1994), pp. 78–82. Unless otherwise noted, scriptural texts are from the Revised Standard Version, including those that are offered without notice in place of Vulgate quotations. Contractions and abbreviations are silently expanded.

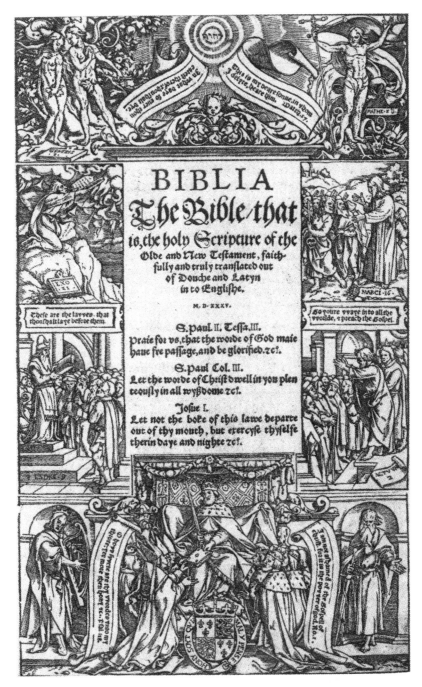

Plate 23. Henry VIII with the Sword and the Book, a woodcut by Hans Holbein the Younger; part of the border of the title-page of the Coverdale Bible (1535).

authorized, it was brought to completion under the patronage of Thomas Cromwell, the king's chief minister.[2] Crowded with biblical images and inscriptions, the intricately carved compartments of this border present the Henrician Reformation as a return to the new dispensation brought by Christ. Flanking the Tetragrammaton at the top are Adam, who stands with Eve at the left as the Old Testament type or figure who foretokens the resurrection of Christ at the opposite side. The commanding figure of Henry VIII in the bottom compartment wields the Sword and the Book as a worldly manifestation of divine revelation.[3] His authority 'descends' from the Old and New Testament models for sacred kingship depicted elsewhere on the page: Moses receiving the Ten Commandments, David with his lyre, and Christ preaching.

The border of the Coverdale Bible addresses the hierarchy of spiritual versus secular functions, legitimation, and the nature of kingship. As a consequence of his separation from the Roman Church, Henry VIII superseded the pope to become, as head of the English Church, the intermediary between temporal society and the divine order. Cromwell, as the effective patron of the Bible translation, presumably intended the Holbein image to validate, by a universally available means, Henry's claim to govern as an English 'pope'. Miles Coverdale's preface (sig. + 2v) comments on the symbolism of this scene by explaining that the Bible

declareth most abounddauntly that the office, auctorite and power geven of God unto kynges, is in earth above all other powers: let them call themselves Popes, Cardynalles, or what so ever they will, the worde of god declareth them (yee and commaundeth them under payne of dampnacion) to be obedient unto the temporall swerde: As in the olde Testament all the Prophetes, Pr[i]estes, and Levites were.

The figures of David and Paul flanking Henry VIII represent sources of spiritual authority that derive from the scriptures rather than from ecclesiastical tradition. (David was commonly believed to have composed the Psalms.) As major authors of the Old and New Testaments, David and Paul respectively symbolize divine revelation before and after the advent of the New Dispensation brought by Christ. They carry iconographical attributes that identified them in medieval art. The image of David and his lyre serves primarily as a type for Henry VIII's claim to govern by divine sanction. David's image is particularly useful in portraying Henry as the intermediary between heaven and earth, because the Hebrew king was regarded by Christians as a prototype of the Messiah.[4]

[2] Roy C. Strong, *Holbein and Henry VIII* (1967), p. 14. See also J. B. Trapp and Hubertus Herbrüggen, *'The King's Good Servant': Sir Thomas More, 1477/8–1535* [catalogue of the exhibition at the National Portrait Gallery, London] (1977), p. 75.

[3] This 'image was to be definitive one for the Tudor and Stuart Kings', according to Strong, *Holbein and Henry VIII*, p. 14. See also Pamela Tudor-Craig, 'Henry VIII and King David', in *Early Tudor England: Proceedings of the 1987 Harlaxton Symposium*, ed. Daniel Williams (Woodbridge, Suffolk, 1989), pp. 183–205.

[4] On the medieval origins of praising Henry as a new David, see King, *Tudor Royal Iconography*, pp. 56, 60.

In accordance with Holbein's portrayal of king rather than pope as the apostolic successor to Christ, St Paul's dominant presence denies Petrine supremacy. His chief attribute, a sword, was employed throughout the Middle Ages as a martyr's device commemorating his decollation. Protestants revered Paul as the paramount saint, not for his martyrdom, but for his authorship of New Testament epistles and promulgation of the crucial distinction between faith and works. Thus Paul's assertion 'that a man is justified by faith apart from works of law' (Rom. 3:28) provided the basis for Luther's doctrine of justification by faith alone as the fundamental religious tenet. No longer a simple martyr's symbol, the sword of Paul's hands came to be identified during the Reformation as an evangelical symbol for the Bible.[5]

Although the sword in King Henry's hand is an ancient symbol for royal authority and the administration of justice, its close proximity to the sword borne by St Paul identifies it, moreover, with 'the sword of the Spirit, which is the word of God' (Eph. 6:17). The reformers reinterpreted the regal sword as an evangelical device for the exercise of royal justice in line with scriptural precepts when Henry denied the pope's claim of divine authority to delegate temporal power to emperors and kings. Thomas Cranmer accorded with this shift when, during the reign of the king's daughter, Mary, he proclaimed that

contrary to [the pope's] clayme, the emperial crowne and jurisdicion temporal of this realme is taken immediately from God, to be used under him only, and is subjecte unto non[e], but to God alone . . . As the pope taketh upon him to geve the temporall sworde, or royall and Imperiall power to kynges and princes, so dothe he likewise take upon hym to depose them from their Imperiall states, yf they be disobedient to him.[6]

The base of the Coverdale Bible border resolves the one-time rivalry of Church and state by subordinating kneeling hierarchies of Henrician prelates and lords to an omnicompetent king. The woodcut inverts the conventional pattern of the dedication portrait in which an author or translator kneels before a patron to present a copy of a work. The 'upward' movement found in standard portraits is reversed in the Coverdale Bible to show Henry VIII handing the Bible down to the prelates and nobles who kneel before him. These recipients personify the clerical and magisterial estates who are delegated to disseminate the scripture to the population at large.

The side compartments of Holbein's border portray royal permission for the Coverdale Bible as a recapitulation of pivotal biblical events. Cromwell's role as patron of the volume suggests that he may have chosen the scenes to include in the artist's design as a compliment to King Henry. Moses's reception of the Ten Commandments on the left side furnishes a type for a divinely inspired leader capable of delivering God's chosen people out of bondage to the tyrannical Pharaoh, whom the reformers interpreted as a figure for the pope. Beneath this

---

[5] Strong gives less emphasis to the evangelical origins of this figure in *Holbein and Henry VIII*, pp. 14–16.

[6] *The copy of certain lettres sent to the Quene . . . from prison in Oxeforde* (c. 1556), sig. A3ᵛ, B2ᵛ.

scene, Esdras preaches the Old Law. In the balanced New Testament scenes at the right, Christ first commissions the apostles with the words 'Go youre waye into all the worlde, & preach the Gospel' (Mark 16:15; quoted from the border of the Coverdale Bible). With tongues of flame upon his head and those of this associates, St Peter then preaches after Pentecost (Acts 2:3). Christ's delegation of the apostles as his successors establishes a direct line of spiritual authority that descends to Henry VIII without any intervention from the ecclesiastical hierarchy. As the occasion of the birth of the Christian Church, Pentecost supplies a type for the alleged rebirth or renewal of the Church during the Reformation.

Holbein's woodcut amalgamates the portrait of Henry VIII and the scriptural images above it, with their accompanying texts, into a complex portrayal of the liberating power of the vernacular Bible. The evangelical images in the New Testament panels are compatible with the Reformation emphasis on gospel preaching, in contrast to the legalism of Old Testamental worship, which the reformers interpreted as a type for the formalistic religion of the late Middle Ages. The proliferation of keys in the inset portrait of Christ and the apostles at the right-hand side undermines the papal claim to primacy as the inheritor of the keys of St Peter. By appropriating a symbol that had been identified with the primacy of the Church of Rome, the image suggests that the 'keys of the kingdom of heaven' (Matt. 16:19) function as a symbol for Reformation kingship rather than the papal power to loose and to bind.[7]

The propagandistic image of Henry VIII on the title page of the Great Bible of 1539 (plate 24) was the direct successor of Holbein's portrayal of the monarch bearing the Sword and the Book in the Coverdale Bible. The publication of the Great Bible under royal patronage as the first authorized English scriptural translation represented a revolutionary victory for protestant ideology, one that had a direct effect upon the transformation of the book, symbolic of the scriptures, into a distinctive new device for Tudor protestant royalism. This title page symbolizes complex relations among concepts of authorship, authority, and authorization, for it represents not only official sanction of the Bible translation, but also the royal control over Church and state from which it stems. Carved by a member of the school of Holbein, the illustration reflects the title page of the Coverdale Bible in its inversion of the conventional 'movement' of the dedication portrait, in which a patron characteristically receives a presentation copy of a manuscript or book from its author or translator. Henry VIII's posture in the Great Bible woodcut therefore combines that of both artist and patron as he assumes the quasi-authorial role of transmitting *Verbum Dei* ('the Word of God') to the flanking figures of Thomas Cromwell, the king's chief minister, and Thomas Cranmer, the archbishop of Canterbury. As the

---

[7] See Strong, *Holbein and Henry VIII*, p. 16, and King, *Tudor Royal Iconography*, pp. 64–70.

Plate 24. Henry VIII as a Reformation king, a woodcut by the School of Holbein; part of the border of the title-page of the Great Bible (1539).

king's vicegerent for religious affairs, Cromwell instigated publication of the Bible translation.

Holbein's original design for the Coverdale Bible (plate 23) was loosely adapted for the Great Bible title page, which symbolizes the royal supremacy over Church and state by depicting a graded hierarchy in which the king replaces the pope as the temporal intermediary between heaven and earth. Henry's reception of the divine Word directly from God embodies the reformers' belief that the vertical process of reform is a royal prerogative, because the king alone can transmit the Bible to the bishops and magistrates in the second level. The rigid stratification of the scene enacts a tense balance between freedom and control, because its orderly ranks reflect Henry's cautious retention of traditional doctrine and ritual during the early stages of the English Reformation. The image ambivalently endorses the protestant commitment to the priesthood of all believers in a realm where the monarch maintained tight control over religion. Accordingly, the bottom compartment portrays members of a congregation hearing the English Bible from the lectern rather than reading it for themselves, because they are still passive recipients of scriptures that are transmitted by a priestly élite operating under political instructions from the Crown. The ability of those who call out the Latin words of homage, '*Vivat Rex*', distinguishes them as superiors of the childlike figures who shout out 'God Save the King'.

The complicated symbolism of this woodcut border applies different scriptural guises of Henry VIII in a heavily layered and overlapping fashion. The most prominent visual allusion is to his instrumental role in the transmission of *Verbum Dei*, an apostolic image for the dissemination of the Bible in the post-Pentecostal world of the early Church; it offered protestants a figure for the renewal of the 'true' Church during the Reformation. The image of the sacred Book, as it descends through various levels of the political and social hierarchy, objectifies the utterance emanating from God in the banderole at the top of the border: 'So shall my word be that goes forth from my mouth; it shall not return to me empty, but it shall accomplish that which I purpose' (Isa. 55:11). In the New Testament, *Verbum Dei* refers specifically to the preaching of the divine word and missionary activity of the apostles (Acts 8:14). The tag-phrase *Verbum Dei* affords a visual analogue to the inset scenes in the Coverdale Bible showing Christ's delegation of the disciples and the inspiration of the apostles at Pentecost.

Key scriptural texts inscribed in sinuous banderoles present the iconographical programme of the woodcut border. Although Henry VIII's pre-eminent role is that of David,[8] he also voices King Darius's acknowledgement of the power of Yahweh and speaks to Cromwell in the voice of Moses and to Cranmer through words uttered by St Paul. With the exception of Darius, all of these regal

---

[8] Tudor-Craig concurs that 'in the Great Bible David is subsumed into Henry, the Lord's Anointed'; 'Henry VIII and King David', p. 193.

prototypes also appear in the border of the Coverdale Bible. The praying figure of the king in the upper right corner utters words attributed to David in celebrating the power of the divine word as a guide for royal conduct: 'Thy word is a lamp to my feet' (Ps. 119:105; Vulg. Ps. 118:105). God reciprocates in his selection of Henry as David to govern over England as a new Israel: 'I have found in David the son of Jesse a man after my heart, who will do all my will' (Acts 13:22). The largest banderole attributes to Henry's enthroned figure the response of Darius the Mede to the miraculous survival of Daniel in the lion's den, whereby he proclaimed: 'I make a decree, that in all my royal dominion men tremble and fear before the God of Daniel, for he is the living God' (Dan. 6:26). The Bible's presentation of the unhistorical figure of Darius as the conqueror of Babylon may be interpreted as a prefiguration of the English king's rejection of the authority of papal Rome.

Henry VIII's balanced actions at the right and left sides of the border present him as a figure who unifies the role of Moses, one who imparts law to judges, and St Paul, an authority who offers counsel to an apostle on the conduct of Christian missions to the Gentiles. In the second register of the border, Cranmer is empowered to 'command and teach' religious doctrine (1 Tim. 4:11), casting him in the role of a new Timothy who, as the favoured colleague of Pauline Henry, is entrusted with converting the English to an evangelical religious programme. Cromwell in turn receives a Mosaic charge to 'judge righteously' and to 'hear the small and the great alike' (Deut. 1:16–17). In the third register these servants of the crown transmit *Verbum Dei* to figures representative of the clergy and magistracy, respectively. Cranmer instructs the cleric at the left by repeating St Peter's injunction that pastors fulfil their obligation to 'tend the flock of God' (1 Pet. 5:2); according to protestant teaching, the Bible is the worldly source of spiritual 'feeding'. Cromwell outlines the responsibility of civil authorities by quoting from Psalm 34:14 (Vulg. Ps. 33:15): 'Depart from evil, and do good; seek peace, and pursue it.' As is the case in the Coverdale Bible, a congregation gathers at the base of the title-page border. Representative of the English people, this gathering hears a biblical text that was interpreted as a foundation of the political doctrine that subjects must obey royal authority: the cleric enjoins them to pray for 'kings and all who are in high positions' (1 Tim. 2:2).

The image-making strategies of the Coverdale Bible and the Great Bible were well suited to the initial phase of the English Reformation, when the monarch sponsored an adminstrative revolution that placed himself at the apex of an ecclesiastical structure that now excluded the pope, cardinals, and the monastic establishment. Liturgy and theology remained virtually intact, however, despite expectations for an evangelical government that had been aroused by Cranmer and Cromwell.

At Henry's death in 1547, Edward VI's accession to the throne posed the radically different problem of how to justify the introduction of thoroughly

Plate 25.   Unknown artist, *Edward VI and the Pope*. Oil on panel (*c.* 1570). Portrait no. 4165, National Portrait Gallery, London.

protestant changes in theological doctrine and Church ritual during a royal minority. Unlike the commanding figure of Henry VIII, who so often dominated portraits as a divine right monarch wielding absolute power, Edward often shared his portraits with his father, his uncle, Protector Somerset, or some other authoritative figure like Hugh Latimer. Regardless of whether the boy-king exercised real power, the inclusion of powerful adults in his portraits served to validate his claim to govern, in at least an implied reponse to the widespread quotation of a verse from the Bible that had not been applied to England since the disastrous minorities of Henry VI and Edward V: 'Woe to you, O land, when your king is a child' (Eccles. 10:16). Basing Edward's official image on his father's portraits may have represented another response to this iconographical problem. When the king's painter, William Scrots, portrayed Edward, he modelled the figure and its powerful legs-astride posture on the well-known Holbein painting of Henry VIII at Whitehall.[9]

The image of Edward as a zealous ruler was identified with the Book, symbolic of the Bible that 'upheld' his ability to govern. An open Bible is accordingly positioned near the centre of *Edward VI and the Pope*, an anonymous courtly portrait that epitomizes the iconographical shift that followed Henry's death (plate 25). This allegorical portrayal of the Edwardian Reforma-

---

[9] Roy C. Strong, *Tudor and Jacobean Portraits* (2 vols., 1969), i, p. 93.

Plate 26. Hugh Latimer preaching before Edward VI, a woodcut in John Foxe, *Actes and Monumentes* (1563), p. 1353.

tion transposes to King Edward a variation of the royal stance on the title page of the Coverdale Bible (compare plate 23). Although Edward carries sceptre rather than sword, he is still flanked at his left-hand side by magistrates and clerics. The sacred book at the focus of his portrait is a commonplace pictorial figure for Edward as a zealous ruler. The scene depicts the transfer of power from the dying monarch to his zealously protestant son. At Edward's left stands Protector Somerset, who held power during the early years of the king's reign (January 1547–October 1549). Although Edward exercised no genuine authority during his brief reign as a minor, this painting idealizes the king as one who governed under the guidance of members of the privy council, who surround the table. The inset panel in the upper right-hand corner depicts an outburst of the kind of iconoclasm that accompanied the thorough programme of protestant reform implemented following Henry's death; an iconoclast is toppling a religious statue from the top of a column. The smouldering ruins contrast the destruction of idolatry with the reformist regime of Edward VI.[10]

[10] For further discussion of this portrait, see Roy C. Strong, 'Edward VI and the Pope: A Tudor Anti-Papal Allegory and Its Setting', *Journal of the Warburg and Courtauld Institutes*, 23 (1960): 311–13; and King, *Tudor Royal Iconography*, p. 163. Strong and King have assumed that this painting was composed *c.* 1547–49. On the basis of new evidence, Margaret Aston, in

A Bible similarly commands attention in the foreground of a woodcut in Foxe's 'Book of Martyrs', an image epitomizing an Elizabethan protestant view of preaching at the court of Edward VI. In this view, Hugh Latimer's popularity and influence was so great that it was necessary to set up a wooden pulpit in the privy gardens at Whitehall Palace to accommodate the overflow crowd that gathered to hear him preach (plate 26).[11] In what looks like a revision of the congregational scene at the bottom of the title page of the Great Bible, which includes women among the hearers of scriptural tests (plate 24), the central location of the solitary woman at the foot of Latimer's pulpit focuses attention on her as she reads from the Bible during the sermon. This scene incorporates an Erasmian-protestant appeal for the literacy of women as well as men so that all people may understand the scriptures for themselves. (The more conservative border of the Great Bible portrays ordinary people as *hearers* of scriptures that are read aloud by the cleric.) King Edward's sharing of a casement window with three adult men constitutes a symbolic dilution of his authority. The royal uncle, Protector Somerset, occupies the same position at the king's side that he has in the allegorical portrait of Edward VI toppling the pope (plate 25). Edward himself appears as a monarch receiving religious instruction under the guidance of his powerful regent and an influential cleric. The scene suggests that the boy's ability to govern is circumscribed by a pre-eminent lord and a prominent cleric.

Royal iconography filled the artistic vacuum left by outbursts of Edwardian iconoclasm, because images of the king and royal heraldry inherited the veneration that statues of the Virgin and Child, saints' images, and other cult objects had acquired by the late Middle Ages.[12] The woodcut allegory of Edward's reign that John Daye inserted into Foxe's 'Book of Martyrs' portrays this iconographical shift (plate 27). The top panel juxtaposes the pulling down of a statue from the wall of a church (plate 28) with the scene at the lower left in which adaptation of the Henrician device of the Sword and the Book provided a striking means of styling Edward as a Reformation king and of sanctioning his ability to embark on a programme of religious reform despite his status as a minor. Portrayal of sword-bearing Edward distributing the Bible to the prelates (plate 29) functioned as an implied image of dynastic continuity, because the evangelical stance of the young king alludes to the well-known image of his father in the Coverdale Bible (plate 23).

The King's Bed-post: Iconography and Reformation in a Tudor Group Portrait (Cambridge, 1993), indicates that the events took place *c.* 1547; that they were depicted retrospectively at the end of the first decade of the reign of Elizabeth I; and that the portrait represents Edward VI as a second Josiah, the iconoclastic monarch who inherited the throne of Judah as a boy. According to this redating, *Edward VI and the Pope* is roughly contemporary to the woodcuts in Foxe's 'Book of Martyrs' that are discussed in the following passage.

[11] John Foxe, *Actes and Monumentes* (1563), p. 1353. Although this woodcut first appears in the second part of *27 Sermons Preached by . . . Maister Hugh Latimer* (1562), Sig. D1, the publisher, John Day, incorporated it as an integral part of the 'Book of Martyrs'.

[12] John Phillips, *The Reformation of Images: Destruction of Art in England, 1535–1660* (Chicago, IL, 1973), p. 88.

The stark simplicity of the new protestant church service at the lower right portrays the Edwardian religious settlement, which reduced the sacraments from seven to the two associated with the communion table and baptismal font (plate 30). The new order denied sacramental status to confirmation, penance, ordination, marriage, and extreme unction. As it supplants the allegedly idolatrous images depicted above, the preaching of the gospel alludes to the woodcut of Latimer preaching before Edward VI (plate 26). The second congregational scene (plate 30) positions three Bible-reading women at the base of the pulpit. In an allusion to Josiah's cleansing of the Temple and, possibly, to Christ's expulsion of the money changers, captions at the top contrast 'The Temple well purged' with the packing away of Roman 'trinkets' (plate 28).

The fervour of the Edwardian attack against 'idolatry' extended to an attempt to eradicate the royalist cult of St George, when the boy king considered replacing the saint's image with scriptural symbols in the insignia of the Order of the Garter. Proposals that received his initial approval would have supplanted St George with protestant iconography symbolic of or drawn from the Bible. Although they never received final approval, draft revisions of the Garter statutes would have substituted for the patron saint a king holding the composite image of the Sword and the Book, the respective elements of which would have borne the label *Ivstitia* and *Verbum Dei*. This badge would have corresponded to title pages of the Coverdale Bible, where Henry VIII bears the sword of Justice as he disseminates the divine Word, and the Great Bible, with its ubiquitous portrayals of *Verbum Dei* (plates 23 and 24). An alternative proposal would have substituted for St George a horseman holding a sword in one hand and a shield in the other. The sword was to support a book inscribed *Verbum Dei*, and *Fides* was to be inscribed on the shield. Yet another proposed symbol was the Shield of Faith (*Scutum Fidei*) with a red cross on the other side; it would have combined a protestant image for justifying faith with the shield of St George. The usage of the sword and shield as symbols for Christian governance derives from the allegorical Armour of God in Eph. 6:10–17. Alterations in the hands of Edward VI and Sir William Cecil provide some indication of how seriously these proposals were considered.[13]

The revised statutes of the Order of the Garter that went into effect on 17 March 1553, shortly before Edward's death, deleted all references to St George and excluded essential heraldic elements that defined his cult. The crucial change was the deletion of the dragon as the embodiment of evil. The new Garter pendant was to bear instead a 'golden Image of an armed knight sytting on horseback with a drawne sworde in his right hande all compassed within the garter'. Although this knight differed in no material respect from the standard visualization of St George, the absence of the dragon-slaying incident eradicated all reference to the old saint's cult. The replacement of St George's spear with

[13] Edward M. Thompson, 'The Revision of the Statutes of the Order of the Garter by King Edward the Sixth', *Archaeologia*, second ser., 4 (1895): 179–80.

Plate 27.   The Reign of Edward VI, a woodcut in John Foxe, *Actes and Monumentes* (1570), p. 1483.

Within the image labels read:
Burning of images.
The ship of the Romish Church.
Shippe over your trinkets and be packing ye Papistes.
The Temple well purged.
The Papistes packyng away their paultrye.

Plate 28.   'The Temple Well Purged', a detail of plate 27.

Plate 29.   'King Edward delivering the Bible to Prelates', a detail of plate 27.

Plate 30. 'The Edwardian Worship Service', a detail of plate 27.

the drawn sword in the knight's right hand was a vestige of the purely evangelical iconography under consideration in the earlier draft proposals. Edward's death on 6 July 1553 prevented the full implementation of these revised statutes, which were abrogated by his elder sister and successor, Mary I, in the following September. The St George's Day celebration was thus one of the few forms of pre-Reformation pageantry to survive without modification into Elizabethan England.[14]

Queen Mary rejected protestant royalist iconography as part of her effort to further the Counter-Reformation in England. She tried to return to the state of Catholic orthodoxy that prevailed in the time of her mother, Catherine of Aragon. Because a government that banned the vernacular Bible could not praise the Tudor sovereigns as 'liberators' of the scriptures, a tableau of Henry

[14] BL, Royal MS. 18 A. I, fos. 9ᵛ, 10ᵛ–11; 18A. II, fos. 2ᵛ–3. On the refounding of the Order, see Roy C. Strong, *The Cult of Elizabeth: Elizabethan Portraiture and Pageantry* (1977), pp. 166, 182.

VIII and the Nine Worthies for the London entry of Mary I and Philip II (18 August 1554) had to be altered. Its designer, Richard Grafton, had evidently planned to praise Henry VIII as a monarch bearing *Verbum Dei*, the evangelical symbol familiar from the title page of the Great Bible (plate 24). Grafton had published that text in partnership with Edward Whitchurch, another well-known protestant partisan. But Grafton lost his position as royal printer soon after the death of Edward VI, because he had issued the proclamation of Lady Jane Grey as queen. Grafton's designation as a designer of pageantry in August 1554 suggests that the City of London authorities who were responsible for this royal entry harboured residual protestant sympathies. The implied protestant-ism of one of the elements of Grafton's design prompted the lord chancellor, Bishop Stephen Gardiner, to order the censorship of a decorated niche in a cross at the Conduit in Gracechurch Street:

This year the ix worthies, at graces church was paynted, and the king henry the eight emongst them w[i]th a bible in his hand, written uppon it Verbu[m] dei. but com-[m]andement was geven ym[m]ediatlye that [it] should be put out, and so it was, and a paier of gloves put in the place.

Because it violated 'the quenes catholicke proceedinges', Gardiner ordered the repainting of the familiar device, *Verbum Dei*, and had it covered over with the innocuous image of a pair of gloves.[15] The Marian regime thus redefined its iconographical legacy from Henry VIII and Edward VI (who was also present in that mural) in order to efface all reference to alterations in religion. The revised pageant provided a noncontroversial image of dynastic succession from Henry VIII to his Catholic daughter.

Of course, the queen had no intrinsic objection to portrayal of the Bible so long as it was subject to the traditional controls of the Church of Rome. This explains why Philip and Mary did not object to a different tableau that greeted them at St Paul's Cathedral. In a pageant where *Misericordia* and *Sapientia* paid homage to the royal couple, the arming of *Veritas* with *Verbum Dei* subord-inated the scriptures to Church tradition; Truth alone bore the Bible without any form of royal intercession. Actors representing the king and queen appeared at the centre of this tableau. They were honoured on one side by personifi-cations of '*Iusticia* with a swerd in her hande, and *Equitas* wyth a payre of ballaunce. And of theyr left side *Veritas* wyth a boke in her hande, whereon was written, *Verbum Dei*.' The personification of *Veritas* was related to Queen Mary's motto – *Veritas Temporis Filia* ('Truth is the Daughter of Time'), a phrase that crystallized her hostility to religious innovation.[16] Because of the

15 BL, Harleian MS. 419 [John Foxe Collections, vol. 4], fo. 131, mistakenly dated 1555. See also J. G. Nichols (ed.), *The Chronicle of Queen Jane, and of Two Years of Queen Mary, and Especially of the Rebellion of Sir Thomas Wyatt*, Camden Society, first ser., vol. 48 (1850), pp. 78–9; and Sydney Anglo, *Spectacle, Pageantry, and Early Tudor Policy* (Oxford, 1969), pp. 329–30, 350–4.
16 John Elder, *The Copie of a letter sent in to Scotlande, of the arrivall and landynge, and moste noble marryage of the moste Illustre Prynce Philippe, Prynce of Spaine, to the moste excellente Princes[s]*

notoriety of *Verbum Dei* as a symbol for the free circulation of the Bible under Henry VIII and Edward VI, it is possible that the tableau referred obliquely to the restoration of the Vulgate Bible as the only acceptable version of the scriptures in England; in that case, the scene would have represented an inversion of a well-known Reformation slogan.

Cardinal Reginald Pole reversed biblical iconography dear to protestant reformers when he reinterpreted the device of the Sword and the Book, applying it to Philip and Mary in his inaugural speech to parliament as papal legate on 27 November 1554. His return to England in itself epitomized the progress of the Counter-Reformation. Just as the exile of this descendant of royalty had demonstrated the existence of highly placed resistance to the Reformation, his return from Rome and assumption in 1556 of the office of archbishop of Canterbury typified England's renewed submission to the papacy and Mary's refusal to assume the title of Supreme Head of the Church. Applauding the separation of the ecclesiastical and temporal powers that Henry VIII had united in the person of the monarch, Pole distinguished between 'the Temporall swerde' of Philip and Mary and the power inherent in papal control of the holy scriptures and ecclesiastical tradition. He thus separated the compound symbol of the Sword and the Book into its constituent parts. Pole's imagery squared with the pageantry for the royal entry of Philip and Mary in that he identified ancient Church tradition with Truth, regardless of whether that virtue was considered an abstract personification, the queen or the pope. The cardinal's definition of ecclesiastical authority assumed that the pope was the rightful custodian of both the Bible and the keys of St Peter:

The other power is of ministracyon whyche is the power of the keies, and order in the Ecclesiastical state, which is by the authoritie of gods word and examples of the Apostles, and of all olde holy fathers from Christ hitherto attributed and geven to the Apostolike Sea of Rome, by speciall prerogative.[17]

A crucial element here is Pole's Catholic definition of the ministry. In place of the Henrician and Edwardian conception of a caesaropapal monarch who unites secular and ecclesiastical authority, Pole returned to the medieval separation of the two powers. He demoted monarchs because they altogether lacked spiritual authority and received divine sanction through the intercession of the pope and the clerical hierarchy. Unlike protestants, who brought the 'keys of the kingdom of heaven' in line with the royal supremacy (see plate 23, upper right inset), Pole restored the keys of St Peter as a symbol of the pope's exclusive power in spiritual affairs.[18]

Elizabeth I's accession at the death of her sister, Mary I, in 1558 was accompanied by a return to the iconography of the Sword and the Book. Images

Marye Queen of England (1555), C3ᵛ–4, transcribed by Nichols (ed.), *Chronicle of Queen Jane*, pp. 136–66. See also Anglo, *Spectacle*, pp. 329, 337–8.
[17] Elder, *Copie of a letter sent in to Scotlande*, Sig. D7v–E1.   [18] *Ibid.*

of Elizabeth that display that composite symbol are relatively rare because the sword tends to disappear or undergo subordination in portrayals of the queen as the protestant heroine and saviour of England who reads or carries a Bible or evangelical book. The prototype of this reconfiguration was to be found in Elizabeth's histrionic gesture of kissing and embracing an English Bible, or '*Verbum veritatis*, the woorde of trueth', when she entered London prior to her coronation. This spectacular gesture constituted a public announcement of England's return to protestant ecclesiastical practices. She restored the Bible to the place it had enjoyed as a means of spiritual instruction and as a device symbolic of royal authority under her late father and brother.

The queen's active participation in a tableau set up for this entry at Cheapside was intended to break down any division between the real world and symbolic ideals. She had already identified herself as Truth by remarking upon the portrayal of Time at an earlier pageant: 'Tyme hath brought me hether [sic].' By kissing and embracing the scriptures – a response that was actually written into the scripted account that appeared in print only ten days after the event – Elizabeth also played the role of Faith, whose conventional attribute is an open Bible (see plate 31, upper right). The queen thus provided a living enactment of the eulogistic iconography incorporated into so many woodcuts of her reign: 'But she as soone as she had received the booke, kyssed it, and with both her handes held up the same, and so laid it upon her brest, with great thankes to the citie therefore.' The queens's enthusiastic response to an appeal lodged by the 'Interpreter' of this pageant – 'We trust O worthy quene, thou wilt this truth embrace' – revealed her as the restorer of 'true' religion through the unification of temporal authority with knowledge of the divine Word.[19]

The pageant series was staged according to custom by the City of London and its guilds. Richard Grafton's inclusion among the four devisers is noteworthy, because less than five years earlier he had designed the censored tableau that was to have shown Henry VIII displaying the Bible during the London entry of Philip and Mary. The presentation of Elizabeth I as Truth may have referred obliquely to the Marian pageant, but the allusion that most observers would have recognized is to the woodcut showing Henry VIII transmitting *Verbum Dei* on the title page of the 1539 Great Bible (plate 24); Grafton had published the work in collaboration with Edward Whitchurch. At the Cheapside tableau, Elizabeth may have embraced an edition of that text, which would soon be reauthorized for use in England. In effect, Truth returned to her alter ego, the queen – and to the English people – the translation of the scriptures once authorized by her father and containing his powerful image.

The explication of the pageant series provided by Grafton and Richard Mulcaster show that these protestant ideologues conceived of the spectacles as allegorical scenes conveying a fully developed political programme. Grafton

---

[19] Richard Mulcaster, *Quenes Majesties Passage*, ed. James M. Osborne (facsimile reprint, New Haven, CT, 1960), Sig. C2v, C4^{r-v} (pp. 44, 47–8). See also Anglo, *Spectacle*, p. 355.

and Mulcaster incorporated overtly reformist sentiment into most of the tableaux. For example, Grafton praises 'the conjunction and coupling together' of Elizabeth 'with the Gospell and veritie of Goddes holy woord, for the peaceable government of all her good subjectes'.[20] Grafton's protestant zeal was well known, as was that of Mulcaster, the composer of verses for the 1559 entry and compiler of the published account in *The Quenes Majesties Passage*, which appeared within two weeks of the event. Mulcaster had studied with Nicholas Udall, who collaborated with John Leland on the 1533 entry for Anne Boleyn. As a London schoolmaster, Mulcaster belonged to the traditional profession of pageant devisers. The handiwork of Grafton and Mulcaster is a prominent example of a Reformation adaptation of a traditional form, because it assimilated protestant ideology and iconography into a medieval dramatic mode instead of looking to the classical models that Leland and Udall had infused into Queen Anne's pageantry. The stridency of this pageantry represents a throwback to the kind of propaganda nurtured by Thomas Cromwell and Protector Somerset.[21]

Queen Elizabeth's pre-coronation pageantry established a precedent for renewed imitation of her father's use of the English Bible as a symbol for governance by a 'godly' monarch. When the Bishops' Bible succeeded the Great Bible as the official Elizabethan translation (1568), its allegorical title pages looked back to the Henrician Bibles by using the sovereign as a nexus for symbols of authorship, authority, and authorization. Visible at the front of Bibles available by law in every parish church, the entire series of monarchal figures must have been thoroughly familiar to the English population as images of royal permission and control.

By positioning Elizabeth I between flanking female personification of Faith and Charity, the title-page border of the first edition of the Bishops' Bible makes it clear that the queen completes St Paul's triad of theological virtues (1 Cor. 13:13) by personifying the Hope brought by gospel faith (plate 31). Although the image of Charity suckling her two babies is conventional in late medieval art, the portrayal of Faith holding a Bible and a cross represents a variation of her traditional presentation with a cross and a chalice; that she bears an open copy of the scriptures constitutes an endorsement of the protestant insistence on the free circulation of the vernacular Bible. (The cross rests upon an open Bible in Counter-Reformation representation of Faith.) The epigraph offers the Latin text of Rom. 1:16 as a gloss: 'Non me pudet Evangelii Christi. Virtus enim Dei

---

[20] Richard Grafton, *Abridgement of the Chronicles of Englande* (revised edn, 1570), Sig. Z2ᵛ–3. See Anglo, *Spectacle*, p. 350–1, 354.
[21] For further discussion of the 1559 London entry, see David Bergeron, *English Civic Pageantry: 1558–1642* (Columbia, SC, 1971), pp. 11–22; David Norbrook, 'Panegyric of the Monarch and Its Social Context under Elizabeth I and James I' (unpublished D.Phil. dissertation, Oxford University, 1978), pp. 21–5; Roy C. Strong, 'Elizabethan Pageantry as Propaganda' (unpublished Ph.D. dissertation, University of London, 1962), p. 38; and his *Art and Power: Renaissance Festivals, 1450–1650* (Woodbridge, Suffolk, 1984), p. 11.

Plate 31. Elizabeth I as Hope (engraving), part of the border of the title-page of the Bishops' Bible (1568).

est ad salutem Omni credenti' ('I am not ashamed of the Gospel of Christe, because it is the power of God unto salvation to all that beleve'). This verse supplies a textual link to the Coverdale Bible border, where it appears in the banderole at the left of Henry VIII (plate 23). Depiction of the queen as England's only 'Hope' for resolution of religious discord clearly praises her as the embodiment of peaceful and godly government; the scene surely refers to the Elizabethan religious settlement of 1559.[22]

A handsomely bound folio volume of the 1568 Bishops' Bible that presumably occupied a prominent place in Queen Elizabeth's library[23] could have provided a 'prop' for the queen's private 'dramatization' of her public role as an evangelical monarch, one who had physically embraced the Bible as a devotional example to her subjects during her pre-coronation entry into London. Should she have opened the volume to read its contents for herself, the title page would have taken on special meaning. The queen would have seen her own portrait, reflected as it were in a mirror image. To Elizabeth alone, the title page would portray the queen, not in her public capacity as a permitter and advocate of the free circulation of the divine Word, but as a private individual who takes it upon herself to read and understand the scriptures. Only in this private royal copy of the Bishops' Bible could the queen's portrait have functioned as an image of personal religious conviction and piety.

An allegorical title page introduced in the 1569 quarto edition of the Bishops' Bible (plate 32) transposes the royalist iconography of the Sword and the Book into yet another allegory that praises Elizabeth as a faithful queen who wields royal authority over Church and state. Adopting the conventional monarchal pose established in the Coverdale Bible (plate 23), Elizabeth in her royal magnificence appears as the summation of the virtues personified in the corners of the woodcut: Justice, Mercy, Prudence, and Fortitude. With the transposition of Temperance into Mercy, this modification of the four cardinal virtues of the classical world is particularly appropriate to Elizabeth I because it associates the imperial virtues of Justice and Mercy, portrayed in the act of crowning the queen, with symbols of divine revelation. Thus Justice, at the queen's right side, carries the sword linked by the reformers to the Holy Spirit. Explained by Edmund Spenser as the 'sacred pledge of peace and clemencie',[24] the sceptre carried by Elizabeth appears to weight the Tableau in the favour of Mercy, who is identified by the Bible in her hand as the pre-eminent virtue. Fortitude, at the lower left, carries a broken pillar, possibly alluding to Samson's destruction of the Philistine Temple (Judg. 16:29–30); whether broken or whole, the pillar is the traditional image of fortitude. If the bough behind Prudence bears laurel leaves, it may call attention to the synthesis of pagan and divine inspiration. A disparity therefore existed between the queen's public image, as it was fashioned by protestant apologists for propagandistic purposes, and claims that Elizabeth made on her own behalf: in one speech she laid claim to the virtues of justice and

[22] On a precursor of this allegory, see Jan van Dorsten, 'Steven van Herwyck's Elizabeth (1565) – A Franco-Flemish Political Medal', *Burlington Magazine*, 111 (1969): 143–7.

[23] This is the copy in the Folger Shakespeare Library (STC 2099, copy 3); see King, *Tudor Royal Iconography*, p. 107.

[24] *The Faerie Queene*, 5.9.30. The *Sieve Portrait* (c. 1580) attributed to Cornelius Ketel also employs Temperance as a symbol for Elizabethan majesty.

Plate 32. Elizabeth I and the Four Virtues (woodcut), part of the border of
the title-page of the Bishops' Bible (1569).

temperance, while acknowledging that the remaining regal virtues – prudence
and magnanimity – were appropriate only to men.[25]

The details of the Bishops' Bible title page coalesce to identify the queen with
divine Truth, by analogy to the Four Daughters of God derived from Psalm

25 David Norbrook, *Poetry and Politics in the English Renaissance* (1984), p. 114.

Plate 33.   Attributed to Lucas de Heere, *Allegory of the Tudor Succession*, oil on panel (*c.* 1570). Collection of Lady Ashcombe, Sudeley Castle, Winchcombe, Gloucestershire.

85:8–13: Truth, Mercy, Righteousness (or Justice), and Peace. The interpretation of that Psalm as 'a figure of Christs kingdome, under the which shulde be perfite felicitie', according to the headnote in the Geneva Bible, easily permitted English protestants to apply the text to the new Israel of Elizabethan England. It should be noted, however, that such imagery was traditional and well known. The strong association between spiritual truth and Christian queenship extends into the inset beneath the cartouche containing the title 'The holi bible'. The divine revelation claimed for the English church service 'descends' on an axis from heaven above through the queen to the people below. The title page personifies the queen's endorsement of the free reading and preaching of the vernacular Bible as portrayed in the inset. The inset's conventional congregational scene is a variation of the vignettes that are set into the base of the Great Bible title page and the portrayal of the Edwardian worship service in Foxe's 'Book of Martyrs' (plates 24, 26, and 30); the major difference is the replacement of Henrician apparel with Elizabethan garb.

   The deliberate undoing of Marian iconography may be noted in the *Allegory of the Tudor Protestant Succession*, a painting (oil on panel) of *c.* 1570 that Elizabeth presumably commissioned as a gift to Sir Francis Walsingham (plate 33). The oversize figure of the queen stands at the viewer's right in a direct line of succession passing from Henry VIII, who sits enthroned at the centre as he hands the sword of justice to the kneeling figure of Edward VI. While the presentation of Elizabeth, her father, and her brother offers a conventional image of the protestant succession (compare plate 25), the allegorical focus of the tableau is the stark contrast between the antithetical Tudor queens. The isolation of Philip and Mary at the viewer's left suggests that Mary's reign represented a deviation from the course of Tudor religious and dynastic history; their companion, warlike Mars, defines the Marian Counter-Reformation as a divisive time of bloodshed and rancour. Elizabeth's reign is envisioned as a time of domestic tranquillity, on the other hand, as Peace, who tramples upon weaponry symbolic of discord that includes the sword, spear, and shield of Mars, is led by the queen. The cornucopia held by Plenty, who attends Peace, lodges a claim that the reign of Queen Elizabeth has brought an end to a period of privation. Verses inscribed on the picture frame this dynastic allegory:

> A Face of muche nobillitye loe in a little roome,
> Fowr states with theyr conditions heare shadowed in a showe,
> A father more than valyant, a rare and vertuous soon [i.e., son],
> A zeal[o]us daughter in her kynd what els the world doth knowe,
> At last of all a vyrgin queen to Englands joy we see,
> Successyvely to hold the right, and vertues of the three.

Elizabeth is seen to inherit the respective virtues of her predecessors, including her father's valour, her brother's virtue, and even her sister's zeal.

If, indeed, Elizabeth commissioned this allegory, she involved herself in the fashioning of her own image as a peaceful protestant ruler. The painting was made about the time that Pius V's bull of 1570, *Regnans in Excelsis*, raised the spectre of Catholic peril by excommunicating the queen and urging her overthrow. The Northern Rebellion of the previous year had demonstrated the strength of sentiment to return to her late sister's Counter-Reformation settlement in religion. The inscription at the base, 'The Quene to Walsingham this Tablet sente / Marke of her peoples and her owne contente', suggests that the portrait may have functioned as an admonition to those like Walsingham who advocated militant English support for the Huguenots and the protestant cause in the Low Countries. It may embody the queen's assurance to a staunch reformer and one-time Marian exile that her cautious brand of protestantism was better served by a policy of peace than one of military intervention.[26] This painting may therefore represent a response to the 'unofficial' cult of protestant queenship that was already 'being built up without the approval of the goddess herself. Indeed, the role of Protestant champion which it assigned to her was one deeply repugnant to the secular-minded Queen.[27]

---

[26] Roy C. Strong connects this portrait to Walsingham's instrumental role in 'the signing of the Treaty of Blois on 21 April 1572'; *Gloriana: The Portraits of Queen Elizabeth I* (1987), p. 74.

[27] Wallace MacCaffrey, *Queen Elizabeth and the Making of Policy, 1572–1588* (Princeton, NJ, 1981), pp. 265–6.

Plate 34. Elizabeth Regina, a woodcut (frontispiece) in Richard Day, *A Booke of Christian Prayers* (1578).

The queen's name is associated with two collections of prayers attributed to Richard Day and printed by his father, the eminent publisher John Day (or Daye). Also known as 'Queen Elizabeth's Prayer Book', *Christian Prayers and Meditations* (1569) contains a frontispiece portrait of 'Elizabeth Regina' kneeling devoutly in prayer. Nearly a decade later, the Days transferred the title page, frontispiece, and woodcut borders to *A Booke of Christian Prayers* (1578: plate 34). Elizabethan heraldic devices figure prominently in both of these collections. Richard and John Day collaborated in the production of what are, in effect, protestant books of hours that pay tribute throughout to Elizabeth as a Reformation queen. In an outstanding example of literary 'iconoclasm', Elizabeth receives the place of honour in collections of prayers comparable to the *Horae* in which the Blessed Virgin Mary once reigned supreme as Mother of God and Queen of Heaven.

The modification of the royalist device of the Sword and the Book in the frontispiece (plate 34) provides a superb compliment to the queen.[28] The epigraph offers the Vulgate text of 2 Chr. 6:14 as a caption for this woodcut image of the queen: 'O Lord, God of Israel, there is no God like thee, in heaven or on earth, keeping covenant and showing steadfast love to thy servants who walk before thee with all their heart.' Solomon uttered this prayer after his completion of the Temple, when he knelt as a pious king before the congregation of Israel to dedicate the structure. This epigraph suggests that Elizabeth, like Solomon, is an ideally religious ruler. The great Hebrew king prefigures Christ in the Tree of Jesse depicted in the title-page border of both texts,[29] and he offers a biblical model for the queen's capacity as a wise governor who has reestablished the Lord's Temple by imposing a protestant settlement of religion and bringing peace to England. A prayer in *Christian Prayers and Meditations* (sig. P2v–3) that is tailor-made for Elizabeth puts into the queen's mouth words that relate directly to her frontispiece image:

whereas the wisest king Salomon plainly confesseth him self unable to governe his kingdome without thy helpe and assistance: how much lesse shall I thy handmaide, being by kynde a weake woman, have sufficient abilitie to rule these thy kingdomes of England and Ireland.

The subtle variation of the motif of the Sword and the Book in the woodcut of 'Elizabeth Regina' (plate 34) transforms Holbein's definitive image of monarchal power in the Coverdale Bible (plate 23) into a portrayal of the queen as a Christ-like Prince of Peace. In contrast to the prayer book that is displayed clearly on the prie-dieu, the sword in front of the cushion upon which the queen kneels is cut short by the lower edge of the picture. A book of divine invocation receives priority over a weapon symbolic of Elizabeth's punitive capacity as an instrument of retributive justice. The truncation of the sword may be intended to suggest an optimistic belief that her protestant settlement of religion has brought an end to the discord that wracked the reigns of her father and siblings. The cutting off of the sword beneath the kneeling queen suggests that she may be more devoted to the arts of peace associated with the prayer book in front of her than the punitive capacity of royal justice. This weapon is analogous to the unused and rusted sword that Elizabeth was known to have kept in her private

[28] See Samuel C. Chew, 'The Iconography of *A Book of Christen Prayers* (1578) Illustrated', *Huntington Library Quarterly*, 8 (1945): 293–305. He notes that the use of the first person in the prayers in foreign languages indicated that *Christian Prayers and Meditations* (1569) was expressly designed for the queen (p. 293). The Elizabethan connection is personal and explicit in a copy of *Christian Prayers and Meditations* that was tailor-made for the queen's own use. See S. W. Kershaw, *Art Treasures of the Lambeth Library* (1873), pp. 87–9; and King, *Tudor Royal Iconography*, pp. 112–14.

[29] See the illustration in King, *Tudor Royal Iconography*, pp. 113.

apartments as a reminder that her desire for peace was ever tempered by the corrective power that she kept in reserve. The subordination of the sword recurs in other portraits of the queen (see plate 33, lower right).[30] Unlike her father Henry VIII, who rarely hesitated before applying harsh measures, Elizabeth styled herself as a Solomonic ruler who was slow to anger, but always capable of stern action. This woodcut accords with the image of a cautious queen who in her own life adopted the pose of a ruler who prefers reading the book symbolic of divine wisdom and mercy to wielding the sword of military and judicial power.

A memorial portrait of Queen Elizabeth by Crispin van de Passe the Elder (plate 35) incorporates a final revision of the Sword and the Book as a Tudor royalist device. The coat of arms and the complete regalia of the gem-encrusted queen – crown, orb, and sceptre – refer to her secular authority and might, just as the motto 'Posui Deum Adiutorem Meum' ('I have made God my help') alludes to her role as a divine instrument. Her alignment with the 'imperial' virtues of Justice and Peace mirrors the biblical iconography of the Sword and the Book at her left, which are respectively termed 'IUSTITIA' and 'VERBUM DEI'. Although the conjunction of these symbols suggests the equivalence of Justice and Mercy, the reference to 'Misericordia' in the inscription at the queen's right implies that the latter is the pre-eminent royal virtue. The capital letters in this phrase, 'Mortua anno MIserICorDIae' ('Died in the year of Mercy'), contain an anagram for the year of Elizabeth's death: MDCIII, or 1603. The balanced reference to the date of her birth at Greenwich ('6 Id. Sept.' [*sic*], i.e. 7 September 1533) to the left completes a portrait symbolizing the entirety of her life, from birth to death, and a reign that might be conceived of as the worldly embodiment of the millennial virtues of Justice, Mercy, Truth, and Peace. That the queen was born on the eve of the Nativity of the Blessed Virgin and then died on 24 March, the eve of Mary's Assumption into heaven, was to reformers an incontrovertible mark of providential intervention.[31]

This retrospective image of the queen whose death marked the demise of the Tudor dynasty fittingly recalls iconographical themes that can be traced back to the presentation of Henry VIII in the title page of the Coverdale Bible. However, the displacement of the composite symbol of the Sword and the Book to the margin of the portrait corresponds to the modulation of the strident polemicism that this figure had once implied in representations of her father's subordination of the Church to state authority and of the heyday of iconoclasm under her

---

[30] William Nelson cites a recurrence of this motif in *The Faerie Queene*, 5.9.30, in 'Queen Elizabeth, Spenser's Mercilla, and a Rusty Sword', *Renaissance News*, 18 (1965): 113–17. See also the painting (*c.* 1585) attributed to Marcus Gheeraerts the Elder of the queen standing above a sword and holding the olive branch of peace; cited in Frances Yates, *Astraea: The Imperial Theme in the Sixteenth Century* (1975), pp. 71–2; and Roy C. Strong, *Portraits of Queen Elizabeth I* (Oxford, 1963), paintings, no. 85.

[31] See Yates, *Astraea*, pp. 78–9; Strong, *Cult*, p. 125.

Plate 35. Crispin van de Passe I, after Isaac Oliver, *Elizabeth I Memorial Portrait*, engraving (*c.* 1603–4). Henry E. Huntington Library, San Marino, California.

brother, Edward VI.[32] From the time that a youthful Elizabeth embraced the Bible during her pre-coronation pageantry – an uncommonly controversial gesture for this politique queen – the book symbolic of Mercy and evangelical Faith tended to supplant the sword of Justice in her increasingly complicated portrayals. This iconographical shift appears to have resulted from a deliberate strategy of styling Elizabeth as a Christ-like Prince of Peace, in contrast to the sister whose persecutions of protestants have earned her the harshest epithet of any British monarch: Bloody Mary.[33] One must recognize that the modification of the Sword and the Book represented only one vein of an iconographical network that became increasingly complex as the queen aged. The abstruse virginity symbolism of her late portrayals as a new Diana or Venus-Virgo, for example, had little if anything to do with biblical imagery. Despite its increasingly classical manner and esoteric symbolism, however, Elizabethan iconography never lost its connection to partisan themes and devices that flourished during the early phase of the English Reformation.

[32] The Sword and the Book are similarly crowded into the background in Simon van de Passe's frontispiece portrait of James I in the 1619 edition of James's *Workes*. See Arthur M. Hind, *Engraving in England in the Sixteenth and Seventeenth Centuries* (3 vols., Cambridge, 1953–64), ii, plate 154.

[33] Although the *Oxford English Dictionary* ('Bloody', adj. 6) cites Charles Dickens' *Child's History of England* (1853) as the first example of this usage, vilification of Mary I originated during her own age.

5 Political culture and the built environment of the English country town, c. 1540–1620

ROBERT TITTLER

If the concept of political culture has to do with the goals, strategies, and behavioural conventions of political groups, then English towns in the decades following the Reformation of the 1530s provide a fruitful opportunity to observe its operation. It has become apparent that the political culture of many such communities, along with their defining political structure, underwent a substantial transformation during the course of the sixteenth century. Though most medieval towns were hierarchical in their social and political structure, and therefore oligarchic in one sense of the word, a great many also remained relatively open, widely participatory and politically accessible. Their political cultures recognized and honoured the integrity of the whole community and worked to encourage the harmonious interaction of its parts.[1]

During the sixteenth century however, urban governing structures moved in greater numbers and more steadily towards the truly oligarchic as well as the structurally hierarchical. They lost many of their traditional harmony-inducing devices and became more narrowly focused on the powers and interests of the dominant few. Though the significant changes were often more matters of degree than of actual innovation, the resulting transition had numerous dimensions and derived from elements of economic, social, and political change in the nation as a whole.

This broad and sweeping shift has been observed from a variety of perspectives. Some have seen it in the emergence of a more rigidly hierarchical structure in many towns at this time. This view reminds us that, though oligarchy was by no means new as a form of urban government, it now became more common.

The author would like to thank the Social Sciences and Humanities Research Council of Canada for funding which facilitated research for this chapter.

[1] This is not, of course, to deny the existence of oligarchic rule in many medieval towns. See, for example, Susan Reynolds, *An Introduction to the History of English Medieval Towns* (Oxford, 1977), pp. 171–7; Stephen Rigby, 'Urban Oligarchy in Late Medieval England', in J. A. F. Thompson (ed.), *Towns and Townspeople in the Fifteenth Century* (Gloucester, 1988), pp. 62–86; Jennifer I. Kermode, 'Obvious Observations on the Formation of Oligarchies in Late Medieval English Towns', in Thompson, *Towns and Townspeople*, pp. 87–106 and, illustrating the economic and social aspects of urban oligarchy, Maryanne Kowaleski, 'Commercial Dominance of a Medieval Political Oligarchy: Exeter in the Late Fourteenth Century', *Medieval Studies*, 46 (1984): 355–84.

For this there were several reasons. The growing financial burdens of office proved increasingly prohibitive to all but the wealthiest few. The intensifying social and economic pressures of the period created greater demands for stronger local government. The proliferation of charters of incorporation from *c.* 1540 facilitated the hegemony of those who had come to the fore. In consequence, senior officers, drawn from the wealthiest citizens, gained greater authority, election gave way to co-option, and a growing chasm developed between the ruling élite on the one hand and the freemanry on the other.[2]

Others have adopted a more anthropological approach to the same phenomenon. They have shown how, e.g. the Reformation brought to an end the heavily liturgical ceremonial which had so effectively bolstered civic morality and sustained harmonious interaction amongst townsmen of diverse status groups. The work of Charles Phythian-Adams and Mervyn James has shown how those ends had been encouraged by the Corpus Christi celebrations, while that of Susan Brigden has made similar observations regarding links between traditional religion and the ethos of social obligation in pre-Reformation London.[3] Though such observances by no means disappeared all at once, they either faded into disuse before the wave of reformed religion and the burden of excessive costs or they changed their character to embrace a more secular format. Finally, historians of the English drama have shown how the shared appreciation of traditional performance, held in public street and marketplace and often expressing anti-authoritarian views in a ritualized and constructive manner, gave way at the same time. In its place, on the one hand, there emerged elements of what we might call a 'high civic culture' (taking the term to denote forms of artistic and creative expression, often with political overtones). This included both an officially sanctioned theatrical tradition, removed from the open air to the controlled space of specific buildings and licensed by civil authorities, and the perpetuation of a more secular and narrowly shared civic ceremonial, devoted less to expressing a popular voice than to displaying the power of civic authority. While on the other hand, a *popular* culture continued to flourish, it did so as an often illicit, unsanctioned, and sometimes subversive activity pursued by the 'common sort'.[4]

---

[2] For this and the following paragraph, see, e.g., Peter Clark and Paul Slack, *English Towns in Transition, 1500–1700* (1976), pp. 129–33; Clark and Slack (eds.), *Crisis and Order in English Towns* (1972), pp. 21–5, 127–34; W. G. Hoskins, *The Age of Plunder* (1976), pp. 100–4; A. D. Dyer, *The City of Worcester in the Sixteenth Century* (Leicester, 1973), pp. 224–6; Charles Phythian-Adams, *Desolation of a City, Coventry and the Urban Crisis of the Late Middle Ages* (Cambridge, 1979), pp. 271–2; R. Tittler, 'The Incorporation of Boroughs, 1540–1558', *History*, 62 (Feb. 1977): 24–42.

[3] Phythian-Adams, 'Ceremony and the Citizen, the Communal Year at Coventry, 1450–1550', in Clark and Slack (eds.), *Crisis and Order*, pp. 57–85; Mervyn James, 'Ritual, Drama and Social Body in the Late Medieval English Town', *Past and Present*, 98 (February 1983): 3–29; Susan Brigden, 'Religion and Social Obligation in Early Seventeenth Century London', *Past and Present*, 103 (May 1984): 67–112, and, more generally, Susan Brigden, *London and the Reformation* (Oxford, 1989).

[4] E.g. Virginia Gildersleeve, *Government Regulation of English Drama* (New York, 1908, reprinted, 1961 and 1975), especially Book IV, pp. 259–345; M. C. Bradbrook, *The Rise of the Common Player* (1962), ch. 3; Jonah Barish, *The Anti-Theatrical Prejudice* (Berkeley, CA, 1981), ch. IV; Mikhail Bakhtin, *Rabelais and His World*, trans. Helene Iswolsky, (Cambridge, MA, 1968); Jean-Christophe

The reasons for this multi-faceted shift of emphasis in the political culture of English towns in the sixteenth century are numerous and largely familiar, and they need only be summarized briefly. Most emanate directly from the changing social and economic circumstances of the time: an increased national population amplified in urban society by large-scale net migration from countryside to town; rising consumer prices; probable declines in the urban housing supply; sharp (and sharply felt) increases in rootlessness, poverty, and crime.[5] Such developments vastly increased the burdens of government as well as the expectations placed upon the governors, both by fellow townsmen, on the one hand, and the Crown, on the other. Tolerance for a more authoritative approach grew steadily.[6] Seen in this light, we must not impose the pejorative connotations that oligarchy holds for us today, but instead ought to evaluate its emergence and operation in its proper historical context. As it persisted in the towns of Elizabethan and Jacobean England, fully formed oligarchy was often both appropriate and inevitable. It held its own promise and bore its own problems. It played a dominant role in defining the political culture characteristic of towns at this time.

One of the chief problems facing the governing élite in most towns of this era was the need to create deference and respect for its members and for the offices which they held. Like the 'new men' who rose to prominence at the Tudor court, very few of these newly emergent urban leaders held any of the claims to deference or obedience which commanded popular loyalties elsewhere in the realm. For the most part merchants and master craftsmen, few of them enjoyed any titles, hereditary status, regional bases of support, statutory rights to social or legal distinctions, ties at court or to the regional power bases of the countryside, or palaces or manor halls in which to preside. In addition, as has been noted, the liturgically based ceremonial which had formerly served to identify their role had substantially waned within a few decades of the Henrician Reformation. Finally (and save for recorders and some town clerks) the senior officials amongst them (the mayors especially) conventionally held office for but one year at a time with almost no chance (or, one imagines, inclination) for immediate re-election.

Under these circumstances, it should come as no surprise that these urban leaders, whether in the simple market town or the great provincial centre, placed

Agnew, *Worlds Apart, The Market and the Theatre in Anglo-American Thought, 1550–1750* (Cambridge, 1986) and Michael Bristol, *Carnival and Theatre. Plebeian Culture and the Structure of Authority in Renaissance England,* (New York and London, 1985).

[5] Excellent summaries are provided by W. G. Hoskins, *The Age of Plunder* (1976) and D. M. Palliser, *The Age of Elizabeth, England under the Later Tudors, 1547–1603* (1983). For specific issues, see E. A. Wrigley and R. S. Schofield, *The Population History of England, 1541–1871* (1981); A. L. Beier, *Masterless Men, the Vagrancy Problem in England, 1560–1640* (1985); Paul Slack, *Poverty and Policy in Tudor and Stuart England* (New York and London, 1988); J. A. Sharpe, *Crime in Early Modern England, 1550–1750* (1984).

[6] Clark and Slack (eds.), *Crisis and Order*, pp. 20–2; J. M. Martin, 'A Warwickshire Town in Adversity: Stratford-upon-Avon in the Sixteenth and Seventeenth Centuries', *Midland History*, 7 (1982): 26–42.

a great deal of emphasis on display and appearance: on those activities, material objects and, indeed, aspects of the physical environment which could identify their standing and advertise their authority to their fellows. These elements created the all-important illusion that the power of these leaders rested in something more than the temporary contrivance of circumstances. Many of the devices conventionally employed toward these ends are familiar, some are less so. Few were new in kind, but many received a greater emphasis than ever before, as befit the conditions of the time.

Civic processions and feasts were still often held on days with liturgical significance, but many now emphasized themes which were predominantly civic. These included, *inter alia*, the beating of the bounds,[7] the annual lawday,[8] the mayoral election or oath-taking,[9] the midsummer watch or fair,[10] the mayor's breakfast or dinner,[11] the reading of the charter,[12] the 'day of the reconciliation',[13] and the 'parade of civic formalities'.[14] Mayors wore their gowns as much as ever, though not always on the same occasions as before, while the ceremonial attire of other officials, even down to livery for waits, paviours, and plumbers, remained unchanged or even became more elaborate.[15] Similarly, the use of civic regalia – coats of arms, maces and swords of office, hats of maintenance, and the like – may also have grown more common and more elaborate.[16] Some such regalia changed from the time of the Henrician

[7] E.g. in Norwich, David Galloway (ed.), *REED, Norwich, 1540–1642* (Toronto, Buffalo, NY, London, 1984), p. 101. For civic festivities observed on a national basis, see David Cressy, *Bonfires and Bells. National Memory and the Protestant Calendar in Elizabethan and Stuart England* (Berkeley and Los Angeles, CA, 1989).

[8] E.g. at Guildford, Enid M. Dance (ed.), *Guildford Borough Records, 1514–1546* (Surrey Record Soc., vol. 24, 1958), p. 131.

[9] E.g. in Oxford, H. E. Salter (ed.), *Oxford Council Acts, 1583–1626* (Oxford Hist. Soc., 1928), p. 81; Norwich: Galloway (ed.), *REED, Norwich*, pp. 53–4; Coventry: R. W. Ingram (ed.), *REED, Coventry* (Toronto, Buffalo, NY, London, 1981), p. 149.

[10] E.g., Coventry: Ingram (ed.), *REED, Coventry*, pp. 149 and 181; Chester: L. M. Clopper (ed.), *REED, Chester*, (Toronto and Buffalo, NY, 1979), p. lii; Much Wenlock: Much Wenlock Borough Minute Book, Corn Exchange, Much Wenlock, MS. no. B3/1/1, p. 432. I am indebted to Mr Vincent Deacon for allowing me access to this source at Much Wenlock.

[11] E.g. Coventry: Ingram (ed.), *REED, Coventry*, p. 567; Chester: Clopper (ed.), *REED, Chester*, p. 56; Cambridge: J. W. Cooper (ed.), *Annals of Cambridge* (5 vols., Cambridge, 1842–1908), ii, pp. 91–2 and 279.

[12] E.g. Boston: John F. Bailey (ed.), *Transcriptions of the Minutes of the Borough of Boston* (3 vols., 1980–83), i, p. 25.

[13] E.g. King's Lynn: S. Battley, 'Elite and Community in Sixteenth Century King's Lynn' (unpublished Ph.D. dissertation, State University of New York at Stony Brook, 1981), p. 245.

[14] E.g. Winchester: Adrienne Rosen, 'Economic and Social Aspects of the History of Winchester, 1520–1670', (unpublished D.Phil. dissertation, Oxford University, 1975), p. 229.

[15] J. J. Anderson (ed.), *REED, Newcastle upon Tyne* (Toronto and Manchester, 1982), pp. 68–138; Ingram, *REED, Coventry*, p. 201; Bailey, *Minutes of Boston*, pp. 2, 188; W. Devon Record Office, MS. Worth 131 (Plymouth Borough Accounts), fo. 5r and MS. Worth 132, fo. 165r; Devon RO, MS. 1579 a/7/3 (Totnes Accounts for 1554); Humberside RO, Borough of Beverley, 'Small Order Book, 1575–83', MS. DDHE/26, fo. 131v; M. Stanford (ed.), *The Ordinances of Bristol, 1506–1598* (Bristol Record Society, vol. 41, 1990), pp. 27, 32–3, 44, 97 and 105–6.

[16] Llewellyn Jewitt and W. H. St John Hope, *The Corporate Plate and Insignia of the Cities and Towns of England and Wales* (2 vols., 1895). Specific examples include: Carmarthen: PRO, STAC 8/Bundle 20/14; Winchester: Rosen, 'Economic and Social Aspects', p. 229; Alexandra Johnston and Margaret Rogerson (eds.), *REED, York* (2 vols., Toronto, Buffalo, NY, London, 1979), i, pp. 194–5; H. Lloyd

Reformation to emphasize augmented civic authority, as with the seal of the City of Norwich on which the device of the City's arms replaced the image of the Trinity.[17]

In addition, and less familiarly, it became much more common to employ elements of the built environment to reflect the appropriate physical setting for the operations and display of civic authority. We find greater attention being paid to the symbolic as well as the functional role of numerous types of man-made structures, and to the furnishings and division of space within them. It is to this aspect of the civic political culture that we now turn.

The invocation of the built environment in what follows is meant to suggest that the design, construction, furnishing, utilization, and both the symbolic and practical significance of such structures formed an integral and representative part of the political culture of Elizabethan and Jacobean towns as, by extension, analagous structures did (and do) in almost any political ethos. It is meant to affirm the view that the palace has much to tell us of the monarchy; the castle and manor house of the feudal system; the shop, market, and warehouse of commercial activity; and, e.g. the civic hall (as well as the town grammar school, workhouse, prison, parish church, mayor's parlour, and marketplace) of urban society. Above all, this approach is meant to suggest that the use of the built environment made by the civic authorities represents an element in the emergence at this time of a 'high political culture': the goals, strategies, and behavioural conventions, not of the whole community, but of that minority which came to exercise hegemony over the rest. In this sense, some formerly 'public' buildings and spaces became more tightly controlled. In other cases specific buildings, spaces, and even furnishings were created anew, by and for those who ruled.

Perhaps the most obvious and ubiquitous application of this premise may be found in the marked proliferation of town halls in the period under consideration. By definition, the town hall – by whatever term it may have been known in a specific town – formed the administrative headquarters of the community. By the end of the sixteenth century we would expect such edifices to contain, at the very least, the council chamber housing the aldermanic council and the court room housing the town court or courts. Though in the smallest halls one large room may have served both functions, these two chambers more frequently remained spatially as well as functionally distinct. They were becoming even more so as the century progressed.[18]

In addition, many halls held a mayor's parlour, a second council chamber, a kitchen, gaol cells for short-term confinement or prison cells for longer incarcer-

Parry, *The Exeter Guildhall and the Life Within* (Exeter, 1936), pp. 156–7; W. Devon RO, Plymouth Receivers' Accounts, MS. Worth 132, fo. 172v.

[17] Basil Cozens-Hardy and E. A. Kent (eds.), *The Mayors of Norwich, 1403–1835* (Norwich, 1938), p. 56.

[18] This and the following paragraphs derive from Tittler, *Architecture and Power, the Town Hall and the English Urban Community, 1500–1640* (Oxford, 1991), chs. 1 and 2.

ation, an armoury, guild offices, or a muniment room. A few came to hold such amenities as a jury room, a residential room for a caretaker, town clerk or even the recorder, storage areas for the paraphernalia of market regulation, a school room, and even a common bake-house. A great many and probably a majority were constructed in the marketplace and with an open ground floor to shelter market traders and customers from the elements: this is the familiar pillared hall, or 'box on stilts', of which some fine examples survive. These were often called 'market halls', though if they also housed the institutions of town government they obviously exceeded their literal meaning. They were the most common type constructed between 1540 and 1620 and their influence readily crossed the ocean to the urban foundation in the New World.[19] (See plates 36–9.)

Though we shall never know how many halls pre-date the sixteenth century, a great many were obviously extant in 1500. The earliest documented town hall *per se* is that at Exeter, which is known to have existed by the mid twelfth century on the same site as today's edificial palimpsest. Its image rapidly took centre place on the city's medieval seal.[20] It appears that the building of town halls – an activity in which we may include purchase and renovation, substantial addition or actual construction from scratch – fell off distinctly by the middle of the fifteenth century, and that this slump continued on for three or four decades of the sixteenth.[21] Yet from about 1540, halls sprang up or 'grew' at a rate which seems unprecedented. It has been reckoned that roughly half the 650 or 700 towns in England acquired (by purchase or construction) or substantially expanded their civic hall between 1500 and 1640 – and some of them acquired more than one hall in that span. The overwhelming majority of these came between 1540 and 1620, dates forming the boundaries of this paper.[22]

Such expansion accrued for a variety of reasons. Naturally enough, some existing halls had become derelict and needed to be replaced. Some had become too small to accommodate the growing demands placed upon them. Some resulted from the sudden availability of ecclesiastical buildings which came on the property market following the ecclesiastical dissolutions of the 1530s and 1540s. But the first of these developments and to some extent even the second were no more or less likely to occur after *c.* 1540 than before. The third development still begs the question of motivation: even given the wider availability of convertible buildings, why would townsmen rush out to purchase and refurbish them as town halls, especially at a time when many towns seem to have been economically distressed?

[19] Historic American Buildings Survey, *America's City Halls*, ed. William Lebovich (Washington DC, 1984), pp. 14–15.
[20] Lloyd Parry, *The Exeter Guildhall*, pp. 1–20 and the illustration opposite p. 4.
[21] R. B. Dobson, 'Urban Decline in Late Medieval England', *Transactions of the Royal Historical Society*, 5th ser., 27 (1977): 7; Tittler, 'Late Medieval Urban Prosperity', *Economic History Review*, second ser., 37 (1984): 551–4.
[22] Tittler, *Architecture and Power*, appendix I.

The answer seems to lie in concerns which were political, and which entailed assumptions central to the urban political culture of the post-Reformation era. Simply put, halls constructed and/or controlled by the townsmen demarcated and symbolized the emergence of civic authority from seigneurial control. Hence the town hall often replaced the castle or manor hall as the symbol of local hegemony. In addition, town halls represented the ruling element within towns in the eyes of their fellows, the symbol of controlled space of the hall perhaps replacing the shared space of the marketplace. In both contexts, halls provided the essential requirement of dignity and appearance for the urban leadership of the day, a leadership, as we have seen, which was very much more ascendant, active, and aggressive in these years.

Several kinds of evidence support this view. We know that a substantial number of halls were acquired shortly following the acquisition of incorporation,[23] and (as many towns sought incorporation after victories in litigation against the claims of seigneurial authorities)[24] some halls may have been built then, too. Both events often marked a greater assertion of governing authority. What little evidence we have concerning conflicts over hall building in specific towns points to a ruling élite making the decision over the reluctance or even opposition of the general freemanry, who were often expected to pay for the construction.[25] We know, too, that when serious conflicts arose over jurisdiction or hegemony in the community, jurisdiction over or even physical control of the hall often formed the chief strategic objective.[26] Finally, we can observe the development of the hall as the increasingly exclusive preserve of the ruling élite through the strict regulation of public entrance and use which became more common in the decades at hand.[27]

Many of these strategies were intended to do more than to create new office space for civic officials. The establishment of 'hall decorum', for example, could be both extreme and pointed in its objective of creating deference – even reverence – for those who presided within. The ensuing behavioural injunctions were directed to the officials themselves as well as to those who came before them. In many towns, the proceedings in the hall were to be treated in strict

---

[23] Abingdon, Bideford, Boston, Chipping Sodbury, Droitwich, Gloucester, Great Dunmow, Gravesend, Hartlepool, Hereford, High Wycombe, Kendal, Lyme Regis, Macclesfield, Maidenhead, Maidstone, Maldon, Newbury, Penzance, Poole, Reading, Ripon, Romsey, Saffron Walden, St Albans, Sheffield, Sutton Coldfield, Tewkesbury, Tiverton, Warwick, and Weymouth/Melcombe Regis (the two having been amalgamated in *c.* 1572).

[24] Tittler, 'The Incorporation of Boroughs, 1540–1558', *History*, 64 (February, 1977) p. 28 and n. 17.

[25] E.g. Poole Borough Archives, Civic Centre, MS. 26(4), 'The Great Boke, 1568–78', fos. 118–130; MS. 108(63), 'The Answere of Christopher Ffarwell'; MS. 25(3), 'Old Record Book no. 3', fos. 100–01; and MS. TDW/5, 'Settlement toward Building the Market House'.

[26] E.g. Evesham: PRO, E 134/29 Eliz./East. 12, fos. 7r and 15r; E 123/12/275v; Shaftesbury: PRO, E 134/18/James I/East. I; Hythe: PRO, E 134/19/Jas. I., Mic. 25.

[27] Clark and Slack, *English Towns in Transition*, p. 131; Bedford Town Hall, 'Black Book of Bedford', MS B1, fo. 5v; J. M. Baines, *Historic Hastings* (Hastings, 1955), p. 55; Clopper (ed.), *REED, Chester*, p. 451.

Plate 36.   Evesham 'Booth Hall', mid sixteenth century.

Plate 37.   Burford 'Tolsey', first cited in 1561.

Plate 38. Newent 'Market Hall', late Elizabethan or early Jacobean. A typical small market town's pillared hall, sheltering the market below and providing a single room hall above for conduct of the town's affairs.

Plate 39. Hereford Town Hall, *c.* 1600; a drawing by John Clayton, 1846. The 'state of the art' in late-Elizabethan town halls, with market space, town chambers and meeting rooms, and offices for guilds.

confidentiality.[28] Participants in business conducted in the hall were prohibited from uttering 'unseemly words',[29] or from leaving the building before the conclusion of business.[30] In many towns, too, it became common (and thus apparently necessary) to order all officers 'to come in decent order in ther gownes . . .'.[31] When townsmen who were not holders of local office were permitted at hall proceedings – as they were less often in our period – they were enjoined to refrain from behaviour considered undeferential. We find frequent injunctions for quiet and orderly conduct, observance of confidentiality, and even for waiting on the mayor from his house to the hall itself for those having business to bring before him.[32] In such ways as these the town hall came more than ever in the era at hand to represent the environment of civic hegemony. In so doing, it provided a compelling setting for an élitist-led or 'high' political culture in the Tudor town.

Though we may not conventionally regard it in that light, the parish church also served as a civic building, and one which was also usefully and variously employed to reinforce the dignity of the town élite. In the medieval town, of course, the church sometimes served as the town hall where no suitable alternative existed.[33] In the unincorporated town of Melton Mowbray, for example, townsmen met in the church for the conduct of official business. They kept the town muniments in a chest next to the Altar of Our Lady, and then elsewhere in the same building until well into the Elizabethan era. The same commodious church held the town grammar school, run after the Reformation by the 'town trust' which ruled the community. This met in the eastern side of the north transept, which had been walled off for the purpose.[34] In Cirencester, the town council met in the expanded first floor of the church porch, which it considered and sometimes even referred to as the town hall.[35] In towns too numerous to mention the church had of course served as the focal point for pre-Reformation civic ceremonial in which the standing of virtually everyone in the freemanry gained public display in the order of procession and the livery worn for the occasion.

As these occasions faded from view or underwent transition to more secular observances, the civic role of the church took on new forms. The most common

[28] St Albans Public Library, Mayor's Account Book, MS. 152, fo. 94r; Dorset RO, Bridport Borough Court Book, MS. B8/C83, a 'grand inquest' of 21 April 1578.

[29] Battley, 'Lordship and Community in King's Lynn', p. 267; Berkshire County RO, Abingdon Borough Minute Book, MS. D/EP 7/84, fo. 7d; Humberside RO, Hedon Borough Records, MS. DDHE/26/fo. 132r.

[30] Humberside RO, Hedon Borough Records, MS. DDHE/26, fo. 132v.

[31] Bailey (ed.), *Minutes of Boston*, order of 11 October 1555, p. 2; Ingram (ed.), *REED, Coventry*, p. 201; Humberside RO, Hedon Borough Archives, MS. DDHE/26, fo. 131v.

[32] Dance (ed.), *Guildford Records*, pp. 10, 36 and 37.

[33] For an interesting, if somewhat eccentric treatment of this link, see Sidney Oldham Addy, *Church and Manor, a Study in English Economic History* (1913, reprinted, New York, 1970), chs. 8–9.

[34] Dorothy Pockley, 'The Origins and Early History of the Melton Mowbray Town Estate' (unpublished Ph.D. dissertation, Leicester University, 1964), pp. 105, 140 and 210.

[35] Anon., *History of Cirencester* (Cirencester, 1863), p. 65; BL, Add. MS. 36362, fo. 176 (Buckler Drawing).

and important of these was the emerging use of church seating to exhibit the relative status of community members, both officials and freeman. Here again a practice with pre-Reformation precedents became more fully developed and widespread – indeed almost universal – in the period at hand. In church services throughout most of the Middle Ages, parishioners either stood or they knelt. Seats were not employed in the church until the mid-fourteenth century, when they were first available for clergy and choristers. They became common in most churches only in the early or mid-fifteenth century.[36] In the sixteenth century the practice of church seating had become virtually universal, as did the concomitant practice of seat rental or assignment.

In most communities, this important ancillary development seems to have progressed in three stages. To begin with, which is to say even in the latter half of the fifteenth century in most urban areas, some parishes rented out a handful of seats, typically for 4d or 6d a year, to men and especially women who were aged and/or infirm.[37] This occurred without very pronounced regard for their social standing, so long as renters belonged to the congregation.

Following the early years of the Reformation and continuing into the beginning of Elizabeth's reign, we find a second phase of this practice. Seat rentals became more widespread, both from church to church and region to region, and within individual churches themselves. In addition, we find a wider differentiation of rental costs and clear signs – for the first time in all but the larger communities – of a new priority in seating: not for the infirm and aged of both sexes, but for men of stature, and sometimes for their families.[38]

Finally, in a phase which commonly began as early as the 1570s in some areas and not until the early seventeenth century in others, we find both a substantive and often quite sudden increase in the number of seats rented, up to several hundred in some cases, and in the social prestige attached both to their possession and to their location in the church building. Here, too, rentals came to be extended from individual seats to whole pews, and were more regularly taken up not merely by the *pater familias* himself, but by his family as well.[39]

---

[36] Alfred Heales, *History and Law of Church Seats* (2 vols., 1872) i, pp. 30–1; John Mirc, *Instructions for Parish Priests*, ed. John Peacock (Early English Text Society, rev. edn, 1902, reprinted, 1975), p. 9; A. H. Thompson, *The Historical Growth of the English Parish Church* (second edn, Cambridge, 1913), p. 109; W. J. Hardy, 'Remarks on the History of the Seat Reservation in Churches', *Archeologia*, second ser., pt. 1, 52 (1892): 104.

[37] Betty R. Masters and Elizabeth Ralph (eds.), *The Church Book of St Ewen's, Bristol, 1454–1584* (Bristol and Gloucestershire Archeological Society, Records Section, vol. 6, 1967), p. 25; J. Charles Cox, *Churchwardens' Accounts from the Fourteenth Century to the Close of the Seventeenth Century* (1913), pp. 67 and 189; Rev. J. R. Beresford, 'The Churchwardens' Accounts of Holy Trinity, Chester, 1532–1633', *Journal of the Chester and N. Wales Architectural, Archeological and History Society*, 38 (1951): 112–16.

[38] Cox, *Churchwardens' Accounts*, p. 189; PRO, SP 14/112/83; J. E. Foster (ed.), *Churchwardens' Accounts of St Mary the Great, Cambridge, from 1504 to 1635*, (Cambridge Antiquarian Society, vol. 35, 1905).

[39] Foster (ed.), *Accounts of St. Mary the Great, Cambridge*, pp. 572–3; Joseph Amphlett (ed.), *The Churchwardens' Accounts of St. Michaels in Bedwardine, Worcester, 1539–1603* (Worcester His-

Some urban parishes even came by then to emulate the rural parish practice of 'manor pews', whereby the owners of certain country properties came to hold church seats which were considered to 'belong to' their houses.[40] In addition, many, and by 1600 perhaps most, major civic parishes allotted specific seating to town officials by dint of their office alone.[41] By the early seventeenth century, therefore, the characteristics of church seating which would endure in many parishes right into our own century were well and widely in place.

How do we account for this common three-stage development? First, there was a financial motivation. It is clear that the Reformation reduced the number of church ales and similar activities which had provided revenue for the parish, making some alternative means of fund raising very welcome. With the precedent of occasional rentals in place from pre-Reformation days, churchwardens throughout the realm quickly recognized this opportunity for its fiscal potential. Secondly, the changing nature of the church service itself, and especially the emergence of the sermon at its centre, made it more important to sit in some degree of comfort. And, since the sermon-centred service needed to be heard as well as witnessed, seating location, preferably nearest the pulpit, also gained a new importance.[42]

And thirdly, there was a social dimension. At the same time that the actual physical display of social standing, formerly provided in the liturgically based ceremonial, came under attack, the potential for public seating in a particular sequence and location provided a very welcome substitute device. Where once the community could identify its leaders by their order of procession out of doors, now they could do so by their order of seating within. The device applied

torical Society, vol. 7, 1896), pp. xv–xvi; Orders of 9 and 23 Eliz., cited in PRO, SP 14/112/83; Bailey (ed.), *Minutes of Boston*, i, pp. 81 and 643.

[40] The practice was specifically disallowed when two parishioners tried to insist on it in Holy Trinity, Chester, as late as 1575, but it had become common there three or four decades later and was taken for granted by the late seventeenth and early eighteenth century. The great ecclesiastical lawyer Richard Burn considered the title to a seat triable at the common law in 1763. Beresford, 'Accounts of Holy Trinity, Chester', p., 126; J. Boulton, *Neighbourhood and Society, a London Suburb in the Seventeenth Century* (Cambridge, 1967) p. 286; J. Charles Cox, *English Church Fittings, Furniture and Accessories* (1923) pp. 115–16; Richard Gough, *History of Myddle* (1701, 1834), ed. D. Hey (1982); Richard Burn, *Ecclesiastical Law* (2 vols., 1763), i, pp. 256, 259.

[41] K. R. Adey, 'Aspects of the History of the Town of Stafford, 1590–1710', (unpublished M.A. thesis, Keele University, 1971), p. 97; Bailey (ed.), *Minutes of Boston*, i, pp. 81, 643; Henry F. Hillen, *History of the Borough of King's Lynn* (2 vols., Norwich, [1907]), i, p. 310; H. E. Salter (ed.), *Oxford Council Acts, 1583–1626* (Oxford Historical Society, 1928), p. 408; F. A. Carrington, 'The Old Market House and the Great Fire at Marlborough', *Wiltshire Archeological and Natural History Magazine*, 3 (1857): 112.

[42] The most desirable seats in most churches were in the east end of the nave, and especially on the north side, nearest the pulpit. The least members of the parish sat at the other extreme, if they sat at all. In St Edmunds, Salisbury, the parish poor were made by the 1620s to sit together in forms on which were painted in big, red letters, 'for the Poore'; A. Tindal Harte, *The Man in the Pew* (1966), p. 129; Mark Knight, 'Religious Life in Coventry, 1485–1558' (unpublished Ph.D. dissertation, University of Warwick, 1986), pp. 132–4; Cox, *Churchwardens' Accounts*, pp. 67–9.

both to the social élite and, though they were often one and the same, the officials of the community.[43]

Along with the town hall and parish church, and often in close proximity to them, lay the physical structures for enforcement and coercion: the gaol or prison cell(s), the mechanisms for punishment and – by the early seventeenth century in some towns – the workhouse as well. If the dignity required by the hall and the church represented the carrot for the encouragement of civic order, these represented the stick. Again, such facilities were not novel. Virtually every medieval town worth its salt had at least a cage or a lock-up and many had more extensive facilities as well.[44] (See plates 40 and 41.) Yet it could be argued that the need for such facilities, and hence their appearance, grew in the sixteenth century. Certainly the perception of growing crime and the reality of increased population, migration, and poverty, all of which supported that increase, point toward that view.[45] The concurrent notion that idleness was sinful, particularly prominent amongst many of the more committed protestants of the age, adds further to it.[46] In addition, it seems likely that improved trial proceedings made prosecution more effective in cases of felony.[47] Finally, it may well be that many misdemeanours which had been punishable by fine or by either fine or imprisonment before more commonly resulted in incarceration in the sixteenth century, if for no other reason than the increasing inability to pay a fine on the part of the poor.

These tendencies had significant bearing on the augmentation of civic authority in two respects. First, brief incarceration became an increasingly common response for offensive words or actions against town officials.[48] It thus served to enforce required deference. Second, the greater emphasis on punishment, both incarceratory and otherwise, relied upon the officials of the town for its application: an extension of the general tendency of the Tudor and Stuart monarchy to delegate powers of enforcement to officials upon whom it felt it could rely.[49]

---

[43] Dr Vanessa Harding has raised the prospect that the position of burial in some London parishes served as a similarly important indicator of social status, though this subject seems 'beneath' the scope of the 'built environment' as employed in this paper; see V. Harding, '"And One More May be Laid There": the Location of Burials in Early Modern London', *The London Journal*, 14 (1989): 112–29. My thanks to the author for bringing this to my attention.

[44] Ralph B. Pugh, *Imprisonment in Medieval England* (Cambridge, 1968), p. 101.

[45] See note 5 above.

[46] Summarized in R. L. Greaves, *Society and Religion in Elizabethan England* (Minneapolis, MN, 1981), pp. 383–95.

[47] Thomas Andrew Green, *Verdict According to Conscience, Perspectives on the English Criminal Trial Jury, 1200–1800* (Chicago, IL, 1985), p. 107.

[48] E.g. Boston: Bailey (ed.), *Minutes of Boston*, i, p. 80; Hedon: Humberside RO, Hedon Borough Records, MS. DDHE/26, fo. 132r; J. M. Guilding (ed.), *Reading Records* (4 volumes, Reading, 1892–96), i, p. 188.

[49] Clark and Slack (eds.), *Crisis and Order*, p. 22. This is also widely reflected in statutes specifying punishment, and in the scores of charters of incorporation granted to towns by the Crown in the period at hand. See especially the powers given to commit rogues and vagabonds in 39 Eliz., c. 4.

Plate 40. Amersham Market Hall, ground floor lock-up. Though probably dating from about a century after the death of Elizabeth I, this typifies a type which was already several hundred years old when built.

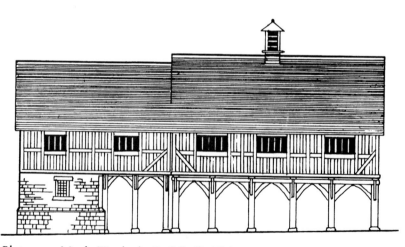

Plate 41. Much Wenlock Guildhall. This anonymous, modern drawing shows the 1577 extension of the five-bay pillared hall on the right over the earlier stone prison cell on the left.

In addition to the gaols and prisons *per se*, facilities for punishment included the ducking stool, stocks, pillory, and other such devices. Perhaps the most common position for these devices of public humiliation lay in the marketplace. This area, usually abutting or containing the hall, was extremely public and increasingly under the eye of civic authorities both literally and figuratively. This spatial juxtaposition kept the stick as well as the carrot of orderly government closely connected in the public gaze.

The ultimate expansion of such facilities in this period was of course the house of correction. This, too, was often adjacent to and sometimes even an extension of the town hall,[50] though near many halls the required space was simply not available. Houses of correction were given over by statute to the administrative jurisdiction of town mayors and their 'brethren', at least in incorporated towns, as the legal representatives of the borough corporation. As is well known, these were first, though ineffectually, called for in the Vagrancy Act of 1547, then in the (only slightly more effective) Act of 1576, and finally in the substantially successful Act of 1610.[51] It has usefully been argued that the greatest effect of the last statute, in addition to prompting the actual construction of many bridewells, was the power it afforded local authorities to command a subservient labour force at little cost.[52] It is hard to imagine a more effective tool for the cultivation of order for the ruling elements in towns with such facilities, or one which symbolized more clearly the coercive potential implied in the high political culture of towns at that time.

Interestingly, the power given to civic authorities to commit to prison, granted progressively during the course of the century, applied not only to the population in general, but also to officials themselves if they acted in ways which could undermine respect for their offices. Like the injunctions to wear proper livery and observe confidentiality in official proceedings, there is an element of self-policing in this, suggesting that dignity, like charity, was considered to begin at home. Thus we may note that imprisonment was widely permitted as a deterrent to the evasion of office or as a sanction against chamberlains failing to render proper account of the revenues in their care.[53] To be sure, these powers were controversial and it is difficult to measure their actual enforcement. Yet recorded incidents of opposition to them – including

---

[50] E.g. Hadleigh and Oxford: W. A. B. Jones, *Hadleigh Through the Ages* (Ipswich, 1977), p. 33; Salter (ed.), *Oxford Council Acts*, p. 117.

[51] 1 Edward VI, c. 3; 18 Eliz., c. 3; 7 James I, c. 4.

[52] Christopher Harding, Bill Hines, Richard Ireland, and Philip Rawlings, *Imprisonment in England and Wales, a Concise History* (1985), pp. 55–6; J. Thirsk, *Economic Policy and Projects* (Oxford, 1978) p. 66.

[53] Guilding (ed.), *Reading Records*, i, p. 188. Another common offence treated in this manner was the refusal to serve in office once elected. E.g. Warwick: *Calendar of Patent Rolls, Philip and Mary*, vol. ii [1554–55] (1935), p. 20; Worcester: *ibid.*, ii, p. 82; Abingdon: *ibid.*, iii [1555–57] (1938), p. 382 (two references); Brecon: *ibid.*, iii, p. 78; Ilchester, *ibid.*, iii, p. 529; Launceston: *ibid.*, iii, p. 176; Thaxted: *ibid.*, iii, p. 155.

suits for false arrest and imprisonment or orders taken by town councils to guard against the same – affirm their application.[54]

These three types of structure, the hall, the parish church, and the facility for punishment, provided in one way or another a physical environment which helped the community define and display its social hierarchy and both the identity and authority of its leaders. In so doing, they formed an essential setting for the 'high political culture' which grew substantially in urban communities at this time. One way in which this theme may be illustrated is by examining how particular participants in that burgeoning ethos employed elements of that setting both to carry out their responsibilities and, more importantly, to display their dignity, power, and authority. One might usefully accomplish this end with reference to characteristic social types, especially the master merchants who usually dominated the urban hierarchy, or political leaders in their official capacities.

Yet perhaps the most obvious subject for this exercise is the mayor, the chief executive and judicial officer in most towns of any standing by the mid-sixteenth century, and more often than not a leading merchant in his private life. No office better exemplifies the growth of oligarchy than his, none better illustrates the adaptation of the built environment for political ends.

Mayoral office in England may be traced to before the thirteenth century and came more commonly to be recognized after the reign of King John. From that time forward it may be taken as a sign of urban autonomy (as opposed to the jurisdiction of, e.g. the bailiff, reeve, or steward on behalf of a manorial lord) or of the emergence of a more distinct hierarchy (as opposed to government by a council of, typically, twelve). As such tendencies became more widespread, so did the mayoralty.[55] There can be little doubt that in the urban community, the mayor was the chief recipient of the central government's broadened delegation of judicial and administrative authority which characterized the period from the High Middle Ages through the sixteenth century.[56] This was especially true in the older and often larger communities, which had established self-rule at an early time or which, in some cases, had never been under seigneurial jurisdiction. But with the increased use of charters of incorporation in the fifteenth century and then their rapid proliferation from the middle decades of the sixteenth, mayoral office became more widespread and potent than ever. Even by the fifteenth century mayoral power was sometimes sufficient to provoke resentment or even revolt, especially in larger and more politically developed towns.[57] Where in most cases the medieval mayor had been little more than

---

[54] Hedon: Humberside RO, Borough Order Book, MS. DDHE/25, fo. 132v (1555); Barnstaple (temp. 32–34 Henry VIII): PRO, STAC 2/13/88–91.
[55] Reynolds, *History of English Medieval Towns*, pp. 109–20.
[56] John Bellamy, *Criminal Law and Society in Late Medieval and Tudor England* (Gloucester and New York, 1984), pp. 14, 21–4, 47, 100–2.
[57] Colin Platt, *The English Medieval Town* (1976) p. 122, citing examples from Southampton (1460) and Northampton (1489).

primus inter pares with fellow councillors[58] his elevation to far greater status and authority was everywhere evident in the age of the Tudors.

On the shoulders of the mayor more than of any other public figure rested the responsibility for maintaining law and order in the community. He directed the aldermen and/or common councillors, the recorder, clerks and chamberlains, and such lesser officials as their serjeants of arms, constables, waits, ale-conners, market inspectors, and the rest. He presided over the town courts, serving as arbiter of justice in their equity jurisdiction, as well as over the councils and assemblies. He often represented the crown as coroner, escheater, clerk of the market and, with increasing frequency as justice of the peace. He came to hold the power to fine and imprison or otherwise punish, to regulate the markets and fairs, to license (or refuse to license) visiting players, and to conduct parliamentary elections. Depending on the status of the community, he often represented a direct administrative link with the Crown, the privy council and parliament, without the intermediate jurisdiction of shire officials.

Though the stipend he received in recognition of his burdens could rarely if ever constitute a true salary, he commanded a great deal of ceremonial homage. This befitted a man of his rank, proved a necessary buttress to his authority, and perhaps served to make up in prestige what he rarely received for his services in the coin of the realm. Thus the mayoralty served as much or more than ever before as the focal point for civic ritual, civic processions, banquets and feasts, for the wearing of raiment, and the display of regalia. On major holidays the mayors of most towns expected to be waited on by aldermen, common councillors, and the like, suitably turned out. In most towns, too, the mayor continued to preside at major holidays and celebrations, host dinners, review processions, review the stilted verses of local school children, attend burials of local worthies, and host visiting dignitaries.

Even in his most mundane functions, the mayor received extensive homage and ceremonial respect. In the town of Guildford, and even as early as 1520, all men having business at the mayor's court were to wait upon the mayor 'from hys house unto the hawle' upon pain of fine.[59] In Beverley the mayor was to walk in his gown on virtually every public appearance with the mace borne before him.[60] And in Coventry the mayor's daily routine began when the officers of the corporation met him at his door at seven in the morning, escorted him for services at St Michael's Church, thence home again, and finally to and from the market to inspect goods for sale.[61]

In the largest and most important communities the mayor attained a status tantamount to the landed aristocrat, at least during his term in office, and the Crown found numerous symbolic means of recognizing that standing. As early

---

[58] B. Wilkinson and R. C. Easterling, *The Medieval Council of Exeter* (Manchester, [1931]), p. xxxiii.
[59] Dance (ed.), *Guildford Records*, p. 10.
[60] Humberside RO, Beverley Borough 'Small Order Book, 1575–1583', MS. BC/II/4, fo. 3r.
[61] Mark Knight, 'Religious Life in Coventry, 1485–1558', pp. 129–30.

as Henry VII's reign the mayor of Exeter received the king's sword and a hat of maintenance as symbols of royal support for his power (and as reward for the city's ability to withstand the Cornish Tax Revolt of 1497).[62] By the early seventeenth century the lords mayor of York – one of two such officials in the realm to enjoy that honorific – were regularly knighted during royal visits in recognition of their authority.[63] A local antiquary of mid-seventeenth-century Winchester could, with perfect impunity, liken the role of the mayor to that of gods and kings over his people, as the 'God of Order', as the 'head' to which 'the laws are the soul and the people the entrails of the Republic'.[64]

In the cultural context of the age, both the mayoral authority and its attendant prestige demanded reinforcement, not only in the ceremonial display of vestments and use of regalia, but in the built environment itself. With the emergence of the mayoral role, we find a corresponding emergence of 'mayoral space' as a specialized development within the civic halls and structures noted above. This consisted of buildings and rooms within buildings which were specifically designed to identify and enhance that role. It also consisted of furnishing designed towards the same end. To a degree we could observe similar accoutrements devoted to at least a few of the other senior officials of most towns – aldermen, common councillors, recorders, clerks, chamberlains, and the like – but none so extensive as for the mayor.

Without doubt, the mayor's most important place of work was the town hall itself, and contemporaries would more easily have associated the hall with his office than with any other. Here the mayor conventionally (and in some cases, exclusively) took his oath of office, presided over the courts and councils, mediated disputes, received litigants, favour-seekers, visiting players, and other entertainments. In some towns the very legitimacy of his official duties could be called into question if carried out elsewhere than in the hall.

Within the hall itself there came to be several devices fashioned to recognize and display the mayor's status or that of specific incumbents. These may have included the representation of the mayor's mace of office over the main

[62] Lloyd Parry, *The Exeter Guildhall*, pp. 156–7; John Vowell *alias* Hooker, *The Description of the Citie of Excester*, eds. Walter J. Harte, J. W. Schopp, and H. Tapley-Soper (Devon and Cornwall Record Society, 1919–47), p. 793.

[63] Johnston and Rogerson (eds.), *REED, York*, p. xi. This was occasionally true elsewhere in the same period: e.g. Robert Wood, Mayor of Norwich in 1569, was knighted during a visit by the queen in that year. Yet it should be noted, by contrast, that when Prince Arthur wished to distinguish a mayor of Chester just a few decades earlier (in 1498) he named him a mere esquire; BL, Add. MS. 29780, fo. 63r; Cozens-Hardy and Kent (eds.), *Mayors of Norwich*, pp. 59–60.

[64] John Trussell, in his unpublished poem, *c.* 1647, 'Benefactors to Winchester', cited in Adrienne Rosen, 'Economic and Social Aspects of the History of Winchester, 1520–1670', p. 234, from Bodleian Library, MS. Top. Hants. c. 5, pp. 83–90.

Plate 42. Thomas Layer, Mayor of Norwich in 1576 and 1586. A print of 1841, from a contemporary oil portrait.

doorway,[65] the furniture,[66] and possibly even his portrait.[67] (See plate 42.) But the two main devices which seem to have emerged chiefly in the period at hand were the mayor's parlour and the mayor's chair.

As the derivation of the term suggests, a parlour was essentially a place in which to carry on conversations. In medieval monastic usage where it first

[65] E.g. Macclesfield: C. S. Davies, *A History of Macclesfield*, (Manchester, 1961), frontispiece.
[66] E.g. Salisbury: Victor Chinnery, *Oak Furniture, the British Tradition. A History of Early Furniture in the British Isles and New England* (Woodbridge, Suffolk, 1979), p. 40 and plate 1.
[67] Henry Harttop (ed.), *The Roll of the Mayors of the Borough of Leicester*, (Leicester, [c. 1935]) pp. 76–7; Cozens-Hardy and Kent (eds.), *Mayors of Norwich*, pp. 42, 43, 45, 48–9, 65, 69 and 79; Lloyd Parry, *The Exeter Guildhall*, pp. 150–5. This interesting topic is the object of continuing investigation.

appeared, it was a place set aside for visitors, and by the late fourteenth century it turns up in references to the homes of wealthy laity. Perhaps the earliest reference to a mayor's parlour is that in Canterbury in 1438;[68] but with the exception of Nottingham, where a mayor's parlour is cited in 1486,[69] other references that have come to light all date from the mid-sixteenth century or later.[70] While most of these were situated in town halls, a few were located in inns, and we may well imagine that many inns held some sort of back room in which the mayor could meet people informally and carry out at least quasi-official business.

A few of these records afford some idea of the activities which went on in mayoral parlours. In Coventry the mayor conducted interviews with, and rendered payment to, players who had performed with his permission in the chamber of the hall itself. He celebrated public events in the close company of his senior aides and officers. He heard disputes and tried to resolve them. He entertained visiting royalty in the intimate setting not available in the market-place, the inn, or the cathedral, though he may have honoured them more formally in those venues as well.[71]

We have less difficulty surmising what such rooms looked like, for the mayor's parlour in the Leicester Guildhall is well restored for our inspection.[72] This room, first built in 1563 and refurbished in 1637, opened off a front corner of the main hall chamber, allowing easy access for the mayor from the parlour to the dais of the hall. The slightly irregular, ground floor parlour is approximately 20' × 35', a substantial size. Its two long walls are dominated by stained glass windows on the west side and a wainscotted wall, furnished with a bench and mayor's chair in the middle of the east wall (plate 43). The short north wall is dominated by a large fireplace and elaborate mantle, the remainder of the wall itself being wainscotted (see plate 44), while the south wall, also wainscotted, bears the door to the great hall which runs along the south or street side of the building. At least in the twentieth century this has been furnished with a conference table running a good part of the length of the room, and no doubt some such table would have been a likely part of the hall in the sixteenth and seventeenth centuries.

The mayoral parlour provided some of the amenities of an official residence, an honour which few if any towns could afford to provide in the period at hand.

[68] S. I. Rigold, 'Two Types of Court Hall', *Archeologia Cantiana*, 83 (1968): 3.
[69] *Oxford English Dictionary*, see 'parlour'.
[70] E.g. Southwark (after 1550): D. D. Johnson, *Southwark and the City* (1969), pp. 222–3; Leicester (1563–1637): N. Pegden, *Leicester Guildhall* (Leicester, 1981), pp. 2, 4; Coventry (1572–73): Phythian-Adams, *Coventry*, p. 275; Warwick (by 1576): Peter Borsay, 'The English Urban Renaissance, Landscape and Leisure in the Provincial Town, *c.* 1660–1770' (unpublished Ph.D. dissertation, Lancashire University, 1981), p. 169; Lostwithiel (mid-seventeenth century): Historical Manuscripts Commission, vol. 55: *Various Collections*, vol. i, (1901), p. 331.
[71] E.g. Ingram (ed.), *REED, Coventry*, pp. 396, 439.
[72] See also T. H. Fosbrooke and S. H. Skillington, 'The Old Town Hall of Leicester', *Transactions of the Leicestershire Archeological Society*, 13 (1923–24) and N. Pegden, *Leicester Guildhall*.

Plate 43.   Mayor's cushioned seat with seal and flanking columns, Mayor's Parlour, Leicester Guildhall, 1637.

In addition, mayors virtually always in the sixteenth century and almost always in the seventeenth made their principal residence in the town in which they served, and therefore had not the same need of an official residence as, for example, did the master of a college, the bishop of a diocese, or, indeed, a king or queen.[73] At least the parlour served as an official place of conference, counsel, and entertainment.

[73] There are instances in which town officials were provided lodging with their office if, as occasionally with town clerks and frequently with recorders, they did not reside in the community; Norfolk RO, Wymondham Town Book, MS. 12.12.66/Q173B, fos., 87–8; Bailey (ed.), *Minutes of Boston*, i, p. 53. In Leicester, the Recorder's Bedroom has been restored or recreated to represent the original.

Plate 44. Fireplace and Mantle, Mayor's Parlour, Leicester Guildhall, 1637.

Our last mayoral amenity, important both for its practical and its symbolic applications, consisted of mayoral seating. This is exemplified in several official settings and certainly in both the town hall and the parish church. Though we may readily take for granted today that seating may have held deeply symbolic values, and that high officials might well have enjoyed a distinctive form of seating, the concept was not as highly developed in the medieval period as we might imagine in either town halls or parish churches. Mayoral seating, for example, seems to have come along slowly, with the mayors of almost all towns even in the fifteenth century sitting shoulder to shoulder with aldermen or fellow councillors on long benches, along a wall of the council chamber or assembly room, with little to distinguish their place from the rest. At a time when most mayors were little more than first amongst equals, this was not inappropriate. For the most part, it is only in the sixteenth century that we find the emergence of true mayoral seating, albeit in several forms.

In some cases, this emergence meant that the mayor continued to sit on the shared bench but that his place became distinguished by the addition of some sort of symbolic furnishing or device: cushions at his place alone, the royal arms on the wall behind his place, or even classical columns along the wall flanking his position (see plate 43).[74] The mayor's seat in Beverley, probably a unique piece, seems to represent an intermediate phase of development between a shared bench and a free-standing chair, a three-seat settle with the mayor's place raised above the other two (plate 45). In other cases this meant the development of a free-standing chair, usually with arms and a high, carved back, and often with some iconographic indication of its purpose.[75] Some such chairs were constructed specifically at the behest of certain mayors, who gave them to the corporation.[76] This does not, therefore, seem a parallel to the custom, for example, whereby the speaker of the House of Commons eventually got to take his chair with him at the end of a parliament, but it may indeed suggest a parallel to forms of gift-giving in English and other contemporary societies in which the gift bestowed to the community reflected, and was intended to reflect, the dignity and status of the donor.[77]

As one might already assume, mayoral seating also became distinct and important in the parish church. In most cases this came to consist of a particular pew or individual seats in the choicest part of the church, though there were variations on this according to local custom and the architectural peculiarities of specific churches. In St Botolph's, Boston, for example, there was a loft '. . . where ye maior useth to sytt in sermons tyme', and anyone intruding on that space could be fined severely.[78] A reference of 1603 enhances the novelty of mayoral seating arrangement in the same church by citing a stool, not a bench or a pew, on which the mayor sat in his loft.[79]

---

[74] In Leicester the mayor's place on the parlour bench is set off by both the royal arms and flanking columns, as may still be seen.

[75] Chinnery, *Oak Furniture*, pp. 40–55 and plate I; A. Raine (ed.), *York Civic Records*, vol. 6 (Yorkshire Archeological Society, CXII, 1948 for 1946) p. 55, and vol. 7 (Yorks. Arch. Soc., CX, 1950 for 1949), p. 168; John Gloag, *The Englishman's Chair* (1964), p. 43.

[76] Chinnery, *Oak Furniture*, p. 42 and plate I.

[77] See, e.g. Richard Trexler, 'Ritual Behaviour in Renaissance Florence: the Setting', *Medievalia et Humanistica*, new ser., 4 (1973): 128–9, and Clifford Geertz, 'Centers, Kings and Charisma, Reflections on the Symbolics of Power', in J. Ben-David and T. N. Clark (eds.), *Culture and its Creators* (Chicago, IL, 1977), pp. 150–71.

[78] Bailey (ed.), *Minutes of Boston*, i, pp. 81, 463.   [79] *Ibid.*, p. 674.

Plate 45.   Mayor's Seat-and-Settle, Beverley Guildhall, 1604.

Like most other dignitaries, the mayor's pew rapidly obtained the sundry accoutrements which denoted his status within the parish and hence, the community. These commonly included pew doors,[80] cushions,[81] or even curtains of lace and silk.[82] And, notwithstanding the usual chronological progression of assigned seats described above, some urban parishes designated mayoral pews at a remarkably early date: by 1490 at St Martin's, Leicester.[83]

Many of the observations made above may bring to mind the growing embellishment of the monarchy itself in the Renaissance era. Such a connection, so far as it goes, is entirely appropriate. Yet it may be misleading to think of the connection between the built environment and the political culture of English towns as merely imitative of royal precedents and forms. The evidence before us would suggest instead a parallel development of physical and environmental features, borne of a similar political imperative but drawn from the rich political experience of towns themselves.

[80] Beresford, 'The Churchwardens' Accounts of Holy Trinity, Chester, 1532–1633', *Journal of the Chester and N. Wales Architectural, Archeological and History Society*, 38 (1951): 149.
[81] Foster (ed.), *Churchwardens' Accounts of St. Mary, Cambridge*, p. 432.
[82] E.g. St Martin's, Leicester: Cox, *Churchwardens' Accounts*, p. 193.
[83] *Ibid.*

6   *Country into court, court into country: John Scudamore of Holme Lacy (c. 1542–1623) and his circles*

W. J. TIGHE

John Scudamore, a son and eventually the head of a powerful Herefordshire family,[1] was an Elizabethan courtier. In 1571 or 1572[2] he became a member of the band of gentlemen pensioners, a fifty-man élite royal guard and court military corps. On 19 June 1599 he became standard-bearer of the gentlemen pensioners, the third-ranking of the band's three officers. In May 1603, when the formal establishment of James VI and I's new English court came into effect, he retired to his Herefordshire estates. An examination of Scudamore's various connections, familial, marital and professional, and the circles in which he moved, as well as his own interests and ambitions, reveals a distinct picture of the 'compenetration' of court influence and country authority in Elizabethan England.

---

[1] The Scudamores of Holme Lacy were a cadet branch of another Herefordshire family, the Scudamores of Kentchurch. The younger branch had settled at Holme Lacy by 1383. Earlier on, the Kentchurch Scudamores appear to have been the more prominent family of the two, but the uncompromising recusancy of two successive heads of the family, John Scudamore (1522–93) and his son Thomas (1543–1606), crippled the family during Elizabeth's reign. Thomas Scudamore's son John (1579–1616) conformed to the established church shortly after his father's death. In the next generation the family's head, another John Scudamore (1603–70), was to be a militant protestant, ever keen to detect and eradicate popery. Such protestant militancy was a rarity in Herefordshire at this period: the Harleys of Brampton Bryan are another, and a better-known, example. The relaxed, conservative conformity of the Holme Lacy Scudamores was more typical of the time and place. (The Elizabethan Sir John Scudamore was undoubtedly a conformist, yet for his sons' tutor he chose Thomas Holford, who in 1582 was reconciled to the Roman Church and went abroad to become a priest. He was hanged at Clerkenwell on 28 August 1588.) During the Civil War, John Scudamore of Kentchurch, like Sir Robert Harley, sided with Parliament. This was another rarity among gentry families in strongly royalist Herefordshire. (I wish to thank the American Philosophical Society and the National Endowment for the Humanities for the grants supporting my research in 1989 and 1990, respectively, and Mr Warren Skidmore of Akron, Ohio, and Mr George Hunt of Potton, Bedfordshire, for so freely sharing with me their own materials on the Scudamore family.)

[2] Scudamore's name does not appear on a check-roll of the band's members which covers the last quarter of 1570 (PRO, E 407/1/6) but it does occur on the next roll to survive, a fragment covering the second quarter of 1572 (PRO, E 407/2/187). Before he 'entered into ordinary' by being sworn into the band, Scudamore probably served for some time as a gentleman pensioner extraordinary, as did most aspirant gentlemen pensioners in Elizabeth's reign (W. J. Tighe, 'The Gentlemen Pensioners in Elizabethan Politics and Government', unpublished Ph.D. thesis, Cambridge University, 1984, pp. 25–8, 46–8).

Let us begin with passages from two letters to Scudamore which date from opposite ends of his career. On 21 January 1570 one Richard Willison wrote from Hereford to Scudamore at Croft Castle, the home of Sir James Croft, father of Scudamore's recently deceased first wife and newly appointed Comptroller of the Household to the queen.[3] The tone of Willison's letter appears to reflect a close familiar friendship between the writer and the recipient. His purpose in writing was to solicit Scudamore's support for a clergyman named Cooper who aspired to become a chaplain to Sir James Croft. The request made, Willison continued:

And if you doe pleasur Mr. Cooper in this sute, I will cause your grandfather to saie God have marcie to you. And one thing I will tell you Mr. Cowrtier, that we carles doe looke that promocion shold not make them to forgett theire owlde freendes. And yet *Honores mutant mores*. But that proverbe was made in the scornyng of hawghtie men. I mistruste not goodman John but that you will make your ffatherlawe and your grandfather presidentes of courtesey, whiche hathe woon unto them bothe the hartes of theire cowntrie. But this is more then neede. It is the lest feare that we have in you . . .[4]

The second letter was written over forty years later, on 10 December 1610. Its author was one of the great friends of Scudamore's mature years, Gilbert Talbot, earl of Shrewsbury. It was a brief, familiar letter of no great importance, written from the Jacobean court to the old Herefordshire knight. At one point, a tincture of melancholy stole into the earl's letter. 'Oft', he wrote

doe we remember the former worlde in this place, and the difference that is now betweene this and that, which is suche, as no man that lyves not in hit can conceave, but all worldly thynges are subiect to change and alteration and therfore in the generall not to be wondred att . . .[5]

It is the purpose of this essay to discuss Scudamore's career as an Elizabethan courtier of some consequence and as a Herefordshire gentleman of ever-increasing eminence in the hope that, by focusing on his career, some facets of the political culture of Tudor England in general and Elizabeth's reign in particular might emerge. In particular, it will be seen that far from being a consequence of the virgin queen's capricious glance and his own talents – undoubted though these were – Scudamore's entrée to court, the opportunity which he had to become a courtier, emerged almost willy-nilly from a great web of relationships, ancestral, marital, and familial, in which Scudamore chanced to be fortunately positioned. Once these circumstances opened him a way into the court,

---

[3] Croft was appointed unexpectedly ('*preter spem multorum*') on 7 January 1570, as Sir William Cecil wrote to Sir Ralph Sadler (*The State Papers and Leters of Sir Ralph Sadler, Knight-Banneret*, ed. Arthur Clifford (2 vols., Edinburgh, 1809), ii, p. 98). On 25 November 1569, however, the earl of Leicester, at that time Croft's patron, had written to Croft to summon him to court and to inform him that the queen was 'mynded to imploye you here about her owne person' (PRO, C 115/M19/7536). Scudamore's wife, Eleanor Croft, died early in December 1569.

[4] BL, Add. MS. 11,042, fos. 80–1.

[5] PRO, C 115/N2/8519. This letter (like so many others in the one-time Holme Lacy archive) was written jointly by the earl and countess (one of Bess of Hardwick's daughters).

however, Scudamore now had to match *fortuna* with his *virtù*, and in this daring and risky conjunction he emerged a winner. His success had its most significant consequences, however, not at court (he seems never to have sought or desired high state office there), but in the country, as he rose to become (after the death of Sir James Croft in 1590) probably the single most eminent local figure in the affairs of his shire. It is at this point, though, that the limits of Scudamore's strength begin to become apparent. If he lacked outright enemies, in Herefordshire and elsewhere, as seems, remarkably, to have been the case, he was not without rivals, and when one of these rivals was able to bring the influence of a great magnate in the person of Robert Devereux, earl of Essex, into these local disputes, Scudamore's sun had to suffer an eleven-year eclipse, one which was not, however, total; and the clouds parted for him in the end.

Scudamore was born 1 February 1542, according to the inquisition post mortem taken after his father's death on 22 April 1560.[6] Little information about the career of the father, William Scudamore, has come to light, but William's father, another John Scudamore, often termed 'the elder' in letters addressed to him during the 1560s[7] to distinguish him from his grandson, had been a courtier during the reign of Henry VIII. This John Scudamore, who was probably born between 1485 and 1490 (he married in 1511) had become a gentleman usher quarter waiter at some point prior to the sixth year of Henry VIII's reign (April 1514–April 1515).[8] For over twenty more years he remained a gentleman usher at court, rising in the course of time from quarter waiter to daily waiter.[9] Late in 1537 he resigned his court office after striking a bargain with Richard Blount of Mapledurham, Oxfordshire, whom he arranged, no doubt for a consideration, to succeed him in his office.[10]

The elder John Scudamore exercised a good deal of influence in Herefordshire down to his death in 1571.[11] He served as sheriff there in 1524–25,

<hr/>

[6] PRO, C 142/126/82.

[7] PRO, C 115/M15/7342 (Sir James Croft to John Scudamore 'th' elder,' 18 July 1562); BL, Add. MS. 11,049, fo. 7 (Sir James Croft to John Scudamore 'the yonger', n.d.).

[8] HMC, *Twelfth Report, Appendix, Part IV. The Manuscripts of His Grace the Duke of Rutland, G.C.B., preserved at Belvoir Castle* (3 vols., 1888), i, p. 21.

[9] *LP*, ii, pt. 1, no. 2735 (p. 872).

[10] BL, Add. MS. 11,042, fo. 45. Blount, later knighted, remained a gentleman usher for the remainder of Henry VIII's reign. In the course of Edward VI's reign he became one of the three gentlemen ushers of the privy chamber. Blount lost his court offices in Mary's reign but in 1560 he was appointed lieutenant of the Tower of London, an office which he held until his death in 1564. Michael Blount (d. 1609), Sir Richard's eldest son, was also to be lieutenant of the Tower between 1590 and 1595.

[11] He died 25 September 1571 (PRO, E 150/456/1). His tomb survives in Holme Lacy church. The inscription, below alabaster effigies of Scudamore and his first wife, Sybil Vaughan, describes Scudamore as 'sometyme one of the foure gentyllmen usheres unto our late sovaryne lord King henry the eighte & afterwarde admytted one of the esquiers for his highnes body'. A gentleman usher who became an esquire for the body would be making an advantageous move: his new office would be more prestigious and its duties less demanding. There is, however, no other evidence that Scudamore was an esquire for the body between 1537 and 1547. The tomb itself must date from between Henry VIII's death in 1547 and Scudamore's wife's death in 1559 since the spaces left for the insertion of both individuals' death dates remain blank to this day. (Scudamore subsequently remarried.) The inscription ends by requesting passers-by to 'say for ther soules a Pater Noster and Ave Marie'.

1536–37, 1543–44 and 1552–53, was a justice of the peace by 1528 and served as *custos rotulorum* of the Herefordshire commission of the peace for many years until his death. Upon John Rudhall's death in 1532 Scudamore replaced him as junior knight for the shire in Henry VIII's Reformation parliament. As a receiver of the court of augmentations he was active in the task of surveying, valuing, and managing the monastic lands in the west country which came into the Crown's hands in the last decade of Henry VIII's reign: his eldest son, William, served as his deputy in these tasks, and the elder Scudamore himself secured notable additions to his own estate in these years. For many years prior to his death in 1571 he was steward of Hereford: Holme Lacy is only four miles southeast of the city. In religion he was (as his will reveals) a strong conservative, and as such he was denounced more than once in the 1560s by John Scory, Edwardian bishop of Chichester, Marian exile and finally Elizabethan bishop of Hereford. Yet he was no recusant: when the privy council ordered all the justices of the peace to swear to uphold and practise the state of religion as by law established in November 1569, Scudamore complied.[12] The family was to remain conformist, but conformists of a highly conservative sort, shading off into recusancy in its cadet branches.

More important than Scudamore's grandfather in understanding how he came to be a courtier was Sir James Croft (b. 1517 or 1518, d. 1590), the heir of one of the oldest Herefordshire families.[13] The paths of Croft and John

---

[12] PRO, SP 12/19/26; SP 15/11, fo. 74v; SP 12/60/22, 22I, 22II. In his will, drawn up on 20 July 1571, the elder Scudamore commended himself to the prayers of the Virgin and all the saints and left to the poor a bequest of twenty pounds to pray for his soul (PRO, PROB 11/53, fos. 314r–15r [PCC 44 Holney]).

[13] Croft came to court in the early 1540s. In the parliament of 1542, when his father and paternal grandfather were both still living, he sat as junior knight for Herefordshire, and about the same time he formed a connection with Sir John Dudley, the future duke of Northumberland, who was senior knight for Staffordshire in the same parliament. Although he did not inherit his family estate until his father's death in January 1562, he had by that time experienced a full range of fortune and misfortune. Dudley's patronage facilitated Croft's steady rise in the Crown's service between 1543 and 1553. From April 1551 to April 1553 he served as Lord Deputy of Ireland, and by November 1551 he had become a gentleman of Edward VI's privy chamber. Early in Mary's reign he involved himself in the plots which led to Wyatt's Rebellion and, as a result, he was condemned to death for high treason on 28 April 1554. Released from the Tower some months later, he was spared execution but was not completely rehabilitated until a private act in Queen Elizabeth's first parliament restored him in blood and enabled him to inherit his patrimony. At first it seemed that the way to rapid advancement opened to him at the new queen's accession, and in April 1559 he was appointed governor of Berwick. Disaster followed: in the Scottish campaign of 1560 the duke of Norfolk, the English commander, managed to shift the blame for the lacklustre English performance at the siege of Leith onto Croft's shoulders. The result was that by the end of 1560 Croft had been ejected from his governorship of Berwick and had to spend the next nine years in discontented retirement in Herefordshire. However, early on in this period he had won the influential support of Robert Dudley, soon to be earl of Leicester and a son of Croft's former patron, the one-time duke of Northumberland. In the 1570s Croft and Leicester were to suffer a wrathful parting of the ways, but in the 1560s Croft was reputed to be one of Leicester's 'particular friends' who might (in Mr Secretary Cecil's informed opinion) expect rapid advancement if the earl managed to marry the queen. Possibly it was Leicester who effected Croft's return to court as Comptroller of the Household in 1569. Notwithstanding this disgrace, however, Croft was senior knight for Herefordshire in every parliament from 1562 down to his death in 1590. For all this concerning Croft (including more ample

Scudamore the younger crossed in 1561 when Croft was granted the wardship of the eighteen-year-old Scudamore some months after Scudamore's father's death in April 1560.[14] Within a matter of months Croft had arranged a marriage between his daughter Eleanor and his ward Scudamore, only to find that Scudamore's grandfather, John Scudamore the elder, had made some stringent financial demands as a condition of his agreement. Croft besought Robert Dudley's aid and Dudley wrote to the elder Scudamore on 1 December 1561 to urge on the marriage. In the course of his letter Dudley observed in passing that it was in order to further the marriage that he had procured Scudamore's wardship for Croft.[15] The letter had results, it seems: by July 1562 Croft could write to the elder Scudamore about the detailed arrangements for the imminent marriage.[16] Less than a year later Scudamore came of age and received licence to enter upon his lands from the court of wards.[17]

The marriage of John Scudamore and Eleanor Croft ended at the latter's death in December 1569. The couple produced five children, three sons and two daughters. The match appears to have cemented a close personal friendship between Scudamore and his father-in-law Croft, to judge from the numerous letters from Croft to Scudamore which survive among the Scudamore family papers.[18] Most of these letters are undated and many of them are not of great consequence: they include a mixture of gossip, tidings of disturbances in France and the Netherlands, requests by Croft to borrow money or to delay payments of instalments of his daughter's marriage portion, and the like. Perhaps Croft became a surrogate father for young Scudamore: there is more than a hint in some of these letters that Scudamore found his grandfather troublesome to deal with, and at one point Croft had to write to his son-in-law advising him to 'bere with youer grandfather for many respectes'.[19] When Croft was received back into the queen's favour in 1569 and was appointed comptroller of the Household in succession to Sir Edward Rogers in early 1570, it was a safe assumption that Scudamore would follow him thitherwards.

---

references) see W. J. Tighe, 'Courtiers and Politics in Elizabethan Herefordshire: Sir James Croft, His Friends and His Foes', *HJ*, 32 (1989): 257–79.

[14] PRO, C 66/968, m. 40.   [15] BL, Add. MS. 11,049, fo. 2.   [16] PRO, C 115/M15/7342.

[17] PRO, C 66/994, mm. 3–4.

[18] BL, Add. MS. 11,049, fos. 5–6, 24 November (1568?); fo. 7 (no date); PRO, C 115/M15/7335 (10 September 1568), 7336 (6 October 1568); M19/7546 (n.d.; 1568?), 7549 (6 November 1568). As a result of litigation over the descent of the Holme Lacy estate after the childless death, following over forty years of lunacy, of Frances Scudamore (1750–1820), wife of Charles Howard, K. G., eleventh duke of Norfolk (d. 1815), and last direct heir of the Holme Lacy Scudamores, the greater part of the family papers were deposited as evidence in the court of chancery, at which time an outline index, which remains the only catalogue or guide to these papers, was prepared. The eventual heirs not caring to reclaim the documents, save for a few deeds and wills which were destroyed in 1940 during the Blitz, they were eventually deposited with other chancery records in the Public Record Office where they became known as the 'Duchess of Norfolk Deeds'. At some point prior to the removal of the papers from Holme Lacy to London in 1817, certain items were abstracted from the family archive and eventually came into the possession of the British Museum, where at the present time they constitute BL, Add. MSS. 11,041–11,059. Other volumes among the Add. MSS. (11,407, 11,689, 11,816, 35,207) possibly contain material originally from Holme Lacy.

[19] PRO, C 115/M15/7341 (10 September n.y.).

Scudamore probably accompanied Croft to court late in 1569 or early in 1570. The earl of Leicester had written to Croft to summon him to court on 25 November 1569 and had instructed him to be there by the following Wednesday ('for that is your day', the earl wrote). Croft's appointment was announced on 7 January 1570 and a fortnight later Richard Willison wrote the letter to John Scudamore as 'Mr Courtier' which appeared at the beginning of this account. Scudamore was at Croft Castle when Willison wrote to him, but the letter's tone certainly suggests that Scudamore had recently been at court. In any event, he was to be there soon enough. On 4 July 1570 Croft wrote to Scudamore from London. After remarking on the uncertainty concerning the queen's intended progress, Croft added that if Scudamore could finish his business in the country and obtain his grandfather's permission: 'I woold you were heare againste the progresse, for the queene asked for you sens your departure, and therfore it is thought that she will looke for your attendannce about that tyme.'[20] The progress began shortly afterwards, for on 10 August 1570 Croft wrote again to his son-in-law from the court 'at chenynys' to call him to court. 'As my lord of leycester writethe to you', Croft began,

of her maiesties speeche towardes you wherof hys lordshyp heretofore informed, so was hyt her hyghnes pleasure to use the lyke speeche to me . . . with better wordes than I thynke your yonge yeres can yett deserve, and therefore hys lordshyp and I thought more than tyme to advyse you to come to the court which wylbe at rycott aboutes the xxvth of thys monthe. You most bryng some good spanyels with you for I have a hawke or two but I have no dogges . . .[21]

One might suppose that Scudamore did go to court shortly thereafter, although there is no evidence to substantiate this supposition. At some point in 1571 or early 1572 Scudamore became a gentleman pensioner.[22] It was during this period, on 25 September 1571, that Scudamore's octogenarian grandfather died and the newly established courtier came into his inheritance.[23] It is impossible to date the beginning of the bitter split between Scudamore's father-in-law Croft and the earl of Leicester beyond noting that it was well advanced by 1578, but it may be significant that the captain of the gentlemen pensioners (who normally proposed the names of new members of the band to the queen) was Thomas Radcliffe, earl of Sussex, the lord chamberlain, who was no friend of the earl of Leicester.[24]

---

[20] BL, Add. MS. 11,049, fo. 4.

[21] PRO, C 115/M15/7337. The omitted section is barely legible because of the decay of the paper. It may read 'apon [illegible] last'. No letter from the earl of Leicester corresponding to Croft's reference survives among the Holme Lacy papers.

[22] See note 2 above.   [23] PRO, E 150/456/1.

[24] HMC, *A Calendar of the Manuscripts of the Most Hon. the Marquess of Salisbury, K. G., preserved at Hatfield House, Hertfordshire* (22 vols., 1883–1971), ii, p. 214; R. E. Ham, 'The Autobiography of Sir James Croft', *BIHR* 50 (1977): 57. The split may have been occasioned by differences over foreign policy, more specifically, over the correct attitude to take towards the Dutch Revolt. Leicester was an interventionist from early on while Croft, who later became a Spanish pensioner, strongly disagreed. Croft was a definite protestant, although his admiration for the duke of Alba's wisdom in dealing

Scudamore remained Croft's friend for the rest of the comptroller's life. After some few years at court, however, Scudamore boldly made a marriage which, once the queen's initial, and characteristic, fury had subsided, immeasurably increased his standing at court and his influence generally. Scudamore's new wife was Mary Shelton, a daughter of Sir John Shelton of Shelton, Norfolk. Sir John had died in 1558, two days before Queen Mary; his mother, Anne (or Amy: the accounts differ) Boleyn, had been a sister of Sir Thomas Boleyn, Queen Elizabeth's maternal grandfather. At about the same time as Scudamore had become a courtier, so had Mary Shelton: on 1 January 1571 she entered into ordinary as a chamberer of the queen's privy chamber. A chamberer was the female equivalent of a groom, and received a groom's wages of twenty pounds a year. How the two began to consider marriage, or when, cannot be discovered, but by June 1573 matters had advanced sufficiently for the lord keeper, Sir Nicholas Bacon, to be counselling mistress Shelton about the proposed match, and indicating his approval of Scudamore's person and prospects, while at the same time Croft was offering Scudamore his encouragement. It was Croft, moreover, who hit upon the major dilemma: how to tell the queen. The queen's reluctance to countenance the marriage of her female familiars was already well-known by 1573, and the example of those who had contracted surreptitious marriages in the 1560s, like the Grey sisters, was far from encouraging.[25] To seek the queen's permission to marry might be an equally discouraging alternative: when Frances Howard sought the queen's permission in the late 1570s to marry Edward Seymour, earl of Hertford, the queen kept Howard, a gentlewoman of her privy chamber, waiting for nearly a decade before she allowed the marriage to take place.

Scudamore and Shelton presented the queen with a *fait accompli*. The marriage took place at some point between 10 November 1573 and 26 October 1574, probably in January 1574 or late December 1573. In a letter which Eleanor Bridges, a maid of honour at court, wrote to Edward, earl of Rutland, a letter dated only 'January' and consisting of court news and gossip, Bridges described the ill-temper that the queen had fallen into upon learning of the marriage. 'The queen hathe usid mary shelton very yell for hir mariage', Bridges wrote, 'she hath telt liberall bothe with bloes and yevell wordes, and hathe not yet graunted hir consent. I thinke in my consience', she ended, 'never woman bought hir hosbaunt more derare then she hath done', and eight years later the formidable Bess of Hardwick was telling the captive queen of Scots how Elizabeth had broken Mary Shelton's finger when attacking her with a candlestick.[26] By

---

with the first Dutch Revolt of 1568 shows that he was able to separate his religion from his politics to an extent quite unusual at the time (PRO, C 115/M19/7549). For evidence as to how gentlemen pensioners were nominated, see W. J. Tighe, 'Herbert Croft's Repulse,' *BIHR*, 58 (1985): 106–9.

25 PRO, C 115/M21/7611; M15/7338.
26 Janet Arnold (ed.), '*Lost from Her Majesties back*' (The Costume Society, Extra Series, vii, 1980), pp. 10–11, 15, 48 (item 162), 50 (item 179); HMC, *Twelfth Report* app., pt. iv, I, p. 107. I was able to

October 1574, nevertheless, Mary Scudamore had been received back into the queen's favour and was once again part of the privy chamber.

It seems fair to conclude that it was Scudamore's marriage which, more than any other contributing factor, more than the patronage of Sir James Croft, raised him above the body of his fellow gentlemen pensioners.[27] The privy chamber was closed to him, at least as regards an official appointment, as it was to most men during the queen's reign. He might have aspired to become a groom there, but it is difficult to imagine that had he become a groom of the privy chamber he would have been able to play so prominent a part in the affairs of Herefordshire as he did during the remainder of the queen's reign. The examples of the two cases in which a husband and his wife had positions in the privy chamber do not suggest that either partner in these pairs could enjoy much time away from court,[28] and when Scudamore was in Herefordshire, as sheriff in 1581–82, for example, his wife had to remain at court to attend on the queen.[29] How Scudamore divided his time between court and country between his marriage in 1574 and his promotion to standard-bearer of the gentlemen pensioners in 1599 (an office which would have required almost constant attendance) is difficult to discern. The gentlemen pensioners' check-rolls which survive for that period, while more than a few, are not as straightforward as at first sight might appear.[30] Nevertheless, it does appear from them that he spent considerably more time at court during this period than he did away from it. From June 1599 to May 1603 he appears to have been in constant attendance.[31]

It is easier to compose an orderly account of Scudamore's growing prestige in Herefordshire in the 1570s and 1580s, and of the reversal which he suffered at the hands of the earl of Essex in 1590, nevertheless, than it is to describe his

obtain a photocopy of this letter from the Belvoir Castle archive, for which I thank His Grace, the duke of Rutland.

[27] Scudamore was one of the few officers of the gentlemen pensioners who was not of noble extraction. The officers were captain, lieutenant, and standard-bearer. The captains were, successively, Thomas Radcliff, earl of Sussex, 1553–83; Henry Carey, Lord Hunsdon, 1583–96; and George Carey, Lord Hunsdon, 1596–1603. The lieutenants were Edward Fitzgerald, a younger son of an earl of Kildare, 1554/1558–90, and Sir Henry Grey, 1590–1603. But for the attainder of his uncle in 1554, Grey would have been marquess of Dorset. The standardbearers were Thomas Markham, 1559–72; Sir Charles Somerset, a younger son of an earl of Worcester, 1572–99; and Scudamore.

[28] These pairs were (1) John Astley (d. 1596), gentleman of the privy chamber and master of the jewel house, 1558–96, and his first wife, Katharine (d. 1565), chief gentlewoman of the privy chamber, 1558–65; and (2) Thomas Gorges (d. 1610), groom of the privy chamber 1571–1603, and his wife, Helena (d. 1635), marchioness of Northampton, a gentlewoman of the privy chamber from *c.* 1571.

[29] PRO, C 115/M15/7370.

[30] The section headed 'boardwages' appears to list the number of days in the quarter of a year with which the roll deals that each gentleman pensioner gave attendance. This is straightforward enough. However, a gentleman pensioner 'on duty' was allowed to produce one 'off duty' to substitute for him for all or part of his duty period. Some of the clerks of the check of the pensioners recorded such substitutions on the check rolls which they prepared, while others did not. So the attendance record is less clear than it would appear (Tighe, 'Gentlemen Pensioners', pp. 25–8).

[31] PRO, E 407/1/7–35; E 407/2/187. As standard-bearer of the gentlemen pensioners, Scudamore appears to have been in constant attendance from June 1599 onwards, quite possibly an illusion produced by the method of record keeping of the clerk of the check. Scudamore does not appear to have been often in Herefordshire during these years, however.

court career. There are a good many letters in what was once the Holme Lacy archive from some of Scudamore's fellow courtiers, and of these a number suggest the circles in which Scudamore moved, but until the series of letters to Scudamore from Gilbert Talbot, earl of Shrewsbury, begin in 1590 there is little hard information. The nature of the evidence compels the narrator to discuss Scudamore's court career and country interests separately, and his wife's activities at court as a third story, but these distinctions are a narrative strategy rather than an accurate representation of reality.

By November 1569 Scudamore had joined his grandfather on the Herefordshire commission of the peace as one of the quorum. In the 1571 parliament Scudamore served in the House of Commons for the first time as junior knight of the shire; the senior knight was his father-in-law, Croft. Scudamore was to be returned as junior knight (with Croft as the senior) in 1572, 1584, 1586, and 1589. In 1593 and 1601 he was to step aside to allow Herbert Croft (Sir James's grandson) to serve as junior knight, while in 1597 Scudamore was again to be junior knight. On this occasion (as in 1593 and 1601) the senior knight was Sir Thomas Coningsby, one of Scudamore's fellow gentlemen pensioners and, more importantly in this context, a client of Scudamore's competitor for local influence, the earl of Essex. By 1574 Scudamore had become *custos rotulorum* on the Herefordshire commission of the peace and by 1575 he was one of the two deputy lieutenants of Herefordshire to Sir Henry Sydney, lord president of the council in the Marches of Wales; Scudamore's colleague in the lieutenancy was Coningsby. Throughout the 1570s Scudamore was receiving grants of the stewardship of various manors in the Marches from the Crown. He was also purchasing land and, on occasion, Scudamore and his wife received reversionary leases of crown land from the queen for their service. In 1581–82 Scudamore was sheriff of Herefordshire.[32]

As for Scudamore's career at court, the survival of a great number of letters from his fellow courtiers and other officials in the family archive illuminate some of the connections which he made in these years. Most of them date from the decade of the 1580s, and onwards to the end of the reign, while a few continue to within a few years of his death in 1623. Some of them are cool and formal, betokening no great friendship;[33] others suggest that the correspondents

[32] *CPR*, v (1569–72), p. 225; *ibid.*, vi (1572–75), p. 342; vii (1575–78), pp. 300–1, 427; PRO, SP 12/96, p. 113; SO 12/107/15.

[33] Such was the letter which Scudamore's fellow gentleman pensioner, the poet Arthur Gorges, wrote to him on 7 June 1582 to complain of the disrespectful treatment which he had received from one of Scudamore's servants. Other correspondents wrote with straightforward requests: Humphrey Baskerville in 1582 (the first of many who were to make similar requests over the subsequent four decades) for a loan; Lord Henry Seymour, later in the same year, to ask Scudamore to inform the queen about the magnitude of Seymour's debts, and about how he was unable, in consequence, to sustain the expenses of being a courtier; Thomas Harley, a Herefordshire gentleman and father of the parliamentarian Sir Robert Harley, in 1587, to disavow knowledge of a plan to marry his wife's sister to Scudamore's oldest son (Scudamore had other matrimonial plans for him); Camilla Harvey, widow of a recently deceased gentleman pensioner, in 1602, to send Scudamore a mourning garment

were clearly on more intimate terms with Scudamore.[34] More suggestive is the single letter from Sir George Carey to Scudamore. The eldest son of Henry, Lord Hunsdon, Queen Elizabeth's closest kinsman and, at the time, lord chamberlain and captain of the gentlemen pensioners, Carey was both knight marshal of the royal household and captain of Carisbrooke Castle on the Isle of Wight; when he inherited his father's peerage in 1596 he was to be granted the offices which his father had occupied as well. On 15 June 1585, having arrived at Carisbrooke, Carey wrote Scudamore a long friendly letter. After initial salutations and professions of good will, Carey delivered himself of what he termed 'a pleasinge opinion' concerning 'the differences betwixte the places of bothe our presente aboudes' or, in other words, between country life and court life. 'We live here', Carey began,

subiecte to the sodden assaulte of fforren foes to abide the firste brunt of their furye, you in courte dailie in hazarde to be daungerouslie poisoned with the secrette stinges of smilinge enemies: the fource of our foes to be resisted with the like, and revenge to be retourned as we maie and dare, the dartz of your enemies despite as unseene not to be warded, theie stronge, you weake, therfore to be yelded unto: so that in this our advantage I glorye, and that you cannot triumphe in the like giveth cause to preferre the contrie before the courte. But now, Sir, yf we shall have warres, as the kinge of Spaine hathe occasioned us, goode John for youre owne sake comme uppon the firste breakinge out thereof hither, we shall have better booties, richer spoiles and braver roberies here aboutes in one daie, then you shall have in Wales in seven yeres: you shalbe metropolitan of the pirattes, surveigher, controuller and commaunder of a notable sorte of theeves, as, in mine opinion, for their government the fittest capten in Englande. Refuse not my offer. I will performe more then I promiss, and believe me, you shall not be better welcome to home lacye: yf time give me this advantage to pleasure you, you shall finde my goodewill and I your comminge.[35]

This is a fine piece of rhetoric, even if it is difficult to decide how seriously it was meant. If it was a serious offer, Scudamore never accepted it.

Another friend and correspondent of Scudamore was Thomas Kerry. Kerry, a native of Hereford, had become a clerk of the privy seal during the reign of Queen Mary and was to remain one until his death in 1607.[36] Kerry's office

---

which she requested him to wear in memory of her husband; and many others (PRO, C115/M17/ 7430, 7432; M18/7501, 7513; HMC, *Manuscripts of the Marquess of Salisbury*, ii, pp. 536–7).

[34] Witness the familiar, even teasing, letters from John St John extending (not all are dated) from the early 1580s to the early 1590s. St John (b. 1544) was the oldest son of the John St John who had been created first Lord St John of Bletso in 1559. He had been an esquire for the body at court from the early 1570s until he succeeded to his father's peerage in 1582. Writing in February 1582 to Scudamore when the latter was in Herefordshire as sheriff, St John began his newsletter with the comment that 'it is a hardd course to comytt the sheppe to the wolffe to keppe and the foxe to have chardge over pullen. Yf a badd reckening be madde of the floxe the owners must blame them selfes for apointyng suche keppers. And it is no lesse to be loked for when scourers of the plaine and wanderers over Newmarkett Heythe have auctorytty over trew men and are madde the Q. maiesties levetennante over riche fermers . . .' (PRO, C 115/M15-7374).

[35] PRO, C 115/M15/7364.

[36] PRO, LC 2/4(2), fo. 29v; 2/4(4), fo. 49r. Kerry had settled in Hampshire by the time of his death, but in his will he provided for the foundation of an almshouse in his native Hereford (PRO, PROB

made him privy to a good deal of useful information which he proved willing to share with his friends. For example, he was well placed to exercise influence over the distribution of burdens when the Crown had occasion to raise money by privy seal loans.[37] Having a friend in Kerry's position enabled Scudamore to mediate between Herefordshire and the court with no small increase of prestige for himself. Such connections, however, did not necessarily assure that Scudamore himself would be able to secure the favour of the court, a case in point being the local offices which he hoped to obtain on the death of his father-in-law, Sir James Croft, on 4 September 1590. Whatever hopes Scudamore may have entertained of succeeding to Croft's offices in Herefordshire were blasted by the intervention of the earl of Essex and the influence of his followers and friends, in particular his deputy at Leominster, Thomas Coningsby.[38]

In Hereford city Scudamore's friends also had to deal with aggressive opposition from clients of the Essex–Coningsby faction. On 16 September 1590 the mayor of Hereford, Richard Parrott, wrote to Scudamore at court to inform him that since ancient custom gave the privilege of nominating a steward of the city to the mayor, he had, upon learning of Croft's death, nominated Scudamore for the position, despite 'my self being secrettlie sought for my good will to preferre my l. of Essex in the roome', a passage (one of two in the letter) which was subsequently inked out, presumably by Scudamore as recipient,

and have published the same in open Courte to the discontentment of your secret ennemies who wrought by all diligens to crosse you *vizt. olde Mr Church and his sonne the Swordbearer, Brian Newton, and the undersheryfe Mr Pembridge and their chiefest*

11/110, fos. 124v–128r [PCC 63 Huddlestone]). The first surviving letter from Kerry to Scudamore dates from April 1584 (BL, Add. MS. 11,042, fo. 44).

[37] In a letter of 6 October 1589, for instance, Kerry related to Scudamore with obvious pleasure the tale of how he had successfully thwarted Thomas Coningsby's attempt to get one of his friends, Gregory Price, exempted from making any contribution to the loan. Coningsby had first approached Kerry with the request that Price's assessment be lowered from fifty pounds to twenty-five. Kerry agreed to get Price's assessment lowered but was annoyed to discover that Coningsby had gone to Walsingham to get the remainder remitted as well. Kerry assured Scudamore that he would do his best to see that Price's assessment at twenty-five pounds should stand, and in the end Price had to pay (PRO, C 115/M12/7214).

[38] Coningsby had been at court from time to time in the early 1570s as one of the performers on the tilt-yard, although he did not acquire his gentleman pensionership until 1589. Throughout the 1570s and early 1580s he was closely associated with Philip Sydney (with whom he travelled in Europe in the early 1570s) and, to some extent, with the earl of Leicester. In the Rouen campaign of 1591 Coningsby served as Essex's muster master, and it was from the earl that Coningsby received his knighthood on 8 October 1591. Essex was determined to make South Wales and the Marches, an area from which the Devereux family had originally arisen, the focal point of his influence and strength. He dominated the whole region down to his fall in 1601, and in Herefordshire his interests were to match well with those of Coningsby. Coningsby had become recorder of Leominster in 1583, after the death of the previous recorder, James Warnecombe. The borough had selected Coningsby despite the opposition of its steward, Sir James Croft. Warnecombe, who had been serving as recorder upwards of thirty years at the time of his death, had been Croft's brother-in-law, and Croft subsequently intended the office to pass to his step-son, Thomas Wigmore. From the contest over the recordership sprang the ensuing strife between Coningsby and his friends and the Crofts and their kinsmen. The earl of Essex became steward of Leominster late in 1590 or early in 1591, with Coningsby serving as his deputy there. Sir James Croft's grandson, Herbert Croft, expected to be granted a share of his grandfather's many minor local offices, but Essex intervened to block the

countenaunce to further their intent heerein your worship may well know commith from the Priorie, who labored for voices. But nowe your worship being seated let them displace as they maye.[39]

'The Priorie', Hereford Priory, a former Dominican religious house, was at that time the home of Thomas Coningsby's friend and brother-in-law, Gregory Price; Coningsby was later to acquire the property and to convert it into an almshouse for old soldiers. In the 1580s, however, while Sir James Croft was still steward of the city, the Priory was the focal point of opposition to the dominance of civic political life by Croft's friends and kinsmen.

Shortly thereafter Scudamore drafted a letter to the city corporation of Hereford. Thanking the city fathers for their unanimous endorsement of the mayor's nomination, he accepted their offer of the stewardship and sought the continuance of their good will towards him. 'And for that I am now placed in that office of your mere mocion without any seking or suite of myne', he wrote in a final sentence which appears to betray some uneasiness, 'so I trust you will have due consideracion whatt disgrace and indignyte it shold be unto me to be displaced without iust cause of my part yelded, a thing heartofore in that place never used nor fitt to be offord to the menest your Societie'.[40] What Scudamore feared soon came to pass, although in the absence of documentation it is impossible to specify the circumstances and date: displaced he was and the earl of Essex chosen steward in his place. Possibly connected with this reversal of fortune was an affray or riot at Ross-on-Wye in October 1590 in which Henry Scudamore, John Scudamore's eldest son, and at least five companions assaulted the former undersheriff, Pembridge, and his attendants. Essex's prompt complaint to the privy council resulted in the alleged rioters' swift apprehension.[41]

Evidently the bad feeling which these incidents generated was slow to die, since two years later, on 2 August 1592, the earl of Essex wrote a cold letter to Scudamore to complain of 'the obstinate and crosse dealinges of Garnaunce & Clark' in animating their friends to oppose Essex's servants and friends 'especiallie in the citie causes' in which Essex, as steward, had particular interests. 'Yf you desier that I should hold that good opinion of you', the earl concluded

grants, so that, in the end, Croft was unwillingly driven to make a very disadvantageous composition with the earl (see the articles by Tighe cited in notes 13 and 24).

[39] BL, Add. MS. 11,053, fos. 30–1. The phrase italicized in the longer part of the quotation was the second passage in the letter which was inked out. Under an ultra-violet lamp both passages could be reconstructed. The sheriff of Herefordshire in 1589–90 was Thomas Baskerville. Both Baskerville and his undersheriff, Anthony Pembridge, were 'faction-friends' of Thomas Coningsby.

[40] PRO, C 115/M21/7618.

[41] *APC*, xx, pp. 69–70, 76–7, 104–5, 114–16. Among Scudamore's papers are two undated letters, one from his wife, the other from Jane Devereux, his father's sister, widow of Sir William Devereux, both interceding for Henry Scudamore with his father (PRO, C 115/M15/7368, 7369). Possibly they date from early 1591 and allude to the aftermath of the riot at Ross. Henry Scudamore appears to have died in 1591 or possibly 1592, as Scudamore's second son, John, the seminary priest, was describing himself as Scudamore's heir by the latter year.

which in your protestacions you seemed to make account of: you cannot declare it better, then by your carefull endevor to restrayne the insolencies of such as use or abuse your name therein: which if you performe, I will be towardes you, as I have professed: otherwise, if you shall soffer them to continewe this course of crossinge me, and those that depend of me; I must reforme it as I may, and conceyve of you as I fynd.[42]

A suggestion that Scudamore should be added to the council in the Marches of Wales, found among lord Burghley's papers, probably dates from these years: it was not put into effect, probably because the president of the council, the earl of Pembroke, was one of Essex's friends and followers down until 1596 or 1597.[43]

It is my impression that Scudamore was more completely a courtier in the 1590s than in earlier decades, in the sense that he spent more time there and made it rather than Herefordshire the principal focus of his interest for the time being, but it is difficult to verify the impression. His willingness to stand aside in 1593 so that Herbert Croft could become one of the shire knights for Herefordshire in that year's parliament may be an indication of this, although there is, again, no clear evidence.[44]

In September 1592, the queen knighted Scudamore.[45] On 12 October 1592, Scudamore's wife wrote a letter to the earl and countess of Shrewsbury which appears to be a response to their congratulations for Sir John's elevation. It is one of the earliest datable pieces of evidence for the friendship, seemingly close and affectionate, which existed between the Scudamores and Gilbert and Mary Talbot.[46] By 1591 Scudamore had become steward of Archenfield and, as such,

---

[42] PRO, C 115/M19/7558. William Garnons and Thomas Clarke were both aldermen of Hereford and friends of Scudamore. Clarke was later to be mayor of Hereford and was, throughout the period Scudamore's receiver of rents (BL, Add. MS. 11,053, fos. 41r, 58r, 65r, 68r).

[43] HMC, *Manuscripts of the Marquess of Salisbury*, xiii, p. 457. The document is undated, but it can be no earlier than September 1592, when Scudamore was knighted.

[44] Lambeth Palace Library, Talbot MS. H., fo. 519. Sir Thomas Coningsby was senior knight in 1593, 1597, and 1601. In 1597 Scudamore was once again junior knight. In 1601 Herbert Croft and Sir James Scudamore, Sir John's son, banded together in an unsuccessful attempt to defeat Coningsby. The result was that Croft had the junior seat a second time.

[45] Information on the dating of Scudamore's knighthood – his name does not appear among the individuals listed in W. A. Shaw's *Knights of England* (1906) – has been communicated to me by Dr Ian Atherton of the University of Sheffield. In all likelihood, according to Dr Atherton, Scudamore was knighted by the queen on 14 September 1592 at Sudeley Castle, the Gloucestershire seat of Giles, Lord Chandos, at which the queen was staying in the course of her westward progress. I am grateful to Dr Atherton for his kind assistance.

[46] 'For that Mrs. Skidmors sake who was ever bound to you, I do offer myself, Ladiship & all, to be at your service', she wrote at the beginning of the letter. Following remarks about the queen's grateful acceptance of the Shrewsburys' recent letter, her intention to go on progress next year and to visit the earl and countess in the course of it, all of which was, no doubt, of great interest to the pair, she concluded 'as for my husband Sr. John my Ladiship never sawe him sence the Q. did him that favor. I doubt me, he hath playd me a walch trick, for except he be with you, I know not what is become of him' (Lambeth Palace Library, Talbot MS. H., fo. 441). That the earl and countess reciprocated these sentiments can easily be discerned among the many letters which they wrote to Scudamore and his lady. As an example we may take a letter of which the earl and countess each wrote a part before sending it to Scudamore. The letter is undated, but since it was endorsed by the countess ('to my good cosen and assured frend Mr. John Scudamore esquier give this') it must date from between the death of the earl's father in November 1590 and Scudamore's knighthood in September 1592. It appears from the contents that Scudamore was at Holme Lacy, which might allow a tentative dating of *c.* July/August 1591 when, from the evidence of Robert Compton's letter of 31 July 1591 to

was responsible for the general oversight of the earl's estates in the Welsh Marches.[47] In all likelihood, and despite the absence of evidence in his surviving papers, Scudamore had probably become acquainted with Gilbert Talbot, the future earl, at court, earlier on in his career as a gentleman pensioner.[48] As for Scudamore's wife, we have already seen some evidence of her influence and of her importance in the advancement of her husband's career. Her influence proceeded from her intimate service upon the queen at court, where she retained her position in the privy chamber from 1571 to the queen's death in 1603.[49]

The rebellion of the earl of Essex in February 1601 and his subsequent execution transformed the political scene in the Marches. Herbert Croft hoped to succeed Essex as steward of the borough of Leominster, and successfully sought Sir Robert Cecil's support for his candidacy. But Sir Thomas Coningsby had already prevailed upon Leominster to choose him as town's steward by the time Cecil's letter on Croft's behalf arrived there.[50] Coningsby and Croft had been at odds for nearly twenty years by 1601 and Croft, as the weaker party, had been cultivating Cecil for some time. Cecil, however, accepted the *fait accompli*

Scudamore's friend, and alderman of Hereford, William Garnons (BL, Add. MS. 11,053, fo. 40), Scudamore had recently left the court at Greenwich and 'toke his cooche homewardes'. It is not clear from whence the letter was written. 'Sir', they began, 'the best construction we can make of your not visityng us her according to your promis is that you are in expectation of the cummyng of the good wyfe of the signe of the Lylly pott at the Tyltyard to her other John at homlacy now her Maiestie is so nere you: which if you be, then it is sumwhat honestly to be answered, or els not, and if that gentellwoman doe cum thither, yet I suppose her abode ther will not be so longe, as bothe she and your selfe wolde wyshe, and then we will hope to see you here after her departure whether you shalbe as wellcumm to the good wyfe of this house as casebobby can make you' (PRO, C 115/M19/7560). 'Casebobby', Welsh for 'toasted cheese' (*caws bobi*), probably indicates that the earl and countess were somewhere in the Welsh Marches also, and not at Sheffield Castle, their principal seat. The countess, in her part of the letter, inquired whether Scudamore's wife was at Holme Lacy and asked them to visit the earl and countess before returning to London. In December 1583 the Dean of Lichfield, George Boleyn, wrote a letter to the earl in which he expressed some doubt about Lady Scudamore's ability – though not her willingness – to succeed in advancing her friends' suits at court (Lambeth Palace Library, Shrewsbury MS. 707, fos. 221–2).

47 Lambeth Palace Library, Talbot MS. H., fo. 293; M., fo. 133; Shrewsbury MS. 701, fo. 171; 704, fos. 21–2; 707, fo. 209; BL, Add. MS. 11,053, fos. 80–1. At court, both Scudamore and Thomas Kerry became deeply involved in the negotiations concerning Shrewsbury's purchase of the Welbeck Abbey estate in Nottinghamshire from the Crown, and Kerry in particular appears to have acted as a financial counsellor and business agent for the earl since his succession to the title in 1590 (Lambeth Palace Library, Shrewsbury MS. 698, fos. 153–4; 701, ff. 9–11).

48 Thomas Kerry, for instance, had written to the new earl immediately upon hearing of his succession to the title to offer him both congratulations and financial advice – and a warning to beware new friends, since Shrewsbury's great wealth will mean that 'everie man now will sing placebo' (Lambeth Palace Library, Shrewsbury MS. 701, fos. 173–4). There is some evidence, moreover, that around 1593 Scudamore played a part in attempting to secure better terms for his cousin Sir John Pakington, who had recently received a reversionary grant of the controversial starch monopoly, by acting as an intermediary between Pakington and Lord Burghley (BL, Lansdowne MS. 73, fos. 32, 33).

49 A full treatment of the nature and extent of the influence which Lady Scudamore exercised at court, or was believed to possess, as of the profits she was able to derive from her situation, must await another occasion. Let it suffice to observe that throughout the 1590s suitors were constantly attempting to enlist her efforts on their behalf with the queen or with high court officials. Nor did she escape being tainted with the general accusations of rapacity which were hurled at the privy chamber staff from all quarters during the last decade of the queen's reign. A fair amount of manuscript material that bears upon Lady Scudamore's career as a courtier survives in various collections, but it does not permit so detailed a reconstruction of her career as is possible for that of her husband.

50 HMC, *Manuscripts of the Marquess of Salisbury*, xi, p. 114, 160–1.

and the cautious expressions of respect and deference which subsequently Coningsby offered him.

In Hereford there was a great struggle over the vacant stewardship of the city. To construct a coherent account of the struggle is far from easy, since the sources are few and, more importantly, all of those of which I am aware represent the communications, complaints, and opinions of the partisans of one side only among the two contending factions: Scudamore's. No doubt the other side would have had a significantly different tale to tell, but in the absence of further evidence my account will have to rely on these sources.[51]

In the bill of complaint which Richard Parrott, an alderman of Hereford and long a friend of Scudamore, lodged in star chamber after Scudamore had been chosen and confirmed as the city's steward, Sir Thomas Coningsby was singled out as the principal cause of the recent troubles. His malice and hatred of Scudamore, and his envy of the credit, estimation, and love which Scudamore enjoyed in Hereford had, the complainant alleged, impelled Coningsby to confederate himself with Henry Vaughan, the sheriff of Herefordshire, Anthony Pembridge, a former undersheriff and a solicitor to the late earl of Essex, James Smith, mayor of Hereford, and other aldermen and citizens of Hereford to prevent Scudamore's choice as steward. That Coningsby was the moving spirit behind the attempt to keep Scudamore out is both possible and plausible, but Parrott's complaint is the only direct allegation, and the absence of related material in the star chamber records probably indicates that the case there did not proceed much beyond the initial stages.

Some sort of faction fight was in prospect virtually from the time of the earl's death. When a group of ten aldermen and some other citizens of Hereford wrote to Scudamore on 27 March 1601 to announce their intention 'to honor you with the title of our Stuardshipp as far forth as in us lyeth', they went on to observe that 'some hart burninge and faccious people doe live amongeste us, crossing our intencions in what they cane'. Late in the afternoon of 21 April 1601, at a routine meeting of the city council, the mayor nominated, unexpectedly and (according to a letter which some of Scudamore's friends wrote to him on 28 April 1601) contrary both to his promise and to the charter and customs of the city, a steward: William Herbert, earl of Pembroke. Pembroke, a young man not a fortnight past his twenty-first birthday at the time, had little standing on his

---

[51] The sources for the account which follows are: (1) PRO, C 115/M20/7581: various aldermen and others of the city of Hereford to Scudamore, 27 March 1601. (2) BL, Add. MS. 11,053, fos. 68–9: various aldermen and others of the city of Hereford to Scudamore, 28 April 1601. (3) BL, Add. MS. 11,042, fos. 9–10: Thomas Clarke, alderman of Hereford, to Scudamore, 4 May 1601. (4) PRO, C 115/M21/7614: Herbert Croft to William, earl of Pembroke, undated. (5) PRO, C 115/M21/7615: 'Observations of dyvers misdemeanors commytted by Sir Thomas Coningsby, knight, Henry Vaughan, esquier, sheriff of the Countie of Hereff, Anthony Pembrige, sollicitor to the late Earle of Essex, Epiphanie Haworth, John Davys and others their accomplices sithence the decease of the said late Earle', undated, but seemingly a preliminary short draft version of (6) PRO, STAC. 5/P 44/22: bill of complaint to the court of star chamber by Richard Parrott, citizen and alderman of Hereford, against Sir Thomas Coningsby and others, undated. The undated documents all date from 1601.

own account in Herefordshire. However, his father, the second earl of that creation, Henry Herbert, had been lord president of the council in the Marches of Wales from 1586 to his recent death on 19 January 1601, and it is possible that the young earl or his supporters hoped to capitalize on the memory which the earl's father left behind before it faded. The speculation aside, it is clear, from both Thomas Clarke's letter of 4 May 1601 to Scudamore and Herbert Croft's undated letter to Pembroke, that the earl responded with an eager affirmative to the prospect of obtaining the office. In vain did Croft attempt to warn Pembroke against 'the overweening error of those that by usinge your lordships name desired to create an opinyon of their owne power which they have not' and who would abandon Pembroke, he claimed, when his candidacy had served their turn.

Clarke's letter asserted that only eleven persons were present at the council meeting on 21 April 1601 at which the mayor nominated Pembroke: four of these Clarke noted as 'your ffrendes', the rest as enemies.[52] He also noted that the earl had written to the city to designate Pembridge as his deputy steward. Clarke wrote on the evening of the city's 'lawday', 4 May 1601, after a tumultuous meeting of the city court at which the mayor and his friends had tried to rush through the confirmation of Pembroke's nomination under the pretext that the city could not transact its ordinary affairs without a steward. The mayor's attempt, and attempted justification, caused a great uproar. Most of the aldermen present stood up to contradict the mayor who 'after many speaches . . . was driven unto a non plus' and had to defer the selection of a steward to the customary day, the Monday after Michaelmas, which in 1601 fell on 5 October.

James Smith, the mayor of Hereford, was, as we have seen, a strong proponent of Pembroke's selection as steward. His term of office was approaching its end, however. A new mayor was to be nominated on 3 August 1601 and sworn into office on the same day that the steward should be elected, the Monday after Michaelmas. Parrott stated in his star chamber complaint that Thomas Clarke was to be nominated mayor in August, but also that when Pembroke's partisans discovered that he would stand fast for Scudamore, they resolved to employ all the means that they could to disenfranchise Clarke so as to render him ineligible for the office and to substitute for him Thomas Crumpe, an alderman of their own faction. First (according to Perrott's complaint) they so inflamed an old quarrel between Smith and Clarke that the outgoing mayor called for a session of the city court on the last day of July to proceed against Clarke who, having been out of the city the whole time, knew nothing of what was happening. The next problem which they faced was the fact that the supporters of the 'Pembroke faction' included only a minority of the alderman and chief citizens of the city. Some method had to be devised to procure or

---

[52] Among Scudamore's friends on the list was Richard Parrott, whose star chamber complaint is the only source for subsequent developments in the controversy.

enforce their absence from the session of the city court which the mayor had just called to oust Clarke.

The solution to their dilemma involved the sheriff of Herefordshire, Henry Vaughan, one of Coningsby's friends. At the beginning of Trinity Term 1601, Pembridge (it appears) procured four writs of *latitat*, each one in the name of a different alderman of Hereford, from the court of queen's bench. The aldermen in whose names the writs were issued were all (perhaps with one exception) confederates of Smith, and the writs were each directed against one or more of the supporters of Scudamore on the city court. Immediately upon receipt of the writs, and without disclosing them or acting upon them, Vaughan returned a false certificate to the court which alleged that he had delivered the writs to the 'head officer' of Hereford, to whom the execution of writs in the city precincts belonged, who had not executed them: this so that the sheriff could obtain new writs containing a clause of *non omittas* which would enable him personally to enter into the city liberties in order to execute the writs. The better to bolster their attempt, the agents of Coningsby, the mayor and their associates appear, moreover, to have searched in the records of the court of common pleas for outlawries against individuals bearing the same names and surnames as the aldermen of Hereford who supported Scudamore. Early on the morning of 31 July, Coningsby, Pembridge, and the sheriff arrived in Hereford where they assembled sixteen 'ryotous and disordered armed persons' who 'did marche upp and downe the streetes & markett place of . . . Hereford and with lowde voices did proclaime, publishe & give oute that they had process of outlarie to attache fifeteene of the said Aldermen and cheif Cittizens' while Smith and Pembridge stationed themselves at the doors of the market house where the city court was to be held in order to arrest their opponents as they arrived. In vain did they labour, for their opponents had gotten wind of the plot against them and had installed themselves in the market house during the preceding night. Clarke was not disenfranchised and subsequently became mayor. The immediate consequence of the plot's failure was a riot in the course of which the sheriff's 'posse' attacked the house of an alderman and Scudamore supporter, George Hurdman. Despite this failure of their first attempt, the sheriff and his men were back in force again after Michaelmas. On 3 October, as Parrott alleged, they arrested, beat, and imprisoned him by virtue of writ of outlawry against one Richard Parrott of London. Nevertheless, on 5 October 1601 Scudamore was elected steward of Hereford.

The successful conclusion of this struggle may be regarded in some respects as the happy climax of Scudamore's dual career as a courtier and a countryman. On 20 May 1602 Scudamore was appointed a member of the council in the Marches of Wales (Coningsby had to wait until 1617 for his appointment).[53] At

---

[53] PRO, C 115/M24/7749.

the same time as the struggle for the city stewardship was being played out in Hereford, Scudamore's son, Sir James,[54] and his nephew, Herbert Croft, had joined together in a determined effort to prevent Coningsby, who had been senior knight for the county in the 1593 and 1597 parliaments, from representing Herefordshire in the 1601 parliament.[55] The attempt failed after an intense faction fight of which little detailed evidence has survived: once again Coningsby was senior knight with Croft as junior, but it was to be the last time that the lame, turbulent, and eccentric knight was to sit in the House of Commons.[56]

Queen Elizabeth died on 24 March 1603. When her household was dissolved after her funeral on 28 April both Sir John and his wife lost their court offices. It is possible, even likely, that they went willingly: Lady Scudamore had been ailing for some time and was, in the event, not long to outlive her former mistress and kinswoman.[57] Sir John, on the other hand, had two decades left to live before he died full of years at the age of eighty-one on 14 April 1623.[58] These years were not wholly free from troubles: the decade after 1603 saw the bitter break-up of Sir James Scudamore's second marriage, and in 1619 Sir James died. In the final years of his life Sir John appears to have been troubled by both failing eyesight and the desire of Lord and Lady Grey of Ruthin to dispossess him of the various offices which he had received from Lady Grey's father, the

---

[54] Sir James Scudamore (1568–1619) was Sir John's third son by birth but second surviving son after *c.* 1591. (Sir John appears to have wholly ignored his second son, John, the Catholic priest, even after the latter returned to England and to protestantism in 1606.) The absence of his correspondence and papers from the surviving Scudamore material makes it difficult to trace his career. He was often at court in the 1590s, but he does not appear to have held an official position there. He is often confused with his father in secondary accounts, or else described as a gentleman pensioner, which he never was: see Lisa Hopkins, *Queen Elizabeth I and Her Court* (New York, 1990), p. 79 for the most recent of many examples. Beginning in March 1595 Scudamore served regularly for some years as a tilt-yard combatant, appearing at the accession day festivities in 1596, 1597, 1598, 1599, and 1600: Roy Strong, *The Cult of Elizabeth* (1977), appendix 1. Sir James received his knighthood during the Cadiz expedition of 1596. If he received it from Essex it would imply that the unpleasant affair of the Hereford city stewardship in 1591 had left no permanent legacy of antagonism between the earl and the Scudamores, but Essex, although lavish in distributing the honour whenever he had an opportunity to do so, was not the only commander who conferred knighthoods during the expedition: Charles, Lord Howard of Effingham, the lord admiral, was another, and he was no great friend of Essex.

[55] P. W. Hasler (ed.), *The Commons 1558–1603* (3 vols., 1981), pp. 174–5. In the 1604 and 1614 parliaments Sir James Scudamore was senior knight for Herefordshire with Sir Herbert Croft as junior. By 1621, with Sir James dead and Sir Herbert, a convert to Catholicism, a religious refugee in France, Sir John Scudamore (1601–71), Sir James's eldest son, a baronet and future viscount, sat as senior knight in that year's parliament although not yet twenty-one years of age, with Sir Thomas Coningsby's only son, Fitzwilliam Coningsby (*c.* 1595–1666) as his junior companion.

[56] HMC, *Manuscripts of the Marquess of Salisbury*, xi, p. 441; PRO, PROB 11/148, fos.. 291v–96r (PCC 38 Hele). The figure of Puntarvolo in Ben Jonson's *Every Man Out Of His Humour* was supposed to have been modelled on Sir Thomas Coningsby; C. J. Robinson, *A History of the Mansions and Manors of Herefordshire* (1873), p. 146. (I have been unable to trace the manuscripts to which Robinson refers in his account of Coningsby.)

[57] HMC, *Manuscripts of the Marquess of Salisbury*, xi, p. 538. According to the Holme Lacy parish register (now in the Hereford Record Office), Lady Scudamore was buried there on 15 August 1603.

[58] The Holme Lacy parish register records that Scudamore 'died 14 April about 4 a clocke in the morninge Easter mundaye 1623'. The date of his burial is illegible.

earl of Shrewsbury, after the earl's death in 1616.[59] When compared with the quarrels and enmities which followed Scudamore's erstwhile colleague and rival, Sir Thomas Coningsby, to the grave, however, it was a peaceful end to a long and successful life.

What was the significance of Scudamore's career as courtier and local notable? Does the answer reveal anything of his own character and disposition? There is no evidence that Scudamore aspired to high office or that he was disappointed that the summit of his court career was becoming standardbearer to the band of gentlemen pensioners in 1599. Had he not made his daring second marriage with Mary Shelton late in 1573 or early in 1574 it seems doubtful that he would have gone beyond being a simple gentleman pensioner. In fact, Mary Scudamore was probably more important as a courtier than her husband, in terms of her potential to exercise influence effectually. Without the marriage, Scudamore's court career might have been briefer and less distinguished – or no more distinguished than his grandfather's court career might have been during Henry VIII's reign. Scudamore's career as a courtier, we may conclude, is significant for what it reveals about the road to success at the queen's court. It is difficult to imagine, though, that without his court career he could have achieved the pre-eminent status in local Herefordshire affairs which was his by 1603. Indeed, I wonder whether Scudamore lacked a certain aggressive pushfulness which, had he possessed it, might have enabled him either to rise higher at court or else dominate his native county in such a way that other gentry families would have faced the choice of cooperating with his network of friends and allies or experiencing impotent isolation. Despite his court office and his wife's influence, Scudamore probably could not have averted his humiliation at the hands of the earl of Essex in 1591 even had he been keen to stand and fight, but it is difficult to believe that he could not have waged a tough fight against Coningsby for the senior knight's seat in 1593, 1597, and 1601 had he been intent on gaining it. Instead, he stood aside in 1593 and willingly accepted the junior seat in 1597, just as after 1603 he allowed his son Sir James to occupy the senior knight's place which could have been his own for the asking. Even earlier in his career, at court, he seems to have been averse to taking risks from which he might have benefited – apart from the risk involved in his second marriage. He did not wander abroad in Europe (as did Coningsby, for example, with Philip Sydney in the 1570s), nor is there evidence that he ever involved himself in the displays of the tilt-yard (as did, at various times, both Coningsby and Scudamore's own son, Sir James). He showed no interest in experiencing warfare at first hand, and if there was a genuine offer latent in the letter which Sir George Carey wrote him in 1585, he never did anything to take it up.

Scudamore's career clearly illustrates one important aspect of the political

[59] BL, Add. MS. 11,689, fo. 7; Add. MS. 11,053, fos. 80–1. Elizabeth, Lady Grey of Ruthin, was the second of the three daughters and co-heirs of the earl and countess of Shrewsbury. Lord Grey of Ruthin succeeded his father as earl of Kent in 1623.

culture of late Tudor England, the reciprocal nature of the relationship between courtiership and country status. The relationship was not one of simple equivalence, however. It would be idle to pretend that all courtiers gained an advantage in the contest for prestige and influence in their local communities from the mere fact of enjoying a court position. Those who were younger sons, for instance, or offshoots of junior branches of major gentry families often maintained only minimal links with their localities of origin, and of those who did attempt to maintain a connection, most appear to have enjoyed no great standing there.[60] Others might attempt to establish themselves in counties far from their native soil. Some of these succeeded in their attempt, but normally not until some two or three generations had passed did the more fortunate of such successfully transplanted families manage to enter the circle of their counties' élite families. Still other courtiers held offices whose requirement of virtually constant attendance at court – the grooms of the privy chamber under Elizabeth, or the gentlemen ushers, are two of the groups to which this appears to apply – was an effective barrier to the attainment of high status and great influence in their local communities, even in those cases where individual courtiers did acquire a substantial landed estate and did endeavour to plant their progeny upon it: in such cases it would be later generations which would benefit from their ancestors' efforts. Of all the 'outer chamber' offices whose personnel have been the subjects of my research, only the gentlemen pensioners and the much smaller group of esquires for the body seem to have carried sufficient prestige to make their acquisition and retention worthwhile while at the same time allowing those among them who headed established country families to play a prominent part, if they wished, in the affairs of their county communities.[61]

If the status which the Elizabethan Sir John Scudamore stood to inherit from his grandfather within the county community of Herefordshire was augmented by his court office, and his wife's, his entry into the gentlemen pensioners, on the contrary, cannot be attributed to his family's position and status, nor to any influence which his grandfather might be thought to possess as a quondam courtier. It was due, rather, to his father-in-law, Sir James Croft, whose own political resurrection in 1569 was seemingly effected through the earl of Leicester, and through Leicester's ability to influence the queen. The initiative, in other words, came from the court. For the country to enter the court, the court had first to fetch Croft out of the country by rehabilitating him, and Croft drew Scudamore in with him. Soon Scudamore, in turn, displayed initiative of his own by marrying the queen's kinswoman and familiar, Mary Shelton.

---

[60] This generalization is based on my study of the band of gentlemen pensioners during the reign of Elizabeth I and on my current research on the personnel of the queen's privy chamber and outer chamber.

[61] It may be relevant to note here that the family papers of the Scudamores of Holme Lacy contain very little correspondence of John Scudamore 'the elder' from the years when he was a gentleman usher at the court of Henry VIII (c. 1514–37); there is much more from the period after the late 1530s.

Back in Herefordshire, Scudamore's augmented status as a courtier (combined, perhaps, with the added advantage of an agreeable temperament and personality, if there is more to Richard Willison's letter, excerpted at the beginning of this essay, than a desire to flatter) manifested itself in various ways, most obviously in his repeated selection as junior knight for the shire over a quarter century and in his eventual, if delayed, election as steward of Hereford. But 'junior' and 'delayed' bear witness both to the limits of what Scudamore's status could effect, and to the fact that, courtier though he was, he could be outfaced, and his desires dashed, by others – themselves, significantly, courtiers as well. To Essex Hereford had to yield, to Essex Scudamore had to defer, and thus it was that Scudamore remained junior knight in the 1597 parliament, junior knight to his junior, to his fellow gentleman pensioner and fellow knight, Sir Thomas Coningsby, Essex's client. The friendships which Scudamore formed at court – with the Shrewsburys, with Lord St John, Sir George Carey and the rest – could not alter this. Nor could Lady Scudamore. The one position for which there is evidence that he had a strong desire was the Hereford stewardship – the detailed accounts of city politics and factions surviving in Scudamore's papers sufficiently proves this (and, in addition, offers a fascinating glimpse of Tudor political culture at another social stratum) – and he took its loss in 1590 badly. His reaction may stand, perhaps, as an indication of where Scudamore felt his enduring interests to lie, at home in Herefordshire and not at court.

In conclusion, let us take Scudamore as an archetype of a successful Elizabethan courtier. At the very beginning of his court career the queen (as Croft wrote) spoke of him in words of high praise, and despite the storms attendant upon Scudamore's second marriage, there is no evidence that the queen was anything but *semper eadem* in her opinion of him. Judging by his few surviving portraits,[62] Scudamore appears to have been a fine figure of a man, such a one as often attracted the queen's glance, and other sources show him as a dutiful gentleman pensioner and a capable servant of the Crown in discharging the duties of the positions which he occupied. Few of his own letters survive, but those written to him reveal a winning ability to attract good will and friendship. Ambitious he was, but apparently not consumed by ambition: a man whose estate was such, or ability to husband it, that success at court, and ever greater successes, were not needed to sustain his livelihood, to keep him from falling. In the end his career was an asset for the fortunes of his family rather than their ruin. His augmented estates and his status he bequeathed to his grandson, in

[62] I know of two portraits of Sir John Scudamore. Both are presently at Kentchurch Court, Herefordshire, the seat of the Lucas-Scudamore family. One is a full-length portrait of Scudamore as standard-bearer of the gentlemen pensioners, carrying his staff of office and finely dressed. The other shows Scudamore in old age (the viewer should ignore the later painted caption describing the portrait as one of 'John Scudamore ob. 1571'). A portrait of Scudamore's second wife, Mary (Shelton), dated 1601, was once at Holme Lacy, but has since been sold: Roy Strong, *The English Icon: Elizabethan and Jacobean Portraiture* (London and New Haven, CT, 1969), p. 292, fig. 291.

1623 a twenty-two year old baronet, soon to be the recipient of an Irish peerage, who, as Viscount Scudamore of Sligo, was to experience a full share of the vagaries of fortune in his varying roles as King Charles's ambassador, Archbishop Laud's friend, defender of episcopacy, sequestered delinquent royalist and restoration grandee. Only the extinction of the male line of the family in 1716 and the ensuing difficulties, marital and personal, of two successive generations of heiresses, were to dissipate the influence which earlier generations of the Scudamores of Holme Lacy had garnered in Herefordshire.

7   *Death be very proud: Sidney, subversion, and Elizabethan heraldic funerals*

J. F. R. DAY

Goe to the Heralds Office, the spheare and element of Honour, and thou shalt finde those men as busie there about the consideration of Funerals, as about the consideration of Creations: thou shalte finde that office to be as well the Grave as the Cradle of Honour: and thou shalt finde in that Office as many Records of attainted families and impoverished and forgotten, and obliterate families, as of families newly created and presently celebrated.[1]

Such an observation from John Donne may ill accord with his more famous injunction that 'Death be not proud', but certainly it is more accurate, at least as regards the political and cultural role of heraldic funerals in his time. During the reign of Elizabeth I and even after, the elaborate panoply of the medieval aristocratic funeral flourished, not only at court but in the City. In death, every bit as much as in life, Tudor political culture used the iconography of honour – the heraldic symbols of tradition and rank – to bolster the position of the gentry and to link the governing classes with the feudal past, even at the mouth of the grave itself.

  Undoubtedly the most famous of these funerals, probably even more famous to literary scholars than Queen Elizabeth's own, was that of Sir Philip Sidney.[2]

I wish to thank the Troy State University's Faculty Development Committee for research support for this chapter. For their assistance at the College of Arms in London, I am particularly indebted to the former librarian, J. P. Brooke-Little, C.V.O., Norroy and Ulster King of Arms, and the archivist, Robert Yorke. Dale Randall, Jeff Nelson, and William Tighe read the chapter and offered helpful advice, for which I remain very grateful.

1 John Donne, from a sermon preached at St Paul's on Christmas Day, 1627, quoted in Sir Anthony Wagner, *Heralds and Ancestors* (1978), p. 79. As Dean of St Paul's, Donne would have had occasion to see a good deal of heraldic show; that he may not have always been pleased by the prospect is suggested by sermon LXXII of his *LXXX Sermons* (1640), in which he sniffs (p. 730) that 'mothers are ready to goe to the Heralds to know how Cradles shall be ranked, which Cradle shall have the highest place . . .'. Apparently birth, too, should not be too proud.

2 For Sidney, see below. BL, Add. MS. 35324 is a painted record of the queen's cortège. For more about heraldic funerals and their depiction in the period, see Michael Neill, 'Exeunt with a Dead March': Funeral Pageantry on the Shakespearean State', in David Bergeron (ed.), *Pageantry in the Shakespeare Theater* (Athens, GA, 1985), pp. 153–93, which displays black and white photographs from BL, Add. MS. 35324 showing the above representation of the queen's funeral as well as that of Lady Lumley. Neill's major concern is the relationship of ceremonial funerals to the stage, but he also discusses that other famous artistic example of a heraldic funeral, Sir Henry Unton's in the National Portrait Gallery; see note 43 below. (It was this funeral that presumably prompted Dowland to write 'Sir

This funeral has attracted notice in the last few years, especially as a result of the quadricentennial of Sidney's death in 1986.

The scholarship arising from that anniversary has been copious and occasionally provocative – none more provocative than the suggestion that somehow Sidney's funeral was, instead of being a triumph of the established order, really, if unintentionally, subversive of that order. On the face of it, the idea of subversion may seem absurd. How could a grand funeral compromise social order when it was for an aristocrat who epitomized the best that order could produce?

The death of Sir Philip Sidney in the thick of the fight for the protestant cause in the Netherlands is an important moment in Tudor political culture for several reasons, but reasons having as much to do with the continuation of aristocratic and courtly traditions as with politics or even poetry. John Buxton points out that the number of prominent Elizabethans killed in action in Sidney's generation could be numbered on the fingers of one hand – but it is probably neither Sidney the warrior nor Sidney the writer who is principally the man mourned so extravagantly. Sidney's remarkable writings – *Astrophil and Stella*, *Arcadia*, *A Defence of Poesy* – were still only being circulated in manuscript, as was customary for Elizabethan aristocrats exhibiting their literary *sprezzatura*. Even the role of warrior, one central to the old idea of knighthood, is not solely responsible for the outpouring of grief for Sidney, though the legends of Sidney's gallantry that soon sprang up help to explain the emphasis we place on that role ourselves. But in 1586, it seems that the grief felt for Sidney was primarily for Sidney the courtier, the *preux chevalier* not only in battle but in breeding, as Buxton has said: 'Sidney was mourned not for what he had done but for what he was, not for the achievements for which we admire him, but for his personality. He seemed to his contemporaries to exhibit to perfection those qualities which went to make up the ideal courtier of Castiglione's description, which they wished to emulate . . .'.[3]

Thus whatever political uses Sidney's grieving father-in-law, Sir Francis

Henry Umpton's [*sic*] Funeral' for his *Lachrimae* of 1604.) For the queen's funeral, which certainly was 'among the more splendid public spectacles of her reign' (Neill, 'Exeunt with a Dead March', p. 161), there is, among other records, a second, less-elaborately illuminated account in College of Arms, Vincent MS. 151, 'Vincent's Presidents [*sic*]', pp. 522–33. The MS. dates from the early seventeenth century and is partly in Vincent's own hand, according to the indispensable *Catalogue of Manuscripts in the College of Arms, Collections, Vol. I* (1988), eds. Louis Campbell and Francis Steer, pp. 376ff. A portion of it was reproduced in *Armada: 1588–1988, An International Exhibition to Commemorate the Spanish Armada*, by M. H. Rodríguez-Salgado and the staff of the National Maritime Museum (1988), p. 281, showing the queen's hearse (the canopied catafalque set up in church to receive the body during the service). Henry VIII (like Henry VII) had three hearses, one for lying in state, one where the corpse rested on its journey, and one for the service at Windsor; Paul S. Fritz, 'From "Public" to "Private": the Royal Funerals in England, 1500–1830', in Joachim Whaley (ed.), *Mirrors of Mortality: Studies in the Social History of Death* (1981), p. 63. See also, Clare Gittings, *Death, Burial and the Individual in Early Modern England* (1984), ch. 10 (on royal funerals) and ch. 8 (heraldic obsequies).

[3] John Buxton, 'The mourning for Sidney', *Renaissance Studies* 3 (1989): 47.

Walsingham, might make of Sidney's funeral, either for the family's fame or for the advancement of the protestant cause, both for Walsingham and for Tudor society at large, Sidney's obsequies primarily were meant to honour a man who epitomized the best that aristocracy could produce, an aristocracy which theoretically rooted its privileges in virtue and was still keenly aware of its role in society at large. The famous, if apocryphal, story of the wounded Sidney offering his water bottle to a dying soldier is attractive not only as an example of *noblesse oblige* but also of human compassion which would appeal to all classes.[4]

If Sidney's funeral subverted the natural order of Tudor political society, the members of that society were unaware of it. Mourning for Sidney was mourning for the loss of the ideal aristocrat, and that mourning was one that affected all of society.[5] The outpouring of popular grief that culminated in Sidney's funeral in St Paul's on 16 February 1587 was remarkable: aside from some 700 mourners and hosts of onlookers, there were scores of published elegies. There was also the unprecedented (in England) roll engraving of the procession drawn by Thomas Lant (plates 46 and 47), who himself had a connexion with Sidney and Walsingham (and was eventually to gain a place in the College of Arms). Finally, when the funeral was over, mourning for Sidney continued long after: it was 'accounted a sin' for ordinary gentlemen to wear colourful or festive clothing in London for months after.[6] Even the great Catholic composer

---

[4] Fulke Greville, 'The Water Bottle Story', from *The Life of Sir Philip Sidney* (1633), reprinted as appendix E in Katherine Duncan-Jones (ed.), *Sir Philip Sidney* (Oxford, 1989), p. 329. This volume also includes examples of elegies for Sidney. 'The Water Bottle Story' may be apocryphal, but it is telling even so. As Joan Rees points out in 'In Memory of Sir Philip Sidney', *Essay by Divers Hands, Being the Transactions of the Royal Society of Literature*, Vol. 45 (Woodbridge, 1988), pp. 128–30, the story was not one that could be told of all aristocrats.

[5] Joan Rees, 'In Memory of Sir Philip Sidney', p. 129, suggests that the effect of Sidney's death on the populace at large can be compared to the impact of the assassination of President Kennedy in our own time. If this analogy is useful, it may help to explain why charges of 'subversion' levelled at Sidney's funeral do seem very odd. One might as well argue that President Kennedy's funeral was 'subversive': as an example of American military funeral practice, it apparently owed almost as much to the funeral of Edward VII as it did to that of Abraham Lincoln, itself an elaborate precedent.

[6] *DNB*, 'Sir Philip Sidney', points out the number of mourners and the popular affectation of mourning thereafter. The *DNB* also mentions two separate volumes of elegies published by the two Universities, one of which included an elegy by King James VI of Scotland, Elizabeth's successor. See also Ronald Strickland, 'Pageantry and Poetry as Discourse: The Production of Subjectivity in Sir Philip Sidney's Funeral', in *English Literary History*, 57 (1990): 19–36, which cites evidence for some 700 mourners, p. 28. Strickland also discusses Sidney's elegies, including that of John Phillip's *The Life and Death of Sir Philip Sidney* (1587), reprinted in A. J. Colaianne and W. L. Godshalk (eds.), *Elegies for Sir Philip Sidney* (Delmar, NY, 1980). This volume also reprints Thomas Lant's funeral roll for Sidney, *Sequitur Celebriatras & Pompa Funeris . . .*, known as 'Lant's Roll'. The College of Arms' copy of 'Lant's Roll' (College of Arms, MS. Sidney's Funeral Roll) is the original roll described by Sander Bos, Marianne Lange-Meyers, and Jeanine Six, 'Sidney's Funeral Portrayed', in *Sir Philip Sidney: 1586 and the Creation of a Legend*, eds. Jan van Dorsten, Dominic Baker-Smith, and Arthur F. Kinney (Leiden, for the Sir Thomas Browne Institute, 1986), p. 42, which quotes Aubrey's reference to seeing Lant's engravings as a roll. Bos, Lange-Meyers, and Six also discuss continental examples of similar rolls, like that of the obsequies for Charles V in the Netherlands, now in the College of Arms; the style of 'Lant's Roll', relating the work of the engraver, Theodoor de Brij (or Theodore de Bry) to that of his Dutch contemporaries; and a list of mourners compiled by another witness of the funeral connected to

Plate 46. Heralds in their tabards of the royal arms and wearing mourning gowns and hoods, led by William Segar and followed by Clarenceaux King of Arms, carry Sir Philip Sidney's insignia of knighthood in his funeral procession. From 'Lant's Roll' of the funeral, College of Arms, MS. Sidney's Funeral Roll, membrane 15.

William Byrd took part in the general sorrow, writing three laments for the dead Sidney.[7]

However that may be, the charge of subversion must be taken seriously, not only as an interesting example of New Historicist thought but also as a thought-provoking historical contention; Sidney was, after all, technically a commoner, and yet his funeral was grander than that of many peers. In an age which placed much store on deference given and received, the potential for subversion cannot be dismissed out of hand, even in the case of the funeral of an extremely popular aristocrat.[8]

I should like to begin not with a New Historicist model but with Tudor funeral practice itself. I realize that to some this approach could result in what

the College of Arms, Richard Lea (which Bos, Lange-Meyers, and Six also compare with 'Lant's Roll' and the account in John Stow's *Annals or a generall Chronicle of England* . . . [1631]).

[7] The *DNB* entry on Sidney mentions William Byrd's mourning songs for Sidney in *Psalms, Sonnets, and Songs* (1588). Of the three mourning songs Byrd composed on Sidney, the most famous, 'Come to Me, Grief, Forever' for voice and viols has been recorded by Fretwork on *Armada* (Virgin VC 7 90722–2) with Michael Chance, counter-tenor. The programme notes by David Pinto suggest the Byrd songs may have been commissioned, a likely guess given Byrd's notorious Catholicism. On the other hand, Byrd set to music more Sidney poems than any other composer, as Patricia Adams Nordstrom points out in her notes to *As I Went to Walsingham* by 'The Musicians of Swanne Alley', directors Lyle Nordstrom and Paul O'Dette (Harmonia Mundi USA HMC 905192), on which there is another version of 'Come to Me, Grief, Forever'.

[8] Although it will be clear in this chapter that I disagree with Professor Strickland's conclusions (in his 'Pageantry and Poetry', cited above), I have found his work extremely valuable in clarifying certain New Historical viewpoints. I thank Jeff Nelson for bringing Strickland's published article to my attention.

has been dismissively termed 'naive historicism'.[9] However, the detailed records of aristocratic funeral practice need to be examined in detail in order to put Sidney's funeral in proper context.[10]

These records are associated with the royal officers of arms, the heralds. This came about because aristocratic funerals in early modern England were 'public' rather than 'private' events; they were considered to affect the state as well as the deceased's family and dependents. Thus the sovereign's officers of arms were in attendance, wearing their tabards of the royal arms to testify to the deceased's honourable death and the monarch's approbation of his virtue. In this way hierarchy and social order were publicly upheld in death as well as in life. Although during the seventeenth century 'private' funerals without the heralds in attendance would become the norm, Elizabeth I and her government were whole-hearted supporters of heraldic funerals.[11]

The heralds' funeral records include elaborate paintings of funeral heraldry, funeral certificates, guidelines for marshalling funerals, and records of fees not only for the heralds but also for the herald painters who supplied the numerous shields and banners for the burial procession and the stationary 'hearse', or catafalque, set up to receive the corpse in church.[12] These heraldric accoutrements recalled the ideals of the age of chivalry, and indeed the origins of the heraldic emphasis at an aristocratic funeral were originally rooted in the connexion between the feudal lord and his following. In the case of a great peer,

---

[9] I borrow the term from Jean E. Howard, 'The New Historicism in Renaissance Studies', the *Studies in Renaissance Historicism* issue of *English Literary Renaissance* 16 (1986): 18, n. 10. For Howard, this involves among other things the assumption of historical objectivity and the knowability of history. For a discussion of some of the problems in interdisciplinary relations between history and literature, see Dominick LaCapra, 'On the Line: Between History and Criticism', in the Modern Language Association's *Profession 89*, pp. 4–9.

[10] For guides to the two principal collections of such materials, see Campbell and Steer (eds.), *Catalogue of Manuscripts in the College of Arms, Collections, Vol. I* (1988); Sir Anthony Wagner, *Records and Collections of the College of Arms* (1952); and C. E. Wright, *English Heraldic Manuscripts in the British Museum* (1973).

[11] For the attendance of the officers of arms in their tabards, see Gittings, *Death, Burial and the Individual*, p. 174, also cited from Segar in Nigel Llewellyn, *The Art of Death* (1991), p. 63. See College of Arms MS. S. M. L. 29, 'Ceremonials II', p. 19, which answers the question 'Why the Kings Coate of Arms is worne at Beryalls' with the response that the deceased died honourably as the 'kings trew subject'. (See Sir William Segar, quoted in Neill, 'Exeunt with a Dead March', p. 755.) Llewellyn (*Art of Death*, p. 61) stresses the hierarchical stability represented by the heralds. For Elizabeth I's support of heraldic funerals, see Gittings (*Death, Burial and the Individual*, pp. 182–3). For an approach to aristocratic funerals based not on the heralds' records but on wills, see David Cressy, 'Death and the Social Order: The Funerary Preferences of Elizabethan Gentlemen', *Continuity and Change*, 5 (1989): 99–119.

[12] In addition to 'Vincent's Presidents' (in College of Arms, MS. Vincent 151), see, for example, College of Arms, MS. Dethick's Funerals, vol. i, pt. 2, pp. 243v ff., accounts of the earl of Shrewsbury's funeral in 1590, which include charges for the painter's work per item, the heralds' fees, etc. Between pp. 247v–248 of this manuscript account is a printed copy of 'A True Reporte of a Gentleman's Letter'; intended for a London audience (the earl's funeral was held in Sheffield), the 'Reporte' sheds light on the often considerable charitable expenditure at such funerals (at this one, some 1,100 'blacks' were given out, a considerably larger number of mourning garments than for Sidney's cortège, and 6,000 poor each received 4d and a loaf of bread and some beef). For an overview of Elizabethan funerary practice, see Richard L. Greaves, *Society and Religion in Elizabethan England* (Minneapolis, MN, 1981), ch. 16 ('Last Rites and Monuments').

Plate 47.   Sir Philip Sidney's immobile hearse set up to receive his coffin in old St Paul's. As with the funeral of a lord mayor of London, Sidney's hearse almost amounted to a postmortem promotion to the peerage. Detail of 'Lant's Roll' of the funeral, College of Arms, MS. Sidney's Funeral Roll, membrane 1.

for instance, Mervyn James has pointed out that the lavishly expensive funerary display marked a rite of passage that affected not only the peer and his heir, but all his household and his following. The funeral ceremony, with all its chivalric panoply, thus stressed continuity, just as the heraldic symbolism stressed family and connexion. Beyond that, such a display increased the importance of the dead man's dependants; 'all the brilliance and pageantry was, in due measure, theirs as well as the dead man's'.[13]

Not only was the deceased's body given particular deference in such a scheme, but it was intimately connected with the armorial display on the hearse as well as with the display of his shield, crest, helm, sword, spurs, etc. (plate 51). These accoutrements not only marked his rank in society but associated him with the great tradition of chivalry.[14] The armorial goods carried with the deceased in procession – helm, sword, shield, the spurs of knighthood (if a knight), etc. – had symbolic significance (plate 46).[15] The persistence of bearing these armorial trophies in the funeral procession long after the abolition of the old Requiem Mass, where they would have been presented at the offertory, is indicative of their continued symbolic import.[16] All these chivalric symbols were carried with the coffin in a procession to the heraldically bedecked hearse in a ceremony which included the solemn proclamation of the dead man's style, as at the funeral of the earl of Derby in 1572. The ritual proclaimed the dead man not only a gentleman of rank but also a man of honour and godliness:

All honour laude and praise to Allmightie God, Who through his diuine mercy, hath taken out of this transistorie life to his eternal ioy and blisse, the right Honorable Edward Earle of Darby, Lord Stanley, Strange, and of Man, one of the Q[ueen's]

[13] Mervyn James, 'Two Tudor Funerals', in his *Society, Politics, and Culture: Studies in Early Modern England* (Cambridge, 1986), pp. 176–7. I am grateful to Dale Hoak for this reference.

[14] The provisions of 'Vincent's Presidents' (College of Arms, MS. Vincent 151) clearly indicate a prescribed form of funeral for each rank, even to which of the heraldic 'props' (shield, sword, etc.) should be carried according to the deceased's title. Such items were prepared by painters and craftsmen at the behest of the heralds. See John Brooke-Little (Norroy and Ulster King of Arms), *Royal Ceremonies of State* (1980), pp. 106–9.

[15] James (*Society, Politics, and Culture*, pp. 178–80) makes a distinction between personal and family symbols (personal armour as opposed to family emblems). He also makes a distinction between the significance of the great banner, symbolizing family and continuity, and the standard, or battle flag. A full discussion of this topic involves not only vexillology but also the question of the 'character' imposed by knighthood. I hope to return to this topic in my 'Iconography of Honour: Heraldry Treatises, Chivalric Theory, and English Literature in the Age of Shakespeare'.

[16] For the attention paid to the offering in 'Vincent's Presidents', it seems that something very similar generally occurred after the Reformation, though obviously not in the context of a requiem; however, Communion is still a feature of the English obsequies held for Henry II in 1559: College of Arms, MS. S. M. L. 29, 'Ceremonials II', p. 291. Certainly this aspect of the service had disappeared by 1564, the date of the English obsequies for the Emperor Ferdinand; *ibid.*, p. 292. James (*Society, Politics and Culture*, pp. 180–1) discusses the possible use of the armorial accoutrements during a post-Reformation heraldic funeral, though clearly he sees the original role in armorial symbols presented at the offertory of a Requiem Mass in associating the deceased with the sacrifice of the Mass. Greaves, citing the funeral of the earl of Derby in 1572 (*Society and Religion*, p. 726), states that the heralds gave the new earl his father's arms, sword, shield, etc. at the offering, when each herald was offered gold. Brooke-Little, in discussing the first detailed account of a heraldic funeral, mentions that the accoutrements of the earl of Salisbury were offered to the celebrant at the offertory of the Mass, and were then delivered to the heir of the deceased, Warwick 'the Kingmaker', who returned them to the Officers of Arms to lay on the tomb. (*Cf.* the display of the deceased's heraldic accoutrements over the tomb of the Black Prince at Canterbury.) With the accoutrements came a caparisoned horse – an equine motif that one usually finds in higher aristocratic funerals and also in Sidney's. In Salisbury's case, the horse and trapper were offered to the Church, and the heralds were well rewarded: Brooke-Little, *Royal Ceremonies of State*, pp. 105–6. On the choreography of the offering, see Gittings, *Death, Burial and the Individual*, pp. 176–7. The offertory at Henry VII's funeral has been described as a 'climax which was more heraldic than liturgical'; Sidney Anglo, *Images of Tudor Kingship* (1992), p. 102.

ma[jesti]es most hono[ura]ble privie Councell, and knight and companion of the most Noble order of the Garter.[17]

The cost of this display could be exorbitant. The earl of Leicester's funeral the year after Sidney's ran to more than £3,000; the earl of Rutland's, in the same year as Sidney's, was £2,297.[18] Sidney's funeral may well have cost twice as much as either of these obsequies.[19] Although the expenditure may have undermined Walsingham's fortunes, it is likely he felt the expense worth it. Only a change in funeral fashion – chiefly a result of puritan attitudes – persuaded Tudor Englishmen that such expenses were unjustified.[20]

Certainly the queen's officers of arms would have thought the expense fitting, since as the organizers of heraldic funerals they collected considerable fees for their services, not to mention funeral droits, such as the funeral furniture.[21] Thus they took a great interest in enforcing heraldic funerary precedents. In the reign of Henry VIII, Thomas Wriothesley, Garter King of Arms, sought to regulate funeral display,[22] though perhaps his concern was as much to protect heralds' fees as to prevent incorrect procedure. The heralds' pursuit of their legal rights seems more indicative of their usual concerns, rather than any *ultra vires* attempt to upgrade funerals. Heraldic funeral offences were punished by the high court of chivalry. In 1619, for example, the court heard the case of the funeral of Sir George Smith, whose obsequies at Exeter displayed too many heraldic hatchments for a knight, and even worse, a mere painter had presumed to act as a herald.[23] For the heralds, here was the real problem, an encroachment on their prerogatives and emoluments. Hence the officers of arms 'relentlessly pursued painters and craftsmen who were not employed by them and who threatened their monopoly by producing funeral accoutrements without the licence of a King of Arms'.[24]

I have found few criticisms of the heralds' organization of funerals. Partly this may be because such ceremonies were generally well regulated by traditions

---

[17] College of Arms, MS. Vincent 151, p. 351.

[18] Strickland, 'Pageantry and Poetry', pp. 20–1, quotes Lawrence Stone, *The Family, Sex, and Marriage in England, 1500–1800* (New York, 1977), p. 208, noting that an earl's funeral could cost as much as a year's income from his estates.

[19] *DNB*, 'Sir Philip Sidney', suggests the total cost at something like £6,000, which mainly fell on Walsingham, Sidney's father-in-law, nearly ruining him. See Strickland, 'Pageantry and Poetry', pp. 29–30. The greatest expense of an aristocratic funeral was for black cloth for the hearse, rail coverings, mourners' gowns, etc.; Strickland, 'Pageantry and Poetry', p. 21; Gittings, *Death, Burial and the Individual*, p. 181.

[20] James, *Society, Politics, and Culture*, p. 176. See also Lawrence Stone, *Crisis of the Aristocracy, 1558–1641* (Oxford, 1965), ch. 10 ('Conspicuous Expenditure'), where Stone analyses the decline in heraldic funerals as evidence of a change in aristocratic attitudes towards costs and benefits – an approach which might have struck a great medieval or Elizabethan magnate as somewhat ignoble. Greaves, *Society and Religion*, ch. 16 extensively analyses costs and discusses reasons for the decline of heraldic funerals in the decades following Sidney's obsequies.

[21] See Sir Anthony Wagner, *Heralds of England* (1967), p. 113ff.

[22] Strickland, 'Pageantry and Poetry', p. 22.

[23] For the legal regulation of heraldry, including funerals, see G. D. Squibb, *The High Court of Chivalry*, (Oxford, 1965), where Sir George Smith's case is noted on p. 35.

[24] Brooke-Little, *Royal Ceremonies of State*, p. 109.

such as those Augustine Vincent cites for the use of his brother heralds in an early seventeenth-century manuscript in the College of Arms known as MS. Vincent 151, 'Vincent's Presidents', or, 'Precedents'. Criticism of the heralds' funerary practice clearly yields place to more common animadversions on their supposed faults, most particularly the potential (and, according to some conservative writers in the period, disgusting) subversion of social order arising from the Kings of Arms' right to grant coats of arms, a right which the Kings of Arms are accused of abusing by granting arms to 'vile men'.[25]

That social upstarts might acquire arms, the recognized insignia of gentility, doubtless was perceived as subversive by many writers. Perhaps the most sensible account of the basis of granting arms is in Sir Thomas Smith's *De Republica Anglorum*:

But ordinarily the king doth only make knights and create barons or higher degrees: for as for gentlemen, they be made good cheape in England. For whosoever studieth the lawes of the realme, who studieth in the universities, who professeth liberall sciences, and to be shorte, who can live idly and without manuall labour, and will bear the port, charge, and countenaunce of a gentlemen, he shall be called master, for that is the title which men give to esquires and other gentlemen, and shall be taken for a gentleman: for true it is with us as is saide, *Tanti eris alijs quanti tibi feceris* (and if neede be) a king of Heraulds shal also give him for mony, armes newly made and invented, the title whereof shall pretende to have been found by the sayd Herauld in perusing and viewing of olde registers, where his auncestors in times past had bin recorded to beare the same: Or if he wil do it more truely and of better faith, he will write that for the merittes of that man, and certaine qualities which he doth see in him, and for sundry noble actes which he hath perfourmed, he by the authoritie which he hath as king of Heraldes and armes giveth to him and his heires these and these armes, which being done I thinke he may be called a squire, for he beareth ever after those armes. Such men are called sometime in scorne gentlemen of the first head.[26]

Smith's description reflects the increasing demand for armorial ensigns of gentility, which peaked in the 1570s and 1580s with nearly 1,500 grants in twenty years.[27]

The major legal action taken against the heralds for these alleged abuses seems to have come from other members of the College of Arms themselves during the feuds that occurred in the College in the sixteenth and early seventeenth centuries; though some of these disputes involved funeral fees, the

---

[25] Sir Anthony Wagner discusses the right of heralds to grant arms and the accusations that Garter King of Arms gave coats of arms to 'vile', or ungentle, men; *Heralds and Heraldry in the Middle Ages: An Inquiry into the Growth of the Armorial Function of Heralds* (second edn, Oxford, 1956), ch. 9.

[26] Thomas Smith, *De Republica Anglorum: A Discourse on the Commonwealth of England*, ed. L. Alston (Cambridge, 1906), pp. 39–40.

[27] Edward Elmhirst, 'The Fashion for Heraldry', *Coat of Arms*, 4 (1956–58): 48. These figures are not complete, but they do accord with those in Stone, *Crisis of the Aristocracy*, p. 67. Any free man with £10 per annum in land or £300 in movables could be registered by the heralds; the number of grants between 1560 and 1640 was nearly 4,000; D. M. Palliser, *The Age of Elizabeth: England under the Later Tudors* (1983), p. 70. The historical sociology of this increase, which was linked to the heralds' visitations, awaits further study.

worst quarrels were over charges of armorial or genealogical abuses where the evidence of the official inquiries may be more the result of malice than of malfeasance.[28] Clearly, though, there was criticism: literary satire aimed at the heralds is not hard to find, though as already noted, it also deals mainly with the heralds' activities other than marshalling funerals. Again, the most common complaints are similar to the heralds' own quarrels, that the heralds falsify pedigrees and grant arms to social upstarts. These complaints occur occasionally throughout Elizabethan drama, and most particularly in Ben Jonson. For instance, in *Every Man Out of His Humour*, a bumpkin named Sogliardo is blazoned a brainless boar by a witty herald, who nonetheless takes his money for this ironic coat of arms. In *The Staple of News* there is a 'heraldet' named Piedmantle, clearly a play on Bluemantle, actually one of the junior officers of arms or pursuivants. Jonson, at one time a student of Clarenceaux King of Arms Camden, knew a good deal about heraldry and satirized not only improper grants and dubious pedigrees but also funerals. He makes a specific reference to the practice in *The Staple of News*, where one of his characters dismisses heraldic funerals as 'all that idle pomp'.[29]

The character book writers, whose popularity begins twenty-one years after Sidney's funeral with Joseph Hall's *Characters of Vertues and Vices*, also generally exhibited a lack of concern with funerals, though they were definitely concerned with perceived heraldic abuses. Such works are prime sources for social satire, though again the concern expressed in them comprehends upstart armigers more than anything else.[30]

Whatever other potential subversions, if any, the heralds were perpetrating, it is hardly likely that they got up such a spectacle as Sidney's funeral on their

---

[28] Wagner, *Heralds of England*, p. 203, cites College of Arms, MS. WZ on the accusation by the herald Ralph Brooke that Garter Dethick had given arms to ignoble men, including William Shakespeare's father, a case also discussed in C. W. Scott-Giles, *Shakespeare's Heraldry* (1950), p. 39.

[29] The quotation and discussion of the problem can be found in Arthur Huntington Nason, *Heralds and Heraldry in Ben Jonson's Plays, Masques and Entertainments* (1907; reprinted New York, 1968), pp. 105–8, where he cites (from Mark Noble's *History of the College of Arms*) a case in which Jacobean heralds received compensation for *not* marshalling a gentleman's funeral. See also his discussion of heraldic funerals, pp. 70–2. Nason is a useful compendium of all of Jonson's references to heraldry.

[30] See my 'Venal Heralds and Mushroom Gentlemen: Seventeenth-Century Character Books and the Sale of Honors' (unpublished Ph.D. dissertation, Duke University, 1985), serialized in consecutive issues of *The Coat of Arms*, n.s. 8, no. 149 (spring 1990) to n.s. 9, no. 156 (winter 1991). An early Elizabethan view of upstart armigers and their inclination to spend less on funerals for their forbears is in Gerald Legh, *The Accedens of Armorie* (1562), Preface, n. p., in discussing types of churls: 'The second sort, are vngentile gentlemen, who beeing enhaunced to honour by their fathers, on whom (though it were to their owne woorship) yet can they not keepe so much money from the dice, as to make woorshipful obsequies, for their saide fathers, with any point of armorye: But despise the same, because (say they) those his armes were purchased for slippers. Most of these desire the tytle of woorship, but none doo worke the deedes that appertaine therunto. And of these that runne so farre as wil not turne, old weomen wil say, such youth will haue their swinge, and it be put in a halter: But God keepe them from that.' The only specific heraldic funeral reference I know of in the character books is the Overburian 'An Ordinary Widdow [who] Is like the Heralds Hearse-cloath: shee serves to many funerals, with a very little altering the colour'; W. J. Paylor (ed.), *The Overburian Characters, To Which is Added A Wife by Sir Thomas Overbury* (Oxford, 1936), p. 71.

own, however lucrative it should prove. While the heralds were courtiers usually somewhat removed from court in their own establishment, the authorities exercised some control over their activities.[31] Thus it is clear that the origin of Sidney's funeral pomp emanated from a more powerful source than the heralds' greed. It seems likely that the moving force was Walsingham and his circle; this might also help explain that even though the funeral was unusually grand, there was apparently little objection to its grandeur, even in a court composed of different factions. Curiously, Walsingham does not appear among the lists of participants at his own son-in-law's funeral, and it is possible that he was lying low following the execution of Mary, Queen of Scots, only a few days earlier.[32] There were in any case other reasons why Sidney's elaborate funeral caused no repercussions.

The tacit acquiescence of the queen's government in possibly inappropriate funerary display might seem surprising if the hierarchy of funerals were as rigid as has been assumed. Certainly at the very least it does imply that the queen and Burghley were not opposed to the proceedings for reasons of their own.[33] Whatever the impetus for the splendour of the funeral, it is evident that Sidney's funeral procession was very far from what Augustine Vincent later sets down as appropriate for 'A knightes funerall':

> Two conductors with staues
> Poore men in gownes
> Yeomen in clokes
> > The Standard borne
> > by one near in bloud [sketch of a standard]
> Seruantes of gentlemen
> Seruantes of Knightes
> Seruantes of Lordes
> Seruantes of the defunct
> Gentlemen in blackes
> Esquires in blackes
> Knightes in blackes
> The preacher for the time

---

[31] Wagner (*Heralds of England*) discusses the nature and origins of the heralds' authority as well as their status under the control of the earl marshal or the commissioners for that office.

[32] Bos, Lange-Meyers, and Six, 'Sidney's Funeral Portrayed', p. 39. There is also the theory that Elizabeth I and Burghley deliberately used Sidney's funeral as a grand spectacle to divert attention from the execution of Mary, Queen of Scots, and military failures on the continent, though of course plans for Sidney's funeral must have been long underway. John Aubrey even suspected a false coffin; *Brief Lives*, ed. Andrew Clark (Oxford, 1898), ii, p. 249. In any case, since men like Fulke Greville were consciously fashioning Sidney's image as the protestant champion, it seems likely that some sort of propagandistic motive for the grandeur of Sidney's funeral remains plausible. For this alternative approach to Sidney and the propangandistic uses of his death, see Alan Hagar, 'The Exemplary Image: Fabrication of Sir Philip Sidney's Biographical Image and the Sidney Reader', in *Sir Philip Sidney: An Anthology of Modern Criticism*, ed. Dennis Kay (Oxford, 1987), pp. 53–5.

[33] Joan Rees has pointed out that although Elizabeth I had not treated Sidney well, she was touched by his death; 'In Memory of Sir Philip Sidney', p. 129. However, the queen's view of heroic gestures was less sanguine: witness her reproof to Lord Mountjoy, when she called Sidney 'that inconsiderate [rash] fellow' for getting killed; cited in Buxton, 'The Mourning for Sidney', p. 47.

The Penon borne by
One neare in bloud [sketch of a penon]
Helme and creast
Sword and targett [that is, the shield]
Coate of Armes
[sketched outline of a coffin]
Chiefe mourner next the body
ffoure assistantes
Knightes on horsbacke
Lordes on horsbacke
Two yeoman
Gentlewomen in blackes
Yeomen in coates
Gentlewomen without blackes
Parish and others.[34]

Furthermore, the hearse Vincent depicts for a knight is nothing like the elaborate one erected in St Paul's to receive Sidney's body (plate 47). Instead of having a canopy, the ordinary knight's hearse is merely an enclosure bedecked with escutcheons within which the coffin will be placed (plate 50).[35] As impressive as this may have been, even a cursory glance at 'Lant's Roll' will show that Vincent's description is hardly the model for Sidney's procession and hearse, even though generally the elements in all heraldic funerals are similar. Professor Ronald Strickland, pointing out what he terms Sidney's 'peculiarly ambiguous status as an aristocrat', discusses these heraldic excesses as problematic in the funeral of a man he correctly, if technically, terms a commoner. Before turning to a consideration of Sidney's funeral itself, it will be necessary to consider the problems inherent in the term 'commoner' as applied to a man like Sidney.[36]

The ambiguity of Sidney's position is almost peculiarly English in that it rests on a discrepancy between legal and social definitions of nobility. In English law, only the peer himself is legally noble; the titles of his wife and children are courtesy titles. Leaving aside the exception of so-called 'burgher arms' on the continent, in general the category of *nobiles minores* would apparently include anyone who bore arms – the very people who in England would be termed

---

[34] College of Arms, MS. Vincent 151, p. 175. And see College of Arms, MS. S. M. L. 28, 'Ceremonials I', p. 118, for 'Proceedings to the Funerall of a Knight in London'.

[35] College of Arms, MS. Vincent 151 contains two drawings of a knight's hearse, one a sketch with a single enclosure (p. 174) and another (p. 177) with a double enclosure. Both hearses have two openings opposite each other, apparently lined up with the church's nave. A painting of a hearse opposite 'The Definition of a [Knight] Bachelor' (p. 185, reproduced here as plate 50) shows pyramids topped with balls at the four corners of a single-walled enclosure in which there is a black-draped platform for the coffin. The following page shows the knight's draped coffin bearing his crested helm, sword, shield ('target'), sword, and tabard of arms with his penon and standard erected at either end of the coffin (plate 51).

[36] Strickland, 'Pageantry and Poetry as Discourse', pp. 24ff., adheres to a broad definition of the aristocracy, making the major distinction between those who were gentlemen and those who were not.

'gentlemen' would thus correspond to lesser nobility elsewhere.[37] Sidney was certainly at the very least a gentleman and a knight; he was as well potential heir to two earls, which further elevates his place in society.[38] Thus while it is correct to term Sidney a commoner, the designation has something of the flavour of referring rather discourteously to the earl's daughter who married the present Prince of Wales as 'that commoner who married into royalty'. In fact, the 'ambiguity' of Sidney's status was shared by a number of gentlemen, and if the punctilio of an Elizabethan peer insisting on his prerogatives was, well, punctilious, the right of a Sidney to be termed aristocratic is also very much to the point.[39] The relationship in England of nobility to gentility and of both to the definitive symbol of a coat of arms has nuances that need not concern us here. Suffice it to say that Sidney, aristocrat, gentleman, and commoner, would not normally have been expected to receive the funeral of a baron, yet it seems from all the accounts that it was a baron's funeral he had (plates 47 and 48). It is for that reason that his funeral exhibited a 'great banner' and the appurtenances that appear so out of place for a 'mere' knight, which, of course he never was.[40]

---

[37] In this I have been guided by Palliser (*The Age of Elizabeth*, pp. 68–9), who follows Sir Thomas Smith in calling the peerage *nobilitas maior* and the gentry, *nobilitas minor*.

[38] Preface to *Sidney in Retrospective: Selections from English Literary Renaissance*, ed. Arthur F. Kinney and the editors of *English Literary Renaissance* (Amherst, MA, 1988), p. vii. Sidney's knighthood was further elevated by his having served as an ambassador. In Queen Elizabeth's funeral procession (BL, Add. MS. 35324), ambassador knights have separate precedence.

[39] Much has been made of Sidney's rebuke by Elizabeth I when he challenged the earl of Oxford to a duel; Strickland, 'Pageantry and Poetry', p. 25. Surely the discrepancy in rank was rather less an issue than a useful pretext for the queen to stop the fight. Sir William Segar, in discussing 'The Equalitie and disequalitie of great Nobilitie, and of the priuiledges due to all men professing Armes', argues that a gentleman may fight with a nobleman in cases of treason, but that otherwise the nobleman may use a proxy; *The Booke of Honor and Armes* (1590; reprinted Delmar, NY, 1975), p. 57. The challenge was still allowed. The point is that being a gentleman was to be noble, and the greater nobility 'are (besides their dignity) none other then Gentlemen, and Gentilitie or Nobilitie is hereditary and cannot be taken away, but dignitie may'; Sir William Segar, *Honor, Military and Ciuill, Contained in Foure Bookes* (1602; reprinted Delmar, NY, 1975), p. 122. According to Fulke Greville, Sidney, though not then a knight, answered the queen's objection very much in this spirit. Sidney is supposed to have reminded the queen that Oxford 'was no lord over him, and therefore the difference of degrees between free men could not challenge any other homage than precedency'; quoted in Katherine Duncan-Jones, *Sir Philip Sidney, Courtier Poet* (New Haven, CT, 1991), p. 165.

[40] Following Wagner, Bos, Lange-Meyers, and Six, ('Sidney's Funeral Portrayed', p. 51) clearly state that Sidney's funeral was that of a baron, which explains the presence of the great banner and the other anomalies that we see in 'Lant's Roll': compare the ceremonies for a knight described by Vincent (College of Arms, MS. Vincent 151, pp. 174–7), cited above. The hearse in 'Lant's Roll' (plate 47) may look even grander than that befitting a baron (plate 48), since it, like the later hearse for Henry, Prince of Wales, has six columns. However, it is not clear that the number of columns is definitive in determining the rank of a hearse, and it is also difficult to know how much deviation there may have been from the plans given by Augustine Vincent. Vincent is clearly citing precedents, and as each hearse would have been made for the occasion, one should expect a certain amount of variation in construction and shape. In his discussion of the heraldric funeral, Julian Litten says that the four bannerols carried about Sidney's coffin is the number prescribed for a knight, and that 'it was rare to see the regulations of the College of Arms flouted' in such matters; Julian Litten, *The English Way of Death: The Common Funeral since 1450* (1991), pp. 176–7. How much of an anomaly was created by the number of bannerols in this case remains doubtful; as will be seen, 'baronial' funerals breveted other persons, like a lord mayor of London dying in office, to a higher rank in death. The fact remains that Sidney's funeral, which was marshalled by the College of Arms, was given the form befitting a baron.

Plate 48. 'A Baron's hearse fully furnished' similar to Sidney's. College of Arms, MS. Vincent 151, p. 260.

One possible pretext for this baronial burial is Sidney's foreign title, which he could use abroad. Walsingham, who probably orchestrated this sombre show for political purposes of his own – including increased support for the prot-estant cause in Holland[41] – may have justified his son-in-law's funerally elevated rank on the grounds that Sidney, who was knighted to serve as proxy for Prince John Casimir's installation as a Garter Knight, also held the title of baron from

[41] Bos, Lange-Meyers, and Six, 'Sidney's Funeral Portrayed', pp. 50–1.

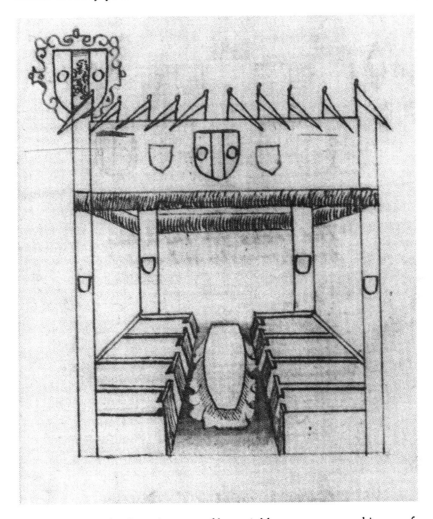

Plate 49. Sketch of another sort of baronial hearse constructed in 1591 for the funeral of Sir John Allot, Lord Mayor of London, who died in office and was buried as a baron. Because 'the Seats were Standinge' in the parish church, there could be no rails or double bars. Detail of College of Arms, MS. Vincent 151, p. 178.

the king of France.[42] While this title was of little use to Sidney in England at least while he was alive, it might afford the technical rationale allowing him to qualify for the postmortem promotion inherent in his politically impressive aristocratic funeral. This pretext would certainly take some of the potentially

---

[42] On the queen's commission for Sidney's knighthood, see *Sir Philip Sidney: Life, Death and Legend. An Exhibition to Commemorate the 400th Anniversary of the Death of Sir Philip at the Bodleian Library, Oxford* (Oxford, 1986), p. 19, and *DNB*, 'Sir Philip Sidney'. John Buxton also cites the French title as a reason for Sidney's baronial funeral: 'The mourning for Sidney', *Renaissance Studies* 3 (1989): 49.

subversive anomaly out of the affair, especially since there are other precedents that indicate similar exceptions were made under particular circumstances. For example, Sir Henry Unton, pictured as one of Sidney's mourners in 'Lant's Roll', died in 1596 and was buried 'with a Baron's hearse, and in the degree of a Baron, because he died Ambassador Leger for France'.[43]

Another example of an exceptional funeral 'promotion' is that of Sir John Allot (d. 1591), Lord Mayor of London, who although a commoner, was also buried as a baron (plate 49). Allot's 'promotion' may have been engineered by the City, which had already enhanced the status of its aldermen with heraldic funerals, but also by Garter's desire to have a share in the fees, since he marshalled nobles' funerals.[44] However, it was Clarenceaux King of Arms, Robert Cooke, who marshalled Sidney's funeral.[45] Whether this is more indicative of the status of the funeral or an arrangement within the College of Arms is difficult to say. Perhaps Clarenceaux argued that Sidney's English rank gave him the right to marshal the funeral, while the form honoured Sidney's French title. Whatever the pretext for upgrading Sidney's funeral, Sidney was given the honours due a baron, *nemine contradicente*.

[43] Memorandum from the College of Arms quoted in Neill, 'Exeunt with a Dead March', p. 160. Unton's postmortem promotion was welcome not only to his family but to the heralds, who thereby increased their fees. Unton was himself the subject of the funeral portrait in the National Portrait Gallery, a painting that became a permanent memorial to Unton's newly won quasi-baronial status. In 'Sir Henry Unton and His Portrait: An Elizabethan Memorial Portrait and Its History', *Archaeologia* 99 (1965): 51–76, Sir Roy Strong points out that Unton was knighted after Zutphen and walked in Sidney's funeral procession. Though not as elaborate as Sidney's funeral procession, the partial (not 'fairly modest', as Strickland terms it in 'Pageantry and Poetry', p. 36, n. 24) procession wending its way prominently across the middle of the Unton portrait is self-consciously impressive: it ends not in the hearse, which was, after all, a temporary housing for the corpse, but in an elaborate tomb. For the importance of such tombs, see Nigel Llewellyn, 'Claims to Status through Visual Codes: Heraldry on Post-Reformation Funeral Monuments', in Sidney Anglo (ed.), *Chivalry in the Renaissance* (Woodbridge, Suffolk, 1990), pp. 145–60. The attempt to give Sidney an appropriate tomb proved abortive; Walsingham was quietly interred in the same grave; *ibid.*, p. 158. This lack of a tomb made for some gibes when Sir Christopher Hatton's vast memorial was erected: 'Philip and Francis haue no Tombe / For great Christopher takes all the roome'; quoted in the Preface to *Sidney in Retrospect*, pp. vii–viii. Nigel Llewellyn even suggests that the splendour of the funeral's images obviated Sidney's need for a tomb; Nigel Llewellyn, *The Art of Death: Visual Culture in the English Death Ritual c. 1500–c. 1800* (1991), p. 68.
[44] College of Arms, MS. Vincent 151, pp. 178–81. There follows (*ibid.*, pp. 182–3) 'A Remembrance of the controversie w[hi]ch grew between Garter and Clarenceaux concerninge the right of serveinge the funerall aforegoeinge of Sir John Alote who died in his Maioralitie . . .'. The dispute was apparently as much a matter of fees as of rank; regulations in 1568 clarified Garter's rights to marshal the funerals of peers, prelates, Garter Knights, and their wives; Wagner, *Heralds of England*, p. 197. This later controversy, decided by Burghley, added to Garter's rights, while preserving Clarenceaux's. The point is that this commoner's funeral was to be ordered 'like to a Baron'; College of Arms, MS. Vincent 151, p. 183. See College of Arms, MS. S. M. L. 28, 'Ceremonials I', p. 121, which states that the position of lord mayor represents 'a barons roome' and therefore affects funeral rank, possibly to a lesser degree, even for former lords mayor.
[45] Bos, Lange-Meyers, and Six, 'Sidney's Funeral Portrayed', p. 38. Richard C. McCoy, 'Sidney and Elizabethan Chivalry', in M. J. B. Allen, Dominic Baker-Smith, Arthur F. Kinney, and Margaret M. Sullivan (eds.), *Sir Philip Sidney's Achievements* (New York, 1990), p. 39, points out the Clarenceaux was the protégé of Sidney's uncle, the earl of Leicester. This certainly might help explain not only why Clarenceaux marshalled the funeral but why it was so very splendid.

The baronial character of the ceremony explains many of the apparent anomalies in Sidney's funeral, including the presence of his 'great banner', usually reserved for peers, and the increased number of assistants to the chief mourner, Sir Robert Sidney.[46] It does not, however, explain other allegedly irregular features, including especially the presence of noble mourners.

For some critics, the presence of four earls (all of them Sidney's kinsmen) in the contingent following the corpse[47] is held to contravene Garter Sir William Segar's observation that 'no man of greater title than the defunct should be permitted to mourne'.[48] The presence of the nobility here is seen as a threat to the social hierarchy; Sidney's funeral, it is argued, is therefore 'unconventional and perhaps unique'.[49] It seems to me, however, most unlikely that this is the case. I am not at all sure that Segar's injunction means that no one of higher rank than the deceased was allowed to *attend* a funeral. The subversive interpretation here may be based on a misunderstanding – the terms 'mourne' or 'mourner' must apply in this context not to the entire body of those attending the funeral, but rather to the chief mourner and his assistants. The context in which Segar's injunction is applied seems to bear this out. In arguing against 'superfluous' expense Segar says:

To auoid which excesse I could wish, that excepting the number of poore who are commonly so many as the defunct was yeeres olde, her Maiestie or Lord Marshall would be pleased to prescribe a certain number of Mourners to euery degree, and that no man of greater title then the defunct should be permitted to mourne, so as the chiefe mourner may euer be *in pari dignitate* with the defunct, and all the rest of meaner qualitie.[50]

From this it would appear that the precise meaning of 'mourner' depends largely on context; by 'Mourners' Segar here seems to mean only the chief mourner and his assistants. The evidence for this reading comes from clear references in other heraldic accounts to the number of assistants to the chief mourner specified according to the deceased's rank, just as Segar describes. For instance, in the cortège of a knight quoted above, the 'Chiefe mourner next the body' is accompanied by 'ffoure assistantes'. This is precisely the sort of enumeration according to rank discussed by Segar, and the number of assistants increases as the rank of the deceased becomes higher. Sidney, buried as a baron, has six assistants to the chief mourner, and they are all of Sidney's English rank of knight or under. It seems clear that the term 'mourner' in this case is rather more specific than it first appears. Thus it would be proper to say that Sir Philip Sidney had no 'Mourners' in Segar's sense higher than his own rank of knight, despite the presence of noblemen in the funeral procession.

---

[46] Strickland specifically mentions the great banner; 'Pageantry and Poetry', p. 30.

[47] Bos, Lange-Meyers, and Six, 'Sidney's Funeral Portrayed', p. 43.

[48] Strickland 'Pageantry and Poetry', p. 31. There is a fuller version quoted in Neill, 'Exeunt with a Dead March', pp. 154–5. The original passage is in Segar, *Honor, Military and Ciuill*, quoted below.

[49] Strickland 'Pageantry and Poetry', p. 31.

[50] Segar, *Honor, Military and Ciuill* (1602; reprinted 1975), p. 253. The passage is in Book Four, cap. 27, 'Of Funerals'.

Plate 50. Painting of a knight bachelor's hearse – a knight bachelor being one 'not married unto some higher dignity'. However, this knight apparently was married to a woman who survived him, since, like later hatchments, her half of the impaled marital coat is shown on white. College of Arms, MS. Vincent 151, p. 185.

To make this case even stronger, there is clear evidence in the heralds' rules for marshalling funerals for the presence of mourners who clearly outrank the deceased. For instance, there is Vincent's reference to 'Lordes on horsbacke' in the funeral procession of a knight quoted above, which makes no sense if Segar is taken to mean that no one of higher rank than the deceased may even be present at a funeral. Then there is the notation in the 'Instructions' for 'The funerall of a Countesse', also in 'Vincent's Presidents', which further clarifies the point: 'The lady cheife mourner only hath a mantell, the other ladies none, though they be of higher degree, the reason is because there is but one Estate kept that day'.[51]

The 'Estate' being officially kept is that of the deceased, which limits his chief mourner and assistants to his degree or under. It does not necessarily mean that no higher noble might attend. Now in fact all of Sidney's official mourners are knights or esquires, and while there are six assistants to the chief mourner (as for a baron) rather than four (as for a knight), the tradition is apparently being followed punctiliously. Thus it seems that the presence of the higher nobility at a knight's funeral is neither consciously or unconsciously subversive; they are there to honour their kinsman or friend in full accord with heraldic practice, following the group of 'official' mourners but not technically a part of it.

Much less in accord with usual practice is the presence, before and after the corpse, of military units. Among these are fellow officers from Holland, who follow the traditional poor recipients of funeral charity (thirty-two of them, traditionally one for each year of Sidney's life) who precede the corpse. These officers might well be expected to attend the funeral of a comrade. But this does not explain why after the corpse come 300 citizens of London armed with a variety of muskets, 'small shot', pikes, halberds, and the like, accompanied by fife and drum.[52]

This military display is apparently unusual in any heraldic funeral of the period – even the queen's! In her exceptionally elaborate funeral in 1603, there is hardly any mention of military units, except the knight marshal's men, who whiffle, or clear the way, for the procession, and the gentlemen pensioners 'with their axes downward', escorting the queen's body. Only at the very end do we find 'The Captaine of the Guard' and 'All the Guard following five and five in a Rancke'.[53] Now however long it may have taken the guard to pass, the reference takes up about three lines in a list of mourners covering ten pages (including, to be sure, space for small paintings of banners and horses and armorial accoutrements). In best feudal form, the procession includes all the queen's servants, given by office, their numbers further swollen by the servants of participating noblemen in order to make the greatest possible impression – but not necessarily a military one.[54]

---

51 College of Arms, MS. Vincent 151, p. 380.
52 See 'Lant's Roll', which is also enumerated in Bos, Lange-Meyers, and Six, 'Sidney's Funeral Portrayed'.
53 College of Arms, MS. Vincent 151, 'The proceeding at Queene Elizabeths funerall . . .', p. 532. The pictorial record of Elizabeth I's funeral (BL, Add. MS. 35324) shows the guard and its captain (Raleigh) merely bringing up the rear of the procession. Litten, *The English Way of Death*, p. 160, credits Oliver Cromwell for the military display associated with royal funerals. Apparently the association was rare before Cromwell's time, though an analogy to Sidney's case might be found in the burial in 1629 of John Whitson of Bristol, who was colonel of the 'trained band'. Whitson was buried with his troops present, carrying black-decked pikes and drums; *ibid.*, p. 155.
54 Vincent's account of Elizabeth I's funeral (College of Arms, MS. Vincent 151, pp. 522–37) includes both a painting of the queen's hearse (pp. 534–5) and an engraving of her tomb, a juxtaposition suggesting once again, as in Sir Henry Unton's funeral portrait, that the tomb should be considered a permanent hearse, or monument of the deceased's heraldic status. The display of status is, as Llewellyn points out (in 'Claims to Status through Visual Codes') clearly the point of

Plate 51. The knight bachelor's coffin covered with a black pall and his heraldic insignia. At either end of the coffin are his penon and his standard (with the cross of St George for England). The escutcheons are apparently painted on squares appliquéd to the presumably reusable pall. College of Arms, MS. Vincent 151, p. 186.

Thus I would contend that the military presence at Sidney's funeral has no particularly 'subversive' subtext; it is perhaps simply an anomaly, an *ad hoc* tribute to a popular fallen warrior. Such a martial display certainly does not seem to be subversive of the social order *because* of its apparent unusualness; it seems to be the sort of tribute appropriate for an extraordinary war hero. The

both funeral and tomb. See Neill, 'Exeunt with a Dead March', pp. 155–67, and Sir Roy Strong, *The Cult of Elizabeth: Elizabethan Portraiture and Pageantry* (1977), ch. 3. For the tomb as permanent hearse, see the countess of Derby's tomb by Maximilian Colt (1636), illustrated in Gittings, *Death, Burial and the Individual*, plate 7, p. 127.

military presence added to the show, reinforcing Sidney's military role, but it seems to have had no sinister implication.

Another anomalous group in Sidney's funeral is the party of delegates from the Lowlands, who are associated with a rather different set of implications. These representatives of Holland and Zealand received their invitations late,[55] but their presence has suggested an official cast to the funeral. It has even been argued that Sidney's funeral was a state funeral, which might 'unsubvert' a good many excesses. But as Bos, Lange-Meyers, and Six argue, this does not seem to be the case: the governments of neither England nor Holland paid for the funeral (despite the rumours of an offer from Holland to the queen, who refused), and there was apparently no official representative of either state present. The Dutch who marched as 'the States of Holland' may well have been present in a private capacity, at Walsingham's request.[56] Of course, as Bos, Lange-Mayers, and Six also point out, it 'is a question of speculation whether anything comparable to state funerals existed in Elizabethan England . . .'.[57] This is surely the case. State funerals so defined – officially paid for and officially attended – will not occur for nearly a century more.[58] Even so, the very grandeur of Sidney's funeral, attracting so many viewers in the heart of London that 'the mourners had scarcely rome to pass',[59] seems to make it almost a proto-state funeral – something, to use an anachronistic if not improper analogy, somewhere between the state funeral of Sir Winston Churchill and the well-publicized burial of a Hollywood legend. In any case, the question of the event's status as an official state funeral seems to be something of a non-starter, foundering on the retroactive application of a definition for which the age seems to have had no referent.

A third anomalous group represented the City – the lord mayor and aldermen, followed by the Grocers' Company. Professor Strickland thought this most extraordinary for an aristocratic funeral.[60] Sidney's funeral was indeed unusual, but not necessarily irregular. If, according to 'Lant's Roll', Sidney was

---

[55] Bos, Lange-Meyers, and Six, 'Sidney's Funeral Portrayed', p. 39.

[56] Although Bos, Lange-Meyers, and Six ('Sidney's Funeral Portrayed', pp. 47–50) could find no evidence of a Dutch offer to pay for Sidney's funeral in extant collections in Zealand or Holland, John Buxton ('The Mourning for Sidney', p. 48) noted a reference to such an offer from the states of Zealand in Holinshed's *Chronicle* (1587), iii, p. 1555, a reference which originated with Edmund Molyneux who presumably would have known, as he was Sir Henry Sidney's secretary at the time.

[57] Bos, Lange-Meyers, and Six, 'Sidney's Funeral Portrayed', p. 49.

[58] I refer to state funerals other than those of the royal family, though at this time the term may seem odd even for them. According to Robert Yorke, Archivist of the College of Arms, the first state funeral in the modern sense of particularly honouring distinguished service to the Crown was that of George Monck, duke of Albemarle, in 1670. An account of this funeral is in Francis Sanford, *The Order and Ceremonies Vsed for, and at, the Solemn Internment of the most High and most Noble Prince, George, Duke of Albemarle* (1670). It is also mentioned in Thomas Woodcock and John Martin Robinson, *The Oxford Guide to Heraldry* (Oxford, 1988; reprinted 1990), p. 179.

[59] Lant, quoted in Strickland 'Pageantry and Poetry', p. 27.

[60] Strickland 'Pageantry and Poetry', p. 32, who cites Greaves, *Society and Religion*, p. 727, n. 6.

'free' of the Grocers' Company,[61] the presence of the lord mayor and the livery company in the procession is very much in line with usual funerary practice for a member of a guild. At 'The funerall of a Knight or Alderman of London', the lord mayor and aldermen were expected to attend, along with the company of which the deceased was a member.[62] Guildsmen would not normally march *en masse* in funerals of non-members; the explanation for the absence of guilds at aristocratic funerals is perhaps that peers may not often have joined livery companies. (In any case, a peer's funeral might well occur at his family's country seat, rather a long way for a guildsman to travel, even if we found other 'gentle' Grocers amongst the noble lords.) It seems therefore quite likely that the Grocers simply wished to share in Sidney's glory by stressing their relationship to him – not entirely unlike those feudal dependents who felt that 'all the brilliance and pageantry was, in due measure, theirs as well as the dead man's'.[63] In the socially mobile world of Elizabethan England, it seems likely that the Grocers would want to claim Sidney, just as Sidney might not have wanted to snub them. While Sir John Ferne might consider marriages between merchants' daughters and gentlemen's sons disparaging in the original sense of the word, these strictures were perhaps rather more theoretical than practical.[64] In any case, one doubts that the Grocers' presence is likely to have been thought subversive by anyone watching the procession.

Only New Historicist critics have found 'subversive' elements in Sidney's funeral; none of Sidney's contemporaries can be said to have done so. True, 'subversion', like 'irony' before it, has sometimes been applied to anything critics want to appropriate for their own use, but in the case of the 'unconscious subversion' in Sidney's funeral, the ascription seems to me to be historically improbable.[65]

Instead of looking at the various 'texts' of Sidney's funeral as examples of an emerging 'middle class' subjectivity or as evidence of an incipient class struggle, as has been done, I should like to suggest that the funeral was staged for a different effect – to glorify Sir Philip Sidney, knight and champion of the Faith.

---

[61] Bos, Lange-Meyers, and Six, 'Sidney's Funeral Portrayed', pp. 51–2) point out that no proof of Sidney's affiliation with the Grocers has yet been found in guild records. The presence of the guildsmen, however, makes Lant's claim believable, especially as no other guild marched with the procession.

[62] College of Arms, MS. Vincent 151, p. 171.

[63] James, *Society, Politics and Culture*, p. 177. By recontextualizing this quotation, I do not mean to imply that the Grocers were somehow Sidney's 'men'. I mean that their co-option of Sidney is closer to the older feudal sensibility than it may first appear.

[64] Sir John Ferne, in *The Blazon of Gentrie* (1586), pp. 10–11, argues that a gentleman should not marry a merchant's daughter, even if she has a large dowry, for their offspring will be 'greatly blemished', just as if someone had badly bred his hunting dogs! One suspects, however, that contemporaries frequently found such marriages more profitable than subversive. Subversive or not, the City was not about to let its 'gentility' be impugned. Over forty years after the Grocers marched behind Sidney's coffin, the City was still associating itself with the gentry: see *The Cities Advocate, In this Case or Qvestion of Honor and Armes. Whether Apprenticeship Extinguisheth Gentry* (1629), attributed to either John Philipot or Edmund Bolton.

[65] I refer of course to Professor Strickland's interpretation in 'Pageantry and Poetry'.

This is likely to have been the 'text' consciously presented to Tudor readers and viewers in the various accounts of the funeral, one that they understood very well. Whatever 'unconscious subversion' there may have been was minimal. Consider the alleged difference, for example, in George Whetstone's titles for his elegy for the earl of Sussex and his elegy on Sidney in which Professor Strickland sees an 'unconscious' ideological subversion and an incipient individualism. It is true that the title of Whetstone's elegy on Sussex refers to Sussex's hereditary honours, while that for Sidney is distinctly individualistic; the latter stresses Sidney's personal merits, just as the title of his elegy for the earl of Sussex stresses the honour of Sussex's rank. But rather than reading into this difference a theoretical change from traditional subservience to individual merit, thereby demonstrating a change in subjectivity,[66] I would suggest an alternative decoding, especially since it is not at all clear that this emphasis on Sidney's individual merit necessarily subverts aristocratic ideology. In fact, when the writers of heraldry books wish to discuss the origins of the class system, they usually fall back on the idea that individual virtue *creates* nobility. Why else would Francis I of France choose to be knighted by Bayard, the *chevalier sans reproche*?[67] Surely it is this individualistic, but chivalric, symbolism that is behind Sidney's funeral 'text', not the presumed rise of bourgeois subjectivity.

It is almost an essential justification of the class system in most heraldry books and treatises on nobility that nobility begins in virtue, and, if only in theory, the 'natural noblemen' was every bit as worthy of praise as the man of birth – more so, if birth was not matched by deeds.[68] To argue that 'heroic apotheosis of a particular individual was counterproductive to the social and political goals of traditional funeral pageantry'[69] thus seems to me highly unlikely. I would argue instead that the chivalric model encouraged individual subjectivity as well, though I concede that acting in the service of one's lord is not exactly the same as individualistic, bourgeois 'subjectivity', even if one credits the historical authenticity of an emerging bourgeois 'subjectivity' in the late sixteenth century. In any case, such a putative development does not seem to make much immediate difference in the case at hand. Even with heraldic

---

[66] Strickland 'Pageantry and Poetry', pp. 25–6. The problem with this analysis of Sidney's funeral as subversive stems (in my view) from the application of Louis Althusser's model for defining class relationships and consciousness. Strickland applied Althusser's model to Sidney's funeral in order to discuss the funeral as 'text' and to discover the underlying, unintentionally subversive elements in Sidney's funeral elegies – particularly those elements, it was said, that reinforce the emerging, autonomous subjectivity of incipient capitalism, a capitalism that was struggling to replace paternalistic feudalism. In my view, the questionable nature and application of the model renders such a reading unhistorical. Gittings (*Death, Burial and the Individual*, pp. 175–6) discusses the rise of individualism in relation to the decline of heraldic funerals, which, even if credited, would hardly include Sidney's obsequies.

[67] Maurice Keen, *Chivalry* (New Haven, CT, 1984), p. 78.

[68] See my discussion of the theories of class origin and the 'natural nobleman' in *The Coat of Arms*, new ser. 8 (1990): 263ff.

[69] Strickland 'Pageantry and Poetry', p. 26.

funerals, the decline is slow – Oliver Cromwell himself still gets the full treatment.[70] None the less, it is the chivalric model which underlies not only Renaissance social class theory (however anachronistic) but funeral heraldry as well. Even as the urban middle class was experiencing a theoretical change in its subjective consciousness, it was reading romances like *Amadis of Gaul* (or seeing itself pilloried for reading them in Beaumont's *Knight of the Burning Pestle*) and watching City aldermen being buried like the gentlemen of coat armour they had become. An alderman buried with armorial pomp may be subversive of the social order, though I doubt few aldermen thought so; it is a subversion that seems to have had little practical effect. Whatever the theory of a static society may have been in Elizabethan England, the reality was change, and time and chance had been subverting the aristocracy far longer than any change in middle-class subjectivity.[71] In short, unless all social change is credited to subversion, conscious or unconscious, I see rather less subversion in English Renaissance society than is currently fashionable, at least in the case of heraldic funerals.

Furthermore, I would not read the 'text' of civic participation in Sidney's funeral as suggesting that commoners were vying with the nobility for power and place; much less does the 'text' equalize the poor mourners and the rich. Nor, I think, does Sidney's funeral provide evidence of the unconscious 'bourgeois' competition with the aristocracy that Professor Strickland reads into both 'Lant's Roll' and John Phillip's elegy on Sidney.[72] For all its great length, Sidney's funeral procession was marshalled by rank and function like any other heraldic funeral. Thus I see the presence of citizens in the funeral more as the co-option of the citizens' support for the social order in general and Sidney and

---

[70] Wagner, *Heralds of England*, p. 114. Cromwell's funeral cost an extraordinary £28,000 – Litten (*The English Way of Death*, pp. 159–60) put it at a staggering £100,000 – and featured, in addition to the armorial accoutrements, the crown he had refused as Protector (Wagner, *Heralds of England*, p. 84). Henry Ireton, another regicide, also had a heraldic funeral of considerable pomp (*ibid.*, p. 258). Gittings (*Death, Burial and the Individual*, p. 207) cites the heraldic funeral for the duke of Buckingham in 1735 as the last of its type.

[71] See K. B. McFarlane, *The Nobility of Later Medieval England, The Ford Lectures for 1953 and Related Studies* (Oxford, 1953), appendix B, 'The Rate of Extinction of Noble Families', where he argues that the remarkably high turnover in the peerage was occurring long before the changes noticed in Elizabethan society.

[72] Professor Strickland compares 'Lant's Roll' and Philip's elegy in 'Pageantry and Poetry', pp. 28–33, even suggesting that the poor wear black cloth so fine that the demarcation of dress by rank is lost, which socially has an equalizing effect. This would have surprised an alderman of London, not to mention an earl. Although the ascription of an 'unconscious' attitude is impossible to refute, the class competition Strickland finds here seems very laboured indeed. For instance, even if the quality of the cloth could be judged from the engravings in 'Lant's Roll', the niceties of funeral protocol and dress do not seem to be violated in Sidney's case. It is apparent that, except for the official mourners and those carrying heraldic accoutrements, all of whom wear mourning hoods, the majority of gentlemen in the procession wear mourning cloaks, which seems to be standard. While the manner of wearing funeral dress can get very technical (e.g. at 'The funerall of a Knight or Alderman of London', 'The Standard [is] borne by a gent in his gowne and hood on his head', while he is followed by 'Gentlemen in gownes with hoodes on their left shoulders': College of Arms, MS. Vincent 151, p. 169), there is clearly a difference between the traditional poor men walking before the corpse and the higher ranks – the nobility, the states of Holland and the City dignitaries – riding behind according to their degree. Everyone is placed in a traditional, carefully regulated order in relation to the corpse.

his aristocratic faction in particular. The City had always been eager to claim its just due, and by participating in Sidney's funeral, City-men increased their own prestige.

Thus I return to a reading of the 'texts' of Sidney's funeral with a different, more traditional approach. Traditional answers are not necessarily wrong answers. The chief beneficiary of Sidney's funeral was not an emerging class of citizens unconsciously subversive of the traditional order; it was the traditional order itself. Burghley and the queen did not object to the 'apotheosis' of a loyal subject who exemplified chivalric virtue in the queen's service, and Walsingham and his circle had staged a propaganda spectacle that, whatever practical effect it may have had, was nonetheless a 'triumph' for Walsingham's house and faction, however much it may have drained Walsingham's financial resources.[73] The political uses of Sidney's death and funeral are borne out in other ways. For instance, Sidney left his best sword to the earl of Essex, a clearly symbolic political legacy.[74] This legacy was remembered four years after Sidney's death: George Peele in *Polyhymnia* (1590) explains Essex's black attire for the Ascension Day Tilt as the earl's continued mourning for Sidney.[75]

As an aspect of Tudor political culture, the heraldic funeral had not yet lost its importance by 1587. Whether for an earl at his family seat or for an alderman in the City, heraldic funerals emphasized the place of the deceased and his family in society. While the heraldic funeral originally may have flourished in a feudal setting, it remained important in Elizabethan society precisely because it bolstered the social order with the sort of pageantry that defined the individual and his place. The heraldic funeral remained a pageant that consoled the family of the deceased by parading his heraldic 'achievements' to the glory of the dead man's house and in honour of a chivalric tradition which had still not entirely succumbed to a new age. In the case of Sidney's funeral, heraldic funerary pageantry honoured a man who, more than any other aristocrat of his period, epitomized the chivalric traditions that, however anachronistically, still under-pinned many of society's assumptions. Sidney was mourned so extravagantly because he represented what a knight and a courtier should be, and his funeral, though ostentatious, upheld rather than subverted aristocratic ideals. I should also like to believe that at least some of the grief for Sidney so elaborately demonstrated in his funeral was sincerely rooted in an intensely subjective sense of loss that such an exemplary young man had fallen so gallantly in the service of queen and country.

---

[73] For the funeral as 'triumph', see Neill, 'Exeunt with a Dead March', p. 154.

[74] F. J. Levy, 'Philip Sidney Reconsidered', in Kinney (ed.), *Sidney in Retrospect*, p. 12.

[75] Alan Hager, *Dazzling Images: The Masks of Sir Philip Sidney* (Newark, NJ, 1991), p. 24. And, of course, Essex does marry Sidney's widow, which may have cost him the post of queen's champion. McCoy ('Sidney and Elizabethan Chivalry', pp. 39–40) has argued that Essex's entrance in black was an attempt to upstage the queen's champion; the gesture stressed Essex's allegiance to his new bride, Sidney's widow, and his claim to Sidney's legacy as chevalier – a legacy that would end with his execution.

'O, 'tis a gallant king':
Shakespeare's Henry V *and the
crisis of the 1590s*

PETER C. HERMAN

WILL. Let it be a quarrel between us, if you live.
K. HEN. I embrace it.   (IV.i.205–206)

Sometime around 1600, Nicholas Hilliard painted two miniatures of Queen
Elizabeth I that are striking both for their detail and for their infidelity. Both
depict Elizabeth as a beautiful young woman.[1] In one (plate 52), possibly a
visual echo of her coronation portrait, her long hair falls over her shoulders (an
unmistakeable sign of virginity); in the other (plate 53), her hair is bound.
Despite their seeming verisimilitude, these exquisite portraits were not intended
as mirrors held up to nature; they do not reproduce the tired old woman with
blackened teeth who deeply resented any reminder of her physical decline.
These miniatures are, rather, relics of the cult of Elizabeth, and they represent
the 'idea' of Elizabeth as ever youthful, the Queen of Beauty, Beauty's Rose,
Astrea, or Belphoebe, images that she had always assiduously cultivated but
especially so over the last decade of her reign.
   The gap between idea and reality suggested by Hilliard's miniatures can be
read, however, as more than evidence of Elizabeth's personal vanity. Roy Strong
proposes that these works capture that last poignant moment when 'all could
yet join in the paeans to the Divine One', but by 1600 a growing number of
people both inside and outside the court declined to participate in this chorus of
praise.[2] The gap, then, posited by these miniatures also emblematizes the social
fractures characterizing the last years of Elizabeth's reign. Official views of an
obedient, stratified, unified society, ideals expressed or prescribed, for example,
in the Books of Homilies or officially approved reprints of Sir Thomas Smith's

I want to thank Jean E. Howard, Skiles Howard, and David S. Kastan for their help. I especially want to
acknowledge Dale Hoak's editorial acumen, which significantly improved this chapter. I presented a
shorter version of this chapter at the 1991 CEMERS conference, 'Place and Displacement in the
Renaissance', and a longer version at a Folger Shakespeare Library Evening Colloquium. I am grateful
to both audiences for their balanced combination of praise and blame.
[1] The miniatures are reproduced in Roy Strong, *The Cult of Elizabeth* (Berkeley, CA, 1977), p. 49. See
   also John N. King, 'Queen Elizabeth I: Representations of the Virgin Queen', *Renaissance Quarterly*
   43 (1990): 43.
[2] Strong, *Cult of Elizabeth*, p. 55.

Plate 52. Elizabeth I as 'Queen of Beauty', a miniature (2½″ × 1⅞″) painted by Nicholas Hilliard *c.* 1600.

Plate 53. Elizabeth I as Cynthia, 'Queen of Love and Beauty', a miniature (2⅝″ × 2½″) painted by Nicholas Hilliard *c.* 1600.

De Republica Anglorum, rarely, if ever, admitted the extraordinary economic, political, and social tensions of the 1590s.[3] The riots and rebellions of this decade, as much as the government's repeatedly shrill attempts to justify its

---

[3] The title pages of 1583, 1584, 1589, and 1594 editions of Smith's work make a point of declaring that the *De Republica Anglorum* has been 'Seene and allowed', that the censors have passed it. Now this fact that would be of little consequence if most other books of the period carried a similar *nihil obstat*, but they do not, perhaps suggesting that the publishers wanted to advertise the *official* approval of

authority via royal proclamations, testify to the distrust and hostility separating the rulers from the ruled, to the enormous gap between political ideals and socio-political realities.

In 1599, Shakespeare's company performed *The Life of Henry V*, the final instalment of his trilogy (or quadrilogy, depending how one counts the two part of *Henry IV*) on the roots of the Tudor dynasty. The title is misleading, because rather than dramatizing the important events of Henry V's entire life, as Shakespeare did for Henry IV, Henry V concentrates upon the events leading up to and immediately following the invasion of France, and the play reaches a climax with the battle of Agincourt. *Henry V* has the potential to become an exercise in English nationalism and many critics, as well as audiences, have taken it that way. In this essay, however, I shall argue that Shakespeare's *Henry V* challenges such expectations by making the social fissures of the 1590s a constituent element of the play.[4] Superficially, *Henry V* strongly implies that Henry's golden reputation shares about the same relation to reality as do Elizabeth's late portraits to her actual physical appearance; more profoundly, it shows that the idealization of Henry (like that of Elizabeth) has ideological purposes that are masked by providentialist language. Furthermore, *Henry V*'s project of demystification is inflected by the loud and frequently violent expres-

---

Smith's vision. Although I cannot say that I have made a systematic study, I cannot recall any other title pages that make a similar claim.

[4] The question of the place of *Henry V* in Elizabethan political culture is a vexed one. One school, exemplified by E. M. W. Tillyard and Lily Campbell, finds in the Henriad an endorsement of orthodox Elizabethan beliefs about order, rebellion, and kingship. See E. M. W. Tillyard, *Shakespeare's History Plays* (1974); Lily B. Campbell, *Shakespeare's Histories: Mirrors of Elizabethan Policy* (San Marino, 1947). In addition, see Hardin Craig, 'Shakespeare and the History Plays', in Brander Matthews and Ashley H. Thorndike (eds.), *Joseph Quincy Adams Memorial Studies* (Washington DC, 1948), pp. 55–64; Irving Ribner, *The English History Play in the Age of Shakespeare* (Princeton, NJ, 1957); Derek Traversi, *Shakespeare: From 'Richard II' to 'Henry V'* (Stanford, CA, 1957); Robin Headlam Wells, *Shakespeare, Politics, and the State* (1986); F. P. Wilson, 'The English History Play', in Helen Gardner (ed.), *Shakespearean and Other Studies*, (Oxford, 1969), pp. 1–53; Sherman H. Hawkins, 'Virtue and Kingship in Shakespeare's *Henry IV*', *English Literary Renaissance*, 5 (1975): 313–43; Andrews and Gina MacDonald, '*Henry V*: A Shakespearean Definition of a Politic Reign', *Studies in the Humanities* 9 (1982): 32–9; and Lawrence Danson, '*Henry V*: King, Chorus, and Critics', *Shakespeare Quarterly* 34 (1983): 27–43. Over the last decade, however, many Shakespeare critics (generally if not entirely accurately associated with the New Historicism or its English cousin, Cultural Materialism) have begun regarding the play as a complex but none the less forceful intervention into the confused scene of late Elizabethan politics. See Stephen Greenblatt, 'Invisible Bullets', *Shakespearean Negotiation* (Berkeley, CA, 1988), pp. 21–65; Jonathan Dollimore and Alan Sinfield, 'History and Ideology: the instance of *Henry V*', in John Drakakis (ed.), *Alternative Shakespeares* (1985), pp. 206–27; Leonard Tennenhouse, *Power on Display: The Politics of Shakespeare's Genre* (1986). Some, like Greenblatt and Tennenhouse, regard the history plays as shoring up the authority of the state. Others, following the lead of Elizabeth I, regard the theatre as a potentially destabilizing institution. See Dollimore and Sinfield, *Political Shakespeare*; Jonathan Dollimore, *Radical Tragedy: Religion, Ideology and Power in the Drama of Shakespeare and his Contemporaries* (Chicago, IL, 1984); Michael Bristol, *Carnival and Theatre: Plebian Culture and the Structure of Authority in Renaissance England* (New York, 1985). As David S. Kastan puts it, 'The histories expose the idealizations of political power by presenting rule as role, by revealing that power passes to him who can best control and manipulate the visual and verbal symbols of authority'; 'Proud Majesty Made a Subject: Shakespeare and the Spectacle of Rule', *Shakespeare Quarterly* 37 (1986): 469. See also Thomas Cartelli, 'Ideology and Subversion in the Shakespearean Set Speech', *English Literary History*, 53 (1986): 1–3.

sions of anger against authority that had been building up steam since at least 1590. Now, I am not suggesting that *Henry V* passively reflects this widespread discontent. To appropriate Wayne Rebhorn's comment about *Julius Caesar*, a play that was also staged in 1599 and shares *Henry V*'s concern with using the past as a means of critically examining the present, *Henry V* 'is not a *repetition* of its context, but a *re-presentation* of it; it does not simply reiterate what is already known but re-forms it, thereby actually helping to constitute the very context of which it is a part. It is not a mirror but a shaping presence.'[5]

The play's generation of opposing perspectives has genuinely contestatory resonances, for by repeatedly opening up rifts between the Chorus and the play, between Henry and his soldiers, indeed, between Henry's own speeches, Shakespeare's *Henry V* not only reflects the generalized crisis of authority in late Elizabethan England, but actually helps define the very climate of which it is simultaneously product and indicator.

The clearest example of this paradigm may be found in the undermining of King Henry's authority in IV.i.[6] Although Bates and Williams have no intention of deserting, their allegiance to the king does not extend to an unexamined approval of the present 'incursion' into France or to Henry's public pronouncements. Bates grounds his refusal to accept his king's words at face value in his recognition of what Henry tries to erase, that in war the fortunes of the nobility and the common people are not coterminous:

> K. HEN. By my troth, I will speak my conscience of the King: I think he would not wish himself anywhere but where he is.
> BATES. Then I would he were here alone; so should he be sure to be ransom'd, and a many poor men's lives sav'd. (IV.i.118–23)

Michael Williams also refuses to accept Henry's claims that he would not be ransomed, and like Bates, Williams's cynicism arises from his rejection of the very populism that Henry tries to propagate:

> K. HEN. I myself heard the King say he would not be ransom'd.
> WILL. Ay, he said, so, to make us fight cheerfully; but when our throats are cut, e may be ransom'd, and we ne'er the wiser.
> K. HEN. If I live to see it, I will never trust his word after.
> WILL. You pay him then. That's a perilous shot out of an elder-gun, that a poor and a private displeasure can do against a monarch! You may as well go about to turn the sun to ice with fanning in his face with a peacock's feather. You'll never trust his word after! come, 'tis a foolish saying. (IV.i.191–201)

---

[5] 'The Crisis of the Aristocracy in *Julius Caesar*', *Renaissance Quarterly* 43 (1990): 82. Rebhorn appropriates the term 'shaping presence' from Louis Montrose's '"Shaping Fantasies": Figurations of Gender and Power in Elizabethan Culture', in Stephen J. Greenblatt (ed.), *Representing the Renaissance* (Berkeley, CA, 1988), pp. 31–64.

[6] All reference to Shakespeare's plays are to the Riverside edition: *The Riverside Shakespeare*, ed. G. Blakemore Evans (Boston, MA, 1974).

As for Henry's answer to Williams's charge that 'if the cause be not good, the King himself hath a heavy reckoning to make' (IV.i.135), Henry's reply carefully evades the substance of his subordinate's questions.[7] Moreover, although his argument that 'The King is not bound to answer the particular endings of his soldiers' (IV.i.155–5) may bludgeon his interlocutor into silence, it contradicts his earlier charge to the Archbishop to weigh carefully his justifications for war precisely because the guilty party will answer for it:

> We charge you, in the name of God, take heed;
> For never two such kingdoms did contend
> Without much fall of blood, whose guiltless drops
> Are every one a woe, a sore complaint,
> 'Gainst him whose wrongs gives edge unto the swords
> That makes such waste in brief mortality.   (I.ii.23–8)

Henry and Williams decide to settle their quarrel after the battle; the soldiers wander off and Henry is left alone to deliver his soliloquy on kingship which begins with the recognition that authority derives not from a divinely instituted hierarchy but from the exercise of power, from creating 'awe and fear' in other men (IV.i.247). Henry concludes by reversing both his famous 'We few, we happy few, we band of brothers' speech before the battle of Agincourt and the Chorus's assessment of his egalitarianism:

> For forth he goes, and visits all his host,
> Bids them good morrow with a modes smile,
> And calls them brothers, friends, and countrymen   (Pro. 32–4)

Rather than calling attention to any unity of purpose, Henry's speech ends in a Coriolanus-like paroxysm of condescension that justifies his soldiers' scepticism over his public assertions of solidarity:[8]

> And, but for ceremony, such a wretch,
> Winding up days with toil, and nights with sleep,
> Had the forehand and vantage of a king.
> The slave, a member of the country's peace,
> Enjoys it; but in a gross brain little wots
> What watch the King keeps to maintain the peace,
> Whose hours the peasant best advantages.   (IV.i.278–84)

Determining that Shakespeare treats Henry ironically has been a commonplace of *Henry V* criticism since Hazlitt.[9] What has not been noted is how Henry's contradictory statements and the challenges to his authority by his

---

[7] David S. Kastan, *Shakespeare and the Shapes of Time* (Hanover, NH, 1982), p. 68.

[8] Annabel Patterson, *Shakespeare and the Popular Voice* (Oxford and Cambridge, MA, 1989), pp. 90–1.

[9] Robert Ornstein, *A Kingdom for Stage* (Cambridge, MA, 1972); Gordon Ross Smith, 'Shakespeare's *Henry V*: Another Part of the Critical Forest', *Journal of the History of Ideas* 37 (1976): 3–26. See also H. C. Goddard, *The Meaning of Shakespeare* (Chicago, IL, 1951); A. P. Rossiter, *Angel with Horns* (New York, 1961); R. W. Battenhouse, '*Henry V* as Heroic Comedy', in Richard Hosley (ed.), *Essays*

subjects both echo and reinforce the widespread suspicion of established authority among the non-élite elements of Elizabethan society.

Both contemporary reports and modern historians agree that in the 1590s the government's legitimacy came under attack from many quarters. Radical protestants, such as the author (or authors) of the Marprelate Tracts, declared that Elizabeth I's authority in ecclesiastical affairs was misplaced, even illegitimate.[10] In 1591, for example, the appropriately named Tristam Blaby found himself under indictment for delivering a seditious sermon 'against authority' arguing that 'there was never any so high or mighty in authority that could or might rule and govern both sorts of people [sic], both the spirituality and the temporality, . . . in any of their own dominions and jurisdictions'.[11] Tensions between local officials and the central government also contributed to the slippage in prestige of established authority. In particular, squabbles over the raising, training, and provisioning of militias led to friction between court and country gentry. In Norfolk the result was an 'intensely political situation . . . [that led] to frequent debates about who did what and on whose authority'.[12]

Many also believed that the governing authorities were no longer fit to rule. The queen's age and her advancement of men thought to be grasping and amoral prompted Thomas Wilson to remark that the factionalism, even paranoia, of the queen's officers had so crippled government at the top as to render it incompetent:

They [the privy councillors] suffer very fewe to be acquainted with matters of state for feare of divulging it, whereby their practises are subject to be revealed, and therefore they will suffer fewe to rise to places of reputacion that are skillful or studious in matters of pollicy, but holde them lowe and farre of[f] soe that the greatest politicians that rule most will not have about them other then base penn clarkes, that can do nothing but write as they are bidden, or some mecannicall dunce that cannot conceive his Master's drift and polices, for if they have lynces eyes they must looke into their actions.[13]

on *Shakespeare and Elizabethan Drama in Honor of Hardin Craig*, (Columbia, SC, 1962), pp. 169–180; R. W. Battenhouse, 'The Relation of *Henry V* to *Tamburlaine*', *Shakespeare Quarterly* 27 (1974): 71–9; Alexander Leggatt, *Shakespeare's Political Drama: The History Plays and the Roman Plays* (1988); Larry Champion, '*The Noise of The Drum*': Dramatic Strategy and Political Ideology in Shakespeare and the English Chronicle Plays (Newark, NJ, 1990). Some critics recognize that Shakespeare's treatment of Henry is ambiguous at best, but that the play either resolves the ambiguities or refuses to favour one view over the other. See Norman Rabkin, *Shakespeare and the Problem of Meaning* (Chicago, IL, 1981); Paul Dean, 'Chronicle and Romance Modes in *Henry V*', *Shakespeare Quarterly* 32 (1981): 18–27; Joanne Altieri, *The Theatre of Praise* (Newark NJ, 1986).

10 See Lord Chief Justice Puckering's notes of his interrogation of 'puritans' in star chamber, in John Strype, *Annals of the Reformation* (4 vols., reprinted New York: Burt Franklin, n.d.), iv, pp. 197–202.

11 Quoted in F. G. Emmison, *Elizabethan Life: Disorder* (Chelmsford, 1970), p. 57.

12 A. Hassell Smith, *County and Court: Government and Politics in Norfolk, 1558–1603* (Oxford, 1974), p. 334. I am indebted for this reference, and for my sense of the 1590s as a decade of crisis, to Robert Weimann, 'Society and the Uses of Authority in Shakespeare', in Kenneth Muir, Jay Halio and D. J. Palmer (eds.) *Shakespeare, Man of the Theater* (Newark, NJ, 1983), pp. 182–99.

13 Thomas Wilson, *The State of England, Anno Dom. 1600*, ed. F. J. Fisher, *Camden Miscellany* 16 (1934): 42. See also Anthony Esler, *The Aspiring Mind of the Elizabethan Younger Generation* (Durham, NC, 1966). For the suggested importance of paranoia in Elizabethan political life, see Lacey Baldwin Smith, *Treason in Tudor England* (Princeton, NJ, 1986).

By the turn of the century, even Elizabeth I admitted the decline. 'Now the wit of the fox is everywhere on foot', she complained to William Lambarde, 'so as hardly a faithful or virtuous man may be found.'[14]

Such statements by those who, like Wilson and the queen, were familiar with the internal operations of government provide part of the context for understanding why Shakespeare's two soldiers refuse to grant their king unqualified, unexamined support. An equally significant, yet rarely mentioned, part of this context is the overt class hostility of the 1590s, as sharp as anything voiced in 1549, a year of popular rebellion against established authority, local and central. For example, an Essex weaver charged with sedition said that 'it would never be better until men did rise and seek thereby an amendment . . .'.[15]

At Norwich in 1595 the mayor and the justices received an anonymous letter describing how 60,000 London craftsmen were waiting the call to rise up and how in the ensuing revolution 'some barbarous and unmerciful soldier shall lay open your hedges, reap your fields, rifle your coffers, and level your houses to the ground'.[16] In Somerset too someone threatened that 'ther would be old threshing owt of mowes & Cuttynge of throatts'.[17]

Although historians agree that the economic hardship born of dearth and poor harvests caused much of this distress, Elizabethan officials understood such words as an attack on the established social order. The instigator of the Oxfordshire Rising, Bartholomew Steere, averred that 'it would never be well until the gentry were knocked down' with the hedges.[18] Like the Norfolk libeller, he had convinced himself that 'the London apprentices would join them', and that 'it would only be a month's work to overrun the realm . . .'.[19] Unsurprisingly, the judges who convicted Steere of treason – their number included Attorney-General Coke – interpreted this as an assault on the system as a whole, not just hedges.[20]

Discontent with established authority was especially sharp in London, where unemployment and severe inflation prompted talk of assassination. In 1590 a baker said he would kill the queen and drink her blood.[21] In October 1592 Richard Stone's arrest for 'seeking to kill the queen' moved another prisoner in

---

[14] Quoted in J. E. Neale, 'The Elizabethan Political Scene', *Essays in Elizabethan History* (New York, 1958), p. 78.

[15] Quoted in Emmison, *Elizabethan Life: Disorder*, p. 64.

[16] *HMC. Salisbury MSS.* (24 vols., 1915), xiii, pp. 168–9. The editors date the 'Norfolk Libel' as 'after 1578', but John Walter gives 1595 as its date: John Walter, 'A "Rising of the People"?: The Oxfordshire Rising of 1596', *Past and Present* no. 107 (1985): 91.

[17] Quoted in Walter, 'A "Rising of the People"?', p. 91.   [18] *CSP. Dom.*, 1595–97, p. 343.

[19] *Ibid.*, p. 345.

[20] Roger B. Manning, *Village Revolts: Social Protest and Popular Disturbances in England, 1509–1640* (Oxford, 1988), p. 228; Walker, 'Oxfordshire Rising', pp. 128–9. Three judges dissented, arguing that one must specifically resist the queen's authority to be judged guilty of treason, and not merely knock down an enclosure. The majority held that because 'the case here tend[s] to a generality', Steere and his followers were guilty of rebellion against the social order; quoted in Walker, 'Oxfordshire Rising', p. 130.

[21] Peter Clark, 'A Crisis Contained? The Condition of English Towns in the 1590s', in Peter Clark (ed.), *The European Crisis of the 1590s*, (1985), p. 53.

the Marshalsea to say that 'there were many committed for that, but someone
would make an end of her one day, and then all those commitments would be
void, and all would be well'. When the commons found a leader, 'all . . . would
rise, for they all disliked the State and Government'.[22] In June 1595 riots broke
out when a silk weaver appeared before the lord mayor's house making some
'hard speeches in dispraise of his government', and Edward Coke again testified
that the root issue was not so much economic as the rioters' intent to 'take the
sworde of Aucthoryte from the magistrates and gouernours Lawfully
Authorised and there vnto appointed . . .'.[23] Coke's charge finds confirmation in
a 1598 libel urging the apprentices of London to 'be revenged' of the lord mayor
because of his abuse of authority: 'for to se our brethren whypt and set on the
pyllory without a cause, which is a greyf to us'.[24] The city fathers' answer was to
set up a cage outside Newgate for the public display and punishment of
'disordered persons'.[25]

The reproduction in *Henry V*.iv.i of the general distrust of, and hostility
towards, authority in Shakespeare's London takes on even more resonance by
the fact that Elizabeth's government considered soldiers like Williams, Bates,
and Pistol a dangerous, politically suspect class of vagabonds and thieves, one
inherently given to sedition and rebellion. The soldiers were commonly
recruited from the ranks of the criminal underclass, and when those pressed into
overseas duty returned home, they swelled all the more the ranks of the
dispossessed.[26] Of the twelve proclamations directed at remedying social disorder between 1589 and 1600, seven deal specifically with vagrancy and each
one of the seven singles out soldiers for special admonishment, the only
profession so identified.[27]

The government's assumption that soldiers constituted a destabilizing force
in the commonwealth carried some justification, given the veterans' loud,
occasional threats to march on London or raid the countryside.[28] Like some
lawyers, the veterans' leaders knew that forced conscription was of dubious
legality, and when some sought revenge (like the Essex weaver cited earlier) they
tried to use their involuntary military experience to make credible their threats:

---

[22] *CSP. Dom., 1591–94*, p. 282.   [23] Cited in Manning, *Village Revolts*, pp. 207, 208.
[24] J. P. Collier (ed.), *Trevelyan Papers, Part II*, Camden Society, old. ser., vol. 84 (1862): 101, Clark, 'A
Crisis Contained?', p. 54.
[25] M. J. Power, 'London and the Control of the "Crisis" of the 1590s', *History* 70 (1985): 380. James
Shapiro, to whom I owe this reference, calls it a 'bizarrely Tamburlainian scene' ('Revising
Tamburlaine', *Criticism* 31 (1989): 364.
[26] A. L. Beier, *Masterless Men: The Vagrancy Problem in England 1560–1640* (1985), p. 94. One
Barnaby Rich testified that recruiters 'either . . . scour their prisons of thieves or their streets of
rogues and vagabonds'; *ibid.*
[27] Paul L. Hughes and James F. Larkin, *Tudor Royal Proclamations*, (New Haven, CT, 1969), iii,
nos. 716, 725, 735, 740, 745, 762, 777, 779, 789, 795, 796 (repeat of 735), and 800. See, for example,
the proclamation of 1589, *Placing Vagrant Soldiers under Martial Law* (*ibid.*, no. 716), which
typically assumes that such vagrants were frauds, only pretending to have served Her Majesty
overseas.
[28] Clark, 'A Crisis Contained?', p. 55.

'he wished in his heart a hundred men would rise, and he would be their captain to cut the throats of the rich churls and the rich cornmongers for he had served as a soldier divers times beyond the seas and could lead men'.[29] Such men did not distinguish between 'churls' at home or in the field, for many of their superiors believed, to quote Falstaff, that the commoners were 'good enough to toss . . .', mere 'food for powder' (*1 Henry IV* IV.ii.65–6). 'A group of sailors', for example, 'who seemed to be newly come from the sea', denounced their commander, Thomas Lord Howard, because 'he hath cast away a number of men better than himself'.[30] Many ex-soldiers must have sympathized with John Thompson who was hauled into court in 1602 for proclaiming that 'if he were a soldier again as he had been, he would rather fight against his country than for it'.[31]

By explicitly ruling out disobedience, Williams and Bates are clearly not going as far as Thompson or the Essex weaver; even so, their scepticism concerning Henry's solidarity with his troops and their refusal to abandon the proposition that 'if the cause be not good, the King himself hath a heavy reckoning to make' (IV.i.134–5) draws on the same pool of resentment.

The cultural work of dramatizing Henry's interrogation at the hands of his soldiers is complex. The play appears to legitimate authority by illustrating, via Williams and Bates, why Elizabeth I and her councillors viewed soldiers with such suspicion. In Stephen J. Greenblatt's terms, Shakespeare 'records' their dissenting voices only to have them 'contained' by the play's overall celebration of Henry's victories. Like Hal's baiting of the hapless Francis in *1 Henry IV*, 'the commentary glimpse of a revolt against authority is closed off', first by Williams's rejection of rebellion in language that directly echoes the Homily against Disobedience ('to disobey [the king] were against all proportion of subjection' [IV.i.146]), then by Henry's extended rebuttal, and finally by Bates's acceptance of Henry's rebuttal ('Tis certain, every man that dies ill, the ill upon his own head, the King is not to answer it' [186–7]).[32]

But when Henry claims that he has heard the king say that he will not be ransomed, Williams's contemptuous dismissal of this opinion as mere propaganda ('Ay, he said so, to make us fight cheerfully' [192]) reopens the argument. This time, Williams refuses to back down and Henry finds himself agreeing to continue the quarrel after the battle (assuming both survive). Even though Williams grounds his scepticism in the powerlessness of his class, the unsettled nature of this exchange implies that *Henry V*'s interrogations of authority may not be so neatly contained as Greenblatt's highly influential model would

---

[29] Quoted in Emmison, *Elizabethan Life: Disorder*, p. 64.   [30] Quoted in *ibid.*, p. 57.
[31] Quoted in Beier, *Masterless Men*, p. 95.
[32] Stephen J. Greenblatt, 'Invisible Bullets', pp. 44–5. Greenblatt argues that *Henry V* contains its subversions because 'the very doubts that Shakespeare raises serve not to rob the king of his charisma but to heighten it, precisely as they heighten the theatrical interest of the play' (*ibid.*, p. 63). Similarly, Leonard Tennenhouse has argued that the *Henry* plays authorize the power of the state by demonstrating how 'recalcitrant cultural materials [such as Williams and Bates] were taken up and hierarchized within the official rituals of state' (*Power on Display*, p. 85).

predict.[33] Williams refuses to be 'contained' either in this scene or when Henry reveals himself in iv.viii.[34]

However, the play's challenge to established authority also originates in the conditions of dramatic representation in the English Renaissance, conditions which had the effect of levelling *on the stage* the differences between social groups. Just as the privileged are inevitably demoted, the unprivileged inevitably undergo a form of promotion because, as Stephen Orgel puts it, 'the miming of greatness ... employs precisely the same methods [e.g. stage business, props, costumes, etc.] the crown was using to assert and validate its authority'.[35] Although acting the role of the king demystifies the sources of authority by identifying them as extrinsic and therefore appropriatable – to mime a king successfully implies that there is nothing intrinsically special about a king in the first place – miming the disgruntled lower classes works in the opposite direction because the play raises the subaltern group from anonymity to the same status as royalty. Even further, the play valorizes the Williamses and Bateses of Renaissance society by *envoicing* (to coin a term) and thereby endorsing those whom the officially sanctioned chronicles usually silenced or marginalized.[36] The resentment against authority and the sheer

---

[33] Greenblatt has complicated this overly stiff interpretive model in his recent work. See, for example, 'Resonance and Wonder', in *Learning to Curse: Essays in Early Modern Culture* (New York and London, 1990), pp. 165–6, and the brilliantly subtle essays collected in *Marvelous Possessions: The Wonder of the New World* (Chicago, IL, 1991).

[34] When Henry tells William that 'It was ourself thou didst abuse' (l. 49), William shifts the blame back onto Henry:
> Your Majesty came not like yourself. You appear'd to me but as a common man; witness the night, your garments, your lowliness; and what your Highness suffer'd under that shape, I beseech you take it for your own fault and not mine; for had you been as I took you for, I made no offense; therefore I beseech your Highness pardon me. (iv.viii.50–6)

[35] Stephen Orgel, 'Making Greatness Familiar', in Stephen J. Greenblatt (ed.), *The Power of Forms in the English Renaissance* (Norman, OK, 1982), p. 45. See also David S. Kastan, 'Proud Majesty made a Subject', *Shakespeare Quarterly* 37 (1986): 459–75. One of the hallmarks of Shakespeare's drama is its repeated demonstration of how social roles are constructed and fluid rather than inherent and immutable, a concept obviously threatening to a culture that sought to define itself in fixed, hierarchical terms. See David Cressey, 'Describing the Social Order of Elizabethan and Stuart England', *Literature and History* 3 (1976): 29–44. The writers Cressy examines (e.g. Sir Thomas Smith, William Harrison, and Thomas Wilson) all recognize that social mobility exists, but none are happy about it; they wish that everyone would just stay in the place where they were born. Wilson, for example, calls anyone who rises above his origins a 'Covetouse Mongrell gentleman' (*The State of England*, p. 19). Perhaps the best example of Shakespeare's depiction of the social constructiveness of identity and social class would be the Introduction to *The Taming of the Shrew*, in which the tinker, Christopher Sly, is convinced that he is a lord because everyone around him, for a joke, dresses him as a lord and says that he is a lord. See Karen Newman, 'Renaissance Family Politics and Shakespeare's *The Taming of the Shrew*', in Arthur F. Kinney (ed.), *Renaissance Historicism* (Amherst, MA, 1987), pp. 131–45.

[36] Until recently no one questioned the assumption that the chronicles of Hall and Holinshed lend unqualified support to the Tudor myth; see for example Antonia Gransden, *Historical Writing in England* (2 vols., Ithaca, NY, 1986), ii, p. 470. But such accounts are being scrutinized anew. Annabel Patterson argues that Shakespeare's chief source for the history plays, Holinshed's *Chronicles*, does not slavishly endorse the Tudor party line; instead, it emphasizes multivocality and divergences of opinion. See Patterson, 'The Small Cat Massacre: Popular Culture in the 1587 "Holinshed"', *Reading Between the Lines* (Madison, WI, 1993), pp. 117–59; 'Rethinking Tudor Historiography', *The South Atlantic Quarterly* 92 (1993): 185–208; and *Reading Holinshed's 'Chronicles'* (Chicago, IL, 1994). In a forthcoming essay I will argue that Hall's treatment of Henry VIII is more complicated and contestatory than has previously been recognized.

bitterness at pawnhood welling up in Williams's and Bates's speeches would have echoed and reinforced the distrust of actual authority felt by many members of Shakespeare's audience.[37] By having Williams and Bates articulate with impunity resentments that the law rigorously suppressed when expressed outside the theatre (and sometimes when expressed within it), Shakespeare confers on these sentiments precisely the legitimacy that the authorities sought to deny.

If Williams and Bates reify in dramatic terms the rumblings of the commons in the 1590s, Pistol represents an Elizabethan nightmare come true, and Gower execrates him in terms that echo the proclamations against the disruptive swarm of 'false' soldiers:[38]

Why, 'tis a gull, a fool, a rogue, that now and then goes to the wars, to grace himself at his return into London under the form of a soldier. And such fellows are perfit in the great commanders' names, and they will learn you by rote where services were done – at such and such sconce, at such a breach, at such a convoy; who came off bravely, who was shot, who disgrac'd, what terms the enemy stood on; and this they con perfitly in the phrase of war, which they trick up with new-tun'd oaths; and what a beard of the general's cut and a horrid suit of the camp will do among foaming bottles and wale-wash'd wits, is wonderful to be thought on.   (III.vi.7–79)

The history plays provide much evidence to support Gower's view. *2 Henry IV* reveals that Pistol is a pimp and murderer,[39] and in *Henry V*, he proves himself a braggart, a thief, and a coward, urging others to the breach while hanging back himself. The Boy describes Pistol, Nym, and Bardolph as 'three such antics [that] do not amount to a man', and Pistol in particular as someone who 'hath a killing tongue and a quiet sword' (III.ii.31,34). At the end of the play, Pistol declares that upon his return to England he will fulfill Gower's prediction:

---

[37] Phyllis Rackin, *States of History: Shakespeare's English Chronicles* (Ithaca, NY, 1990), p. 203; Bristol, *Carnival and Theatre*, pp. 88–9. On Shakespeare's audience, see Martin Butler's chapter, 'Shakespeare's Unprivileged Playgoers', in his *Theatre and Crisis: 1632–1642* (Cambridge, 1984), pp. 299–302. Because the authorities considered the theatre a potential source of civil discord, it was subject to increasing regulation and censorship. For example, the opening scene of *Sir Thomas More* (usually ascribed to the early 1590s, although the play may have been written as late as 1603) had to be cut because the Master of the Revels, Edmund Tilney, considered it inflammatory. The script begins with a scene that the government would have found all too familiar in 1599 – a mob of citizens protesting their grievances – and so Tilney demanded that the players 'leave out the insurrection wholy and the Cause ther off and begin with Sir Thomas More att the mayors sessions with a reportt afterwards off his good service don being Shrive off London upon a mutiny Agaynst the Lumbards only by A short reportt and nott otherwise att our own perilles'; quoted by Rackin (*Stages of History*, p. 207) who cites Jane Clare, '"Greater Themes for Insurrection's Arguing": Political Censorship of the Elizabethan and Jacobean Stage', *Review of English Studies* n.s. 38 (1987): 171. See also Annabel Patterson, *Censorship and Interpretation: The Condition of Writing in Early Modern England* (Madison, WI, 1984).

[38] See for example the proclamation for placing vagabonds under martial law (1598): 'there are in many parts of the realm . . . wandering in the common highways . . . multitudes of able men, . . . exacting money continually upon pretense of service in the wars without relief, whereas many of them never did serve . . .'; Hughes and Larkin (eds.), *Tudor Royal Proclamations*, iii, no. 796, p. 196.

[39] *Beadle*: 'Come, I charge you both go with me, for the man is dead that you and Pistol beat amongst you' (*2 Henry IV*, v.iv.15–17).

... Well, bawd I'll turn,
And something lean to cutpurse of quick hand.
To England will I steal, and there I'll steal;
And patches will I get unto these cudgell'd scars,
And swear I got them in the Gallia wars   (v.ii.85–9)

But Pistol fulfills a more complex function in *Henry V* than playing the role of
the *miles gloriosus* and confirming the Elizabethan stereotype of the beggar-
soldier. As many critics have noted, Pistol acts as an ironic commentator upon
the main action. For example, Henry's ringing couplet, 'Cheerly to sea! The
signs of war advance! / No king of England, if not king of France' (II.ii.192–3),
Pistol reduces to 'Let us to France, like horse-leeches, my boys, / To suck, to
suck, the very blood to suck!' (II.iii.55–6). Similarly, Pistol's attempt to save his
friend Bardolph's life makes Henry's cold denial of his erstwhile companion all
the more striking, especially since Henry's invasion of France is as much theft as
Bardolph's actions.[40] However, Pistol's role goes beyond that of ironic mirror,
for in addition to providing comic relief, Pistol, like Williams and Bates, also
serves as a vehicle for reinforcing a commoner's critical stance towards
authority.

The conventional dismissal of Pistol as a fustian clown rests on the assumption that the Boy, Fluellen, and Gower are right when they call Pistol a coward,
but Shakespeare carefully impugns the credibility of each judge. It is the *Boy*
who says, 'Would I were in an alehouse in London, I would give all my fame for
a pot of ale and safety' (III.ii.12–13) and Pistol who concurs. Thus the Boy is no
happier about being in France than his master, and so it may not be appropriate
for him to fault Pistol for expressing the same reluctance to fight. Furthermore,
given the cynicism with which the clerics justify the French war and the dying
Henry IV's prescription for avoiding civil strife through a belligerent foreign
policy, their preference to be in a London alehouse rather than on a battlefield
outside Harfleur appears less as a failure of nerve and more as unwillingness to
risk one's neck in Henry's scheme 'to busy giddy minds / With foreign quarrels'
(2 *Henry IV* IV.v.213–14).

Pistol's treatment by his superiors also demonstrates how quickly those in
power can forget the good service of those beneath them when it serves their
purpose. Although Pistol may have disgraced himself (in some eyes) by his
unwillingness to follow Henry unto the breach, Fluellen gives Pistol's soldiering
at another juncture the highest praise. When asked by Gower about the status of

---

[40] Richard Levin finds that 'everything in the subplot points unambiguously to its function as a foil
employed to contrast with, and so render still more admirable, the exploits of the "mirror" of all
Christian kings'; *The Multiple Plot in English Renaissance Drama* (Chicago, IL, 1971), p. 116. Most
critics, however, regard Pistol as an ironic reflection of Henry. See, for example, Goddard, *The
Meaning of Shakespeare*, pp. 226, 233, 248; Smith, 'Shakespeare's *Henry V*', p. 21; Anthony S.
Brennan, 'That within which Passes Show: The Function of the Chorus in *Henry V*', *Philological
Quarterly* 58 (1979): 45; Leggatt, *Shakespeare's Political Drama*, pp. 121–2; and Rackin, *Stages of
History*, p. 144.

the bridge, Fluellen, an authority on proper military conduct, replies that 'very excellent services [have been] committed' and goes on to praise Exeter's bravery. Significantly, Fluellen then adds – without prompting – that Exeter is not the only superb soldier at this engagement:

There is an aunchient lieutenant there at the pridge, I think in my very conscience he is as valiant a man as Mark Antony, and he is a man of no estimation in the world, but I did see him do as gallant service.   (III.vi.12–15)

For Fluellen to equate Pistol's valor to Mark Antony's must be a strong compliment indeed for this humanistically minded captain.

Fluellen alters his opinion only after Pistol asks him to intercede on Bardolph's behalf. In his subsequent report to Henry, instead of repeating what he told Gower, Fluellen revises his earlier description of the battle by enlarging his praise of Exeter and excising all mention of Pistol's 'gallant service':

The Duke of Exeter has very gallantly maintain'd the pridge. The French is gone off, look you, and there is gallant and most prave passages. Marry, th'athversary was have possession of the pridge, but he is enforced to retire, and the Duke of Exeter is master of the pridge. I can tell your majesty, the Duke is a prave man.   (III.vi.90–6)

Similarly, Gower's description of Pistol is not entirely accurate since we know from Fluellen's own mouth that Pistol *has* rendered good service, that his knowledge of at least one engagement comes from first-hand experience. But because Pistol has offended by refusing to favour military discipline over his friend's life, Gower chooses to elide this information and to reconstruct him as the begging mock-soldier of the royal proclamations. The subsequent descriptions of Pistol and the battle at the bridge suggest how quickly the deeds of the lowly can be erased from the record as punishment for challenging authority.

If Williams, Bates, and Pistol embody the distrust of authority so widespread in the 1590s, the Chorus also does so in two different and yet related ways. Shakespeare sets up the Chorus as another authority figure whose assertions are challenged, but the resonances are not restricted to affecting our perception of the dramatic character because the Chorus reproduces the view of Henry in the histories propounding the Tudor myth. To render the Chorus problematic consequently implies rendering problematic one of the pillars of Tudor legitimacy.

In the prologue to the fourth act, the Chorus once more asks the audience to participate in creating the dramatic scene: 'Now entertain conjecture of a time / When creeping murmur and the poring dark / Fills the wide vessel of the universe' (1–3). However, the meanings of his repeated pleas for audience participation become increasingly unstable as the play progresses. At first, what the Chorus says seems straightforward enough; he provides the background scenery for the action about to take place, painting with words how the armies are so close that 'the fix'd sentinels almost receive / The secret whispers of each other's watch' (6–7) and 'through their paly flames / Each battle sees the other's umber'd face' (8–9). The problems arise when he moves from describing the background to describing the action. The 'poor condemned English'

> Like sacrifices, by their watchful fires
> Sit patiently and inly ruminate
> The Morning's danger; and their gesture sad,
> Investing lank-lean cheeks and war-worn coats,
> Presented them unto the gazing moon
> So many horrid ghosts. O now, who will behold
> The royal captain of this ruin'd band
> Walking from watch to watch, from tent to tent,
> Let him cry, 'praise and glory on his head!'
> For forth he goes, and visits all his host,
> Bids them good morrow with a modest smile
> And calls them brothers, friends and countrymen.
> Upon his royal face there is no note
> How dread an army hath enrounded him;
> Nor doth he dedicate one jot of color
> Unto the weary and all-watched night;
> But freshly looks, and overbears attaint
> With cheerful semblance and sweet majesty;
> that every wretch, pining and pale before,
> Beholding him, plucks comfort from his looks.
> A largess universal, like the sun,
> His liberal eye doth give to every one,
> Thawing cold fear, that mean and gentle all
> Behold, as may unworthiness define,
> A little touch of Harry in the night.   (22–47)

Clearly, this speech is a rhetorical *tour de force*, impossible to read or hear without being utterly thrilled by it. However, the speech's rhetorical success only emphasizes one's disappointment when the following scene enacts nearly the opposite of what the Chorus so brilliantly conjures us to see. According to his proleptic description, an entirely unworried King Henry goes among his troops, spreading cheer and joy to all: he is (ostensibly) the fountain of encouragement and 'largess universal'. Richard II may claim that like the sun, his appearance will scatter treason, that his name is 'twenty thousand names' (III.ii.36 *et seq.*), but according to the Chorus, Henry enacts what Richard can only claim: it is Henry's visage, not Richard's, that thaws 'cold fear' like the sun, his name ('a little touch of Harry in the night') that contains all the virtue that Richard's lacked. The problem is that first exchanges in IV.i. dramatize exactly the opposite of what the Chorus says, so much so that the disjunction between the Chorus and the play has forced one distinguished critic to assume that

Shakespeare provides the audience with *two* visits to his troops, one described by the Chorus, the other put on stage by Shakespeare's players.[41]

Although the Chorus asserts that 'Upon his royal face there is no note / How dread an army hath enrounded him', Henry begins by admitting this discouraging fact: 'Gloucester, 'tis true that we are in great danger' (IV.i.1). Moreover, he goes among the troops incognito, having borrowed a cloak from Sir Thomas Erpingham, not, as the Chorus says, in his own person. And he spreads not good cheer among his soldiers but only worry. His first meeting results in Pistol cursing Henry ('The *figo* for thee then!' [IV.i.60]) in response to Henry's claiming Fluellen as his kinsmen. True, Pistol's mistaking Harry le Roy for a Cornish name makes him appear foolish, but we have already noted that Pistol has good reason to hold a grudge, and underneath the humour of the scene, we see the perpetuation of strife within Henry's ranks, not encouragement or the dissipation of rancour. The next meeting, with Bates, Court, and Williams, is a much more serious encounter. Again contradicting the Chorus's version of the king's effect upon his soldiers, Henry draws attention to their extremely dire circumstances:

> WILLIAMS.. . . I pray you, what thinks he [Sir Thomas Erpingham] of our estate?
> K. HEN. Even as men wrack'd upon a sand, that look to be wash'd off the next tide.
>
> (IV.i.97–8)

Like the confrontation with the quarrelsome Pistol, this meeting also ends with the promise of future strife among the English ('*Will.* Let it be a quarrel between us, if you live. / *K. Hen.* I embrace it' [IV.i.205–6]).

The Choric view of the French camp is equally meretricious, although with an interesting twist: the 'confident and overlusty French/ . . . Do the low-rated English play at dice / And chide the cripple tardy-gaited night' (18–20). To be sure, the French do sound confident, and the Lord Rambures does ask 'Who will got to hazard with me for twenty prisoners?' (III.vii.86). But the Chorus elides the sensible comments of the Constable of France, who reminds Rambures that 'You must first go to hazard, ere you have them' (III.vii.87), suggesting that at least one member of the French party views the upcoming battle with a modicum of good sense. Similarly, when Orleans and Rambures claim that the mastiffs, not the men, are the only valiant creatures produced by 'that island of England' and compare Henry's army to 'a valiant flea that dare eat his breakfast on the lip of a lion' (III.vii.145–6), the Constable again reminds them that the English army may be more formidable an adversary than the French lords imagine:

Just, just; and the men do sympathize with the mastiffs in robustious and rough coming on, leaving their wits with their wives; and then give them great meals of beef and iron and steel, they will eat like wolves and fight like devils.

(III.vii.147–51)

---

[41] Anne Barton, 'The King Disguised: Shakespeare's *Henry V* and the Comical History', in Joseph G. Price (ed.), *The Triple Bond: Plays, Mainly Shakespearean, in Performance*, (University Park, PA, 1975), pp. 92–117.

Since the Chorus is describing the preceding scene, the audience has a chance to compare his version of the French camp with the one they just watched, and it should be immediately apparent to all that the Chorus, like Fluellen and Gower, gives only a partial, ideologically inflected, version of events. Significantly, in the only instance in which the Chorus speaks about a previously enacted scene, his rhetoric moves from *asking* the audience to amend the play with their collective imagination to *commanding* them to recreate ('*Now* entertain conjecture . . .') a version of the French camp that contradicts the evidence of their senses. In other words, the Chorus demands that the audience open a gap between the idea and the dramatized reality of the French camp, a gap that mirrors the distance between the lofty justifications of Henry's French invasion and the actual causes, between Henry's populism and its reception by his soldiers; indeed, between the pronouncements of nearly every authority figure in the play and the reality of the situation.[42]

Rather than highlighting the deficiencies of the theatre, as some critics suggest, the glaring discrepancies between what the Chorus tells the audience to expect and what they actually get encourages the audience to use its collective imagination to *question* rather than passively accept the Chorus's version of events.[43] As such, the Chorus forms another instance of *Henry V*'s incorporation of contemporary popular scepticism towards royal authority. Because of Henry V's central importance in the myth of Tudor legitimacy, Shakespeare, by depicting what I might call a 'credibility gap' between the Chorus and the play itself, calls into question the very foundations of that myth.

Henry V enjoyed a reputation as a paragon of kingly virtue. The first chronicle of his life, the so-called 'Chaplain's Account', treats Henry as a king guided in all matters by divine providence, a pattern that reappears in other fifteenth-century versions of his career.[44] Polydore Vergil, 'relaxing for a

---

[42] A tremendous gulf exists between the play the Chorus describes and the play the audience enjoys. Shakespeare created a figure who, in Anthony Hammond's words 'contrives to get, really *everything* wrong'; '"It must be your imagination then": the Prologue and the Plural Text in *Henry V* and Elsewhere', in John W. Mahon and Thomas A. Pendleton (eds.), '*Fanned and Winnowed Opinions': Shakespearean Essay Presented to Harold Jenkins* (1987), p. 138. Edward Berry argues that by alternating between the golden world of the imagination (the Chorus) and the tawdry world of Machiavellian politics, the play illustrates 'not only the truth of our ideals but their inaccessibility . . .'; '"True Things and Mock'ries": Epic and History in *Henry V*', *Journal of English and German Philology* 78 (1979): 16. Anthony Brennan suggests that the Chorus 'represents one extreme of the spectrum of ideas on patriotism, as Pistol represents the other extreme. The King holds the balance'; 'That within which Passes Show: The Function of the Chorus in *Henry V*', *Philological Quarterly* 58 (1979): 43. Alternatively, Alexander Leggatt proposes that the abyss separating 'what we are told to imagine [and] what we actually see . . . alerts us to the inadequacies of the theatre'; *Shakespeare's Political Drama*, p. 123.

[43] Leggatt, *Shakespeare's Political Drama*, pp. 122–3.

[44] The 'Chaplains' Account' begins by estblishing Henry's piety: 'When, young in years but old in experience, he began his reign, like the true elect of God savouring the things that are above, he applied his mind with all devotion to encompass what could promote the honour of God, the extension of the Church, the deliverance of his country, and the peace and tranquillity of kingdoms . . .'; *Gesta Henrici Quinti*, ed. and trans. Frank Taylor and John S. Roskell (Oxford, 1975), p. 3. For other accounts of Henry's life, see Henry Kelly, *Divine Providence in the England of Shakespeare's Histories* (Cambridge, MA, 1970), p. 33.

moment his usual critical coolness', as Tillyard put it, also depicts Henry as a model of all the virtues.[45] Both Hall and Holinshed reproduce Vergil's views, and by the later sixteenth century the myth of the conquering, virtuous king who outshone all other English monarchs was well established. In Raleigh's words: 'None of them went to worke like a Conquerour: saue onely King *Henrie* the fift.'[46]

As Raleigh's comment suggests, Henry V's sterling reputation stemmed as much from his successful if short-lived conquest of France as from his apparently genuine piety. Henry V became a handy tool for those who wanted to promote a hawkish foreign policy; his reputation never went into eclipse and references to him increased significantly whenever England was involved in a foreign venture. For example, in 1513, as part of the propaganda campaign to justify his invasion of France, Henry VIII commissioned an English translation of Tito Livio's *Vita Henrici Quinti*.[47] Although the translator, like Polydore Vergil, constructs Henry V as the epitome of those virtues 'most necessarie to euerie prince' – justice, continence, and humility[48] – he emphasizes Henry V's 'victorious conquests' in order to explain the reason for his commission:

the principall cause of this my paine ... was that our Souereigne Lorde by the knowledge and sight of the pamphile shoulde partlie be prouoked in his saide warr to ensue the noble and chivalrous acts of this so noble, so vertuous, and so excellent a Prince, which so followed, he might the rather attaine to like honnour, fame, and victorie.   (*The First English Life*, p. 4)

Henry VIII took his model sufficiently to heart to ride about his rain-drenched camp in France, encouraging his soldiers on the night before they set out to engage the French.[49] Similarly, Henry V's popularity rocketed between the late 1580s and the early 1590s. A series of patriotic, if not overtly jingoistic, dramas appeared in the wake of the war-fever caused by the Armada crisis, and at least three plays on Henry V, more than on any other historical figure, were produced at that time.[50] Thomas Nashe, in the course of defending the theatre from the charge of encouraging sedition, describes the effect of one play: 'what a glorious thing it is to have Henry the Fifth represented on the stage, leading the French king prisoner, and forcing both him and the Dauphin to swear fealty'.[51]

The legend of Henry V and Agincourt represented a powerful fantasy of an underdog nation prevailing against foreign enemies and fearsome odds through providence and sheer pluck. But Shakespeare is far from endorsing the glorified

[45] Tillyard, *Shakespeare's History Plays*, p. 33.
[46] Quoted in J. H. Walter's introduction to his edition of *Henry V* (1964), p. xxi.
[47] J. J. Scarisbrick, *Henry VIII* (Berkeley, CA, 1968), p. 23; *The First English Life of King Henry the Fifth*, ed. C. L. Kingsford (Oxford, 1911), p. 4.
[48] *The First English Life*, p. 4.   [49] Scarisbrick, *Henry VIII*, p. 35.
[50] David Bevington, *Tudor Drama and Politics: A Critical Approach to Topical Meaning* (Cambridge, MA, 1968), p. 192.
[51] Thomas Nashe, *Pierce Penilesse, His Supplication to the Devil*, in *The Works of Thomas Nashe*, ed. Ronald B. McKerrow (5 vols., Oxford, 1910), i, p. 213.

view of Henry, for by putting the 'official' version of Henry's life into the mouth of the consistently challenged, if not entirely discredited Chorus, the playwright puts into ironic perspective one of the most cherished English monarchical legends. In much the same way that an undercutting treatment of, say, Washington or Lincoln, would indicate grave doubts about present-day American culture, this implicitly ironic treatment of the Henry V myth suggests the generalized disillusionment permeating the 1590s.

Questioning this political myth was itself a pointed statement because Henry V constituted one of the main genealogical nodes through which the Tudors legitimated their dynasty. At Bosworth Henry VII had won his crown from Richard III only by force of arms; he needed to establish his genealogical credentials as king, and he (or his councillors) did so in three ways. The first two are already familiar and therefore need not delay us: the providential – Henry's defeat of Richard III was accomplished by the grace of God, thereby ending England's punishment for the usurpation and murder of Richard II – and the mythological – Henry Richmond is the direct descendent of Cadwalader, and his accession fulfils the ancient Welsh prophecies predicting the return of King Arthur. Henry VII (or his councillors) evidently believed these metaphysical justifications by themselves insufficient to accomplish the purpose; therefore he buttressed them with a physical connection to the Lancastrian line. In order to make good the claim that his marriage with Elizabeth of York would heal England's wounds by binding up the red rose of Lancaster with the white rose of York, Henry first needed to establish that he was indeed related to the Lancastrians, and it is in the genealogical manipulations (which of course are never entirely divorced from the mythological and providential justifications) of Henry's propagandists that Henry V becomes the unstated *sine qua non* of the Tudor myth.

The poets and historians in Henry VII's pay regularly asserted his legitimacy through direct references to Henry VI.[52] In a speech written for a pageant to be performed before Henry VII during his first progress, 'Henry VI' was to appear before the king and say:

> I am Henry VIth, sobre and sad,
> Thy great Uncle, sumtyme of England King.
> Full xxxix Yeres this Realme myself I had,
> And of the People had the Governyng.[53]

By emphasizing the blood relationship between the two, the anonymous author establishes that Henry VII is the legitimate descendent of the saintly Henry VI and, implicitly, Henry V, the only Lancastrian with an undisputed claim to the

---

[52] Kelly, *Divine Providence*, pp. 76–7; Sydney Anglo, *Spectacle, Pageantry, and Early Tudor Policy* (Oxford, 1969), pp. 38–44.
[53] Quoted in Anglo, *Spectacle*, p. 37.

throne.[54] In other words, the cult of Henry VI *assumes* Henry V's importance and centrality to Henry VII's status.

Henry VII also sought to capitalize on the common Welsh heritage that he shared with Henry V by appropriating for himself some of the Welsh legends surrounding Henry V. Tito Livio begins his life of Henry V by recounting how his subject fulfils the Welsh prophecies 'that amongest them shoulde be borne a Prince that shoulde gouerne the vniuersall realme of England . . .'[55] When the king was a child living in exile, King Richard II 'right often in open audience of the Court vsed to saie these words: "Of the greatest of my house shabe borne a childe, whose name shallbe Henrie, which for his knightlie acts and resplendishinge virtues shalbe renowned throughe out the worlde."'[56] Henry VII's propagandists repeated his story, the only differences being the substitution of Henry Richmond for Henry V and Henry VI for Richard II; one finds it in Polydore Vergil, Hall, and Holinshed.[57] Implicitly, then, Henry VII is not only Arthur *redivivus*, but also Henry V *redivivus*.

This claim is especially evident in Henry VII's manipulation of imperial imagery. As Dale Hoak has shown (above, pp. 65–77), Henry VII tried to enhance the perception of his authority by more prominent use of the symbols of imperial rule, in particular that of the closed, or arched, crown. Henry VII's assertion of an 'imperial' status represented an avenue by which he sought dynastic legitimacy, for Henry V was remembered as the first 'imperial' king of England. Moreover, Henry VII's sponsorship of artistic representations of Henry VI (see plate 8) served to promote that dynastic claim: the imperial crown, worn by Henry V and bequeathed to his son and heir, Henry VI, now belongs to Henry VII, the rightful heir and successor of Henry V and Henry VI.[58] By claiming an 'imperial' status, Henry VII reinforces the implicit claim that he is related by blood to Henry V.

Finally, there is the matter of Henry V's wife, Queen Katherine. In addition to claiming Henry VI as a blood relative, Henry VII's propaganda machine also relied on Katherine to provide a key link to the Lancastrian line because she married Owen Tudor, Henry VII's grandfather. Bernard André, Henry VII's poet laureate and official historian, begins his *Vita Henrici VII* with a descrip-

---

54 Obviously, the chroniclers who aligned themselves with the Lancastrians idealized Henry V, but so did nearly all of the Yorkist chroniclers; see Kelly, *Divine Providence*, pp. 47–8.
55 *The First English Life*, p. 8.   56 Ibid., p. 8.
57 'About the same season, Iasper earle of Penbroke went into Wales, to visit his lands in Penbrokeshire, where he found lord Henrie sonne to his brother Edmund earle of Richmon, hauing not full ten years of age; he being kept in maner like a captiue . . . The earle of Penbroke tooke this child, being his nephue, out of the custodie of the ladie Herbert, and at his return brought the child with him to London to King Henrie the sixt, whome when the king has a good while beheld, he said to such princes as were with him: "Lo, suerlie this is he, to whom both we and our aduersaries heauing the possession of all things shall hereafter giue roome and place"'; Raphael Holinshed, *The Third Volume of Chronicles* (1586; reprinted New York, 1976), p. 302. On the court poets and Vergil, see Kelly, *Divine Providence*, pp. 65–81, 103; *Hall's Chronicle*, p. 287.
58 I am grateful to Professor Hoak for bringing to my attention the painted screen at St Catherine's Church, Ludham, Norfolk (plate 8) and for allowing me to consult his paper in advance of publication.

tion of his master's royal descent. After recounting how Henry stands in the
legitimate succession to Cadwalader, André explains how Katherine brings to
the Tudors not only her French entitlements, but also the legitimacy of Henry V
and the Lancastrians.[59] This aspect of the Tudor myth is sustained throughout
the sixteenth and seventeenth centuries, and Michael Drayton gives this story its
most explicit expression in his Ovidian *Heroicall Epistles*, which invents letters
exchanged by Katherine and Owen Tudor.[60] Drayton has the queen assert that
Owen is Henry's rightful, even designated, successor in love:

> When HENRY was, my lover was onely his,
> But by his death, it OWEN TUDORS is,
> My love to OWEN, him my HENRY giveth
> My love to HENRY, in my OWEN liveth.   (11. 17–20)

After establishing Owen's credibility as an erotically appropriate successor,
Drayton's 'Katherine' makes the critical point that when Henry married her,
they shared the crown, and now that both Henry V and Henry VI are dead, that
crown will go to whomever *she* chooses to marry:

> His [Henry's] Princely Bed hath strength'ned my Renowne,
> And on my Temples set a double Crowne;
> Which glorious Wreathe (as HENRIES lawfull Heire)
> HENRY the sixt upon his Brow doth beare.
> At Troy in Chapine he did first injoy
> My Bridall Rites, to *England* brought from *Troy*;
> In England now that Honour thou shalt have,
> Which once in Champaine famous HENRY gave.   (11. 35–42)

'Owen' responds by once more rendering explicit Henry's, and subsequently
Katherine's, centrality to the Tudor myth. Owen 'writes' that Katherine confers
the legitimacy of the House of Lancaster on husband-to-be and their progeny,
starting, of course, with Henry VIII:

> By our great MERLIN was it not fore-told,
> (Among his holy Prophesies enrol'd)
> When first he did of TUDORS Name divine,
> That kings and Queenes should follow in our Line
>
> ....
>
> As CHARLES *his Daughter, you the Lilly weare,*
> As HENRIES *Queene, the blushing Rose you beare;*
> *By France's Conquest, and by England's Oath,*
> *You are the true made Dowager of both;*

---

[59] 'Sed quia de hac genealogia libelli hoc in regno plurimi extant novissime ad examen veritatis
absolutissimeque ab regni peritissimis compositi, a Katherina Henrici Quinti conjuge et filia
Franciae, postea Eduyno [sic] praefati regis avo paterno antememorato, ab regibus Brittanis succes-
sore, legitimo matrimonio copulata initium faciam.' Bernard André, *Vita Henrici VII*, in James
Gairdner (ed.), *Memorials of Henry VII* (Weisbaden, 1966), p. 11.

[60] *The Works of Michael Drayton*, ed. J. William Hebel (5 vol.s, Oxford, 1932), ii, pp. 208–12.

> Both in you Crowne, both in you Cheeke together,
> Joyne TETHERS love to yours, and your TETHER.
>
> (II. 33–46); [my emphasis]

In this way was Henry V mythically idealized as a source of Tudor legitimacy.

These genealogical arguments are of dramatic importance because Shakespeare uses the Chorus as a mouthpiece for the 'official' view of Henry V. But by articulating this tradition, the Chorus also implicitly renders it problematic, because the play consistently underscores the Chorus's unreliability. Thus, by putting the Henry myth into the Chorus's mouth, Shakespeare calls the tradition into question; the audience is invited to view Henry's reputation as sceptically as the Chorus's view of Henry's night-time visit to his soldiers. Since the glorification of Henry V is, as we have seen, in many ways integral to the Tudors' claim to the throne, undercutting Henry V's authority and the veracity of the traditions surrounding him (e.g. that Henry's conquest of France is politically, not providentially, motivated) also meant attacking the genealogical myth at the root. In other words, the disjunctions between the Chorus and the play problematize not only the character of Henry V, but also the basis of Elizabeth's claim to the throne.

Henry V's deconstruction of Tudor legitimacy brings to a head themes that Shakespeare had been developing throughout the Henriad. In 1599 Shakespeare incorporates contemporary socio-political unrest in dramatic form by returning to the scene of English history and writing a play about the sources of the Elizabethan polity. Rather than following convention and using origins as a mechanism of empowerment, Shakespeare treats the events that will eventually result in the 'accession' of Henry VII as an opportunity to question the ideological basis of the Tudor dynasty. In *Richard II*, Shakespeare destabilizes the providential view of history by staging how (to paraphrase the Bishop of Carlisle) the power that made Richard king does *not* have the power 'to keep [him] king in spite of all' (III.ii.27–8), and by portraying the poetic Richard, universally reviled by fifteenth- and sixteenth-century chroniclers, as the sympathetic victim of the politician, Bolingbroke. The next instalment, the two parts of *Henry IV*, further destabilizes the Tudor myth by showing how history is not an objective record of past events but a narrative constructed by those in power in order to consolidate their positions.[61] *Henry V* brings the series to a fitting conclusion in a number of ways. First, Shakespeare calls into question the providential theory of history by refusing to grant closure. Instead of ending with Henry's triumph, the play's last words undo Henry V's triumph and lead the audience back to the *selva oscura* of Henry VI's pathetic reign:

---

[61] For example, in *Richard II* Richard justifies his banishment of Bolingbroke because Bolingbroke has 'Observed his courtship to the comon people' (I.iv.24). But in *1 Henry IV*, Henry IV claims that he was 'seldom seen' (III.ii.44). Obviously, both kings have a vested interest in promoting the veracity of their perceptions. I am currently at work on a much fuller treatment of the relationship between Shakespeare's plays and the political climate of the 1590s. David S. Kastan also treats the subject at length in *Proud Majesty Made a Subject* (forthcoming, Routledge).

Henry the Sixt, in infant bands crown'd King
Of France and England, did this king succeed;
Whose state so many had the managing,
That they lost France, and made his England bleed.   (Ep. 9–12)

In place of a divinely guided progression, Shakespeare ends the Henriad by
figuring history as a cycle of deceit and violence.[62] Secondly, in *Henry V*
Shakespeare gives voice to the general sense of decline – which John Guy
suggestively calls a *fin de siècle* atmosphere[63] – by endorsing the murmurings of
the commons and by undercutting the legend of Henry V, a legend that early
Tudor propaganda had exploited in order to enhance the Tudor's own claims to
the throne.

In conclusion, *Henry V* reflects the widespread distrust of authority in the
1590s; the play itself may have contributed to contemporary notions of decline.
Shakespeare's treatment of Williams, Bates, and Pistol dramatizes the hostility
separating the ruler from the ruled in the 1590s. The ironic brackets surrounding everything spoken by the Chorus, including his idealization of Henry V,
indicates that as Elizabeth's reign drew to a close the Tudor myth was subject to
pressure from those who, like Shakespeare, used the freedom granted by the
stage's liminality to question ideas that the government would have preferred to
place beyond question. Given the play's ending, it is perhaps not surprising that
in *Henry V* Shakespeare concluded his long engagement with English history;
thereafter he began writing the problem comedies and the mature tragedies.
After such knowledge, what forgiveness?

---

[62] Rackin, *Stages of History*, pp. 84–5.
[63] John Guy, *Tudor England* (Oxford, 1988), p. 437.

9   *Parliament and the political society of Elizabethan England*

NORMAN JONES

Speaking against a 1571 bill to repeal the requirement that members of parliament representing boroughs be resident in their constituencies, Thomas Atkins, deputy recorder of Gloucester, delivered a long soliloquy on the necessity of local representation. 'We know', he declared

that such who have spent their whole time in study or have seen alone the manner of government of other nations, and can tell how the crown of France is delivered out of wardship . . . or can paint you out the monstrous governments of the common people in some part of Germany, or the mangled commonwealths of the apes, or shadows of the great cities which now are to be seen in Italy: surely these men all, *except they know also our own homes, are not to be trusted to conclude for our home affairs*.[1]

Atkin's plea for informed representation fell on deaf ears. Thomas Norton's argument that only men 'fit for so great a place, without respect or privilege of place' should be chosen carried the day. Norton's logic was grounded on his belief that 'the whole body of the realm and good service of the same was rather to be respected than the private regard of place or privilege of any person'.[2]

That the greater number of members 'seemed to say yea' to Norton's logic is not surprising. Many members for boroughs could not meet the residency requirement themselves. But the terms of this debate open a window into the concept of representation held by Elizabethan lawmakers, helping us understand parliament's place in their political culture. Neither Atkins nor Norton spoke of representation in terms of a constituency of electors. Both were concerned with the knowledge possessed by the members and the function that knowledge had in the high court of parliament.

For Elizabethans it seems that the multi-faceted activities of parliament demanded that members be chosen for their ability to judge as much as for their ability to represent. There is no suggestion that they felt the members of the two houses of parliament to be representing platforms, parties, or even patrons.

---

[1] My emphasis. Hartley, p. 228. For the identification of Atkins as the speaker see my 'The Anonymous Diarist of 1571: *Alias* Thomas Atkins or Robert Bowes?', in *Interest Groups*, pp. 337–9.
[2] Hartley, p. 226.

They were there, as Norton said, to apply their wisdom in the good service of the realm.

Or so it would seem. The question of the way in which Elizabethan people conceived parliament's role in their political society is a vexed one. The recent historiographic battles on Elizabethan parliaments have turned around whether or not they were the nursery of the modern parliament complete with a self-conscious role in the government and a loyal opposition. Most scholars would now agree that the House of Commons in Elizabeth's reign was not 'rising' as Sir John Neale had maintained.[3] Moreover, most would agree that parliament was not the key political institution that it was to become. It was still, as Sir Geoffrey Elton succinctly put it, 'a secondary instrument to be used or ignored by agencies whose real power base and arena of activity lay elsewhere – at court or in council'.[4]

Why then did Sir Thomas Smith boldly proclaim that 'The most high and absolute power of the realm of England, is in the Parliament'?[5] Writing in the 1560s he was confident of its place in the firmament of Tudor government, as were his contemporaries. It is the purpose of this article to reflect on how it is that in Elizabeth's day parliament could be at once a passive body controlled by the court and council and interested only in consensus, and a power greater than the monarch. The key to the problem is in the assumptions Elizabethans had about representation. What were members of parliament doing there? Did they speak for themselves alone? for their electors? for their places? for their patrons? Was anyone listening when they spoke? Why did Tudor people assume that parliament should speak? And what of the unelected members of the House of Lords?

To begin let us look at the definitions provided by contemporaries. In 1585 Lord Burghley delivered a lesson in government to the members of a Commons' committee. Lecturing them on the bicameral nature of the institution he said:

that their Lordships of the Upper House being of such quality and calling as they are known to be, are one Member of the Parliament: And also that the Knights, Citizens, and Burgesses of this House representing the whole Commons of this realm are also another Member of the same Parliament, and her Majesty the Head; And that of these three estates doth consist the whole Body of the Parliament able to make Laws. And that none of the said two Houses without the other can in any wise make laws.[6]

Monarch, lords, and commons interlocked to make law and it was clearly established that even the queen could not abrogate law without the consent of the other estates of the parliament. The royal commissioners sent to negotiate a trade agreement with the Low Countries in 1564 were reminded in their

---

3 For a review of the historiography of Elizabethan parliaments see my 'Parliament and the Governance of Elizabethan England: A Review', *Albion* 19 (1987): 327–46.

4 G. R. Elton, *The Parliament of England 1559–1581* (Cambridge, 1986), p. 378.

5 Thomas Smith, *De Republica Anglorum*, ed. M. Dewar (Cambridge, 1982), p. 78.

6 Simonds D'Ewes (ed.), *The Journals of All the Parliaments during the Reign of Queen Elizabeth* (1682), p. 350.

instructions that if their opposite numbers demanded the modification of laws, they should inform them of

the manner of our policy, how the same laws are made in this realm by the assent of three estates, and are not to be made void but with their assent . . . that the execution of them may be suspended by her majesty . . . but yet the laws cannot be utterly abrogated without the like authority where with they were made, wherein they may be assured that her majesty both will and can do as much with her estates as any other her progenitors kings of the realm have done.[7]

Sir Thomas Smith, in his classic discussion of parliament, delineated the reason these classes had the right to make laws binding all persons in the realm. Describing the commonwealth as an organic extended household he says its only subjects are free men who might have rule and jurisdiction over others. Bond men, and women in general [a careful exception is made for the queen], are but 'instruments and of the goods and possessions' of the freemen. These freemen of the commonwealth fall into two loose categories: the magistracy, which bears office, and private men, who bear none – a distinction he clarifies by identifying them with patricians and plebians.

The English magistracy consists of the nobility by birth or creation (which includes the *nobilitas minor* of the knights), gentlemen, and burgesses. The private men are two sorts, yeomen and labourers. Yeomen were identified by Smith as the forty-shilling freeholders [worth £6 in 1560s terms] who had the right to elect members of parliament. They are, he said, people who live well and keep good houses, but who do not meddle in public affairs unless called upon and who are 'obedient to gentlemen and rulers'. The labourers 'have no voice or authority in our common wealth, and no account is made of them, but only to be ruled, not to rule other'.[8]

Strikingly, Smith bases part of his argument for the authority men bear in their communities on the wealth at their disposal. Drawing, apparently, on the fact that a financial qualification had always been used to determine the right to participate in a parliamentary election, he extended the principle. If yeomen had a right to participate for reasons of fiscal power, so other members of the parliament drew some of their legitimacy from the same source. Burgesses, who are not gentlemen, nonetheless have the substance to bear the charges of government in their towns. Gentlemen are those who can bear the 'port and charge and countenance' of gentlemen – including, perhaps, buying a coat of arms. A knight should be able to spend £40 per annum [£120 in 1560s terms]. Even the heritable degrees of the upper nobility should have an income worthy of their rank. Tellingly, Smith says that no man is created a baron unless he has a thousand pounds a year and that, although lords' sons might inherit their titles, 'sometimes they are not admitted to the upper house in parliament' if they have insufficient income to maintain their estates.[9]

[7] BL, Landsdowne MS. 155, fos. 126–126v.   [8] Smith, *De Republica Anglorum*, pp. 64–77.
[9] *Ibid.*, pp. 74–5; 73; 72; 67–8; 66.

Smith's insistence that rank was related to income hints at another defining characteristic of magistracy: it had authority because its possessions gave it responsibility. Parliament consisted of this magistracy, either in their persons or through their representatives.

Sitting in the House of Lords were those who inherited their authority from their progenitors, either by birth or by office. All the degrees of the temporal nobility – earls, viscounts, barons, and others – and the spiritual nobility of the Church, assisted by the voteless judges of the common law, met there under the chairmanship of the lord keeper. The lesser magistracy of knights, esquires, gentlemen, and burgesses was represented in the Commons. Together with the monarch they formed the 'principal court of records and first court of justice' in which 'laws are made, mitigated or abrogated'.[10]

These magistrates, whose right to sit in parliament was tied to their larger responsibilities as rulers of their own peculiar commonwealths at home, ultimately took their authority from God, who had ordered society and given them rule over it. The Almighty had expectation of those to whom He had given authority, for the sins of the people would be held against the magistrates, the masters, and the householders who bore authority over them. As Archbishop Sandys announced at the Spittle early in the reign, God would require the blood of the magistrates if through negligence, evil example, or want of correction those in their charge were lost.[11] Francis Darby repeated this warning in 1601, declaring that if parliament did not curb drunkenness the Almighty would 'lay his heavy hand of wrath and indignation upon this land'.[12]

The duty of the magistracy to God was stressed whenever Elizabethans were involved in the legal system, at the top of which stood parliament. Assize sermons emphasized and reemphasized it; members of parliament invoked it; and even jury charges summarized it. In Richard Crompton's reworking of Fitzherbert's book on the office and authority of the justices of the peace a charge to the jury was printed that neatly laid out the place and duty of those invited by the queen to participate in ruling the nation. The exhortation is a complete cosmology beginning with creation and progressing through the Fall, the unruly life in a state of nature, and the Flood, until it arrives at the creation of law by God in the decalogue. After that God set kings over men, who must obey them as the ministers of God who protect the righteous and take vengeance on the sinners. The justices of the peace and members of the jury share in that authority, owing their duty to the queen and to God, a sacred trust sealed with an oath on the Bible. An oath that binds them, among other things, to enforce the 'good laws and statutes, which we have received by the authority of the high

[10] *Ibid.*, p. 78. Richard Robinson, 'A Briefe Collection of the Queenes Majesties most High and Most Honourable Courtes of Recordes', ed. R. L. Richard, in *Camden Miscellany XX*, Camden Society, Third ser. (vol. 83, 1953): 2–5.

[11] Edwin Sandys, *Sermons*, ed. John Ayre (Cambridge, 1841), pp. 264–5.

[12] BL, Stowe MS. 362, fos. 84v–85.

Court of Parliament of this realm, for the common wealth of her Majesty's subjects'.[13]

The right of members of parliament to give consent for the entire realm was believed to descend on them by right of their birth and office, a natural result of their place in the social hierarchy. It was not granted by 'the people'; it came from God through the monarch. From the beginning of parliaments it had been assumed that the commons and ecclesiastics came to them armed with a power of attorney (*plena potestas*) that gave them the authority to bind those who sent them. The three great Elizabethan political theorists – Hooker, Smith, and Lambarde – were in agreement that members of the Commons gave consent on behalf of those *for* whom they were sent, not *by* whom they were sent.[14] Thus consultation with a constituency was not an issue. They could and did speak and vote on any issue freely, without reference to those on whose behalf they appeared. Moreover, it meant that the person representing a group need not be of the group. As Sir John Neale observed, 'there was no incongruity in employing a stranger as attorney'.[15]

Their votes bound the entire nation, but the entire nation was not invited to the selection of members of parliament. The entire Upper House was unelected, with each peer speaking only for himself. Not even the bishops, dividing their time between parliament and convocation, consulted their clergy. Their right to vote came from God, their social position, and, crudely, their power.

In the nether House the members for boroughs held their seats because of choices made according to local customs, but seldom through election. Frequently the aldermen of a borough would make the choice, or at least the nomination, presenting their choice to the common council or the freemen for ratification. Thus we cannot say that the borough representatives sitting in parliament had been elected in the modern sense.

The county members had been returned by the electors of their shires, but the number of men who could meet the financial qualifications for the franchise was small, and deference bade many of them to consent to the choices of their betters. As the privy council put it in 1597, 'we doubt not much but the principal persons of that county will have good regard to make choice without partiality or affection . . .'.[16] Those 'principal persons' were frequently the leaders of the few dominant families, making their selection long before the electors were invited to ratify their choices.

Taken together the ways in which boroughs and counties chose their

[13] 'An Exortation to the Jurye', in Sir Anthony Fitzherbert and Richard Crompton, *L'Office et Aucthoritie de Justices de Peace* (1584), Sig. CCi ff.: facsimile reproduction, ed. P. R. Glazebrook (1972).

[14] Vernon F. Snow (ed.), *Parliament in Elizabethan England, John Hooker's Order and Usage* (New Haven, CT, 1971), p. 182. David Dean and I have argued this point before in D. M. Dean and N. L. Jones, *The Parliaments of Elizabethan England* (Oxford, 1990), pp. 2–4.

[15] J. E. Neale, *The Elizabethan House of Commons* (Harmondsworth, Middlesex, 1963), p. 151.

[16] *APC*, xxvii, p. 361.

members of parliament demonstrate that very few early modern elections were contests. This fact is so striking that Mark Kishlansky has described the choice of MPs as 'Parliamentary selection', making the point that candidates were selected ahead of time and that a contested election was an accident and a social disaster.[17]

Kishlansky argues that to be returned to parliament was to be recognized as a person of worth and authority in one's community. To be selected to parliament did not bind one to a political position or make one answerable to an electorate in any modern sense. That, however, did not mean that the member of parliament considered himself free of responsibility. Sent there to advise and give consent, members expected to apply their knowledge to the problems of the realm, not to parrot the prejudices of their home countries.

To argue that the members of parliament did not answer to a constituency, however, does not necessarily mean that they were independent in their parliamentary activity. A great deal of ink has been expended on the question of why members of the Commons voted as they did (voting in the Lords has, unfortunately, been ignored). One of the most popular theories about voting behaviour in the Commons (if we can speak of it as such when we have no idea how individual members voted because they did not vote individually) is that it was tied to patronage. Inspired by Namier's studies of eighteenth-century parliaments, the concept of blocks of votes tied to patrons seems, at first glance, to have considerable validity because many seats were awarded on the basis of patronage alone. If, scholars reasoned, patrons went to the effort to place clients in the Commons, the patrons must have wanted their friendly votes.

Working on that assumption, Sir John Neale and the team he directed for many years at the History of Parliament Trust constructed a prosopography of the Elizabethan parliaments that, when all else failed, ascribed membership and behaviour to a patronage link. But Neale failed to ask why a patron would want a voice in the Commons. Whether a peer, a bishop, or an urban oligarch, the patron had to have something he wanted from parliament before exerting himself to control a seat – unless controlling a seat had little to do with the political function of parliament.

Several recent studies have looked at the relationship between patrons and parliament, and all of them agree that parliamentary representation had little to do with the reasons a person was sent to Westminster. In his examination of the operation of the clientage network of Robert, earl of Leicester, and his brother Ambrose, earl of Warwick, in the parliaments of 1559, 1563, 1566, 1571, 1572, and 1584, Simon Adams found little evidence that a client's role in parliament was directly influenced by his patron. Although some of the Dudley clients initiated important debates on the succession and Mary, Queen of Scots,

---

[17] Mark Kishlansky, *Parliamentary Selection. Social and Political Choice in Early Modern England* (Cambridge, 1986). There are some problems with this interpretation, but it does help explain the uncontested nature of most elections.

nothing indicates that their participation in parliament was in any way a concerted action on behalf of their patrons. Adams concludes that his look at the Dudley connection leads to a whiggish proposition: 'Active Elizabethan parliamentarians were active because they wanted to be, not because they were the instruments of faction of the men-of-business of the Council.'

Being the client of a magnate did not mean giving your vote in accord with his wishes, but it did free one to speak with greater impunity. Leicester, says Adams, created a 'climate of benevolent tolerance towards Parliament-men (similar to his tolerance towards Puritan agitators) which encouraged them to express their views without fear of the consequences. If things could (and did) get out of hand, that was in the nature of a free Parliament, not the product of factional politics.'[18]

Jim Alsop reached a similar conclusion by looking at exchequer officials who sat in parliament. In a scathing analysis of the History of Parliament Trust's biographies of members of parliament, in which shadowy if not fictitious patronage connections were used as a *deus ex machina* whenever evidence was lacking, Alsop exploded the Nealean idea that connection or office-holding could directly account for either the presence or behaviour of exchequer personnel in the Commons. Exchequer officials who had seats tended to have them for the same reason they were exchequer officials. Both their offices and their seats were expressions of patronage on the part of their patrons.[19]

The good will of their patrons, however, did not demand that they support the parliamentary objectives of their patrons – if there were objectives. Nor did the fact that they held government office cause them to advance government policies or protect vested interests. Of the forty-five exchequer officials who sat in Elizabethan parliaments, twenty-two left traces in the records of the Commons, but few can be tied to the promotion of the interests of the exchequer. In a few cases there was a connection, but even then those connections are so rare that it cannot be argued that a man was sent to parliament in order to influence legislation touching the exchequer.

Like Adams, Alsop deduces that the exchequer men in parliament did not use their seats to promote the interest of either their patrons or their offices. 'By all appearances', he writes, 'selection and performance were essentially personal – established by the individual and not by the common office-holding experience . . . We possess no reason to believe its officials constituted a parliamentary interest group.'[20]

The connections between members of parliament and boroughs is more problematic than that between individual patrons and members. Elton has

---

[18] Simon Adams, 'The Dudley Clientele and the House of Commons, 1559–1582', in *Interest Groups*, p. 233.

[19] J. D. Alsop, 'Exchequer Office-Holders in the House of Commons, 1559–1601', in *Interest Groups*, pp. 242–53.

[20] *Ibid.*, pp. 265–8.

argued that the enfranchised towns saw parliament as a 'point of contact' between them and the central government, but how did this contact work when so many borough members had little personal connection with the towns?

Robert Tittler suggests that it seldom worked, for the simple reason that parliament was too infrequent, too expensive, and too unpredictable to be effective as a political tool. Surveying the ways in which England's nearly 700 towns, both enfranchised and unenfranchised, used the institution, he found that only 8 to 10 per cent of them gained anything for themselves alone from parliament during the sixteenth century. Fewer than 10 per cent even brought bills to parliament in that period. Those that did bring bills 'found the process costly, prone to delays even of several years, and ultimately disappointing almost exactly half the time'.[21]

Towns were frequently reluctant to send members to parliament because the cost of supporting them in Westminster was so great. *Per diem* travel expenses and even reimbursement for lost business income during the sitting made having MPs a luxury that many Elizabethan towns could ill afford. As Neale noticed many years ago, it was not uncommon for a town to choose its representatives on the basis of the member's or patron's willingness to pay the town's parliamentary costs. When the bishop of Winchester secured a Southampton seat for a client in 1572 he informed the town that his nominee could 'do that city and country such service . . . as is required . . ., and also will ease you of such trouble and charge as usually you have been at in that behalf; so that therein you shall further yourselves and also pleasure me . . .'. So concerned were some towns, like Grimsby, about the cost of parliamentary representation that they required a bond of the patron guaranteeing payment of their expenses before granting him the use of their seat.[22] For many towns it was less important that they be represented by someone who knew their interests than that they avoid the expense of being represented.

If parliament did not provide towns with valuable political access their willingness to be represented by outsiders presented to them by patrons is more understandable. In the ten parliaments of the reign only 24.1 per cent of burgesses were residents of the boroughs for which they sat.[23] In short, very few towns took representation in parliament seriously enough to obey the law requiring that boroughs be represented by residents of the borough.

One might conclude from this that towns did not care about being represented in parliament, but they did – although not for reasons directly attached to parliament. Securing a parliamentary franchise was a mark of distinction for a town, helping the 'newly emergent, highly mobil and largely mercantile urban leadership' secure prestige in the county and creating deference in their fellow

[21] Robert Tittler, 'Elizabethan Towns and the "Points of Contact": Parliament', in *Interest Groups*, pp. 279–80.
[22] Neale, *Commons*, pp. 148–9.
[23] P. W. Hasler (ed.), *The House of Commons 1558–1603* (1981), i, p. 58.

townsmen. Having a listening ear in parliament was useful, too. But perhaps the greatest value of the franchise lay in its use in regional patronage networks. Parliamentary seats bestowed on non-residents could secure for a town good lordship elsewhere. A voice in parliament was less important than a friend at court, and that friendship could be cemented by letting a patron choose the town's representatives.[24]

Lastly, towns were not unaware of the greater talent available beyond their boundaries. Frequently the members their patrons gave them were men of experience and talent, so that if the town did need a voice in parliament the voice of an outsider was effective. Local merchants were not as good at speaking on national politics as were many of the carpetbaggers. For instance, in 1572 Oxford chose as one of its MPs William Downing, a London lawyer who hailed from Suffolk. Anxious to get their bill 'for sprats and smelts' (fish) through parliament, the town authorities wanted his professional skill, which he promised them, writing

I will willingly attend the parliament to do any good that may lye in me as concerning your town it self for I hold my self as one of you. I will perform the best office that I can. I pray you take order that I may have good instruction and some body to solicit, as need shall require . . .

He succeeded, only to see the bill vetoed.[25] Downing clearly saw himself as the town's agent in the matter of smelts and sprats. In cases like this the towns were thinking of their members as lawyers representing their interests, not as the voice of their opinions.[26] However, we should not forget that the men returned as 'lawyers' for the towns were expected to vote on all issues before the House. Sent to achieve some specific goal, they were not bound to a platform and were free to give their voices as they saw fit in matters great and small.

The membership of the Commons was not representing a constituency in any modern sense. The members got their seats in ways that belie the idea that they were expected to vote in any way consistent with the views of those in whose names they sat. Only one group in the two houses in parliament could be construed as consistently representing a special interest, the bishops. The only people who sat *ex officio*, they were there, in the first instance, because the Church was too powerful a landlord to ignore, but in the early Elizabethan parliaments they took upon themselves the responsibility of defending the Church.

In 1559 the bishops were all Catholics and voted as a block against the Elizabethan Settlement. When they failed to stop it they were removed and replaced by protestant bishops who assumed they should use parliament to perfect the Settlement. A slate of bills for ecclesiastical discipline was drafted in

---

[24] Tittler, 'Towns', p. 283.
[25] Quoted in D. M. Dean, 'Parliament and Locality', in Dean and Jones, *Parliaments*, p. 149.
[26] *Ibid.*, p. 286.

convocation in 1563 and introduced in parliament in 1566 at the bishops' behest (but not by them personally). The disastrous result was that the queen accused them of infringing her prerogative and they were put firmly in their places. After that they were less willing to use parliament for their ends – though they continued to raise theological issues in the debates.[27] The bishops spoke as God's representatives in the commonwealth, so, although they could defend their occupational interests, they never had to answer to a constituency. They answered to God and God's Supreme Governor of the Church. Petitioning the queen to allow the bill for enactment of the Thirty-Nine Articles to be given a second reading, they outlined their conception of their role:

Whereupon we your Highness' humble and faithful subjects think ourselves bound in conscience as well to the sacred majesty of Almighty God, as in respect of our ecclesiastical office and charge toward your Highness and loving subjects of your realm, to make several and most humble suit unto your Majesty, that it may please the same to grant that the said bill . . .'[28]

Secular lords did not have to speak for God but, because God had given them their places in the hierarchy, they, at least in theory, had to recognize the magisterial duties He had given them. Their charge was the lower orders, their constituency was God.

The lords and commons were two of the three parts of parliament. The monarch was there, too, holding in her hands the power to accept or veto anything approved by the two houses. Parliament, said Smith, 'is the whole universal and general consent and authority as well as the prince as of the nobility and commons, which is to say of the whole head and body of the realm of England'.[29] This trinity made firm, stable, and *sanctum* (holy) law. It therefore behooves us to consider the queen's role in parliament as we seek to know how representation was understood. Although commonly neglected by historians of parliament except as an irritant that might have forced institutional evolution, the monarch controlled and defined much of what parliament did, calling it and deciding which of its acts to accept into law. Furthermore, the queen's privy councillors sat in the two Houses and, to a large extent, managed their business. In whose interest did Elizabeth I believe the members of parliament served?

At the beginning of each session she granted the speaker's petition for the four 'ancient' privileges of the House of Commons: access to the monarch, the right to correct misunderstandings prejudicial to the Commons, freedom from arrest during the session, and 'liberty of speech for the well debating of matters

---

[27] Norman Jones, *Faith by Statute. Parliament and the Settlement of Religion, 1559* (1982); *id.*, 'An Elizabethan Bill for the Reformation of Ecclesiastical Law', *Parliament History* 4 (1985): 171–87; *id.*, 'Religion in Parliament', in Dean and Jones, *Parliaments*, pp. 119–21.

[28] John Bruce and T. T. Perowne (eds.), *The Correspondence of Matthew Parker* (Cambridge, 1853), p. 293.

[29] Smith, *De Republica Anglorum*, p. 88.

propounded'. This grant, however, was not unconditional, for she required them to be 'not unmindful nor uncareful of their duties, reverence and obedience to their sovereign'.[30]

Elizabeth once described the House of Commons as 'the whole realm' because the realm gave 'their common consent to such as be here assembled'.[31] Nonetheless, she had little patience with the idea that the 'realm' could freely determine to what it consented. 'Time and time again', notes Elton, 'she showed her contempt for these little men who dared interfere in the counsels of princes . . .'[32] Certain subjects were, she insisted, reserved to the queen, most notably religion and the succession. However, it became established over the course of the reign that members of parliament could speak freely to anything raised in the proper fashion – in short, that they could freely debate bills of all kinds, but could not start bills touching affairs of state without official blessings. The members were to advise and give consent, but 'do well to meddle with no matters of state but such as should be propounded unto them, and to occupy themselves in other matters concerning the common wealth'.[33] In short, the queen saw parliament much more as a source of consent than as a voice of the people. Their grievances could be aired there, but they were not invited to initiate legislation on matters that belonged to the queen's prerogative. This attitude was not accepted by all members, but for every man who dared challenge the idea there were several who believed that the queen was right. In 1572 Arthur Hall offended the Commons by suggesting that the duke of Norfolk's possible treason with Queen Mary of Scotland was not a matter for the House. In the acrimonious debate that followed many members demonstrated that they valued free speech only if it agreed with the judgment already received from the queen. The session had been called to deal with the treason, and deal they would. As for people like Hall, many believed they should be silenced. Mr Sampole represented their opinion when he commented that 'he never knew in any parliament liberty of speech so freely granted that a man might say what he listed. These words call in question the proceedings of the Lords and overthrow the resolution of this House.'[34] As Michael Graves has put it, while 'the beneficiaries of electoral patronage were not whipped members of a political party or obedient followers of a faction leader, they were likely to demonstrate in parliament the same deference and sense of duty towards their superiors and benefactors as they did at other times'.[35]

Observing the ways men came to sit in the two houses of parliament and the expectations they had of themselves, we can conclude that Elizabethans did not look upon members as speaking with the voices of the people who would be bound by the laws they enacted there. Nor can they be seen as the agents of

---

[30] Hartley, pp. 42–3.   [31] *Ibid.*, p. 94.   [32] Elton, *Parliament*, p. 329.
[33] Hartley, p. 199; Elton, *Parliament*, p. 343.
[34] Hartley, p. 359.
[35] Michael Graves, 'Managing Elizabethan Parliaments', in Dean and Jones, *Parliaments*, p. 50.

parties or patrons in their voting. What, then, guided the way they voted? Pollyannaish as it may sound, it would appear that many of them were guided by the idea that they should apply their knowledge in the service of queen and kingdom, always remembering their places in the hierarchy.

There were good reasons for this belief, deeply rooted in both their self-conception as magistrates of the realm and in the nature of the institution. As the God-given rulers of the nation, they had a duty, consonant with their stations, to serve the queen with advice as well as their lives and fortunes. As the members of the highest court in the land they had a duty to make laws and resolve disputes in accord with the divine principles enunciated by God and embodied in statute and common laws. All of these things required that members speak freely, applying their learning and wisdom to the cases at hand. Moreover, it required that the wisest men be returned.

The nature of wisdom, however, was complicated. It might, as Thomas Atkins argued, depend upon a knowledge of local circumstances rather than education. Or it might depend on experience in the councils of the realm, upon legal training, or upon business expertise. The notion that men should have knowledge of their particular constituencies therefore often ran counter to the ideal that parliament should contain those most fit to give counsel to the monarch.

That parliamentary workhorse Francis Alford tried to reconcile those contradictory principles when he proposed that boroughs be required to return only one resident, encapsulating both sides of the issue. He reasoned:

that above all things necessary care ought to be for the choosing and having fit men to supply the place, that there be no imperfection, and therefore noted one great disorder, that very young men not experienced for learning sake were chosen, through whose default he knew not, whether letters of noble men or affection in the country, their own ambitions or the careless account of the election, or what else was the cause he knew not; but it was not as it should be . . . Whereupon he would that none should be of that House not of xxx years at the least. And for the choice of towns' men he said he was of this mind, that Moses and Aaron should be conjoined together and that there should be one of their own, or some gentlemen near them who had knowledge of the state of the country, and the other a man learned and able to utter the mind of his opinion, since that the knowledge locked up in the breast not being orderly opened, all is to no purpose, and this part is [as] requisite for consultation as the other.[36]

The most important issue for Alford was that parliament men should be 'requisite for consultation'. Joining knowledge with rhetorical skill, the ideal member of parliament was a Ciceronian paragon. He was to be 'well learned, the flower and choice of your [Majesty's] realm', as the new Speaker, Fulke Onslowe, described him in 1566.[37]

Such paragons were needed because of their parliamentary duties. Time and again the assembled houses were lectured on their responsibilities by the lord

---

[36] Hartley, p. 230.   [37] *Ibid.*, p. 126.

keeper at the opening of a session. And each time they were told that they were
called to make and unmake laws and to consider how the realm might be best
preserved in peace and defended in war. Ultimately, they knew, the purpose of
parliament was:

consultation, advise and contentation, for although divers things that are to be done
here in Parliament might by means be reformed without Parliament, yet the Queen's
Majesty, seeking in her consultations of importance contentation by assent and surety
by advise, and therewith reposing herself not a little in your fidelities, wisdom and
discretion, means not at this time to make any resolution in any matter of weight before
it shall be by you sufficiently and fully debated, examined and considered.[38]

It was as a council that parliament was called, and as a council it was expected
to give counsel.

The implications of this definition of parliament's role were spelled out by
Peter Wentworth in 1576 in an abortive speech which got him locked in the
Tower. This speech has been often celebrated as exemplifying 'a tribe much
favoured by whiggish historians – "the people ahead of their time"', says Elton,
and he is correct.[39] Nonetheless, if we read it from a rhetorical point of view we
can see how Wentworth tried to justify his right to speak freely, even offen-
sively, in parliament by echoing beliefs about the role of parliament in the realm.

His first point was that 'All matters that concern God's honor through free
speech, shall be propagated here and set forward and all things that do hinder it
removed, repulsed, and taken away.'[40] This proposition was a socratic trick, for
Wentworth intended to talk about reform of religion against the queen's will.
He knew that the lord keeper always reminded the two houses that 'in all
counsels and conferences first and chiefly there should be sought the
advancement of God's honor and glory as the sure and infallible foundation
whereupon the policy of every good public weal is to be erected . . .'.[41]

The members would have nodded agreement with his first point, and they
would have accepted the next two without complaint, too. There is nothing, he
said, that loving subjects in parliament will not offer to the prince. Moroever,
anything damaging to the prince or state 'shall be prevented even so much as
seems good to our merciful God to put into our minds . . .'.[42] These points also
played off arguments used in the lord keeper's speech, reflecting the language
with which the subsidy was justified and the way in which parliament was called
upon to make laws for the commonwealth. Even his conclusion, that 'in this
House which is termed a place of free speech there is nothing so necessary for
the preservation of the prince and state as free speech, and without it it is a scorn
and a mockery to call it a parliament . . .', was unexceptionable.

---

[38] *Ibid.*, pp. 33–4 [1559], 183 [1571]; D'Ewes (ed.), *Journals*, p. 524 [1597]. Members heard these
platitudes so often that Peter Wentworth used them as the launching point for his plea for free speech
in 1576; Hartley, p. 425.

[39] Elton, *Parliament*, p. 346.   [40] Hartley, p. 426.

[41] *Ibid.*, p. 183. This quotation is from Lord Keeper Bacon's 1571 address.

[42] *Ibid.*, p. 426.

This rhetorical strategy was not what got Peter Wentworth into trouble with the House. The other members could not tolerate his accusation that the queen was wrong in forbidding them to discuss a change in religion. When Wentworth returned to the Commons from the Tower two days before the end of the session he was lacerated by a speech by Sir Walter Mildmay. Mildmay reminded him of the queen's clemency and the House's duty to her before taking up the theme of free speech in parliament. He made a distinction between liberty of speech and licentious speech, insisting that 'though freedom of speech has always been used in this great council of the parliament and is a thing most necessary to be preserved amongst us, yet the same was never, nor ought to be extended so far as though a man in this House may speak what, and of whom he list . . .'.[43] Mildmay was defining a conundrum which was true, even if it was a conundrum. Members of parliament were expected to speak freely, but it was a freedom constrained by loyalty. Some things were reserved for the queen; others were not.

Even if principles of decorum and political good sense helped control the topics addressed, members still believed that they had a duty to speak freely about issues germane to parliament, which included nearly everything. Lacking direct influence from patrons (and even if there was direct influence on some subjects, patrons had no platforms), without party discipline, reporting to no constituency, they were willing to address issues according to their individual lights and vote their consciences. As a member of the Commons put it in 1566, speaking on the succession:

This king, this head, with the consent of the whole body and through the providence of God, weighing that his eye and ear cannot be in every corner of his kingdom and dominions at one instant to view and hearken out the benefits or inconviencies that might grow to the head, body, or any member thereof, has established this honorable counsel of every part of the same absent from the king's eye, and ear, the which is termed a parliament, that is, a speech uttered from the heart, from the mind, yea a free speech wherefore this counsel was ordained to be absent from the king's eye and ear. The reason is that as the office of a king is an high thing, even so he most commonly lists himself on high and can hardly endure plain speech, being inured to pleasing things. Therefore, to prevent the evils of treacherous flattery and devilish dissimulation and many other inconveniences, the providence of God, I say, has ordained by law that in this House every one has free speech and consent . . .[44]

Asserting the Commons' right to discuss the succession despite a message from the palace forbidding it, this may be read as a special pleading, yet it is also, like Wentworth's speech, the reaffirmation of clichéd principles.

In this world that cherished the duty of the individual member to speak freely in order to make his knowledge and wisdom available to the realm, many individuals never said a word, and some seldom attended. However, judging by the evidence in surviving speeches, members assumed that in parliament, as in

[43] *Ibid.*, p. 453.   [44] *Ibid.*, pp. 129–30.

court, the scholastic belief in hearing pros and cons before deriving a conclusion held sway. Whether in argument between lawyers before the bench or in argument between members of parliament before their colleagues, truth could only be established if all sides of a question were heard. Underlying this belief that debate could lead to truth was the assumption that there was a truth to be found – that answers could be absolute, rather than relative, and that the truths embodied in statutes were, in Smith's word, *sanctum* (holy).

This assumption was drawn from their certainty that God had created the world and that human law should mirror God's will for the world. Axiomatic in scholastic theology, most Elizabethans accepted this, agreeing with Hooker who, in his *Laws of Ecclesiastical Polity*, insisted that the laws made by parliament 'do take originally their essence from the power of the whole realm and the church of England, than which nothing can be more consonant unto the law of nature and the will of our Lord Jesus Christ'.[45] From this it naturally followed that religious ideology played a formative role in the way members approached their duty as representatives. So long as they believed it to be the application of divine truth they had no need to consult those below them. Their duty was to consult God, applying their findings to particular problems.

They conceived their duty to be to create law which conformed with God's law and benefited the realm, the two being synonymous. Therefore ideology and theology were as important as politics in shaping the debates in parliament. This is made clear in the preambles of bills and statutes, in the structures of the debates, and in the way parliamentarians increasingly appealed to conscience as the arbiter of their decisions.

The preambles, mini-explanations of legislation that served as both justifications and guides to judges, often confirm that the law is being made with God in mind. The preamble to the 1563 perjury statute states that the law is being made because lying in court is 'to the high displeasure of God'.[46] In 1571 the Act Against Usury declared lending at interest to be illegal because it was forbidden by the law of God, making it sinful and detestable.[47] In these cases and many more the justification, and sometimes the cause, of the legislative action lay in a theological assumption about what deserved to be regulated by human law.

Everywhere one looks in Elizabethan debates, God's name is invoked as a justification for action. God's law was the beginning and end of legislation, so that debates often had a theological assumption as a subtext. A classic (and visible) case of this is the debate over the Act Against Usury in 1571. At issue was the definition of usury. Clearly condemned by scripture and forbidden by the canon law of the Church of England, the members had to decide what it was in order to legislate concerning it. If it touched all loans that bore interest, then it

[45] Richard Hooker, *The Works of Richard Hooker*, ed. John Keble (Oxford, 1845), iii, p. 412.
[46] 5 Eliz. I, c. 14.1.
[47] 13 Eliz. I, c. 8.4.

had to be forbidden in absolute terms. If, on the other hand, it only occurred when borrower and lender were out of charity with one another over the loan, lending at interest might be tolerated within politically determined limits. A debate over theological distinctions rather than economics, the sides split over whether usury was *malum in se*, forbidden by God and therefore undebatable, and those who saw it as only a prohibited evil and open to regulated tolerance. Their positions reflected Aquinian and nominalist assumptions about sin, but both sides still agreed that human law took its cue from God.[48] Thomas Norton, a leading member of the House and draftsman of many bills, summed up the issue of legislating in accord with God's law by quoting Gratian and St Paul: 'We should be mindful of the true old saying *quod dubitas non fecerit* [don't do what is doubtful], and for that *quod non ex fide est, peccatum est* [what is not from faith is sin].'[49]

The direct linkage between the law of God and the making of human law became harder to establish as Elizabeth's reign progressed. Post-Reformation popular scepticism began to destroy the common ground that made agreement about absolute truth possible. This is first visible in parliament in the frustration some members felt over the refusal of the queen to use parliament to create a fully reformed Church. Outside of parliament this had the effect of creating a theology which, taking its cue from solifidian theology, began to exalt individual conscience over human law. In the first instance this was a rationalization which allowed people to dissent from the state Church. In the end conscience came to be widely recognized as the only authority that a person could follow with certainty. For instance, the Cambridge theologian and popular author William Perkins informed his readers in 1596 that if God commands one thing and the magistrate another, God must be obeyed, for if we do otherwise conscience is bound to charge us with sin.[50]

These kinds of arguments began to change the nature of parliamentary debates. Where once the invocation of divine truth could be an effective argument because agreement was assumed to be possible, it became less effective, since access to divine truth was highly individual and behaviour was not a guide to internal righteousness. Instead, pragmatic considerations came to be the neutral ground on which arguments could be proven, even though God was frequently invoked.[51]

As appeals to natural and divine law waned, appeals to conscience became more and more important in parliamentary rhetoric. Now conscience, reflecting

---

[48] Norman Jones, *God and the Moneylenders. Usury and Law in Early Modern England* (Oxford, 1989), pp. 47–65.

[49] Hartley, pp. 236–7.

[50] William Perkins, *A Discourse of Conscience*, in *William Perkins, 1558–1602: English Puritan*, ed. Thomas F. Merrill (Nieuwkoop, 1966), pp. 10–11. My thanks to David Sacks who, in converstaton and in his unprinted studies on liberty and monopolies, has helped me to refine my ideas about the impact of conscience on parliamentarians.

[51] I have argued this at length in *God and the Moneylenders*, pp. 145–205. See also Dean and Jones, *Parliaments*, pp. 9–12, 122–7.

God's will, became a popular source of authority. This had two effects: it undermined the idea that the magistracy spoke on God's behalf, and it exalted the individual over the community. These tendencies began to appear in the 1590s, becoming really visible only in the reign of James, but they prepared the way for a new concept of representation. The more the individual conscience was exalted and the authority of external hierarchies undermined, the more necessary it became to find legitimacy in the fiction of a sovereign people. Divinity was beginning its slow departure from government.

Ironically, the departure of divinity from government undermined the consensus on which English feudal monarchy had been based. The recognition of the right and necessity for the powerful of the realm to give counsel in their own right was diminishing. It was this recognition that had shaped Elizabethan concepts of parliament and the place of parliament in the political society of the realm. As long as magistracy was snugly tied to a hierarchical model of authority that drew its power from God, members of parliament did not believe they spoke with the voices of their constituencies. Instead, they spoke from their own wisdom, bolstered by the authority God had bestowed upon them.

For most members of the two houses of parliament, attending a session was only one of the many duties their social stations imposed on them. They spoke and voted in the high court of parliament as they might have from the bench at the quarter sessions or in the aldermens' chamber. Firmly embedded in patronage networks that served much larger purposes than providing political support in parliaments which were erratic and unpredictable, they generally were free to vote and speak as they saw fit, always remembering their duty to the queen. The way they spoke and voted was informed by their religion, by their political ties and by their wisdom, but they did not form parties or carry out platforms. That could best be done outside parliament. Within it they were to act as judges, sharing with the queen the responsibility of making law, for which they were answerable to God.

Politics certainly had its place in parliament, but not constituency politics in the way we know it. The members sat in the name of a place and might occasionally vote in the interests of that place, but that anonymous, shouted vote in the Commons could have little direct effect on such a place. It was more important that patronage connections be strengthened through the lending of a seat, and that in principle the realm be governed by magistrates who applied laws made according to the wisdom of the wisest and most responsible in the kingdom.

In representing themselves the members of the two houses of parliament were believed to be representing the best interests of the nation.

10 Image and ritual in the Tudor parliaments

DAVID DEAN

Wednesday morning, being the first day for the convocation of the Estates, which they here call Parliament, an order was issued for another mass of the Holy Ghost to be sung in all the churches [of London]. The King went by water to that of the Preachers where Your Imperial Majesty was lodged on his visit to this country, and he heard it accompanied by all the prelates and nobility of this kingdom with all their dresses and 'gran chappes' of scarlet cloth, only that the King's was of crimson lined with ermine. It would be superfluous for me to describe the order and ceremonies on this occasion, inasmuch as Your Imperial Majesty knows very well how fond the people of this country are of such pageants. (Eustace Chapuys to Charles V, 8 November 1529)[1]

It might be said that foreign ambassadors would be more receptive to the spectacle of the opening of parliament than most observers. As aliens they would have had an almost anthropological interest in the customs, rituals, and traditions of the society in which they lived. After all, they were paid to make telling observations and gather information of great interest. Later ambassadors and their informants were no less impressed with parliamentary processions than Eustace Chapuys. In 1559, the Mantuan ambassador at Brussels received a report that Elizabeth's first parliamentary procession was 'neither more nor less than on the entry into London'. It was accompanied by people kneeling as she passed, shouting 'God save and maintain thee'.[2] In 1597 Henri IV's ambassador, De Maisse, noted that the queen travelled 'in great pomp' to Westminster Abbey 'and thence to the chamber of the said Estates, which is very richly adorned'.[3]

A version of this chapter was read at the Anglo-American Conference in July 1991 and the Tudor and Stuart Seminar in January 1992, both at the Institute of Historical Research, London. I am grateful to those present for their comments, in particular Pauline Croft, Peter Lake, and David Starkey.

[1] *CSP Span.*, iv, pt. 1, p. 323.
[2] R. Brown and G. C. Bentinck (eds.), *Calendar of State Papers, Venetian, Vol. VII: 1558–80* (1890), pp. 22–3. One can perhaps compare such public acclaim with an account of the procession of Prince Henry to his installation as Prince of Wales on 4 June 1610: 'the Thames began soone to flote with Boates and Barges, hasting from all partes to meet him, and the shores on either side where conveniency of place would give way to their desires swarmed with multitudes of people, which stood waytinge with greedy eyes to behold his triumphant passage'; College of Arms, MS. Vincent 151, pp. 456–7.
[3] G. B. Harrison and R. A. Jones (eds.), *De Maisse A Journal of All that was accomplished by Monsieur De Maisse Ambassador In England From King Henry IV to Queen Elizabeth Anno Domini 1597* (1931), p. 30.

Nor is there any doubt that parliamentary processions were of great interest to English men, women, and children. Processions were popular enough that railings were needed to keep the crowds back. In 1601 the royal guard protected the queen and her ladies from the 'presse of the people'. The streets of Westminster were decorated with tapestries from Arras 'and other rich stuffe, such as the inhabitauntes had to furnish the street'. On this occasion 'as her highnes passed, the Earle marshall and knight marshall's men did cleare the streetes before her Majestie which was this yeare so well ordered that no bodye receaved any hurt'. Earlier processions had evidently involved injury to spectators.[4]

Although contemporaries were drawn to the pomp and ceremony of Tudor parliaments, historians have been reluctant to give it a central place, preferring instead to concentrate on political developments, managerial strategies, or legislative concerns. The present study is intended as a step towards a fuller understanding of the role of ritual in the Tudor parliaments. It will argue that the royal procession to the opening of parliament and the rituals on the opening and closing days provide a vital and dynamic context to the session itself. To ignore the ritualistic context of such activities as speech-making and bill-making is to ignore an essential ingredient to the success of the Tudor parliament as both event and institution.

Anthropologists and sociologists have paid much attention to the ways in which ritual serves to legitimize authority, to dramatize power or to amplify aspects of power-holding. Rituals of consensus, accommodation or reversal, the use of imagery and allegory, of liturgical ceremonies, of processions and progresses, have been studied. Victor Turner's work explores the dynamics of symbolism and the elements of ritual processes in many societies and times. Edward Shils and Clifford Geertz have examined the ways in which coronations and progresses served to identify and sanctify royal authority.[5] Historians have also drawn attention to the importance of ritual, display, and image in the political process.[6] Recently there have been numerous studies of the displays, ceremonies, portraiture, and theatre of the Tudor and Stuart courts, although only a few have reflected on the wider questions of public performance and perception.[7] Although the sources do not permit analysis of the reception of a

---

[4] Alnwick Castle, Duke of Northumberland MS. 468, fo. 124 (BL microfilm 342); E. R. Foster, 'Staging a Parliament in Early Stuart England', in P. Clark, A. G. R. Smith and N. Tyacke (eds.), *The English Commonwealth. Essays in Politics and Society Presented to Joel Hurstfield* (Leicester, 1979), p. 130.

[5] Victor Turner, *The Ritual Process* (1969) and *Dramas, Fields and Metaphors; Symbolic Action in Human Society* (1974); Edward Shils and M. Young, 'The Meaning of the Coronation', *Sociological Review*, new ser., 1 (1953): 63–81; Clifford Geertz, 'Centers, Kings and Charisma: Reflections on the Symbolics of Power', in his *Local Knowledge. Further Essays in Interpretative Anthropology* (New York, 1983), pp. 121–46. See also David Kertzer, *Ritual, Politics and Power* (1988).

[6] Studies include S. Wilentz (ed.), *Rites of Power: Symbolism, Ritual and Politics since the Middle Ages* (Philadelphia, PA, 1985) and David Cannadine and Simon Price (eds.), *Rituals of Royalty, Power and Ceremonial in Traditional Societies* (Cambridge, 1987).

[7] Two notable exceptions are Judith Richards, '"His Nowe Majestie" and English Monarchy: The Kingship of Charles I before 1640', *Past and Present*, 113 (1986): 70–96, and R. Malcolm Smuts,

parliamentary procession, a good deal of material has survived which enables a reasonably detailed reconstruction of the event itself. Through 'thick description' we should be able to discover some of the elements which made the parliamentary procession an important event in the political calendar of Tudor England.

Lacking pageants and staged allegorical displays, the procession to parliament was undoubtedly less spectacular than a coronation procession or a royal entry, but it nevertheless was a public procession of the monarch which had considerable importance and impact. Moreover, it was a more regular feature of the regnal calendar than royal entries and it displayed the virtues and qualities of monarchical government in a distinctive manner. Whereas royal entries focused on the personal qualities of the monarch and his or her government, a parliamentary procession emphasized royal authority particularly through the representation of the legal, political, and religious élites who processed before the monarch. It was not a progress from one royal palace to another, to a country house or a town, nor was it a procession returning from the country into the City of London. It was a procession from the royal palace to the parliament house where the monarch would make laws for the kingdom with the lords spiritual and temporal and the representatives of the commons of the realm. Culminating in a parliament, this procession may have invoked expectations of problem-solving among the spectators which would have been at least less specifically directed in the royal entry. A parliamentary procession thus had a significance of its own: it had similarities to a royal progress or a royal entry, but it contained elements specific to parliament's function as a meeting of the 'body of the whole realm'.

By this end of the sixteenth century, when Richard Hooker coined this famous phrase, parliament was no longer simply a meeting of the king's council to which members of the Commons had been called to offer their petitions and advice. During the Reformation parliament, the House of Commons became identified as a full member of the high court of parliament, a trinity of equals consisting of crown, lords, and commons.[8] In 1585 William Cecil, Lord Burghley, could inform a Commons' delegation to a joint conference:

their Lordships of the Upper House being of such quality and calling as they are known to be, are one Member of the Parliament; And also that the Knights, Citizens and Burgesses of this House representing the whole Commons of this Realm are also another

---

'Public Ceremony and Royal Charisma: the English Royal Entry in London, 1485–1642', in A. L. Beier, D. Cannadine and J. M. Rosenheim (eds.), *The First Modern Society: Essays in English History in Honour of Lawrence Stone* (Cambridge, 1989), pp. 65–93. Recent studies of court culture and ritual include Sydney Anglo, *Spectacle, Pageantry and Early Tudor Policy* (Oxford, 1969); David Bergeron, *English Civic Pageantry* (1971); Roy Strong, *Splendour at Court* (1973); Stephen Orgel, *The Illusion of Power* (1975); Frances Yates, *Astraea* (1975); Roy Strong, *The Cult of Elizabeth* (1977); D. R. Starkey, 'Representation through Intimacy', in I. Lewis (ed.), *Symbols and Sentiments* (1977), pp. 187–224; Graham Parry, *The Golden Age Restored* (Manchester, 1981); R. Malcolm Smuts, *Court Culture and the Origins of a Royalist Tradition in Early Stuart England* (1987); John King, *Tudor Royal Iconography: Literature and Art in An Age of Religious Crisis* (Princeton, NJ, 1989).

8 See G. R. Elton, *The Parliament of England 1559–1581* (Cambridge, 1986), pp. 16–39.

Member of the same Parliament, and her Majesty the Head; And that of these three estates doth consist the whole Body of the Parliament able to make Laws.[9]

In 1549 the full participation of the Commons was realized in one of the most significant developments in the history of parliament, the moving of the lower house from the chapter house of Westminster Abbey into St Stephen's Chapel in the Palace of Westminster.[10] Yet, as we shall see, the parliamentary procession failed to reflect these developments because members of the lower house were excluded. Properly described as a procession *to* parliament, it was the first of several stages which led to the formation of 'the whole Body of the Parliament able to make Laws'.

Parliament thus held a unique place in the English polity: it combined the transitory impact of an event with the stable, time-honoured, permanent qualities of an institution. Once one parliament had ended, no one knew when the next one would take place, but the clerks gathered up their records in expectation that it would. These records not only provided information about the business transacted, but also told the clerks who should receive writs of summons, assistance, and election when the next parliament was called. Although each parliament was an event, there were important institutional links *between* parliaments. There were thus both static and dynamic aspects to the staging of a parliament in Tudor England. The all-encompassing power of crown-in-parliament, which became a political reality after the Reformation, was revealed both in the closed world of the two Houses and the public world of the parliamentary procession.

It is the static, interior world of the House of Lords which most figures in our images of the Tudor parliament. Although more animated pictures of the Commons were available from the 1620s onwards, Paul Bowes chose to illustrate his uncle's *Journals of all the Parliaments of Queen Elizabeth*, published in 1682, with a frozen image of Elizabeth enthroned in the Lords on the day when the speaker was presented at the opening of parliament (plate 54). The queen sits, almost larger than life, gazing at the viewer in regal splendour. She holds the orb and sceptre under a canopied throne decorated with the arms of England and France, a rich tapestry behind her. Before her sit the assembled bishops and lay peers, the judges, legal assistants, and clerks on the woolsacks, and the noblemen carrying the royal regalia stand before her with Garter, King of Arms. Yet the room seems narrow, the ceiling low; we seem to be treated to a special viewing of a closed and private world. Like the Commons, who crowd awkwardly behind the bar at the end of the chamber (and the bottom of the picture),

[9] Sir Simonds D'Ewes, *The Journals of all the Parliaments During the Reign of Queen Elizabeth, Both of the House of Lords and House of Commons* (1682, reprinted Shannon, Ireland, 1973) p. 350. It is important to note that Burghley was angry that the Commons had rejected a Lords' bill without first consulting the upper house.

[10] J. E. Neale, *The Elizabethan House of Commons* (1949), p. 364.

Plate 54. Elizabeth I in parliament, frontispiece to Sir Symond D'Ewes'
Journals (1682). This is a late seventeenth-century representation of the
Elizabethan House of Lords. The officers bearing the royal regalia stand
with Garter King of Arms immediately before the queen, the bishops sit to
her right and the senior lay peers to her left. The barons sit at the end of the
chamber before her and behind them stand the Commons with their
speaker. The clerks, judges, the legal assistants sit on the sacks in the centre
of the chamber.

Plate 55. Elizabeth I in parliament, from Robert Glover's *Nobilitas Politica vel Civilis* (1608). An early seventeenth-century image, this is the closest to a contemporary view that survives. The feeling here is of a much grander and more specious chamber than that offered by D'Ewes, a point emphasized by the strong use of perspective in the tiled floor.

the viewer is given a momentary glimpse of monarchy and aristocracy in all their glory.

This image, the most commonly reproduced of all the images of the Tudor parliaments, owes much more to the seventeenth-century chamber than to that which it represents.[11] Yet in many respects it owes a good deal to the image of the same scene engraved, possibly by Renold Elstrack, for Robert Glover's *Nobilitas Politica vel Civilis*, published posthumously in 1608 (plate 55).[12] The impression here is of a much grander chamber, more spacious, lighter, less crowded. Yet in essentials it is the same: the closed world of the Lords is opened for the briefest of moments, namely the presentation of the speaker to the monarch. The MPs and their speaker, differentiated by costume and standing as if in suspended animation, stare, as it were, into the space framing the static images of queen and aristocracy. In this majestic world only the clerks seem alive, scribbling away on their woolsacks at the centre of the picture.[13]

Elstrack's engraving was the first published picture of the Tudor parliament but it was not the first image. It is not known whether Glover's manuscript included a drawing upon which Elstrack could have based his engraving, but as Somerset herald from 1570 until his death in 1588, Glover may well have had the same inclination to prepare such an image as other heralds had done before him. All of the Elizabethan examples are plain, simply sketched outlines of the Lords'

[11] D'Ewes, *Journals*, frontispiece. The round window above and behind the throne was a Caroline addition; Arthur M. Hind, *Engraving in England in the Sixteenth and Seventeenth Centuries, Part II, The Reign of James I* (Cambridge, 1955), p. 198. The image is also dated by the presence of the mace-bearer in front of the queen, the large number of barons and perhaps also by the presence of Black Rod, since the first reference to Black Rod as leading the Commons to attend the sovereign in the Lords was in 1614; M. Bond and D. Beamish, *The Gentleman Usher of the Black Rod* (1976), p. 5; M. Jansson, *Proceedings in Parliament 1614 (House of Commons)* (Philadelphia, PA, 1988), p. 12. Glover, in his image of the 1584 parliament, has the speaker accompanied by two men carrying rods on his left and right, which represents D'Ewes's words better than the image that accompanied his *Journals*: 'the said Prolocutor or Speaker being led up by two of the most honourable Personages of the said House, and there having made his excuse according to the usual form at the Bar or Rail at the lower end of the Upper House'; D'Ewes, *Journals*, p. 333. One could surmise that the 'Personages' mentioned were Knollys and Croft, respectively treasurer and comptroller of the household. Two other privy councillors, Chancellor of the Exchequer Mildmay and Secretary Walsingham, may also be possible candidates. The image in D'Ewes also mistakenly places Walsingham behind the throne.

[12] Robert Glover, *Nobilitas Politica vel Civilis* (1608). The British Library has several copies of this work, none of which have the coloured engraving present in the copy held by the Folger Shakespeare Library, Washington, DC. Glover married Elizabeth Flower, daughter of Norroy King of Arms, and he has been described as the most scholarly of heralds; Louise Campbell, *A Catalogue of Manuscripts in the College of Arms Collections* (vol. 1, 1988), pp. 169–70. Glover's nephew, Thomas Milles, published an English translation in 1610 as part of his *Catalogue of Honor*, a lengthy study of royal and noble pedigrees dedicated to the earls of Salisbury and Northampton. Milles updated Glover's work, including an account of James I's coronation, adding names of knights of the Garter created by James and substituting James for Elizabeth I in the picture of parliament.

[13] Elstrack did a separate portrayal of James I in parliament in 1604, which was re-used in 1621 and 1624. He possibly did all the engraving in Glover's volume since he did the title plate to Milles's *Catalogue of Honor*. The image there (depicting James rather than Elizabeth) was used again by Michael Droeshout in his picture of 'The Powder Treason' and by the anonymous engravers in their pictures of the 1628 parliament; Hind, *Engraving in England ... James I*, plates 108, 109, 110, 112–15; plate 213, pp. 341–2 (Droeshout); id., *Engraving in England ... Part III, The Reign of Charles I* (edited from Hind's notes by M. Corbett and Michael Norton, Cambridge, 1964), plates 205, 206b (1628).

chamber, accompanied often by lists of peers, but two outstanding heralds' drawings survive for 1523 and 1553 (plates 56 and 57). That for 1553, at the Royal Library, Windsor, in the papers of Sir Gilbert Dethick, Garter King of Arms from 1550 to 1584, is a rough drawing of the king enthroned, noblemen holding the regalia and Dethick himself standing before him, the lord chancellor and lord treasurer behind, and the bishops, lay peers, judges, assistants, and clerks seated (plate 56). The picture drawn for Thomas Wriothesley, also Garter King of Arms, for the Blackfriars parliament of 1523, is much more polished and finished. It is also more splendid, partly because of the presence of the mitred abbots and of the two archbishops sitting on the royal traverse (plate 57).[14]

Yet both images show interior views only. Unlike the seventeenth-century pictures there is no architectural reference; these are, in effect, seating plans. Why Wriothesley and Dethick saw fit to prepare the more elaborate and coloured versions for the parliaments is not known; perhaps others were made which have since been lost. It was certainly the responsibility of the heralds to ensure that the Lords were seated properly according to rank and precedence. It might be conjectured that this was especially a problem in 1523 when the parliament met at Blackfriars rather than Westminster; it was a unique event. Certain elements confirm this purpose behind the drawing. In this parliament Thomas Wolsey, archbishop of York, held a unique combination of offices. As archbishop, he would have sat to the king's left, and a cushion marks this spot.[15] But as lord chancellor, cardinal, and papal legate, Wolsey assumed a position next to Archbishop Warham of Canterbury on the king's right. Like Warham, Wolsey's status is shown by a heraldic device, the coat of arms, which sits above him; for good measure a cardinal's hat is rather awkwardly suspended over the mitre which he wears. The heralds' concern to show the peers in their proper places is seen also in the depiction of that essential Tudor indication of hierarchy and status: costume. The bishops and abbots, dukes, earls and barons, and judges are differentiated by mitres, ducal crowns, caps, and coifs; eldest sons of peers, masters of chancery and clerks appear bare-headed. The scarlet robes of the bishops, lay peers, and judges, the dark gowns of the abbots

---

[14] The original is in the Wriothesley Garter Book, Royal Library, Windsor (Royal MS. 1B2b), and is described by A. F. Pollard, *The Evolution of Parliament* (1926), pp. 380–3, and more recently by J. Enoch Powell and Keith Wallis, *The House of Lords in the Middle Ages. A History of the English House of Lords to 1540* (1968), pp. 555–7. The herald's description is in College of Arms MS. 2 H 13, fo. 396. The descriptions are not without controversy, for example, over the identity of the earls standing in front of the king and over which staff of office is held. According to Pollard, Norfolk sits holding his lord treasurer's staff, his earl marshal's baton being held by a deputy standing in front of the king. Powell and Wallis maintain that Norfolk holds his baton; the earl in front of the King is Lord Chamberlain Oxford, who is holding his white wand of office. This would at least remove the need to find a deputy for Norfolk; however, in later parliaments it was the earl marshal's rod which was borne before the monarch, with the cap and sword. Pollard suggests, and Powell and Wallis do not disagree, that the bearer of the cap is the earl of Worcester.

[15] According to Powell and Wallis, this meant that the two bishops of the north, Durham and Carlisle, vacated their normal seats on the forms on the temporal side of the chamber. They also note that spaces on the immediate right and left of the monarch were spaces for the king of Scotland and the prince of Wales. These are clearly shown, and labelled, in the later 'Elizabethan' images.

Plate 56. Edward VI in parliament in 1553. This herald's seating plan may have been known to Glover and clearly bears comparison with the image prepared for the posthumous publication of his book. Note how clearly the rank of each nobleman is depicted by the number of bars of miniver.

Plate 57.   Henry VIII in parliament in 1523. This is the most detailed and beautiful of the Tudor heralds' seating plans. Note the careful depictions of the two archbishops to the king's right, with Wolsey's status as cardinal clearly shown.

(and the prior of St John) make them distinct from the varied gowns of the noblemen's sons, from the MPs gathered with their speaker at the bar of the House, and from the two privy councillors standing behind the traverse.[16] Even more distinctive is the way the ranks of the lay nobility are depicted. Dressed in their parliament robes, they are differentiated by the number of miniver bars on their shoulders (four for dukes, three for earls, two for barons); in this drawing, like that for 1553, the bars are shown very clearly indeed.

These drawings represent, then, the static world of hierarchy and order, presided over by imperial majesty. Though more animated, if only by being located in an actual structure, the same qualities are present in the later pictures of Elizabeth's parliaments. In light of the heraldic drawings, it is especially significant that the picture in Glover's book was intended as the conclusion to his description of what he called the 'Parliamentary Pompe'. This is the scene which would have confronted the reader who had followed the 1584 procession from St James to Westminster, described by Glover in great detail. The static but majestic image of the queen and the lords was the end product of the most dynamic aspect of staging parliament as event, the procession.

As the description of the crowds in 1601 indicated, each procession to parliament was carefully marshalled and organized: it was the responsibility of the earl marshal and the heralds to do so.[17] Thus the many accounts of these processions which have survived were compiled by the heralds.[18] The heralds'

---

[16] This is at the place where the lord treasurer (Norfolk) and the lord chamberlain (Oxford) sat in 1510 and was later reserved for the lord treasurer. Powell and Wallis suggest that either the two are duplicated, i.e. pictured behind the traverse as well as beneath the king, a view suggested by the fact that there were only seven earls at the time (thus the three on the carpet of lilies are duplicated on the forms and behind the traverse), or that the two are Sir William Fitzwilliam and Sir Henry Guildford, respectively treasurer and comptroller of the household, who head the commoners, members of the privy council, as prescribed in an ordinance of 1526. The picture does not show the presence of foreign ambassadors noted in College of Arms MS. 2 H 13, fo. 396, which confirms that the image is of the second opening day rather than the first. Certainly the two figures cannot be ambassadors, as they wear chains of office. When the Spanish ambassador attended in 1614, holes were cut through the crimson curtains at the back of the traverse for him to see through, but in 1627–28 a traverse was built for an ambassador; Foster, 'Staging', p. 132 and n. 23.

[17] It thus may be no coincidence that several copies of the *Modus tenendi parliamentum*, the chief medieval tract on parliament, its nature and procedures, survive amongst manuscripts in the College of Arms: MSS. M 2bis, fos. 162v–168v, and Vincent 25, fos. 11–18. Sir Edward Coke's printed copy of the *Modus* was bound with a treatise on the duties of the earl marshal; N. Pronay and J. Taylor, *Parliamentary Texts of the Later Middle Ages* (Oxford, 1980), p. 209, where Coke's copy is listed as missing. It has since been discovered by Dr David Starkey (of the London School of Economics) in the Isabella Gardner Museum, Boston, MA. The volume contains (p. 13) a painting of a monarch in parliament, showing the earl marshal, the lord chancellor, etc. Coke referred to the *Modus* when he was speaker of the Commons in 1593: D'Ewes, *Journals*, p. 515. I am grateful to Dr Starkey for drawing my attention to this copy of the *Modus* and to the archivist, Susan Sinclair, for allowing me to examine it. Dr Starkey has discussed this copy in 'Stewart Serendipity: A Missing Text of the Modus Tenendi Parliamentum', *Fenway Court*, 1986 (Isabella Gardner Museum, Boston, MA, 1987), pp. 39–49.

[18] A useful descriptive list has been compiled by H. S. Cobb, 'Descriptions of the State Opening of Parliament 1485–1601: A Survey', in H. S. Cobb (ed.), *Parliamentary History: Libraries and Records. Essays Presented to Maurice Bond* (House of Lords Record Office, London, 1981). I am grateful to

main concern was to ensure the proper ranking of the participants according to the established rules of precedence.[19] The importance of precedence and status in the parliamentary procession in especially demonstrated by the well-known heraldic processional roll of 1512, which not only shows forty-six spiritual and twenty temporal peers and the king walking in procession, but also their coats of arms (plate 58).[20] Notable are the depictions of the duke of Buckingham, chief high constable, carrying his staff and the cap of estate; of Henry VIII, in a splendid jewelled cap and the collar of the Garter, carrying a sceptre, walking under a canopy carried by four tonsured monks; and of Archbishop Warham with his attendants, carrying a pastoral staff with images of saints. The roll also shows very clearly the role of the heralds: the Garter King of Arms, Wriothesley, is shown walking before Buckingham, resplendent in his coat of the arms of England (plate 59).

Although no other processional rolls of arms are of such beauty (and none contain images of the participants), several of the written lists that have survived, often as seventeenth-century copies, are accompanied by detailed descriptions of the procession; some of the lists are diagrammatic, written on the page as if in procession.[21] The writer of the descriptions for 1563 and 1584 was

the archivists of the College of Arms and the British Library, London, for their assistance with the records in their keeping.

[19] The general order of precedence had been established by the official regulations drawn up in 1429 by the constable and the earl marshal: College of Arms, MS. Vincent 151, p. 127, printed in C. G. Young, *Ancient Tables of Precedency* (n.p., n.d.), pp. 5 and 6, and discussed by G. D. Squibb, *Precedence in England and Wales* (Oxford, 1981), pp. 15–16. Ten years later, at the opening of parliament on 12 November 1439, orders were set out establishing the general rules for parliamentary processions: College of Arms, MS. Vincent 151, pp. 131–2 (and see Squibb, pp. 20–1). In Edward IV's reign the constable issued regulations for the proper placing of peers in parliament and a table of precedence was included in the Black Book of the Household; further rules were gathered under Henry VII: College of Arms, MS. Vincent 151, pp. 117–18, printed by Young, *Precedency*, pp. 7 and 8, and C. G. Young, *Privy Councillors and their Precedence* (n.p., 1860), pp. 46–7, and discussed by Squibb, pp. 16–17, 21–2. An order drawn up for a dinner given for foreign ambassadors at Richmond in 1520 was considered authoritative and was amended by the commissioners executing the office of earl marshal in 1595; Squibb, pp. 17–18, app. 1, pp. 98–100. Finally, the placing of peers in parliament, in star chamber and other meetings of the council was established by a statute of 31 Henry VIII, an act needed in part because of the Crown's assumption of ecclesiastical authority; precedence had to be established for the new vicar general, Thomas, Lord Cromwell; Squibb, pp. 23–5; *Statutes of the Realm*, iii, pp. 729–30. The act was noted at the beginning of a manuscript which contains several processions: College of Arms, MS. Vincent 172, fos. 1–1v.

[20] The best copy is in Trinity College, Cambridge, but the copy held by the British Library, Additional MS. 22306, has more shields painted in. Another copy is in the Bodleian Library, Oxford. The roll is discussed by F. S. Eden, 'Heraldic Parliament Rolls', *The Connoisseur*, 94 (1934): 363–6; Powell and Wallis, *The House of Lords*, pp. 543–4; and A. Wagner and J. C. Sainty, 'The Origin of the Introduction of Peers in the House of Lords', *Archaeologia* 101 (1967): 119–49 (see the plates between pp. 124 and 125).

[21] Two important collections of processions are College of Arms, MS. 2 H 13 (processions from 20 Richard II to 1 Elizabeth I, including most of Henry VIII's parliaments), and BL, Add. MS. 5758 (36 Henry VI to 39 Elizabeth I). Others are in College of Arms, MSS. WD and WY, Vincent 92 and 172; BL, Harleian MSS. 158 and 5758; and single processions are described in manuscripts scattered in the collections of the British Library, the Inner Temple Library and the Bodleian Library, Oxford. A good processional roll of arms is BL, Add. MS. 40078 (for 1515).

Glover, and it will be convenient to draw upon the Elizabethan processions for the discussion which follows.[22]

In one of the earliest treatises on parliament the Exeter MP, John Hooker, remarked:

On the first day of the summons for the Parlement, the King in proper person (unlesse he bee sick or absent out of the Realme) beeing apparailled in his royall and Parlement robes: ought to be conducted & brought by all his Barons of the Clergie and Laitie, and the Commons summoned to the Parlement, unto the Church, where ought a Sermon to be made by some Archbishop, Bishop or some other famouse learned man. The Sermon ended: he must in like order be brought to the higher house of Parlement, and there to take his seat under the cloth of estate, likewise every Lord and Baron (in his degree) ought to take his place.[23]

Hooker thus identifies three distinct parts to the ceremonies which marked the beginning of a new parliament. First was the mounted procession to Westminster Abbey, a colourful and splendid affair marshalled by the heralds. This usually began at the King's Bridge at Westminster, to which the monarch had travelled by royal barge from the palace of Whitehall.[24] On occasion the procession began from St James, which must have been an especially grand affair, creating even more opportunity for viewing by spectators. The procession ended at Westminster Abbey.

Next was the service at the Abbey. This began and ended with the delivery of a sceptre. The monarch processed to the chapel to hear the Mass of the Holy Ghost (or divine service under Edward VI and Elizabeth I). However, Hooker fails to note that the lord steward of the royal household did not participate in the service. Instead, he was busy officiating at the swearing-in of the members of the Commons, who together comprised the third part of the parliamentary trinity which until now had no role to play in the opening events. Once the service was over, the monarch left the Abbey and proceeded to the 'parliament house', i.e. the House of Lords.

Third, there was the opening ceremony itself. The monarch robed in a private withdrawing chamber while the Lords took their places. The monarch was then led to the throne and the Commons were called into attendance. The lord chancellor (or lord keeper if the holder of the great seal held the lesser office) declared the reasons for the calling of the parliament and the Commons were

[22] Some are available in print: D'Ewes, *Journals*, pp. 58–66, 136–42; Hartley, pp. 66–79, 267–9; J. Nichols, *The Progresses and Public Processions of Queen Elizabeth* (3 vols., 1823), i, pp. 299–301; ii, p. 433; iii, pp. 409–10, 415. Glover's copy of the 1563 procession is: BL, Add. MS. 37526. Sir John Neale wrote a brief description of the opening procession in his *House of Commons*, pp. 349–50.

[23] Vernon F. Snow (ed.), *Parliament in Elizabethan England, John Hooker's Order and Usage* (New Haven, CT and London, 1977), pp. 191–2. As will be clear later, I am uncertain why Snow identifies the place of the sermon as being St Margaret's, Westminster, and not Westminster Abbey (n. 134).

[24] The King's Bridge was rebuilt by Lewis Stockett sometime between 1565 and 1574, when the lower parliament house got a new roof at a cost of over £1,000; H. M. Colvin, D. R. Ransome and John Summerson, *The History of the Kings Works, Volume III, 1485–1660* (Pt. 1, 1975), pp. 77–8.

Plate 58. Henry VIII and the lords of parliament, a detail of the painted Processional Roll of the parliament of 1512. The king proceeds under a canopy decorated with the Tudor rose. Before him is the duke of Buckingham with the cap of estate, Garter King of Arms and the archbishop of Canterbury.

Plate 59. The lords of parliament, a detail of the painted Processional Roll of the parliament of 1512. Behind the king are the senior peers followed by the prior of St John and the barons. Note the distinctive parliament robes which were used only for parliamentary processions. The heraldic shields were important as a means of ensuring that peers proceeded in the proper order; other rolls only show shields in procession. ▼

instructed to select a speaker. The monarch then departed, with the Lords in attendance, and returned to Whitehall (or St James).

The highlight of the procession was, of course, the monarch herself. She was distinguished from all others by the splendour of her costume, described in 1563 as a mantle edged with ermine and a kirtle of crimson velvet with ermine cuffs, with an ermine hood and 'over all a rich coller sett with stones and other jewells, and on her head a riche calle'. Elizabeth's spectacular costuming referenced the power and spectacle of majesty. Her God-given status was also emphasized by the presence of the royal regalia (the cap of maintenance or estate, the sword of state, and sometimes a verge or rod of office, usually the earl marshall's baton) carried before her by the chief officers of the realm.

The queen alone travelled by coach, which in 1571 was described as having 'a Canopye very rich over her, with foure pillars in her parlament Robes' (plate 60).[25] In 1584 the coach, drawn by two splendid white horses, had two small silver pillars at the back supporting a rich covering surmounted by a crown of gold; at the front, on two pillars by the queen's feet, stood a lion and a dragon, 'glittering with Gold, made with wonderfull cunning, supporting the Queenes Armes'. The golden throne upon which the Queen sat was covered in silver cloth and cushions.

The monarch was also distinguished by being carefully protected: alongside the queen marched her footmen 'in their rich Coats' carrying halberds; on the outside, and on either side, were the gentlemen pensioners with their poleaxes (plate 61). Following the queen, the master of the horse led a horse of state, followed often by the chamberlain and vice-chamberlain of the household, the ladies of the household, noblewomen and men of the court and, finally, the guard led by their captain.

This was the apogee of the procession in which both the private and public worlds of the monarch were represented. The procession effectively grew outwards from the queen's private household to the most public of royal officials who led it. Thus all were carefully ranked according to their relationship with the Crown. Immediately in front of the queen were the noblemen carrying the regalia, including the lord steward, the lord high chamberlain and the earl marshal. They were preceded, and made distinctive, by the guardians of status and hierarchy: Garter King of Arms in his resplendant heraldic coat, and the sergeants-at-arms with their silver maces covered in gilt. Before them were the principal officers of Church and state: the archbishops of York and Canterbury, the lord treasurer, and the lord chancellor accompanied by a footman, probably his sergeant, bearing the Great Seal of England, the ultimate symbol of the right to make law.

The next group in the procession comprised the political, religious, and social

---

[25] Alnwick Castle, Duke of Northumberland MS. 468, fo. 122 (BL, microfilm 342). In 1563 the queen rode on horseback from Whitehall to Westminster Abbey and on other occasions, as in 1601, she went by royal barge from Whitehall to Westminster and then proceeded to the Abbey.

Plate 60. 'The Procession Picture', a painting attributed to Robert Peake (*c.* 1601). Although a wedding picture, this reveals the splendour of Elizabeth's costume as noted in the herald's description of the parliamentary processions.

elite of Tudor society, essentially the members of the House of Lords who proceeded in front of the lord chancellor, united by their scarlet gowns, but also distinguished by variations in their costume. Immediately in front of the lord chancellor rode the upper ranks of the nobility: dukes, marquises, earls, and viscounts, their status signalled by the bars of miniver on their shoulders. In front of them, riding two-by-two, were the bishops, distinguished by their hoods lined with miniver hanging down their backs.[26] Then came the barons, with two bars of miniver, riding in order of precedence.[27] The members of the upper house were led by the son of a nobleman carrying the queen's hat and

---

[26] In his description of 1584, Glover notes that the bishops of London, Durham, and Winchester were to go next before the archbishops according to the act of 31 Henry VIII, 'but all the rest take their places, according to the ancientesse of their elections'; Glover, *Nobilitas*, p. 119; Milles, *Catalogue*, p. 65.

[27] Glover's list of 1584 notes the peers in order of precedence, as do many of the lists. Glover notes that William Cecil, Lord Burghley, should have been before De La Warr, but 'he went in another place, because he was Treasuror of England'; that between Lord St John and Lord Chandos should have been Henry Carey, Lord Hunsdon, but he was absent because he was governor of Berwick; that between Lord North and Lord Darcy would have been Charles Howard, Lord Howard of Effingham, but he took a more prominent place in the procession as Lord Chamberlain; and that Lord Grey of Wilton would have been preceded by Henry, Lord Scrope of Bolton, had the latter not been absent as governor of Carlisle; Glover, *Nobilitas*, pp. 117–18; Milles, *Catalogue*, p. 65.

Plate 61. A pen-and-ink drawing of Elizabeth's coronation procession. As in parliamentary processions, the queen's carriage was followed by the master of the horse and was protected by two ranks of guards, the queen's footmen on the inside and the gentlemen pensioners with their poleaxes on the outside.

cloak. Of course, what was unique to this procession was that the nobility were dressed in their parliament robes. Once again, costume signalled the special nature of the event.[28]

In front of the nobility, lay and clerical, rode those privy councillors who were commoners (usually the secretary, the treasurer and comptroller of the household); knights of the Garter and of the privy council (those, of course, who did not have a higher status by office or title); the eldest sons or heirs of the nobility; knights of the Bath; and younger sons of the nobility. Before them, more powerful in politics but not in status, were the judges, the master of the rolls, the queen's attorney and solicitor, the queen's sergeant, and the sergeants at law. Before the cream of the legal profession were knights banneret and knights bachelor; then the masters of chancery, the clerks of the privy council and clerks of the signet and chancery. The latter, of course, represented the administrative body responsible for the summoning of parliament and the keeping of its records.[29] Finally, at the front of the procession, were the esquires, gentlemen, and messengers of the royal chamber, led by trumpeters 'here and there sounding' who also punctuated various stages of the procession.

This was also the key role played by the heralds in the procession. Of course, they had to plan the procession to perfection because only a few changes by grant of office or inheritance would alter the order. In addition they marshalled the procession itself and were themselves ranked according to the rank of the participants: the pursuivants rode alongside the gentlemen, judges, and knights, with the heralds accompanying the barons and bishops, and Norroy and Clarenceaux Kings of Arms the higher nobility.[30]

It is worth reminding ourselves that no members elected to the House of Commons took part in the procession as a distinct group, although some took part as privy councillors or royal officials. In other words, of the three estates only two, the crown and the Lords, took part in the procession to the English parliament.[31] This was in contrast to Scotland where the procession or 'riding'

---

[28] A reproduction of the portrait of Thomas Cecil, second Lord Burghley, in his parliament robes, together with a description of the robes of the nobility from College of Arms, MS. Vincent 151, is in H. K. Morse, *Elizabethan Pageantry, A Pictorial Survey of Costume 1560–1620* (1934), p. 89. Glover's book includes portrayals of the gowns of barons, viscounts, earls, marquesses, and dukes.

[29] No lesser officials or messengers of the chamber were noted in the 1563 list; Hartley, p. 66.

[30] This was the scene depicted in the description of 1563. However, this account also notes that Norroy and Clarenceaux separated the archbishops from the sergeant at arms and Garter King of Arms; Hartley, pp. 66–8. If this is what actually happened, in later processions the heralds not only rode alongside but also signalled the end of one group and the beginning of another. Glover notes that heralds separated groups, although a rough plan shows them proceeding alongside: BL, Harleian MS. 5758, fo. 75; Glover, *Nobilitas*, pp. 116–21; Milles, *Catalogue*, pp. 64–6. The list of 1597 shows the heralds walking on both sides, separating gentlemen from the masters of chancery and the legal assistants, the latter from the judges, the judges from the knights marshall and the knights of the privy council, the bishops from the earls and so on; College of Arms, MS. WY, fo. 209.

[31] All but one of the heralds' notes on the processions confirm this. The description for the procession of 24 October 1597 notes 'knights, burgesses of the parliament' riding between esquires and the trumpeters who preceded the heralds and the masters of chancery; College of Arms, MS. WY, fo. 209. This must signify, unless it is simply an error, that on this occasion some of the knights bachelor or knights banneret had been elected as MPs. Perhaps this explains Hooker's generalized

from Holyrood Palace to the parliament house, was led by the burgh representatives followed by the lesser barons, country members, the nobility and the clergy, and it also included their servants.[32]

Thus, as Sir John Neale observed, 'Virtually the whole House of Lords was incorporated in the procession not, however, the Commons except individuals belonging to the Court', but he was wrong to describe the procession as 'the full Court in motion' for some participants, notably the judges and legal officers, were not part of the court.[33] Nevertheless, the participants in this procession were ranked by their relationship to the queen and the procession grew outwards from the royal household. Moreover, it was also framed by the royal household: the messengers of the chamber and esquires of the body led and the royal body-guard brought up the rear. The message seems clear: by demonstrating the awesome power of monarchy in its judicial, political, social, and religious aspects, the procession embodied the stable and ordered universe of Elizabethan England. The failure to include the Commons in the procession emphasized the fact that this was still the medieval parliament in motion. The presence of the royal regalia also signalled continuity with the early Tudor and Plantagenet monarchs: the Great Seal, the verge and the sword of state symbolized lasting royal authority. Another symbol of that authority was the cap of maintenance or cap of estate, a crimson cap trimmed with ermine carried at the end of a rod. Originally symbolic of papal support, the cap now demonstrated the royal supremacy.[34]

One of the key rituals accompanying the opening of parliament occurred at Westminster Abbey once the procession had arrived, 'som of the best estate' dismounting within the yard. The queen was met by the dean of Westminster, his prebendaries and all the choir 'in their Coapes'. She knelt at a platform covered with carpets and cushions and received the golden sceptre of St Edward from the dean. This she laid on a cushion before her and, taking up a book of prayers which she had also received from the dean, 'unto her selfe softly prayed'. After prayer, Elizabeth took the sceptre and entered the church under a canopy

---

comment, cited above, that members of the Commons brought the monarch to parliament along with the Lords.

[32] David Masson (ed.), *The Register of the Privy Council of Scotland* (first ser., 14 vols., 1877–98), Vol. 6: *1599–1604* (Edinburgh, 1884), pp. 170–1, orders for the procession of November 1600. James caused some disquiet when he gave the bishops superior positions to the barons and the archbishops to the earls; James I to the duke of Lennox, Oatlands, 24 July 1609, in *Original Letters Relating to the Ecclesiastical Affairs of Scotland* (2 vols., Edinburgh, 1851), Vol. 1: *1603–1614* (Bannatyne Club vol. 92), p. 382; *The Register of the Privy Council of Scotland*, Vol. 7: *1604–7* (Edinburgh, 1885), pp. 533–4.

[33] Neale, *House of Commons*, p. 349.

[34] The cap (and sword) were gifts from the popes to Henry VII in 1489 and 1496, and to Henry VIII in 1505; Anglo, *Spectacle*, p. 88, n. 1, citing J. Wickham Legg, 'The Gift of the Papal Cap and Sword to Henry VII', *Archaeological Journal*, 57 (1900): 183–203. The Elizabethan cap was presumably that given to Henry VIII in 1514 (College of Arms, MS. L 12 b, fos. 46v–47v) or perhaps that given to Mary in 1554–55.

of silver cloth suppported by six knights.[35] Her train was carried by noble-women and she was supported by her chamberlain and vice-chamberlain. Her heavy robes were lifted off her shoulders by two noblemen as she walked.

This little procession walked to the west door of the choir, led by the 'singing men' and choristers who sang psalms and the lord chancellor and lord treasurer. The canopy was set aside as the queen entered the choir. Here, on the right hand side, stood the royal traverse near to the communion table. The 1563 account notes that this was new: 'other princes have used to be placed in the quire till the offeringe, but not now, for that there was neither Communion nor offeringe'. The account of 1601 notes that 'ther was also within the Chapple dore wher the Tombes be, a little private place hanged richlye wher in was a pan of Coales if her Majestie pleased to repose her selfe'.[36] The noblemen took their places on platforms set up beneath the royal traverse on the south side and the bishops, their places beneath the pulpit on the north side of the choir. The sword and cap were carried before the cleric delivering the sermon and were laid out on the table. The sermon was heard once a psalm had been sung.[37]

During the service the lord steward retired in order to supervise the return of knights, citizens, and burgesses in the lower house, returning to meet the queen as she left the Abbey. Once the service was over, and before leaving, the queen surrendered the sceptre of St Edward to the dean. The canopy belonging to the Abbey was left behind, replaced by another which was also carried by six knights. The lord steward conducted the queen, who in 1584 alone rode on horseback, to a privy withdrawing chamber in the palace of Westminster, where she rested (and sometimes robed) until the Lords were properly seated according to precedence. The canopy which was taken away at the foot of the stairs leading to the parliament house was by tradition 'delivered to the footemen which were reddy there to receyve the same as a fee dewe unto them'.[38]

Perhaps the most distinctive aspect of this ritual was the ceremonial delivery and return of the sceptre of St Edward at Westminster Abbey. This sceptre may well be that held by Henry VIII in the 1512 processional roll; it seems to have been replaced by a rod of equity and mercy sometime in Elizabeth's reign.[39] The

35 According to an undated account of a procession, the six knights were to be noblemen's sons; BL, Harleian MS. 5758, fo. 8ov.
36 Alnwick Castle, Duke of Northumberland MS. 468, fo. 124 (BL, microfilm 342).
37 In 1563 the sermon was delivered by Alexander Nowell, Dean of St Paul's, in 1572 by Bishop Cooper of Lincoln, in 1584 by Archbishop Whitgift, and in 1601 by Bishop Babington of Worcester.
38 Hartley, p. 268. See also Alnwick Castle, Duke of Northumberland MS. 468, fo. 124 (BL microfilm 342); BL, Harleian MS. 5758, fo. 77. In 1601 the queen went from the Abbey to parliament on foot, although 'it Rayned a littell she went the faster'; College of Arms, MS. Vincent 92, p. 266.
39 The sceptres are noted and variously described in Alnwick Castle, Duke of Northumberland MS. 468, fo. 124 (BL microfilm 342); Hartley, p. 267; Nichols, *Progresses*, iii, p. 415; College of Arms, MS. WY, fos. 211–211v, and Vincent 92, p. 266. A drawing in a manuscript which includes heralds' accounts of the opening of parliament shows St Edward's sceptre as having a cross at the top and another 'Sceptre of the dove, all gold excepting the dove which is white', which may be the rod of equity and justice; College of Arms, MS. WY, fos. 267, 269. See M. Holmes and H. D. W. Sitwell, *The English Regalia* (1972), pp. 9–11, and Lord Twining, *European Regalia* (1967), p. 188 (and

surrender of the Abbey's sceptre may have been intended to signal the power of the Crown over the Royal Peculiar of Westminster and, more generally, over the Church as a whole. Its religious associations were enough for the ceremony to be abandoned in the first parliament of Edward VI's reign: the sceptre was neither received nor delivered by the king 'as the Ceremonyes thereof heretofore hathe ben hade'.[40]

The whole ceremony at the Abbey marked the end of any similarity between the parliamentary procession and a royal entry or progress. It was here that the state, embodied in the person of the monarch, sought the blessings of the Almighty in the proceedings which were to follow. Indeed, the link between Church and state, in the person of the monarch, was even realized in a visual sense: the seating in the Abbey, with the bishops on the north side facing the lay peers on the south, mirrored the seating plan in the House of Lords itself. There the bishops sat to the monarch's right facing the lay peers on her left, and the clerks so marked up their journals to make it easier to record attendance.

However, the ceremony at the Abbey also signalled the beginning of a ritual process which culminated in the full creation of parliament as the 'body of the whole realm'. Precisely at the same time as those who effectively constituted the House of Lords heard the service in the Abbey, those who would become the House of Commons were sworn in at the palace of Westminster. Just as the earl marshal had responsibility for the procession, so the lord steward supervised the return of writs and officiated at the oath-taking by MPs. The 1584 proceeding in the Commons was noted by D'Ewes in some detail but, significantly, was given only the briefest mention in Glover's account.[41] The lord steward, Leicester, entered the outer chamber of the Commons where he met the members of the lower house who, according to London's recorder, William Fleetwood, had been 'owt of all order, in troops, standing upon the flowre making strange noises'. Three privy councillors, all commoners, took the oath: Sir Francis Knollys (treasurer of the household), James Croft (comptroller of the household) and Sir Walter Mildmay (chancellor of the exchequer). Leicester then proceeded to the court of requests where Secretary Sir Francis Walsingham took the oath. Then Leicester oversaw the calling and oath-taking of the MPs present, 'the name to be pricked of so many of them as then appeared', and nominated Knollys, Croft, Mildmay, and Walsingham as his deputies to see that the oath was taken by the rest. On this occasion they were not quite

---

p. 51, for the cap of maintenance). The dove sceptre was a disappointment to the 1649 parliamentary commissioners appointed to catalogue the regalia for sale: it turned out to be largely wood with gold and silver gilt.

[40] College of Arms, MS. 2 H 13, fo. 414.

[41] D'Ewes, *Journals*, p. 332. There is a detailed account of this proceeding for 1593, including the fees due for getting entered into the sergeant's book (2s), for the return of the indenture of the election (2s), and for the door keeper ('three Eighteene pence [*sic*]'); BL, Harleian MS. 1888, pp. 1–3.

finished by the time they were called (at around 2 pm) to attend the queen in the upper house.

The final stage of the opening of parliament was the ceremony in the House of Lords. If the Commons had no role in the earlier procession and service in the Abbey, they did play a significant part now. Once the queen had been led to the throne, they were called to attend her and were admitted to the bar at the opposite end of the chamber. As is well known, often there was a scramble to get in and on more than one occasion MPs complained that the door was shut too early or that they could not hear what was being said, typically the speech by the lord chancellor. Standing to the monarch's right, the lord chancellor declared the main reason for the calling of the parliament and instructed MPs (whom Glover describes as 'standing on an heape together below') to choose a speaker. The clerk of the parliament then declared the names of the triers of petitions in the Lords, and with this the opening ceremony was concluded. The queen departed with the Lords in attendance and returned to the palace of residence.

As noted above in our discussion of the images of parliament, the ceremonial presentation of the speaker of the House of Commons had yet to take place. This usually happened three days later and did not involve a procession on the scale of the opening day, nor any service or ceremony at the Abbey. With the regalia carried before her, and the Lords seated around her, the queen was led to the throne. Once seated, the speaker was led to the bar of the Lords by two principal MPs, usually privy councillors. After pleading his insufficiency, which was answered by the lord chancellor, the speaker then 'framed himselfe to another manner of speach', praising the queen and her government and asking for the three traditional petitions of the speaker: freedom from arrest, freedom of speech, and freedom of access to the queen. These were granted by the lord chancellor, at the queen's command, whereupon she retired, disrobed, and was escorted out of the palace of Westminster by the nobility. In 1584 Elizabeth, 'with a greate traine of Noblemen and honourable Ladies attending her (the Earle of Kent carrying the sword before hir) she by Torch-light through the Parke, returned unto her Pallace of Saint James, from whence she before came'. Such was the formal ending of the opening of a parliament.

In the Commons, meanwhile, the ability of members to initiate new law was signalled by the reading of a bill 'pro forma' as soon as MPs returned to their meeting place with their newly approved speaker;[42] in this way Burghley's 'whole Body of the Parliament able to make Laws' can be said to have been fully constituted, and both houses were now able to get down to the business of legislation. It is surely significant that the images drawn for D'Ewes and Glover depicted the day on which the Commons presented their speaker rather than the formal opening a few days earlier in which the Commons enjoyed only a

---

[42] The only time this did not happen in this period was in 1597 when Speaker Yelverton failed to do it, earning a stiff rebuke from D'Ewes (*Journals*, p. 550).

spectator's role. The day on which their speaker was presented was the day they were truly an effective part of the parliamentary trinity.

The ceremonies and procession which opened a parliament are the most obvious and dynamic aspects of parliament as event. By contrast, the ritual of the reading of a bill 'pro forma' was an essential element of parliament as an institution, as a law-making body. Yet the demonstration of authority through hierarchy which was the key message of the procession was not forgotten once parliament's law-making function was assumed. Not only was this function conducted within the ceremonial framework of the opening and closing days, but at all stages of the legislative process ritual reinforced this message.

One of the most obvious of such rituals was the nomination and appointment of the speaker of the lower house. This was an event which had at its heart the insistence that the speaker was 'freely' elected when, as everyone knew, the candidate had already been chosen by the queen and her councillors.[43] Thomas Norton, one of the most experienced of Elizabethan MPs, once cynically wrote:

The House hath used, and as I think will use, to like of such a person as the Councillors present; not arrogating to themselves the right of nomination, but leaving the House to their full liberty, who in their greatest liberty will be most frankly obsequious.[44]

It was always a leading councillor who nominated the speaker although, as D'Ewes noted for 1584, Knollys 'did leave every man to his own free opinion to nominate any other of whom they might think better' after he had suggested John Puckering.[45] Recorder Fleetwood notes on this occasion that Puckering was sitting beside him and that after Knollys had nominated him 'there was not one word spoken. And then I said to my companions abowt me, "crie Puckering"; and then they and I begynniynge, the rest did the same'.[46]

Once nominated, the speaker then with 'a modest and humble Speech disabled himself, yet withal acknowledging the great favour of the House unto him, in that they had been pleased to nominate and chuse him unto a place of so great charge and weight'. This was formally disallowed by the House, whereupon the nominee was led 'between two of the most eminent Personages of the said House unto the Chair, and placed in it'. On his presentation to the

---

[43] Neale, *House of Commons*, pp. 354–8.

[44] *Ibid.*, p. 355, cited from BL, Harleian MS. 253. On Norton's authorship, see Elton, *Parliament*, pp. 322–8.

[45] D'Ewes, *Journals*, p. 333. Neale noted that murmurs were made against the nomination of the privy councillors in 1604, and discusses the problem in 1566 when there was some doubt as to whether Richard Onslow, Solicitor-General, should have been speaker (a division was called); *House of Commons*, p. 356.

[46] BL, Harleian MS. 41, fo. 45. This adds much to D'Ewes's rather frozen account: 'After whose Speech many of the said House named also Mr Serjeant Puckering, and none was heard to disallow or speak against the said choice; whereuppon Mr Treasurer standing up again, did then and there put it to the question, asking them whom they would be pleased to allow of for their Speaker, and to name him. To which the greater part of the House making Answer again, that they did allow of and chuse the said Mr Serjeant Puckering for their Speaker as before . . .'; *Journals*, p. 333.

monarch, Puckering also 'disabled himself', which 'was not allowed by her Majesty', whereupon he asked for the traditional freedoms of arrest, speech, and access.[47]

This elaborate ritual of nomination, selection, protestation, and acclamation disguised the reality that Puckering had been chosen long before the opening day of the parliament; it was a formalized statement of the Commons' right to nominate. The reality behind the appearance was too much for the MPs in 1597. They 'hawked and spat' when Sir William Knollys delivered a somewhat elaborate speech nominating Christopher Yelverton. At hearing his name 'Mr Yelverton blushed and put off his Hat and after sate bare-headed'; whatever their misgivings, the 'whole House' nevertheless cried 'I, I, I, let him be'.[48]

Other rituals embodied within parliamentary procedure served to reinforce the importance of hierarchy and status demonstrated in the opening procession and ceremony. It is often noted that a major contribution of the Tudor parliaments to the development of parliamentary procedure was the joint-conference. This was, it is true, an important means whereby disputes between the two Houses could be discussed and information exchanged. However, it was also a means whereby the Lords could demonstrate their greater social standing. Burghley especially, and particularly in cases where the Commons had rejected or replaced a Lords' bill without prior consultation with the Lords, was very keen to remind the lower House of its inferior status. The Commons were kept waiting when a conference met over Lord Stourton's bill in 1576 and then, even when the Lords had sat down at the conference table, they conferred among themselves before they 'called for those of the nether howse' to listen to Burghley's 'vehement' criticism of their proceedings. Indeed, the very procedure of the joint-conference emphasized the inferiority of the Commons. While the peers sat during the deliberations, MPs had to stand; in 1604 it was reported that the older members of the Commons 'found themselves sicke and lame long after' a conference. Whereas peers simply doffed their hats when greeting the assembled MPs, the MPs had to stand bareheaded, as they did if they ever appeared at the bar of the Lords' chamber, even if they were privy councillors or the speaker himself.[49]

Rituals also abounded in the legislative procedure of the House. Established rules of amendment to bills, the proper placing of endorsements on bills, and such like, were occasions for discussion and debate, even for anger.[50] Sometimes old rituals were abandoned because of the pressure of business. One such ritual, 'according to the Auncient Orderes', was designed to signal the unity of the

[47] D'Ewes, *Journals*, p. 333.   [48] *Ibid.*, p. 549.

[49] E. R. Foster, *The House of Lords 1603–1649. Structure, Procedure and the Nature of its Business* (Chapel Hill, NC, and London, 1983), pp. 12, 131–2. See also D. M. Dean, 'Patrons, Clients and Conferences: The Workings of Bicamerism in the Sixteenth-Century English Parliament', in H. Blom (ed.), *Bicamerism: Proceedings of the 175 Jaar Eerste Kamer der Staten-Generaal* (The Hague, 1992), pp. 209–27.

[50] See, for example, D'Ewes, *Journals*, pp. 575–7.

governing class in parliament: those voting against a successful measure were to carry it out of the chamber and return with it along with those who had voted for it. This may well have been a dramatic demonstration of accommodation and agreement, of harmony and unity, but it was also a very time-consuming one and was eventually abandoned.[51]

It is this everyday context surrounding the making of speeches in parliament that makes the interpretation of speeches, and even the import of debate, difficult for the historian to decipher. Most historians read parliamentary speeches as reported, seeing them rather like poor examples of today's Hansard. Yet the debates which have come down to us are not *verbatim* transcripts but interpretations and summaries by others. It is difficult to assess the speakers' sincerity or the validity of what was reportedly spoken, for the actual context, let alone the legislation to which speakers referred, has been lost to us. Humour, irony, and satire is difficult to detect; the historian has lost the contemporary understanding of devices and desires. Thus, for example, how is one to read the debates on the subsidy, the grant of which was the main reason for the calling of parliament? These debates provided the opportunity for displays of loyalty, by declaring forcefully one's support for the regime, hatred of enemies and, in 1593 and 1601, insistence that the rich should pay up to lighten the burden on the poor. Yet we know, as contemporaries did, that they themselves were the main culprits in being under-assessed. So are these sentiments sincere? Are the changes to the tax system which they suggested serious? Or are such speeches ritualistic, but essential, responses to the demands of authority? Taxes were always granted, but the one Elizabethan MP who ventured to say that the debate was superfluous was severely disliked for so doing.[52]

The end of parliament-as-institution was signalled, like the opening, by the presence of the monarch (plate 62). On the closing day, once again enthroned with her Lords around her and with the speaker and leading MPs standing at the bar, the monarch either gave life to the bills produced by the two Houses, making them law, or vetoed them. This authority was absolute and the very language used for the assent or the rejection, Norman French, emphasized

---

[51] It was certainly done in the case of the 1589 bill for Lincoln, approved by 118 votes to 65 against, but in 1597–98, when a bill prohibiting corn exports passed by 124 votes to 85, a motion was put whether to bother with this procedure or not. There were many speeches 'both pro & contra' before it was finally decided to do so 'for Orders sake'. However, two days later Speaker Yelverton successfully moved that the practice be dropped in the case of a bill on Sussex and Essex cloth, which was approved by 105 votes to 79, 'in regard of the preciousness of this present time, the Parliament being so near an end': D'Ewes, *Journals*, pp. 451, 573, 574. In the busy session of 1601, after four hours of debate over merchants' shopbooks and with the time perilously close to the MPs' dinner-time of 1 pm, the ceremony was dropped: 'because time was past, and it was very late, and there were great Commitments this Afternoon, they were dispensed withal'; *ibid.*, p. 667. The seventeenth-century author of a treatise on parliamentary procedure, William Hakewill, duly noted the ritual, but added that it 'hath not beene used of late tymes'; C. S. Sims, 'The Speaker of the House of Commons, An Early Seventeenth-Century Tractate', *American Historical Review*, 45 (1939–40): 94–5. Indeed, it is possible that the practice was only adopted when a special motion to do so was made, as D'Ewes was careful to note on two such occasions (in 1597 and 1598).

[52] D'Ewes, *Journals*, p. 633.

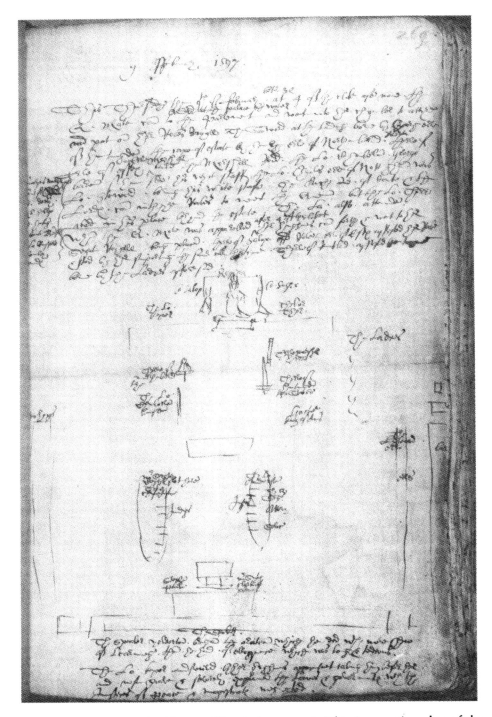

Plate 62. The House of Lords in 1597–98. This is a seating plan of the Lords on the last day of Elizabeth I's penultimate session and was an important part of the herald's preparations for the closing ceremony. Note the stylized rods of office, sword of state and cap of estate immediately before the queen.

continuity with an Anglo-Norman past.[53] Once the list of bills received their fate the queen departed, and another parliament was over.

Professor Lehmberg has described the opening of the Reformation parliament as a 'blaze of splendid pomp and medieval pageantry', and it is proper to emphasize the continuity of the Tudor (including the Elizabethan) ceremony with those of earlier times.[54] Historians of Elizabethan parliaments, whether 'traditionalists' like Sir John Neale (who found parliamentary sessions occasions of political conflict and opposition) or 'revisionists' like Sir Geoffrey Elton and Michael Graves (who placed greater emphasis on the institutions's law-making function), have seen parliament as a secular body, as part of the developing modern state. To view parliament as an event, through ritual and image, reveals that the religious or liturgical dimension to the medieval assemblies was not altogether lost after the Reformation.

Yet parliament after the Reformation was transformed by the emergence of the notion of a parliamentary trinity, by the new location of the House of Commons and by an increasingly important role played by the Commons in the business of making law. The realities of political life meant that the procession to parliament reflected only two parts of the trinity. To many MPs the procession must have seemed like a preliminary, however spectacular, to the main event. To involve them more fully was undoubtedly a concern of Robert Cecil, earl of Salisbury, when he came to stage the installation of Prince Henry in the parliament of 1610. Nevertheless, his decision to revive an old ceremony at a time of political and financial difficulty is testimony to a belief in the power of rituals in parliament.[55]

The Tudor parliament was thus an institution with a real political purpose and function as well as an event in which the virtues of solidarity, honour, loyalty, obedience, and authority could be demonstrated. That authority, surrounded in liturgical ceremony, was vested in the monarch and the aristocracy. Their power was demonstrated in a procession which was centred on the monarch. Like the costumes of the participants, the structure of the procession was determined by status and hierarchy, and marshalled by the heralds. Yet, if this signifies what Victor Turner calls 'structure', confirming the individual's position within this hierarchical authority, it also could very easily display 'communitas', establishing a relationship which suggested shared experience. In 1601 it was noted that 'with great pleasure and contentement unto all her Subiettes' the queen proceeded 'in pryncely estate to the Cathedrall Church at Westminster'. But she also made pauses along the way to greet her subjects and

[53] This especially interested De Maisse; Harrison and Jones (eds.), *De Maisse A Journal*, p. 31.
[54] S. E. Lehmberg, *The Reformation Parliament 1529–1536* (Cambridge, 1970), p. 76.
[55] This is discussed in an article by Dr Pauline Croft, 'The Parliamentary Installation of Henry, Prince of Wales', *Historical Research*, 65 (1992): 177–93.

communicate with them.[56] As with her personal speeches to the Commons, Elizabeth was skilful in animating her fixed image and turning a static spectacle into a dynamic event. The Tudor parliament was not only a key institution offering counsel to the monarch and devising solutions to the nation's problems. It also had all the hallmarks of a successful ritual process.

[56] College of Arms, MS. Vincent 92, p. 266.

11 *The countervailing of benefits: monopoly, liberty, and benevolence in Elizabethan England*

DAVID HARRIS SACKS

By the standards of the age, Elizabeth I's last parliament was a happy one. Laws were enacted, taxes were granted, and grievances were redressed.[1] At its close, the queen and her people were seen to be in affectionate harmony with one another. But it was not a parliament without conflict or acrimony. If consent to taxation had proceeded relatively smoothly, redress of grievances had not. At the heart of the controversy were the royal patents of monopoly granted for the exclusive production and trade of specified manufactures. These patents raised the most fundamental questions affecting the polity and its law. They were the fruits of the royal prerogative, with which no subject could meddle without the monarch's leave, but they touched the common weal, with whose preservation and advancement the members of parliament were especially charged.[2] They arguably encroached on the liberties of the subject, which protected freeborn Englishmen in their property and persons, but they exemplified the role of

Earlier versions of this chapter were presented in whole or in part to the Center for the History of British Political Thought at the Folger Shakespeare Library, the Center for Seventeenth and Eighteenth Century Studies at UCLA, the Early Modern British History Seminar at Harvard University, the British History Colloquium at the Huntington Library, the Department of English at the University of Maryland, College Park, the Department of History at The Johns Hopkins University, and at annual meetings of the American Historical Association and the Renaissance Society of America. The author wishes to thank the following scholars for their helpful comments and criticisms: J. D. Alsop, Bernard Bailyn, John Brewer, Harold J. Cook, Stephen Diamond, Stephen Greenblatt, John Guy, Donna Hamilton, Donald Kelley, Mark Kishlansky, Karen Ordahl Kupperman, Wallace MacCaffrey, John Morrill, John Murrin, J. G. A. Pocock, Paul Seaver, Lois Schwoerer, Gordon Schochet, A. J. Slavin, Susan Staves, Lawrence Stone, and Perez Zagorin.

[1] On the nature of parliament see G. R. Elton, *The Parliament of England, 1556–1581* (Cambridge, 1986), ch. 2; G. R. Elton, 'Tudor Government: The Points of Contact, I. Parliament', in G. R. Elton, *Studies in Tudor and Stuart Politics and Government* (3 vols., Cambridge, 1974–83), iii, pp. 3–21; Conrad Russell, 'The Nature of a Parliament in Early Stuart England', in Howard Tomlinson (ed.), *Before the English Civil War: Essays on Early Stuart Politics and Government* (New York, 1984), pp. 123–50; Conrad Russell, *Parliaments and English Politics, 1621–1629* (Oxford, 1979), pp. 35–64.

[2] For this distinction, see the remarks of the lord keeper in 1571 reporting Elizabeth I's views on freedom of speech in the House of Commons: 'they should doe well to meddle in noe matters of state but such as should be propounded unto them, and to occupy themselves concerninge the commen wealth'; quoted in Hartley, p. 199.

political authority in the regulation of the economy, without which those liberties might become quite valueless. When parliament assembled in 1601, monopolies had been the target of widespread complaints for some time.[3]

A CONFOUNDING OF BENEVOLENCE

From the mid-sixteenth century, when they first were introduced into England, patents of monopoly for manufactures were used by English monarchs not only to protect new industrial processes and new products but to favour their subjects with royal bounty. They quickly took their place alongside the monies, titles, rent charges, lands, offices, and the like which regularly flowed from the prince to loyal courtiers and their clients. By the 1580s, the original promoters of the monopolies – the projectors seeking exclusive rights for their schemes and inventions – typically enjoyed their patents only second hand as the substitutes of the royal favourites who were the actual grantees.[4]

At the same time, the patent system became subject to serious abuse. Patentees, more interested in the income they could derive from their new rights than in the development of their new inventions, simply licensed craftsmen to continue employing older techniques in competition with the patent – in effect introducing an excise tax on their production. The Crown also began using the patents as sources of revenue, reserving to itself a percentage of the patentees' profits, ostensibly in compensation for the income lost to the customs because the manufactures produced under the grants had displaced imports. It also used them to compensate royal creditors among the nobility and gentry or to reward Crown officials for their service. Once these powerful interests became engaged in the system, a more vigorous and systematic enforcement of monopoly rights was instituted. The powers of the privy council and the prerogatives of the Crown were used to intercede on behalf of the patentees, coercing compliance and blocking litigation in the law courts. Informers also appeared in the picture, seeking reward from the beneficiaries of the grants or bribes from those who had violated them.[5]

However, even before 1580 when the monopolies entered what Joan Thirsk

---

[3] For a general account of the parliament of 1601 and the role of the monopolies in it, see J. E. Neale, *Elizabeth I and Her Parliaments, 1584–1601* (1957), pp. 369–423, especially pp. 376–93.

[4] See, e.g. Townshend, p. 250. This paragraph and the following are derived from William Hyde Price, *The English Patents of Monopoly* (Boston, MA, 1906), ch. 1; E. Wyndam Hulme, 'The History of the Patent System under the Prerogative and at Common Law', *Law Quarterly Review*, 12 (1896): 141–54 and 'The History of the Patent System under the Prerogative and at Common Law: A Sequel', *ibid.*, 16 (1900): 44–56; Joan Thirsk, *Economic Policy and Projects: The Development of a Consumer Society* (Oxford, 1978), chs. 1–3. See also David Harris Sacks, 'Private Profit and Public Good: The Problem of the State in Elizabethan Theory and Practice', in Gordon Schochet (ed.), *Law Literature and the Settlement of Regimes* (Washington, DC, 1990), pp. 123–6; David Harris Sacks, 'Parliament, Liberty and Commonweal', in J. H. Hexter (ed.), *Parliament and Liberty from Elizabeth I to the English Civil War* (Stanford, CA, 1992), pp. 95–6.

[5] See Price, *English Patents*, ch. 1; Thirsk, *Economic Projects*, pp. 57ff; Linda Levy Peck, *Court Patronage and Corruption in Early Modern England* (Boston, MA, 1990), pp. 135ff.

has identified as their first 'scandalous phase', they were already a source of complaint. They may have been one of the causes of grievance behind Robert Bell's attack on 'lycenses' in 1571.[6] In 1572, the mere thought that any public action might result in the creation of a monopoly was widely condemned as an evil, even by Sir Francis Knollys, treasurer of the queen's household and a leading privy councillor.[7] By the 1590s the royal patents themselves had become a genuine canker on the body politic.[8] In 1597 a serious attempt to legislate on the matter was forestalled by the promise of remedy made on behalf of the queen by her councillors in the Commons, yet nothing was accomplished – save that some of the loudest complainers seem to have felt the wrath of the queen for their presumption.[9] In 1599 some of the basic legal issues involved in the monopolies had been aired in the case of *Davenant v. Hurdis* concerning certain by-laws of the Company of Merchant Tailors of London issued under its royal charter. In that case, the judges had found any economic regulation that deprived a man of the free exercise of his craft without his consent to be against common right and in violation of chapter 29 of Magna Carta.[10] But this decision did not touch the royal patents, whatever the judges might have intended. The Crown continued to issue or renew its monopoly grants without stint.

When parliament convened again in 1601 a number of members, especially the common lawyers, appear to have come armed with a determination – possibly even a plan – to remedy the matter on their own. Looking at the lists of suspect patents that circulated among the MPs, the petitions that arrived at the privy council from aggrieved craftsmen, the crowds in the streets near the parliament house and at the doors of committee meetings, and at Sir Robert Cecil's enraged outburst complaining of these facts, it is hard to escape this sense that something a bit out of the ordinary was afoot. On 4 November, only a few days after the session had begun, Robert Johnson made a vigorous speech against the 'vile Practices' of the patentees. Their 'abuses' were denounced again on 18 November when the lawyer Anthony Dyott sought to introduce 'An Act against Patents'. On the next day, Lawrence Hyde, another lawyer, introduced

[6] Hartley, pp. 202, 245 (and see also pp. 207, 224, 238, 436); J. E. Neale, *Elizabeth I and her Parliaments, 1559–1581* (1953), pp. 218–19, 221–2; Neale, *Parliaments, 1584–1601*, p. 352. The prospect of monopoly was also angrily complained against in this parliament in regard to the privileges of Bristol's Society of Merchant Venturers; see Hartley, pp. 210–11; David Harris Sacks, *The Widening Gate: Bristol and the Atlantic Economy, 1450–1700* (Berkeley and Los Angeles, CA, 1991), pp. 196–201.

[7] Hartley, p. 372 (and see also, pp. 264, 384).

[8] For this paragraph and those following see Sacks, 'Parliament, Liberty, and the Commonweal', pp. 93–101; Sacks, 'Private Profit and Public Good', pp. 121–33.

[9] Townshend, pp. 103, 234; Simon D'Ewes, *A Compleat Journal of the Votes, Speeches and Debates, both of the House of Lords and the House of Commons Throughout the whole Reign of Queen Elizabeth of Glorious Memory* (1682), pp. 554–5, 558, 570, 573; Neale, *Parliaments, 1584–1601*, pp. 352–6, 365.

[10] *Davenant v. Hurdis*, Moore 576–91, 672 in *The English Reports*, eds. Max A. Robertson and Geoffrey Ellis (reprinted, 176 vols., 1900–30), vol. 72, pp. 769–78, 830; Edward Coke, *The Third Part of the Institutes of the Laws of England* (1644), p. 182; see also *Darcy v. Allen*, 11 Co. Rep. 86b in *English Reports*, vol. 77, p. 1263.

his own bill, entitled simply 'An Act of Explanation of the Common Law in Certain Cases of Letters Patents', which then became the focus of the debate.[11] Most probably this bill sought to limit the scope of the patents in light of the principles laid down in *Davenant*. Even Francis Moore, the lawyer who had represented Davenant in his losing effort to enforce the Merchant Tailors' ordinances, came prepared to restrain the patents. He was one of the most articulate critics to speak against them in this session, as he had been in 1597.[12]

The central arguments against the monopoly patents, as it was articulated in 1601 and in the pleadings in *Darcy v. Allen* the following year, was that by granting exclusive manufacturing and trading rights to a few private individuals monopolies deprived free men of their livelihoods, hence of the liberties they were assured by chapter 29 of Magna Carta. The central idea is that every free man had a godly obligation (not just a right) to earn his bread, a duty which could not be bridged without his consent. Therefore, a monopolist was understood – actually said – to be a *vir sanguinis*, a man of blood who in preventing competitors from exercising their crafts threatened their very existence as free men.[13] As the lawyer Francis Moore put it, monopoly 'bringeth the General Profit into a Private Hand; and the End of All is Beggery and Bondage to the Subject'.[14] Monopolists, therefore, were 'Bloodsuckers of the Commonwealth', as said Richard Martin, another lawyer. They sucked 'up the best and principallest Commodities, which the Earth . . . hath given Us . . . the Commodities of our own Labour, which with the Sweat of our Brows (even up to the Knees in Mire and Dirt) we have labour'd for'.[15] They thereby turned free subjects into bondmen or villeins – deprived them of their ability to use their labour as they chose.

Since human beings were understood not merely to be free to labour but called by God to do so, the opponents of the monopolies believed that they interfered with men's voluntary performance of their spiritual as well as their worldly commitments. They prevented men from pursuing the callings which they were bound in conscience to practise, thereby depriving them of the public and social freedoms necessary if they were to conform themselves to Christian

---

[11] Townshend, pp. 188, 224–5, 229–37; D'Ewes, *A Compleat Journal*, pp. 644–7. Townshend reports Hyde as attempting to introduce his bill on 18 November, only to have it blocked by the Speaker, apparently at Sir Robert Cecil's behest. But according to Townshend's account, the bill seems to have been introduced successfully on 19 November, and to have received its second reading and formal commitment on 20 November, after a commotion in the House to have it read and a long debate on whether to commit or engross it. D'Ewes first mentions the bill only in his account of debate on 20 November, but his treatment of the discussion follows Townshend's as regards commitment. Since D'Ewes makes no mention of two readings on this day, it appears likely that the bill was first read on 19 November and received its second reading and commitment on the following day.

[12] Townshend, p. 233.

[13] Darcy v. Allen, 11 Co. Rep. 84b–88b in *English Reports*, vol. 77, pp. 1260–6; Noy, 173–85 in *English Reports*, vol. 74, pp. 1131–41; Moore, 671–5 in *English Reports*, vol. 72, pp. 830–2; PRO, SP 12/286/47; BL, Add. MS. 25203, fos. 543v and ff; Edward Coke, *The Second Part of the Institutes of the Laws of England* (1641), pp. 46–7; Coke, *The Third Part of the Institutes*, pp. 181–2.

[14] Townshend, p. 233.   [15] *Ibid.*, p. 234.

liberty, which required nothing less than absolute obedience to God's commands. This theory, articulated especially by Nicholas Fuller in defending Thomas Allen against Edward Darcy in the case of the playing-card monopoly, saw the liberties of the subject as securing Englishmen in the performance of their duties, that is in meeting their responsibilities to themselves, their families, and the commonwealth.[16]

Although much else was said in condemnation of the monopolies – for example that they drove up prices and that they resulted in the production and sale of poor quality goods[17] – it was their threat to workingmen's vocations that had the greatest weight. This threat provided the fulcrum on which turned a theory of what liberties a subject enjoyed by virtue of being a freeborn Englishman and not a villein or bondman. From the start, a link was seen between those liberties protected by Magna Carta, especially in chapter 29, and the requirement that consent be obtained for any act that would touch the possessions of the subject, whether material or intangible. Liberty and consent were inextricably interconnected as 'property' is to 'propriety', as what is possessed is tied to the right to possess it.[18]

Understood in this way, the dangers to the liberties of the subject entailed by the monopolies were dangers to the commonwealth at large. They undermined order by threatening the bonds that held society together. In part this was because the number and economic significance of the grants had grown so great by the end of Elizabeth's reign that they risked touching public necessity. When in 1601 Sir Robert Wroth read out a long list of patents issued since the previous parliament – a list that contained iron, glass, vinegar, sea-coal, steel, salt, saltpetre, train oil, and many other items – William Hakewill 'stood up and asked … Is not Bread there? Bread quoth another? … No quoth Mr. *Hakewell*, but if order be not taken for these Bread will be there, before the next Parliament'.[19] Hakewill's point was that in offering patents of monopoly as royal bounty to her courtiers the queen put at risk her duty to provide for the well-being of all her subjects. It is not surprising, therefore, that many members of the House of Commons saw the monopolies as a danger not only to the realm but to the queen's rule as well. 'There is no Act of Hers', said Francis Moore, 'that hath been, or is more Derogatory to her *Majesty*, or more Odious to the Subject, or more Dangerous to the Common-Wealth, than the Granting of these *Monopolies*'.[20]

By breaking down the web of favour and good will that knit the body politic into unity, the monopolies had generated a threat to benevolence, as Sir George More warned.

---

[16] Sacks, 'Parliament, Liberty and the Commonweal', pp. 93ff.

[17] See Townshend, pp. 224–5, 230–6, 238–53; Neale, *Parliaments, 1584–1601*, pp. 377–88.

[18] See *Darcy v. Allen* (1602), Noy 173–85 in *English Reports*, vol. 74, pp. 1131–41, especially Noy 179–80 in *ibid.*, 74, pp. 1136–7.

[19] Townshend, p. 239.   [20] *Ibid.*, p. 233.

There be Three Persons; Her *Majesty*, the *Patentee*, and the *Subject*: Her *Majesty* the Head, the *Patentee* the Hand, and the *Subject* the Foot. Now here is our Case; the *Head* gives Power to the *Hand*, the *Hand* Oppresseth the *Foot*, and the *Foot* Riseth against the *Head*.[21]

In More's view the monopolies risked spreading a disease in the commonwealth, an overturning of proportion and order, a derangement in which the limbs and organs of the social body fell into opposition to one another.

THE GOLDEN SPEECH

The debates over the monopolies continued in the House of Commons for more than a week, but the queen put an end to them with a proclamation which voided a number of the most hated grants – those for salt, starch, train oil, vinegar, *aqua vitae*, and several other commodities – permitting the rest to be tested at the common law, and in the meantime removing the support of the privy council from the patentees. On the day the proclamation appeared, the Commons discussed sending a delegation to thank the queen. But in their joy, they could reach no decision on whom to send, and, as Heywood Townshend tells us, 'At the last, at the Lower-End of the House, they cryed, All, All, All'. And so it came that 140 members of the Commons, led by their Speaker, assembled on 30 November to give thanks to their queen and to hear her response to them.[22]

Elizabeth's speech – her 'Golden Speech' as it later came to be known – survives in four versions: Heywood Townshend's, recorded by him in his diary of the Parliament;[23] an edition of 1601 said to have been taken down by one 'A. B.' and printed by Robert Barker, the royal printer;[24] an edition of 1628, which was subsequently reprinted in 1642;[25] and a manuscript version in a collection of papers belonging to William Dell, apparently found on his desk while he was secretary to Archbishop Laud.[26] In what follows we shall rely primarily on Townshend's version, since as a member of the Commons in 1601

---

[21] *Ibid.*, p. 234.   [22] *Ibid.*, p. 259.

[23] *Ibid.*, pp. 263–6; the original manuscript version is found in BL, Stowe MS. 362, fos. 169–72.

[24] *Her Majesties most Princelie answere deliuered by her selfe at the Court at VVhite-hall, on the last day of Nouember 1601 . . . The same being taken verbatim in writing by A. B. as neere as he could possibly set it downe* (1601). (This is *STC* 7578 and will be referred to hereafter by that number.) A printed copy is in PRO, SP 12/282/67; manuscript versions survive in PRO, SP 12/282/65, 66; BL, Lansdowne MS. 94, fo. 123. If 'A. B.' was a member of the House of Commons, he could only have been Anthony Blagrave, who sat in the parliament of 1601 for Reading in Berkshire and who was closely associated with the Cecils.

[25] *Qveene Elizabeths Speech to Her Last Parliament.* (This is *STC* 7579 and will be referred to by this number.) There is no indication on the title page of the place and date of publication but the second edition of the *STC* identifies this version as being printed possibly before 12 July 1628. This version of the Speech was subsequently republished in different formats four times in the seventeenth century, viz. 1648, 1659, 1679, and 1698.

[26] BL, Harleian MS. 787, fos. 127v–128v. It is unknown whose notes of the queen's speech are recorded here.

he followed the debates on monopolies very closely. But the other versions also will help throw light on the meaning of the queen's words.

The speech as we have it from Townshend falls into three parts: an introduction in which Elizabeth talks about her duty and about her love for her subjects and theirs for her, a middle section in which she shifts to discuss the monopolies issue itself and a conclusion in which she returns with new force to some of the themes of the introduction and speaks especially of her service to God.[27] It would be easy to think of her words as a conventional, though eloquent, statement of the divine sanction for her power, since a good deal of what the queen said concerns her relation to God. But in fact it is not primarily a speech about power, divine or otherwise. What holds the speech together, rather, is the idea of duty, especially the monarch's duty.

To unravel the queen's message, we need to start in the section where Elizabeth explains what went amiss with the monopolies. 'Since I was Queen', she said, 'yet, did I never put my Pen unto any Grant, but that, upon Pretext and Semblance made unto Me, it was both Good and Beneficial to the Subject in general; though a private Profit to some of My Antient Servants, who had deserved well at My Hands'. In treating the functions of her servants, however, the queen acknowledged that something had gone very wrong. 'Shall they think to escape unpunished', she asked, 'that have thus Oppressed you, and have been respectless of their Duty, and regardless of Our Honour? . . . I perceive they dealt with Me like Physitians, who Administering a Drug, or when they give Pills, do Gild them all over'.[28] Note the image of the physician. Elizabeth seems to say some of her advisors supported the patents by colouring their harmfulness – presenting them as beneficial to the subject though a private profit to her servants – as some physicians obscure the true nature of their noxious potions. What kind of physicians are these?

According to the Hippocratic Oath the first duty of the physician is to do no harm and to treat every patient honestly, equally and fairly. Those who violate this oath by placing their own advantage over the good of the patient are false physicians, and so are those who through ignorance or ill-will bring suffering to whom they treat.[29] The classic example of such a false doctor was the empirick, that hobgoblin of the professional physicians of the early modern period. An empirick was an ignorant practitioner who 'fetcheth all his skill from bare and

[27] This same schema is followed in *STC* 7579 and in BL, Harleian MS. 787, but not in *STC* 7578, which concerns itself more than the other versions with accounting for the wrongs done by the patentees and with thanking the Commons for saving her from culpability for their errors.

[28] Townshend, pp. 264, 265. BL, Harleian MS. 787, fo. 128r uses a similar figure in relation to the patents. In *STC* 7578, pp. 3–4, and *STC* 7579, Sig. A3c, the same figure refers to the way in which the outward lustre of a kingly title as it appears to observers covers the cares and burdens of the office borne by its holder.

[29] Hippocrates, 'The Oath', in *Hippocrates*, Loeb edition, tr. W. H. S. Jones (4 vols., 1923–43), i, pp. 298–301. On the nature of the medical marketplace in this period see, Harold J. Cook, *The Decline of the Old Medical Regime in Stuart England* (Ithaca, NY, and London, 1986), ch. 1. I am grateful for Professor Cook's advice and guidance in what follows.

naked experience' and had no learning. According to the professional physicians who condemned them, many 'clothed' their ignorance 'with the outward
garments of knowledge', especially by magnifying their skills and extolling their
strange cures. To conceal the true nature of 'their vile and contemptible
medicines . . . from those that know all vsuall medicines by their colour, smell
or taste . . . they mingle something with them onely to alter these qualities' and
'by this tricke, that sauoreth of cousenage' they enhance their fame 'and increase
their wealth'.[30] Queen Elizabeth's complaint was that her advisers had acted
like 'subtill and deceptfull Empiricks', pretending that established trades were
new inventions and that the monopolists' bitter pills were sweet and beneficial
cures. Her councillors had permitted self-seeking to substitute for the common
good.

What, then, was the proper duty of royal councillors? The model of the
physician again helps us understand what Elizabeth had in mind. Starting in the
later sixteenth century, as the queen and her privy councillors had good reason
to know, the professional physicians, acting through the College of Physicians,
began a concerted effort to establish themselves as the sole practitioners of
medicine in London and its environs.[31] They wished not only to distinguish
themselves from surgeons and apothecaries, who sometimes prescribed physic
as a by-employment, but also – as Thomas Gale said in introducing his
translation of Galen in 1586 – from those 'honest Artists, as Tailers, Shoo-
makers, Weavers or anie other handie occupations, that . . . should Leave their
arte wherein they are perfect, and fall to this art of Medicine'.[32] Thus the
physicians acted on the adage, proclaimed in the mid-century by one of their
learned colleagues: 'Let no man medle with another mannes corne, but with his
owne. Lette the shoemaker medle with his shoes'.[33] To put it crudely, but
accurately, the physicians wanted a monopoly of practice in their art.

The writers on the medical profession in the sixteenth century, and the great
classical writers on physic upon whom they relied, all stressed the necessity of
tempering experience with reason. Without a universal standard against which
to measure experience, there could be no true knowledge and therefore no
certainty of judgment.[34] As with the physician, so with the political councillor.

[30] E[leazar] D[unke], *The Copy of A Letter written by E. D., Doctour of Physick* (1606), pp. 21, 40.
[31] George N. Clark, *A History of the Royal College of Physicians* (2 vols., Oxford, 1964–66), i,
pp. 160–1; Cook, *Medical Regime*, p. 97.
[32] Claudius Galen, *Certaine VVorkes of Galen called Methodvs Medendi*, tr. Thomas Gale (1586),
sig. Aiiib.
[33] John Securis, *A detection and querimonie of the daily enormities and abuses comitted in physick*
(1566), sig. Biia. The ultimate source for this idea is, of course, Plato's *Republic* 370a–c, Plato,
Republic, tr. G. M. A. Grube, revised by C. D. C. Reeve (Indianapolis, IN, 1992), pp. 44–5. But the
commonplaces referred to by Securis arise from later sources which are conveniently summarized
and commented upon by Erasmus in his collection of *Adages*; *Collected Works of Erasmus*,
vol. xxxi, tr. Margaret Main Phillips (Toronto, 1982), pp. 351–2, 411–12; vol. xxxii, tr. R. A. B.
Mynors (Toronto, 1989), p. 14.
[34] John Cotta, *A Short Discoverie of the vnobserved dangers of seuerall sorts of ignorant and
vnconsiderate Practitioners of Physicke in England* (1612), pp. 11–12.

He too faced a world of variable conditions and continually changing circumstance, and thus he too needed to temper his own experience with knowledge of a wider range of occurrences and of the underlying nature of things. Hence in drawing the analogy between the false physicians and those of her advisors who had promoted the monopolies, Elizabeth implied that a true councillor would be professional in the same way as a true physician. He would exercise judgment for the well-being of his charges, based on a firm foundation of learning as well as experience. Like the physician, his role would be as much diagnostic as instrumental. It would be for him to foresee potential problems and prescribe a preventative, as well as to discern the nature of present discontents and recommend a cure.

Conceiving of the governors of the realm as physicians indicated that they had charge of the welfare of a body-politic, with everything organized proportionally and in its proper place. The vision is very much one of a hierarchical division of labour, in which head and members each performed vital functions for the rest. If the realm should fall into 'distemper' or become 'distracted' – words which grew out of the metaphor of the body – the head, the monarch and his councillors, were to restore it to health by reestablishing the proper arrangement of organs and limbs. This understanding was summarized in the concept of *salus populi*, the doctrine that the rulers of the realm were to provide for its social health – its commonweal. *Salus populi* assumes a collective health in which head and body together participate. The monarch is at one and the same time at the head and in the service of the body. As the principal physician of the realm, it is his duty to act disinterestedly in the performance of his function.

Elizabeth recognized this implication in her speech to the Commons. 'Of My Selfe', she reminded them,

I was never any greedy scraping Grasper, nor a straight, fast-holding Prince; nor yet a Waster. My Heart was never set on Worldly Goods, but only for my Subjects Good. What you bestow on Me, I will not hoard it up, but Receive it to bestow on You again: Yea, My own Proprieties I count Yours, and to be Expended for your Good; and your Eyes shall see the Bestowing of All, for your Good.[35]

Unlike the monopolists, pursuing private gain, she gathered wealth in only to put it out again for common purposes and public good. From these considerations came a theory of monarchical duty.

Generally speaking duties arise in three quite distinct ways. They can come from abstract and universal principles of practical wisdom or right action applied to particular circumstances. They can spring from the exchange of words and deeds in the form of a gift or of a contract – that is, from some performance by which we accept an obligation or create one. Or they can derive from our positions, our callings, as is true for ministers, teachers, lawyers, and of course physicians. The doctor's duty was to do everything to save his patient

[35] Townshend, p. 264.

and restore him to health, but the duty was to the ideals of medicine, not to the individual. The queen appears to have conceived of her own duty in a similar way. It arose, she implied, because 'God hath raised Me high' and 'made me his Instrument to maintain his Truth and Glory'.[36] He had put her in the position to rule for her subjects' benefit, and she could do naught but obey this calling. She had a general duty to God, of course, but this duty was the same owed by every Christian, as King James said in *Basilikon Doron*.[37] Her special duties, for which she particularly 'set the last Judgement-Day before [her] Eyes', came from her position, just as the duties of her councillors and as the duties of everyone else in the social order came from theirs. And just as God had put her in this place, so too He gave blessing to her conduct of it, a point she stressed 'to give God the Praise, as Testimony before you, and not to Attribute any thing to My Self'.[38]

In thus stressing her God-given duty, Elizabeth also conceded that she was compelled to act for 'Conscience-sake' against those 'Varlets and lewd persons' who had put her subjects to the 'Errours, Troubles, Vexations and Oppressions' created by her patents.[39] Hence, the Queen expressed her gratitude to the critics of the monopolies because they kept her from the 'Lapse of an Errour', discharging her of guilt for the faults of her advisers and 'Substitutes'.[40]

From these considerations came a theory of the subjects' duty, which properly fell into a coordinated relation with the monarch's. In general, it could be summed up in the 'Loves and Loyalty' they gave her, in part by means of their 'intended Helps' – the grant of subsidies – and in part by their respect for her sovereign rule.[41] Rule belonged to the queen; and with it subjects were not to meddle, any more than shoemakers were to meddle in surgery. It was her responsibility alone to provide for government. But the first requirement of just rule, as Cicero said, was that it do no harm.[42] If faults occurred she was obligated to correct them or to bear herself the burden of the 'crime'.[43] This meant that whenever royal authority erred, her subjects had a duty to her as well as to the commonwealth at large to air them in the public forum. The queen especially praised those members of the Commons who, she said,

spake out of Zeal for their Countries, and not out of Spleen, or Malevolent Affection, as being Parties grieved. And I take it exceeding Gratefully from them; because it gives Us

[36] *Ibid.*, pp. 263, 266.
[37] James I, *Basilikon Doron, Or His Majesties Instrvctions to his Dearest Sonne, Henry the Prince* in *The Political Works of James I*, ed. Charles McIlwain (Cambridge, MA, 1918), pp. 12ff.
[38] Townshend, pp. 265, 266.
[39] *Ibid.*, p. 265; see also *STC* 7578, pp. 5–6; *STC* 7579, Sig. A3c; BL, Harleian MS. 787, fo. 128v.
[40] Townshend, p. 264; *STC* 7578, p. 5; see also *ibid.*, p. 2, *STC* 7579, Sig. A2b; BL, Harleian MS. 787, fo. 128r.
[41] Townshend, pp. 263, 264–5; see also *STC* 7579, Sig. A2b; BL, Harleian MS. 787, fo. 127v.
[42] Marcus Tullius Cicero, *Marcus Tullius Ciceroes thre bokes of duties*, tr. Nicholas Grimalde (1556), ed. Gerald O'Gorman (Washington, DC, 1990), p. 63 (and see also p. 59).
[43] *STC* 7578, p. 5; see also Townshend, p. 266; *STC* 7579, Sig. A3b; BL, Harleian MS. 787, fo. 128r.

to know that no Respects or Interests had moved them other than the minds they bear to suffer no diminution of our Honour, and our subjects Loves unto us.[44]

If every person in the realm held to his proper place in this way, each contributing to the common good as God had called him, the queen would be 'that Person, that still (yet under God) hath Deliver'd you; so I trust, (by the Almighty Power of God) that I still shall be his Instrument to Preserve you from every Peril, Dishonour, Shame, Tyranny and Oppression'.[45]

What then of liberty, which had so much dominated the debates in the Commons? For the queen and her officials, who had recently experienced the earl of Essex's abortive rebellion and who were still fighting an international war with the greatest power in Europe, the freedom of Englishmen depended critically on the capacity of the state to maintain stability at home and protect itself from foreign dangers. For them, peril and dishonour as well as tyranny and oppression could come as easily from within as from without the realm, especially because a state torn by internal strife was vulnerable to foreign conquest. A conquered state was a slave state, since the conquest wiped away existing law and subjected its people absolutely to the conqueror.[46] Hence it was essential that the queen have the necessary authority and means to serve the realm. Only then could she conserve her subjects in safety and be, in the words of a 1628 printing of her speech, 'the Instrument to deliuer [them] from out of seruitude, and from slauerie vnder our Enemies, and cruell tyranny, and vilde oppression intended against Vs'.[47] For those who thought in this vein, there could be no more certain recipe for the loss of freedom than the collapse of authority at home and of power abroad. The queen dwelt very heavily on this theme throughout her remarks, explicitly linking her ability to protect the realm from insurrection and invasion with the monies her people had bestowed upon her.[48]

Elizabeth's defense of royal duties, therefore, was also an apology for the supremacy of her monarchical power. If liberty was in danger, it was the ruler's calling to preserve it. Like the physicians, she claimed a monopoly over the health of the body with whose care she was charged.

RITUALS OF ACCOMMODATION

The Elizabethan monopolies point to the existence in the late sixteenth century of rival outlooks about the nature of the English polity. Those who created them

---

[44] Townshend, pp. 264–5; see also BL, Harleian MS. 787, fo. 128r; STC 7578, p. 3; STC 7579, Sig. A3a.

[45] Townshend, p. 263 (and see also p. 266); STC 7579, Sigs. A2b, A3b; BL, Harleian MS. 787, fos. 127v, 128r.

[46] J. P. Sommerville, *Politics and Ideology in England, 1603–1640* (London and New York, 1986), pp. 66–9; see also J. G. A. Pocock, *The Ancient Constitution and the Feudal Law: A Study of English Historical Thought in the Seventeenth Century; A Reissue with a Retrospect* (Cambridge, 1987), pp. 282–7, 299, 301–2.

[47] STC 7579, Sig. A2b.

[48] This emphasis is especially clear in BL, Harleian MS. 787, fo. 127v; see also Townshend, p. 263; STC 7579, Sig. A2b.

saw the grant of exclusive trading rights in manufactures and other commodities as a fitting means to order the economy and promote the common good through the due exercise of royal authority. To their advocates, these new-found enterprises fit neatly into the hierarchical ranking of offices and callings which made up the commonwealth. If properly administered each contributed in its distinct way to the larger good.[49] As Queen Elizabeth herself argued, there was nothing wrong in granting 'a private Profit to some of my Ancient Servants' through her patents, so long as what she did was 'Good and Beneficial to the Subject in general'.[50] Hence, she wished only to prevent the abuse of patents by those she called, according to the 1601 printed version of her speech, 'the thrallers of our people, the wringers of the poore'.[51]

Those who opposed the monopolies in principle, however, saw something inherently contradictory in the granting of public goods into private hands. It was not only that a private man necessarily pursued his own interests, centred his actions on his own advantage, not the public good. The monopolies also corrupted the body politic. First and most obviously by taking the profits of their skills from certain artisans and craftsmen, which were as land was to a gentleman,[52] they hurt them in their inheritances. Only parliament, it was argued, could ever impose charges of this kind upon the subjects, for this institution alone had the capacity to grant the requisite consent. Moreover, the grant of monopolies undermined the monarch's obligation to provide equal justice to all freemen in the kingdom. They turned what properly belonged to everyone into exclusive private possessions, thereby defeating each man's obligations to perform his duties to God and neighbour.[53] In this formulation, what was private could never be simultaneously public.

Such differences could not readily be accommodated to each other. How, then, did England manage to escape for so long the consequences of such ideological division? How, in particular, did the pro- and anti-monopolists in 1601 achieve resolution of their dispute without turning the parliament into a shambles? To arrive at answers, we must return again to Queen Elizabeth's 'Golden Speech', this time focusing on it as a ritualized acting-out of the principles of social harmony against the threat of disorder and opposition.

The hierarchical image of political society offered by the queen rested on an ideal of reciprocity in which, as Sir Robert Cecil said, 'the Qualities of the Prince, and the Subject' were seen as inseparably 'good for the one and the other'.[54] But, as Elizabeth depicted it, this reciprocity amounted to more than a mere harmonizing of material interests. It created a moral community whose

---

[49] See the remarks of Thomas Fleming, then the solicitor general, on behalf of Sir Edward Darcy; in *Darcy v. Allen* (1602), PRO, SP 12/286/47.
[50] Townshend, p. 264; see also, BL, Harleian MS. 787, fos. 127v, 128r; *STC* 7578, p. 3; *STC* 7579, Sigs. A2b–A3a.
[51] *STC* 7578, pp. 2–3.   [52] *Darcy v. Allen* (1602), BL, Add. MS. 25203, fo. 574v.
[53] See Coke's report of *Darcy v. Allen*, 11 Co. Rep. 84b–88b in *English Reports*, 77, pp. 1260–6.
[54] Townshend, p. 253.

watchword was 'love'. 'I do assure you', she told the assembled parliament men,

There is no Prince that loveth his Subjects better, or whose Love can countervail Our Love. There is no Jewel, be it never so Rich a Price, which I set before this Jewel; I mean, your Love: For I do more Esteem of It, than of any Treasure or Riches; for That we know how to prize, but Love and Thanks I Count Unvaluable. And though God hath raised Me high; yet This I count the Glory of my Crown, That I have Reigned with your Loves. This makes me that I do not so much rejoyce, That God hath made Me to be a Queen, as, To be a Queen over so Thankful a People.[55]

In return for his love, the queen herself bestowed love upon her subjects. 'There will never Queen sit in my Seat', she proclaimed,

with more Zeal to my Country, Care for my Subjects, and that sooner with willingness will venture her Life for your Good and Safety, than My Self. For it is not my desire to Live nor Reign longer, than my Life and Reign shall be for your Good. And though you have had, and may have many Princes, more Might and Wise, sitting in this State; yet you never had, or shall have any that will be more Careful and Loving.[56]

In this way, she argued, mutual love knit the people's hearts to the queen and became the guarantee of stability and order in the realm.[57]

The love spoken of here was akin to the Greek ideal of *philia*, friendship, for which according to Aristotle human beings 'choose to live'. 'Even rich men and those in possession of office and of dominating power', he said, 'are thought to need friends . . . for what is the use of such prosperity without the opportunity of beneficence'.[58] This theme of beneficence lay at the heart of the monopolies affair. The patents originated in the monarch's general obligation to be bountiful in granting favour and reward to those who had shown loyalty and done service to her. They arose, that is, within the economy of favour and gratitude that characterized all patron–client relations in this period.[59]

---

[55] *Ibid.*, p. 263; see also *STC* 7579, Sigs. A2a–b; BL, Harleian MS. 787, fo. 127v.

[56] Townshend, p. 266; see also *STC* 7579, Sig. A3c.

[57] See Townshend, p. 265.

[58] Aristotle, *The Nicomachean Ethics*, 1155a 7–10, tr. W. D. Ross, revised by J. L. Ackrill and J. O. Urmson (Oxford, 1980), p. 192. The earliest English version of the *Nicomachean Ethics*, by John Wilkinson, is based on Brunetto Latini's Italian summary and dates from 1547; Aristotle, *The Ethiques of Aristotle, that is to saye, precepts of good behauioure and perfighte honestie now newly translated into English*, tr. John Wyklinson (London, 1547) (*STC* 774); the passage in question is at Sig. Hiiir. See also Irving Singer, *The Nature of Love* (3 vols., Chicago, IL, 1984), i, pp. 88–110, 198–232.

[59] On this theme see J. E. Neale, 'The Elizabethan Political Scene', in J. E. Neale, *Essays in Elizabethan History* (1958), pp. 59–84; Wallace T. MacCaffrey, 'Place and Patronage in Elizabethan Politics', in S. T. Bindoff, J. Hurstfield, and C. H. Williams (eds.), *Elizabethan Government and Society* (1961), pp. 95–126; Joel Hurstfield, 'Political Corruption in Modern England: The Historian's Problem', in Joel Hurstfield, *Freedom, Corruption and Government in Elizabethan England* (1973), pp. 137–62; G. R. Elton, 'The Tudor Government: The Points of Contact. III. The Court', in Elton, *Studies*, iii, pp. 38–57; Penry Williams, 'Court and Polity under Elizabeth I', *Bulletin of the John Rylands University Libraries*, 65 (1983): 259–86; Peck, *Court Patronage*, chs. 1–3; Linda Levy Peck, 'Court Patronage and Governmental Policy: The Jacobean Dilemma', in Guy Fitch Lytle and Stephen Orgel (eds.), *Patronage in the Renaissance* (Princeton, NJ, 1981), pp. 27–46; Linda Levy Peck, '"For a King not to be Bountiful were a Fault": Perspective in Court Patronage in Early Stuart England', *Journal of British Studies* 25 (1986): 31–61.

This connection is apparent in every version of Elizabeth's speech, but we can see it most clearly in the copy preserved among William Dell's papers. There the queen tells her listeners that she granted her patents by her 'Prerogative royall' to her servants as a 'priuate benefitt' to them 'by way of recompence for theyr good Seruice done'.[60] The world 'benefitt' is crucial in this connection. It links the queen's actions to the analysis and advice given in Seneca's essay, *De Beneficiis*, which to a very large degree provided the vocabulary and grammar for patronage and favour in this period.[61] According to Seneca, the giving and receiving of benefits provides the 'thing that most of al other knitteth men togither in felowship'. A benefit 'is a frendly goode deede'. It is something immaterial, something in our hearts or minds. According to Seneca, the money or offices given by a patron to his client are only the 'badges of benefites'.

> Therefore neither Gold nor Siluer, nor any of the thinges wee receiue of our neighbours, is a benefit . . . These thinges which we handle and looke vppon, and which our greedinesse is so fast tyed vntoo are transitorie. Both misfortune and force may take them from vs. But a good turne endureth still, yea euen when the thyng that was given is gone.

The receiving of benefits also calls forth a need for recompense, initially acquitted by our gratitude when we accept a gift 'thankfully, by powrying out our affections' and witnessing them everywhere. 'He that hath taken a good turne thankfully', Seneca says, 'hath payd the first paiment of it'. Through this exchange the giving of benefits forms the bonds of human society. 'For in what other thing haue wee so muche safetie', Seneca argues,

> as in helping one another with mutuall freendlynes? . . . Put eueryman too himself alone, and what are wee? A pray for beasts, a slaughter for Sacrifice, and very eazie to haue our blud shedde . . . Take away this fellowship, and yee rend asunder the vnitie of Mankynd, whereby our lyfe is maynteined.

What was essential was the exchange of human affections, not just the giving and receiving of material things.[62]

This Senecan way of framing the issues, and some of the same language, permeate the rituals of accommodation in 1601. The speech of thanks given by John Crooke, Speaker of the Commons set the tone for the exchange. He was there, he said, 'to present all humble & dutiful thankes' of the Commons for her Majesty's recent proclamation

60 BL, Harleian MS. 787, fo. 127v; see also Townshend, p. 264, *STC* 7578, p. 3; *STC* 7579, Sig. A3a.
61 See John M. Wallace, 'Timon of Athens and the Three Graces: Shakespeare's Senecan Study', *Modern Philology*, 83 (1985–86): 350ff; Peck, *Court Patronage*, ch. 1.
62 Lucius Annaeus Seneca, *The woorke of the excellent Philosopher Lucius Annaeus Seneca concerning Benefyting, that is too say the dooing, receyuing, and requyting of good Turnes*, tr. Arthur Golding (1578), fos. 4v, 5v, 22r, 55r; Cicero also treats the theme of benefits in similar terms in his *De Officiis*; see Cicero, *Ciceroes thre bookes of duties*, tr. Grimalde, pp. 131ff.

ffor which they confess they are not able to yeild your Majesty either answerable guifts or comparable treasure, but true hearts they bringe, with promise of respect & duty befitting true & dutifull Subjects euen to the spending of the uttermost droppe of blood in theyr bodyes, for the preseruacon of Religion, your Sacred person, & the Realme.[63]

They would make their recompense according to their best abilities, as Seneca had advised. The exchange was not of material things, but of good will, exemplified in loyal and loving service. They were especially 'thankfull', Crooke went on, 'not for Benefitts receyued, which were sued for, & soe obtayned, but for gracious favours bestowed of your gracious mere mocon'. Although they knew her

Sacred Ears are allmost bowed done & open to theyr Suites & Complaints, yet now yo.[ur] Ma[jes].[ty] had ouercome them by your most Royall bounty, & as it were presented them by your magnificent & princely liberality.[64]

Elizabeth picked up on the theme of benefits right away. She 'well understood', Dell's version reports her as saying, that the Speaker and other members had 'come to giue us thankes for Benefitts receyued'. She wanted them to know that she returned them 'all the thankes that can possibily be conceyued in a kingly heart, for accepting my message in soe kinde manner'. She especially thanked the Speaker for delivering it. But, she went on, 'I must tell you, I doubt & cannot be resolued, whether I haue more cause to thank them, or they me. Howsoeuer I am more then glad to see Sympathy between them & me'. She was, moreover, especially grateful 'ffor the money you haue soe freely & willingly bestowed upon me', promising as we have seen to bestow it back to them for their good 'for the defence of the Kingdome, & theyr owne Eyes shall see it, and a just Accompt shall be made of all'.[65] The effect of these words was to cast the speech as part of the ritualized exchange of gratitude given for gratitude received which lies at the heart of the Senecan ethic, binding queen and subject, as she says, in 'sympathy'.

This view spoke expressly to the granting of supply, which was still in process when the queen spoke. The discussion had begun on 3 November, with Sir Robert Cecil's speech on the queen's necessity and the appointment of a large committee to consider the 'greatest matters', including the provision of new taxes. On the following day, Robert Johnson introduced the grievance of monopoly. The main negotiations on the terms of the subsidy were settled by 9 November, yet the finished bill was not voted until 5 December.[66] There was an explicit sense, as Robert Wingfield put it on 9 November, that with the terms of

[63] BL, Harleian MS. 787, fo. 127r; see also Townshend, pp. 263, 264; STC 7578, pp. 1–2; STC 7579, Sigs. A2a, A2b.

[64] BL, Harleian MS. 787, fo. 127r; see also Townshend, p. 262.

[65] BL, Harleian MS. 787, fo. 127v; see also Townshend, pp. 263, 264; STC 7578, pp. 1–2; STC 7579, Sigs. A2a, A2b.

[66] Townshend, pp. 183–5, 188, 197–200, 204–5, 286–7; see also D'Ewes, *Journal*, pp. 623–4, 626, 629–32, 668; Neale, *Parliaments, 1584–1601*, pp. 411–16.

the subsidy effectively settled, 'it would please her Majesty not to dissolve the Parliament till some Acts were passed'. Robert Cecil made it clear that she would. The subsidy may have been 'the *Alpha* and *Omega*' of the parliament, Cecil conceded, but not the entire alphabet.[67] Between the beginning and the end a number of bills indeed were considered and passed, but it was the monopolies that received the most attention. In fact, work on the subsidy proceeded in counterpoint with discussion of the grievances they had stirred. The first reading of the actual bill for four subsidies and eight fifteenths and tenths came only on 26 November, the day following the Speaker's report to the House of the queen's promise to issue a proclamation to remedy the grievance. The second reading came only on the morning of 30 November itself, two days after the issuance of the proclamation and just before members went to Whitehall to thank the queen for her beneficence and to listen to her response.[68] The two matters – redress and supply – proceeded in tandem, the one requiting the other, not formally as a *quid pro quo* but as one benefit answers another in mutual exchange. In Heywood Townshend's account, the first reading is shown to have occurred only after Sir Robert Cecil reported the queen's response to the Commons' expression of gratitude for her promised remedy for their grievance. 'You can give Me no more thanks for that which I have promised You', he quotes her as saying, 'Than I can and will give You Thanks for that which You have already Performed'. Townshend adds that she was referring here to the Commons agreement in principle on taxation.[69]

In the parliament of 1621, Sir George More suggested that redress of grievances and supply should be thought of 'as twins, as Jacob and Esau' going 'hand in hand' through the Commons, with grievances proceeding first but the blessing falling on subsidies at the end.[70] More was an active member of the parliament of 1601, who early in the session had moved for the creation of the committee to consider the subsidy and who was very involved in the monopolies matter.[71] He may well have been thinking of the successful matching of redress and supply at that time. In this understanding, parliament, which brought all the elements of the realm together representatively, was conceived as more than a mere institution for the making of authoritative decisions in the realm. The requesting and granting of consent to statutes or taxes was less the striking of a bargain between competing parties or interests than the ritual recognition that a social and political bond held the governors and the governed together for

---

[67] Townshend, p. 204.   [68] D'Ewes, *Journal*, pp. 654, 658.

[69] Townshend, p. 253. The second reading came only after the Commons, anxious to express their good will to the queen were assured that she would 'welcome' all who would come to give her thanks 'without Restraint or Limit' of number, a matter touching their honour which had been in some doubt until then; *ibid.*, p. 261.

[70] *Commons Debates, 1621*, eds. Wallace Notestein, Frances H. Relf and Hartley Simpson (7 vols., New Haven, CT, 1935), ii, p. 21. Attention has recently been called to this passage in an important article, Thomas Cogswell, 'A Low Road to Extinction? Supply and Redress of Grievances in the Parliaments of the 1620s', *HJ*, 33 (1990): 283.

[71] Townshend, pp. 185, 234.

common profit. As regards taxes, there was no general right of refusal once a case for their necessity had been made. Parliamentary debate was confined merely to determining their size, terms, and conditions, sometimes but not inevitably accompanied by demands for redress of grievances. Completion of the negotiation, as in 1601, signified the renewal of the ties that made the realm a healthy body politic, while failure of monarch and subject to reach concord, as they would frequently fail to do in the early seventeenth century, indicated nothing less than the presence of disease in that same social body.[72]

This sense of the ritualized renewal of the bonds of society was manifested in many of the ceremonies of parliamentary life – for example, in the formalities that opened the session and that accompanied the final presentation of the subsidy and general pardon at its close. Note, for example, the speech of Speaker Puckering at the conclusion of the 1585 parliament when he presented the subsidy bill as an outward token of the subjects' love and gratitude for the beneficial rule they had received from the queen. Note, too, the thanks he gave on his knees for her grant of the general pardon. The queen responded on this occasion, as she would in 1601, by returning her own thanks to the Commons for their care in safekeeping her life, confessing herself fast bound to them through 'the link of your good will' which made her 'heart and head . . . seek forever all your best'.[73] The regime of sympathy evoked in this setting was distinctly hierarchical in character – a regime of deference.

This same kind of reciprocity, hierarchical and deferential, was played out in the council chamber at Whitehall in 1601. When the members of Commons assembled there they found the queen sitting in 'her Seat royall . . . under the Cloth of State at the upper end . . . attended with most of the Priuy Councell & Nobles' whose presence itself honoured her and demonstrated her position.[74] The Speaker began and ended his eloquent address of thanks with 'three low reverences', while the rest of the members of the Commons were on their knees, 'prostrate at her sacred feet', as the Speaker says. At the end of her own speech, moreover, she told her privy councillors 'That before these *Gentlemen* depart into their Countries, you bring them All to Kis My Hand.' It is perhaps no surprise, therefore, that among the gifts for which the speaker thanked the

---

[72] For guidance on this theme, see G. L. Harriss, 'Medieval Doctrines in the Debates on Supply, 1610–1629', in Kevin Sharpe (ed.), *Faction and Parliament* (London and New York, 1978), pp. 73–104; G. L. Harriss, *King, Parliament and Public Finance in Medieval England to 1369* (Oxford, 1979). See also David Harris Sacks, 'The Paradox of Taxation: Fiscal Crises, Parliament, and Liberty in Early Modern England, 1450–1640', in Philip T. Hoffman and Kathryn Norberg (eds.), *Fiscal Crises, Representative Institutions, and Liberty in Early Modern Europe* (Stanford, CA, 1994), pp. 7–66; J. D. Alsop, 'Parliament and Taxation', in D. M. Dean and N. L. Jones, *The Parliaments of Elizabethan England* (Oxford, 1990), pp. 91–116; J. D. Alsop, 'The Politics of Parliamentary Taxation, 1558–1603', (unpublished paper). I am grateful to Dr Alsop for sharing his unpublished work with me.
[73] D'Ewes, *Journal*, pp. 327–29; Neale, *Parliaments, 1584–1601*, pp. 95–101.
[74] See William Harrison, *The Description of England*, ed. Georges Edelen (Ithaca, NY, 1968), pp. 227–32.

queen one was that it had pleased her 'soe freely & willingly to graunt them this access unto your sacred person'.[75]

But there was something more at work here, something more than the reproduction of hierarchy. For along with asserting her own authority, the queen was simultaneously giving her listeners their due. Her speech began with the members of the Commons on their knees, a position in which they remained during its first third while the queen graciously accepted the thanks she had been offered and spoke of her duty to God and the mutual love between her and her subjects. But at this point she stopped and asked the Speaker and the rest of the members of Commons to rise and draw closer because, she said, 'I shall yet trouble you with longer Speech'.[76] Here the matter and tone changed as she took these men, all of them prominent local leaders and officials, into her confidence, explained to them how and why the monopolies had gone so wrong, and thanked them for so disinterestedly bringing the subjects' grievances to her attentions and keeping her from falling into error by having the uncorrected wrongs committed by her servants attributed to her. In this way, she recognized them as participants with her in the ordering of society, men who not only deserved confidence but who could be trusted to aid her in the performance of her duties. Only after doing so did she turn again to the themes of godly duty and love with which she had opened and offer her hand to all those who had attended. The whole speech was accompanied by what Dell's version calls

her Majestes gestures of Honor & princely demeanour used by her, As when the Speaker spake any effectuall or mouing speech from the Comons to her Majesty, she rose up & bowed her selfe, As alsoe in her owne Speech, when the Comons apprehending any extraordinary words of favour from her did any Reuerence to her Ma[jes]ty she likewise rose up & bowed her selfe, etc.[77]

That, 'etc.' speaks worlds, as Sir John Neale noted in commenting on this same passage.[78]

THE POLITICAL CULTURE OF BENEFITS

In making her speech, Elizabeth was not only salving a wound but composing a realm. She was bringing the representatives of her people – and through them her people themselves – into an ordered relationship to her. By her words and gestures, just as by her governmental actions, she was disciplining society into a proportional, that is to say a hierarchical, arrangement of parts. But the resulting unity was not automatic; it could not be achieved without this effort just because it was a unity of parts, each of which had its own existence. Here the language of benefits was especially useful, since it allowed those who

[75] Townshend, pp. 262, 263, 266; see also BL, Harleian MS. 787, fos. 127r, 128v; STC 7579, Sig. A2a.
[76] Townshend, p. 264; see also BL, Harleian MS. 787, fo. 127v; STC 7579, Sig. A2b.
[77] BL, Harleian MS. 787, fo. 128v.
[78] Neale, *Parliaments, 1584–1601*, p. 393.

employed it to refer simultaneously to a world of social and political hierarchy, in which those of differing rank formed a harmony of favour and respect, and a world of independent souls, in which individual acts of good will draw together every man in a unity of thought and feeling. What was important to the theory of benefits was not the material gifts which were its medium, but the mutual and voluntary exchange of beneficence and gratitude which was its spirit. The latter points to every man's capacity to answer voluntarily the gifts he has received with proper gratitude and appropriate actions according to his abilities, even if he has received those gifts from a monarch.

Hence the language of benefits, called up by John Crooke in 1601 and so skilfully used by Elizabeth in response, carried with it two coordinated but distinguishable visions of the commonwealth. According to Sir Thomas Smith, a commonwealth is a 'society or common doing of a multitude of free men . . . united by common accord' for their 'conservation . . . in peace as in warre'.[79] Its very essence depends on their voluntary coming together for mutual well-being. It is 'nothing more than a commencement or continual suppedition of benefits mutually received and done among men', as Sir Arthur Chichester said in 1612.[80] This understanding pointed to the inevitability of difference – the inevitability that some would be greater in wealth and power than others. It endorsed the idea that the present social order was the image of Reason in the world, ordained by God, and that political action involved no more than what has been identified as rituals of 'affirmation and celebration'.[81]

This same theory of benefits also saw the unity of the realm as depending upon positive acts by which ruler and subject knitted their hearts one unto another.[82] No subject could legitimately deny his service to monarch and commonweal once the case for it had been duly laid before him. But the subject had to be asked for his aid in due form, with proper deference to his honour and his rights.[83] In the face of demonstrated need, he was morally bound to consent, but he had to consent voluntarily. Yielding to such an obligation was just the opposite of being coerced. It involved an inward judgment on the rectitude of the demand and an inward agreement to answer it as best one may. Only such voluntary acts were worthy of moral praise. Their performance turned the brute realities of a hierarchically ordered society into a genuine moral community, thereby assuring a place for freedom and consent in making England a common-wealth.[84]

[79] Sir Thomas Smith, *De Republica Anglorum: A Discourse on the Commonwealth of England*, ed. L. Alston (Cambridge, 1906), p. 20.
[80] Sir Arthur Chichester to the Archbishop of Canterbury, 23 October 1612, 'Letterbook of Sir Arthur Chicester, 1612–1614', *Analecta Hibernaca*, no. 8, p. 56 as cited in Peck, *Court Patronage*, p. 13.
[81] Mark A. Kishlansky, *Parliamentary Selection: Social and Political Choice in Early Modern England* (Cambridge, 1986), p. 10.
[82] Townshend, p. 265.
[83] See David Harris Sacks, 'Searching for "Culture" in the English Renaissance', *Shakespeare Quarterly*, 39 (1988): 486ff.
[84] See Sacks, 'Parliament, Liberty, and the Commonweal', pp. 85–121.

The language of benefits allowed two world pictures to co-exist, one a vision of sovereign authority, the other of free community. It resolved the possible conflict between these views through the principle of reciprocity by which good will was exchanged. Accommodation would become difficult, if not impossible, should either side press its claims to the extreme – should either side, that is, insist on the absolute nature of its rights.

12 *The rhetoric of counsel in early modern England*

JOHN GUY

The music of cornets began to play, and a king accompanied by his nobility and gentlemen appeared on stage. The king sat in his chair of estate and was offered a glass of wine by a grave and senior gentleman. This he refused, whereupon a young upstart handed him poison in a golden cup. The king accepted the cup, drank from it, and fell down dead.[1]

Thus was the parable of 'counsel' represented in the allegorical dumb-show that preceded Act II of *Gorboduc*, first performed before Elizabeth I in January 1562. Just as glass contains no poison, but is transparent and holds no art, so a faithful counsellor imparts no treason, but is plain and open and offers wholesome counsel, which the foolish prince declines. By contrast the cup of gold signifies flattery, which bears deadly poison and destroys the prince who credits it.

In this chapter I shall explore the metaphor or vocabulary of 'counsel', which functioned as an 'inspirational myth' and socio-political matrix in early modern England. I shall argue that the phenomena which I believe the term 'counsel' depicted and which it is illuminating to treat in conjunction, underpinned not only the assumptions, but also some of the most important practices and political structures of the Tudor and early-Stuart polity. I shall suggest that 'counsel' ranked high among the paradigms and traditions which informed public discourse and shaped political institutions between the age of Sir John Fortescue and the outbreak of the Civil War. Francis Bacon hit the nail on the head when he said of antiquity, it 'set forth in figure both the incorporation and inseparable conjunction of counsel with kings . . . whereby they intend that Sovereignty is married to Counsel'.[2] A belief that *imperium* and *consilium* were symbiotic sustained the role of 'counsel' as an 'inspirational myth'. An assumption that the vice and passion of rulers could be mitigated by the advice of good

---

[1] J. M. Manly (ed.), *Specimens of the Pre-Shakesperian Drama* (2 vols., New York, 1967), ii, p. 229.
[2] *Bacon's Essays* (Chandos edition, London, n.d.), p. 37. In this mode *imperium* was represented as male and *consilium* as female: their relationship was conjugal. (A married woman shared in the adminstration of her husband's household and mitigated his *imperium* just as equity tempered the rigour of the common law.)

counsellors energized the process whereby the metaphor was refashioned and reinterpreted for rhetorical and political ends.

'Counsel' was neither in itself a neutral concept nor even one suited intrinsically to the orderly conduct of politics. It subsumed competing moral and political values which stimulated at best intellectual debate, at worst political ideology. The politics of 'counsel' were in this sense the unceasing politics of discourse. Ideas of 'counsel' might be couched in 'humanist-classical' and 'feudal-baronial' vocabulary, and in polyglot versions of each. These idioms derived from separate traditions with their own distinctive preoccupations. Despite efforts at assimilation the metaphor failed to achieve internal coherence and was therefore politically vulnerable. This problem was latent rather than apparent under the Tudors and James I, when political practice largely reflected the values of 'counsel' as an ideal. But with the shift towards adversarial politics in 1640–42, the metaphor collapsed into its component parts. Sharp ideological exchanges between the king and the parliamentary propagandists in the summer of 1642 signalled its limitations as a guarantor of order and consensus.

By the vocabulary of 'counsel' I mean *consilium* in both modern senses. An etymological ambiguity existed in early-modern vernacular speech between 'counsel' or 'consaill' meaning the consultative process, and 'council' or 'consaill' denoting deliberative institutions. From the earliest times until the later years of Elizabeth, the two usages were utterly confused. Thereafter, 'counsel' increasingly denoted advice, and 'council' institutions, which signified changing perceptions of the phenomena to which these terms referred. Yet, even for the late seventeenth century, the linguistic evidence is equivocal, and it is clear that analysis of consultative processes on the one hand, and institutional structures on the other, cannot be pursued exclusively. For the period with which I am concerned, a degree of mental overlap existed which offers both a *caveat* and a corrective to assumptions that consultation may be either divorced from, or confined to, the institutions that contained it, or that firm distinctions can be made between conventionally separate institutions which shared consultation as the means to a common end.

'The end of all doctrine and study is good counsel . . . wherein virtue may be found.'[3] So Sir Thomas Elyot began the final chapters of *The Book Named the Governor*. By curbing human passions and mitigating misjudgments, 'good counsel' stands between order and chaos. By instructing in the ways of virtue and honesty rulers who would otherwise become tyrants or near-tyrants, it is the touchstone of government. From the age of Fortescue, writing in the 1460s and early 1470s, to that of Francis Bacon over a century later, the duties of courtiers and counsellors were couched in such terms. Whether as confidential adviser in

---

[3] *The Book Named the Governor*, ed. S. E. Lehmberg (1962; reprinted 1975), p. 238. See also Elyot, *Pasquil the Playne* (1533; revised edns 1533, 1540): *STC* 7672, 7672.5, 7673; Elyot, *Of the Knowledge which Maketh a Wise Man*, ed. E. Johnston Howard (Oxford, OH, 1946).

a prince's household or literary publicist in retirement or exile the counsellor was supposed to be a grave and weighty statesman capable of making events as well as analyzing them. 'Virtue', 'civility', 'self-rule', and the 'commonwealth' were his predominant concerns, and it was axiomatic that rulers should choose 'good counsellors' and disregard flatterers and time-servers.[4]

This was humanist-classical language, the pith of which was that rulers should be suitably advised. It was said of Tarquin the Proud that he passed judgments touching life and limb without counsel; it was less important to discover whether he had done so than to observe that posterity condemned him on these grounds. A ruler's obligation to seek counsel was strictly moral: 'counselling' was a duty and not a right. A ruler was free to choose his own counsellors and could not be bound by their advice, but it was incumbent on him to listen affably because the spirit of 'good counsel' was 'friendship' (*amicitia*).[5] In practice 'friendship' covered everything from genuine personal relationships to courtesies between rivals, but the crux was that it warranted 'liberty of speech'. The counsellor tendered his honest opinion, which the ruler received in a spirit of 'likeness and equality'.

Fortescue invoked this language when he depicted England as a 'mixed' polity and idealized the Augustan Principate on account of its accessibility to counsel. This was an analogue invaluable to theorists seeking to set republican virtue within the context of monarchical rule; but there was a sub-text. For behind closed doors Augustus was counselled by his 'friends'; and according to Fortescue these *amici principis* degenerated into a private *consilium* or cabinet council within the imperial household. As Tacitus wrote, the emperor was 'edging ahead step by step, drawing into his own hands the functions of senate, magistrates and the law'. Or, as Fortescue explained:

So as at Christ's birth the emperor commanded the whole world . . . Which lordship and monarchy the emperor[s] kept all the while they were ruled by the counsel of the senate. But after that, when the emperor[s] left the counsel of the senate, and some of them . . . had slain great party of the senators, and were ruled by their private counsellors, the estate of the emperor fell in decay, and their lordship wax alway since then less and less . . . We also Englishmen, whose kings some time were counselled by sad and well chosen councillors, beat the mightiest kings of the world. But since our kings have been ruled by

---

[4] As in Italian civic republicanism the authoritative source-book was Cicero's *De officiis*, bolstered by Aristotle's *Politics* and *Ethics*. The difference for the English humanists was that they were obliged to mould their material to suit the models of service, benefits, and the *cursus honorum* prevailing at the royal court. Their objective was to define the role of the active citizen as a 'counsellor' of the ruler. John Guy, 'The Henrician Age', in J. G. A. Pocock (ed.), *Varieties of British Political Thought* (Cambridge, 1993); Pocock, 'The Sense of History in Renaissance England', in J. F. Andrews (ed.), *William Shakespeare*, Vol. I: *His World* (New York, 1985), pp. 143–57.

[5] Aristotle, *The Politics*, ed. S. Everson (Cambridge, 1988), Bk. 3, especially pp. 78–9; P. A. Brunt, *The Fall of the Roman Republic and Related Essays* (Oxford, 1988), pp. 351–81; F. W. Conrad, 'A Preservative against Tyranny: the Public Career and Political Theology of Sir Thomas Elyot', unpublished Johns Hopkins University Ph.D. dissertation (1988); J. Crook, *Consilium Principis: Imperial Councils and Counsellors from Augustus to Diocletian* (Cambridge, 1955), especially pp. 21–30. Cf. Vernon F. Snow (ed.), *Parliament in Elizabethan England: John Hooker's 'Order and Usage'* (New Haven, CT, 1977), p. 117.

private councillors . . . we have not been able to keep our own livelihood . . . And our realm is fallen thereby in decay and poverty, as was the empire when the emperor left the counsel of the senate.[6]

Fortescue wrote at the climax of the Wars of the Roses; his objective was to purge private vested interests from behind the throne. He therefore proposed the exclusion from the king's council of nobles who claimed their place by virtue of high birth alone (the *consiliarii nati* or 'councillors born'), and urged the creation of an executive council of thirty-two persons qualified to advise the king and act as an instrument of the 'public good'.[7] But the composition of the king's council was a shibboleth. It was not until the reign of Henry VIII that an executive 'privy' council was shaped. By October 1536 the institutional council had ceased to be an inclusive admixture of nobles, higher clergy, courtiers, civil servants, and legal experts consulting predominantly in the traditional council chamber at Westminster, and become instead a select, executive board of nineteen or so leading office-holders, courtiers, and administrators, known as the privy council and meeting in the king's 'privy' apartments at court.[8]

Despite overwhelming administrative advantages, this political reconstruction had a potential flaw. Membership of the council was seen by those who were excluded to have narrowed in favour of a courtly and bureaucratic élite, a majority of whom by the central decades of Elizabeth's reign were apologists, if not torchbearers of the Protestant Reformation, who owed their positions less to noble birth and rank in society than to their offices and standing in royal favour.[9]

Elyot wrote his *The Book Named the Governor* synchronously with the Pardon of the Clergy (1531) and first promulgation of the royal supremacy.[10] He recognized that the politics of the king's divorce from Catherine of Aragon would impinge on the council after Wolsey's fall. This led him to reinterpret the role of the *amici principis*, whom he cast not as the instruments of private tyranny but as the agents of a strong state. His historical grasp was surer than Fortescue's and he knew that the *amici* had mostly been drawn from the governors who

---

[6] Sir John Fortescue, *The Governance of England*, ed. C. Plummer (second edn, Oxford, 1926), pp. 149–50, 347–53.

[7] *Ibid.*, pp. 145–9, 348–53.

[8] The principal literature includes G. R. Elton, *The Tudor Revolution in Government* (Cambridge, 1953); Elton, *Reform and Reformation: England 1509–1558* (1977); Elton, *Studies in Tudor and Stuart Politics and Government* (3 vols.; Cambridge, 1974–83), i, pp. 173–88; iii, pp. 373–90; Elton, 'The Tudor Revolution: A Reply', *Past and Present*, no. 29 (1974): 26–49; Elton, 'A New Age of Reform?', *HJ*, 30 (1987): 709–16; C. Coleman and D. R. Starkey (eds.), *Revolution Reassessed: Revisions in the History of Tudor Government and Administration* (Oxford, 1986); John Guy, *Tudor England* (Oxford, 1988), pp. 156–64; Alistair Fox and John Guy, *Reassessing the Henrician Age* (Oxford, 1986), pp. 121–47; D. R. Starkey (ed.), *The English Court: from the Wars of the Roses to the Civil War* (1987).

[9] Fox and Guy, *Reassessing the Henrician Age*, pp. 137–45; Guy, *Tudor England*, pp. 161–4, 272–5, 309–19, 456–7.

[10] J. J. Scarisbrick, 'The Pardon of the Clergy, 1531', *Cambridge Historical Journal*, 12 (1956): 22–30; John Guy, 'Henry VIII and the *Praemunire* Manoeuvres of 1530–1531', *EHR*, 97 (1982): 481–503; G. W. Bernard, 'The Pardon of the Clergy Reconsidered', *JEH*, 37 (1986): 258–82.

served the emperor in the localities, and who numbered among his counsellors when they were resident at court.[11] He therefore devised an educational programme designed to create model Tudor equivalents. Concurring with Thomas Starkey and (later) Sir Philip Sidney that a monarchy limited by a strong nobility would insure the state against tyranny, Elyot imitated the *amici* on the grounds that the will of every sovereign was circumscribed to the extent that he needed 'friends' to enact, enforce, and help determine it.[12] These *amici*, in his reading, were the nobility and country gentry; and the merit of his interpretation was that it closely mirrored existing Crown policy since 1461, and therefore seemed authoritative.

Elyot's account made sense because the Yorkists and early Tudors had gone to great lengths to construct political affinities in the counties. By the 1530s it was barely an exaggeration to say that the leaders of 'court' and 'country' were the same people at different times of year: the Crown aimed to subdue existing noble and gentry affinities and replace them with networks of royal power.[13] Leading county landowners and their sons were invited to court for reasons which were not chiefly military or diplomatic, but local. They were not given salaried appointments, but often received annuities and robes. The exact proportion of supernumeraries who attended at court cannot be reconstructed, but their service was assured once they were 'sworn' and their names recorded in the official registers. Moreover, many supernumeraries *did* attend court, and when they did, they and the Crown fully exploited their bilateral relationship for purposes of patronage and mutual security.

Under these circumstances it required little imagination to cast England's social leaders as *amici principis*. It is true that Henry VII and Henry VIII communicated directly with the members of their affinities while Elizabeth relied on networks constructed by privy councillors and courtiers. Court factionalism during Edward VI's minority usurped the networks of the early Tudors, which had to be reconstituted empirically. But this does not affect my point, which is that the narrowing of the institutional council was not accompanied by the stifling of consultation before Elizabeth's death. Only in Mary Tudor's short reign were sections of the nobility and gentry isolated on purely ideological grounds. When due allowance is made after 1558 for Catholic recusancy and protestant nonconformity, the debates over Mary Queen of Scots, and the pressures of the late-Elizabethan war with Spain and conquest of Ireland, the fact remains that lines of political communication stayed open under the Tudors despite the Essex–Cecil feud in the 1590s.

[11] Crook, *Consilium Principis*, pp. 21–30.

[12] F. W. Conrad, 'The Problem of Counsel Reconsidered: the Case of Sir Thomas Elyot', in T. F. Mayer and P. Fideler (eds.), *The Commonwealth of Tudor England* (1992).

[13] D. A. L. Morgan, 'The House of Policy: the Political Role of the Late-Plantagenet Household, 1422–1485', in Starkey (ed.), *The English Court*, pp. 64–7; R. Horrox, *Richard III: A Study of Service* (Cambridge, 1989); Guy, *Tudor England*, pp. 164–73; Guy, 'Wolsey and the Tudor Polity', in S. Gunn and P. Lindley (eds.), *Cardinal Wolsey: Church, State and Art* (Cambridge, 1991), pp. 54–75.

A different paradigm of 'counsel' was invoked by the leaders of the Pilgrimage of Grace. They complained that Henry VIII was surrounded by 'flatterers' of base birth and vicious reputation who subverted the church and pillaged the realm for their own 'private' advantage.[14] They urged him to dismiss these 'evil counsellors' and restore the 'councillors born' to their rightful place at court. Thomas Cromwell, the king's chief minister, and his dependents were the 'evil counsellors' castigated by name. If the king insisted on retaining such 'private' counsellors, then it would be necessary to appoint a 'council for the commonwealth' like the Parlement of Paris, because rulers should be counselled not by favourites but by 'such virtuous men as would regard the commonwealth above their prince's love'. These 'virtuous men' were the 'nobles, baronage and commons for the said commonwealth'.[15] The Pilgrims therefore demanded that a free parliament be summoned to Nottingham or York, one at which Henry VIII would respect the customs of the lords and allow free speech and free elections to the Commons, so that members might be returned who could 'reason for the wealth' of their communities and not for the king's 'private lucre'.

This was feudal-baronial language, the origins of which lay in the attempts of the baronage in the reigns of Henry III and Edward II to render royal government accountable. By the Provisions of Oxford (1258) a committee of twenty-four nominated by king and barons in equal proportions was to reduce itself to four, who were to appoint the king's council of fifteen. The fifteen were to advise the king and vet all his public acts, and were thrice a year to meet twelve baronial nominees in parliament 'to survey the state of the realm and discuss the common needs of the king and the kingdom'.[16] Again, by the Ordinances of 1311 it was held that the *negotia regni* or 'great affairs' of the kingdom should be resolved by the 'common counsel and assent' of the baronage. Edward II's 'evil counsellors', notably Piers Gaveston, were comprehensively attacked, and the Ordainers insisted that the great officers of court and state were to be appointed in parliament and bound by oaths to the performance of their duties.[17]

The assumptions of this vocabulary sprang from contract theory. The process of feudal enfeoffment made the king and his tenants-in-chief parties to a contract. If one partner breached faith, the contract could be renounced, which

---

[14] *LP*, xi, nos. 705 (1, 2, 4), 714 (p. 276), 902 (2), 1211, 1244, 1246; xii, pt. 1, nos. 900 (p. 401), 901 (p. 404), 1022 (p. 466); *State Papers during the Reign of Henry VIII* (11 vols., Record Commission, London, 1830–52), i, pp. 463–7, 507–8.

[15] *LP*, xi, nos. 705 (1), 1211, 1244; xii, pt. 1, no. 901 (p. 404); *State Papers during the Reign of Henry VIII* i, pp. 466–7; Fox and Guy, *Reassessing the Henrician Age*, pp. 121–47.

[16] W. Stubbs, *Select Charters*, revised H. W. C. Davis (ninth edn, Oxford, reprinted 1962), pp. 378–89; C. Stephenson and F. G. Marcham, *Sources of English Consitutional History* (1938), pp. 142–50. See also N. Denholm-Young, 'Documents of the Barons' Wars', in Denholm-Young, *Collected Papers* (Cardiff, 1969), pp. 155–72.

[17] S. B. Chrimes and A. L. Brown, *Select Documents of English Constitutional History, 1307–1485* (1961), pp. 11–19; Stephenson and Marcham, *Sources of English Constitutional History*, pp. 193–8.

was not an act of rebellion but the practical implementation of the purpose behind the contract. The magnates had the right to bridle the king. They also played an essential role in legislation since in feudal society most public rights and duties derived from the tenure of land.[18] Whereas from a humanist-classical standpoint the appointment of royal counsellors was a matter for the king alone, from a feudal-baronial standpoint the magnates were the king's 'natural' counsellors. They were the 'counsel of the realm', and the 'great affairs of the kingdom' were properly concluded with their co-operation.

The cumulative effect was to forge the link with parliament even if this association owed more to baronial ideology than to institutional practice.[19] 'Revisionist' historians have stressed that the ancestry of parliament lay in its role as a feudal court.[20] 'In his parliaments the king in council holds his court', wrote the author of *Fleta* (c. 1296), and by this reading parliament was a 'political' assembly only when exasperated barons turned the king's instrument of government against him.[21] In strictly institutional terms this interpretation may be sustained, but the matter is more complex. Until the reign of Henry VIII the magnates were convened for 'political' business in *magna consilia* or 'great councils' which, like the medieval parliaments, were afforced sessions of the king's council.[22] Moreover, when knights and burgesses were summoned to parliament with 'full and sufficient power . . . to do whatever . . . may be ordained by common counsel', the process began whereby the commons became the 'representatives' of their communities.[23] By 1300 it was established that the magnates by themselves lacked a sufficient mandate to bind the whole realm. A century later parliament had separated into king, lords, and commons, and it was received constitutional wisdom that taxation was granted by the commons alone, the lords merely 'assenting' to what they had agreed.[24]

When, therefore, the leaders of the Pilgrimage of Grace demanded that 'evil counsellors' be supplanted in favour of the 'counsellors born' who were the king's 'natural' counsellors, it was an instinctive reflex that they should also

---

[18] W. Ullmann, *Principles of Government and Politics in the Middle Ages* (second edn, 1966), pp. 150–92.

[19] N. Pronay and J. Taylor, *Parliamentary Texts of the Later Middle Ages* (Oxford, 1980); Vernon Harcourt, *His Grace the Steward* (1907); G. O. Sayles, *The Functions of the Medieval Parliament of England* (1988); Sayles, *The King's Parliament of England* (New York, 1974); Sayles, '*Modus tenendi parliamentum*: Irish or English?', in J. F. Lydon (ed.), *England and Ireland in the Later Middle Ages* (Dublin, 1981), pp. 122–52; H. G. Richardson and G. O. Sayles, *The English Parliament in the Middle Ages* (1981); M. V. Clarke, *Medieval Representation and Consent* (1936); M. Prestwich, 'The Modus tenendi parliamentum', *Parliamentary History*, 1 (1982): 221–5.

[20] Sayles, *Functions of the Medieval Parliament*, pp. 1–58; Richardson and Sayles, *English Parliament in the Middle Ages*, no. 26, pp. 1–49.

[21] Richardson and Sayles, *English Parliament in the Middle Ages*, no. 26, pp. 1–49. *Cf.* H. M. Jewel, 'The Value of *Fleta* as Evidence about Parliament', *EHR*, 107 (1992): 90–4.

[22] P. J. Holmes, 'The Great Council in the Reign of Henry VII', *EHR*, 101 (1986): 840–62; Holmes, 'The Last Tudor Great Councils', *HJ*, 33 (1990): 1–22; Guy, *Tudor England*, pp. 321–3.

[23] J. G. Edwards, 'The *Plena Potestas* of English Parliamentary Representatives', in E. B. Fryde and E. Miller (eds.), *Historical Studies of the English Parliament* (2 vols., Cambridge, 1970), i, pp. 136–49.

[24] G. L. Harriss, 'The Formation of Parliament, 1272–1377', in R. G. Davies and J. H. Denton (eds.), *The English Parliament in the Middle Ages* (Philadelphia, PA, 1981), pp. 29–60.

seek a parliament with free speech and free elections. They believed that 'reform' of the 'commonwealth' was the function of parliament, yet to structure their demands in this way was to formulate a programme of practical and ideological significance. Henry VIII defended his regime in a printed *Answer* which rebutted the Pilgrims' charges and argued that his privy council contained more nobles 'both of birth and condition' than had the council at the beginning of his reign.[25] The king's right to choose his own counsellors was flatly asserted, and Henry advised his critics to remember their duties as subjects and to 'meddle not with these and such like things as they have nothing to do withal'. He reiterated his council's right to act as an executive board, and dismissed as slanders claims that his counsellors were 'subverters' of the laws of God and the realm.

In the light of the Pilgrims' demands it seems paradoxical that the hereditary nobility had all along numbered among Henry VIII's councillors. The outbreak of the Pilgrimage positively enhanced their role since under the early Tudors the lords of the council were also the military élite. It is ironic that the Pilgrims complained of a council packed with 'villeins' at the very moment that Cromwell and his clients were forced temporarily onto the sidelines. But the issue is not, of course, whether the nobility were inadequately represented in the council; it is that the force of the Pilgrims' rhetoric dictated that it must be so. In the autumn of 1536 the regime and its opponents were speaking in different tongues. Within six months the rebels had been dispersed by a mixture of force and false promises. Henry VIII's victory retrieved his security and stifled the debate, but the Pilgrims' leaders had formulated a platform proleptic of that issued by Charles I's opponents in 1642, while the dissonance between the 'humanist-classical' and 'feudal-baronial' components of the metaphor of 'counsel' had momentarily been exposed.

I have so far isolated the most distinctive paradigms of counsel in order to describe them. But political debate is not conducted under laboratory conditions; most contemporaries spoke in polyglot form. Christopher St German's much-discussed parliamentary draft and Thomas Starkey's *Dialogue between Reginald Pole and Thomas Lupset* adopted this approach. So too did late-Elizabethan and Jacobean antiquarians and political commentators who aimed to assimilate the 'inspirational myth' of 'counsel' to practical programmes for limited, responsible, and (in an aristocratic sense) 'representative' government which sought to link the functions of the institutional council to those of parliament in an attempt to restrict the king and his advisers to a form of government that was limited by the authority of parliament and by the judgments of the common-law courts.

---

[25] *Answere made by the kynges hyghnes to the petitions of the rebelles in Yorkshire* (1536): STC 13077; D. S. Berkowitz (ed.), *Humanist Scholarship and Public Order* (Washington, DC, 1984), pp. 177–84; *State Papers during the Reign of Henry VIII*, i, pp. 506–10.

It was a parliamentary version of Fortescue's council of thirty-two which St German advocated. Called the 'great standing council', its members were to be chosen by Henry VIII but 'authorized' by parliament, and its functions were to advise the king and implement a series of religious and socio-economic reforms from the time the sitting parliament was dissolved until the conclusion of the ensuing one.[26] The relationship between the 'great standing council' and the king's privy council was not expressly defined. In a number of specified matters the 'great standing council' was to 'make ordinance' as seemed to it 'expedient', but in general its agenda was to be predetermined by statute, so that it might diagnose and redress grievances upon lines laid down in parliament.

By contrast, Starkey's *Dialogue* endowed a Venetian-style aristocratic council of fourteen with the 'authority of the whole parliament' when parliament was not in session. The fourteen comprised four peers, two bishops, four judges, and four of the wisest citizens of London, who were to 'represent the whole body of the people . . . to see unto the liberty of the whole body of the realm, and to resist all tyranny which by any manner may grow upon the whole commonalty'. They were to ensure that the king and his (privy) council did 'nothing again[st] the ordinance of his laws and good policy', and were given the authority to summon parliament in their own name 'whensoever to them it should seem necessary for the reformation of the whole state of the commonalty'. They were (in Starkey's words) to 'pass all acts of leagues, confederation, peace and war' and were empowered to 'elect and choose' the king's privy council, since 'this may in no case be committed to the arbitrament of the prince – to choose his own counsel – for that were . . . to commit all to his affects, liberty and rule'.[27]

Starkey's proposals revealed what might emerge from a mind able to fuse European traditions of secular and ecclesiastical conciliarism with the English baronial tradition. Had the *Dialogue* been printed, it would have propounded the most systematic programme for limited monarchy before the Nineteen Propositions of 1642.[28] In the context of the royal supremacy it was tantamount to a counter-theory, because the 'royalist' view of the Acts of Appeals and Supremacy was that *imperium* was vested in the ruler alone; parliament simply declared and enforced that pre-existent fact.[29] Unlike Henry VIII, Elizabeth

[26] John Guy, *Christopher St German on Chancery and Statute* (Selden Society, Supplementry Series, vol. 6, 1985), pp. 127–35.

[27] T. F. Mayer, *Thomas Starkey and the Commonweal: Humanist Politics and Religion in the Reign of Henry VIII* (Cambridge, 1989), pp. 44–5, 132–3; Thomas Starkey, *A Dialogue between Reginald Pole and Thomas Lupset*, ed. K. M. Burton (1948), pp. 155–6, 164–7.

[28] Cf. M. Mendle, *Dangerous Positions: Mixed Government, the Estates of the Realm, and the Making of the Answer to the Nineteen Propositions* (Tuscaloosa, AL, 1985), pp. 43–5.

[29] Guy, *Tudor England*, pp. 370–7; Guy, 'The Henrician Age', in Pocock (ed.), *Varieties of British Political Thought*; Guy, 'The Queen, the Court and the Ecclesiastical Polity', in John Guy (ed.), *The Reign of Elizabeth I: Court and Culture in the Last Decade* (Cambridge, forthcoming); Guy, 'The "Imperial Crown" and the Liberty of the Subject: the English Constitution from Magna Carta to the Bill of Rights', in B. Kunze and D. Brautigam (eds.), *Court, Country and Culture: Essays in Early Modern British History in Honor of Perez Zagorin* (Rochester, NY, 1992), pp. 65–87.

conceded that her power derived from 'the laws of God and this realm always annexed to the Crown of this realm', but even on this account parliament's role was auxiliary. In short, the theocratic potential of Tudor kingship should not be underestimated. Henry VIII's advisers could reinterpret Bracton to say that the king was 'under God but not the law, because the king makes the law'; and there were tense exchanges with the common lawyers and in parliament upon whether the king's *imperium* might override statute and common law.[30]

Yet, within the metaphor of 'counsel', where there is *imperium* there is also *consilium*; or as Bacon put it, sovereignty is 'married' to counsel. From St German's *Answer to a Letter* to Richard Hooker's *Of the Laws of Ecclesiastical Polity* the issue was debated with reference to the royal supremacy. The crux was the role of parliament, for the common lawyers maintained that the prerogatives of the Crown were the common-law rights of the ruler, and that the royal supremacy should be exercised only in parliament. Ecclesiastical conciliarism was invoked to advance the argument: the notion that the pope was an officer of the Church charged with specific duties and therefore responsible to the whole Christian people through their representative general council. When amalgamated with Fortescue's theory of a 'mixed' polity, the result was the thesis that the supreme head's *imperium* was limited by the 'assent of the people' in parliament. Moreover, the ruler was bound to resolve the Church's affairs in parliament, because law-making in both its temporal and spiritual dimensions required the 'consent of the whole realm'.[31]

It followed that parliament could be perceived more clearly than before as a locus of *consilium*. This was neither the Crown nor the privy council's standpoint, but the credibility of the interpretation was enhanced by a series of parliamentary debates from the 1560s to the 1580s upon religion, the succession to the throne, and the fate of Mary Queen of Scots. These debates were not spontaneous; they were largely orchestrated by the protestant majority in the privy council who sought to mobilize public opinion in order to push Elizabeth into accepting advice which she had previously rejected.[32] The privy council's motives were strategic, though in the face of Catholic conspiracy and the strength of Mary's claim to the throne, the protestant élite preferred the

---

[30] BL, Cotton MS. Cleopatra E. vi, fo. 28v. See Fox and Guy, *Reassessing the Henrician Age*, p. 159; Guy, 'The "Imperial Crown"' in Kunze and Brautigam (eds.), *Court, Country and Culture*, pp. 72–8.

[31] Christopher St German, *An Answer to a Letter* (1535), Sigs. G3–G6v; STC 21558.5 (discussed in John Guy, Ralph Keen *et al.* (eds.), *The Debellation of Salem and Bizance, Yale Edition of the Works of St Thomas More*, Vol. X (New Haven, CT, 1987 [1988]), Appendix C; W. Speed Hill *et al.* (eds.), *The Folger Library Edition of the Works of Richard Hooker* (5 vols., Cambridge, MA, 1977–90), iii, pp. 315–445.

[32] G. R. Elton, *The Parliament of England, 1558–1581* (Cambridge, 1986), pp. 350–79; Guy, *Tudor England*, pp. 322–5; M. A. R. Graves, *Elizabethan Parliaments, 1559–1601* (1987); Graves, *The Tudor Parliaments: Crown, Lords and Commons, 1485–1603* (1985); Graves, 'Thomas Norton the Parliament Man: An Elizabethan M.P., 1559–1581', *HJ*, 23 (1980): 17–35; Graves, 'The Management of the Elizabethan House of Commons: The Council's "Men of Business"', *Parliamentary History*, 2 (1983): 11–38.

option of limiting the powers of the Crown should Elizabeth unexpectedly die.[33]

When Elizabeth addressed parliament she stressed the limits of its authority to counsel a prince. She invoked 'humanist-classical' language to argue that she needed to be 'advised' on matters touching her Crown and state, thereby turning recognition of the need for 'counsel' into the excuse for rejecting parliament's advice.[34] To insulate her sovereignty she invoked the Tacitean concept of *arcana imperii* (the 'secrets of rule' or 'mysteries of state'). But *consilium* might be assimilated to parliament by a different route. Until the reign of Henry VIII the Crown continued to summon the Great Council of peers to discuss key political or diplomatic business.[35] The Great Council fell into abeyance after 1536 as the privy council assumed the leading executive and consultative role and as the court became the focus of politics. Yet the notion survived that the magnates should be consulted 'in' or 'out' of parliament.[36] Moreover, the late-Elizabethan antiquarians rediscovered that in the Middle Ages the distinction between parliament and the Great Council had been ambiguous. In Elizabeth's reign writs of summons to the House of Lords still invited peers to 'counsel' the queen on religion and the defence of the realm.[37]

Elizabeth and her privy council repudiated the demands of Paul and Peter Wentworth for full freedom of speech, meaning parliament's right to serve as a council of the realm. But parliamentary 'freedom of speech' had never been governed by the principle of *amicitia*, and no one had argued that parliament was a council from a 'humanist-classical' standpoint. The Wentworths were doubly tendentious, because even if 'humanist-classical' criteria were applied, the distinction was between counsel as a right and as a duty. Peter Wentworth exceeded all bounds when he asserted the right of members of parliament to counsel the queen 'by bill or speech' whether their advice was requested or not and regardless of the wishes of the queen, actual or presumed, as communicated by the Speaker and through the mouths of privy councillors.[38] It was

[33] In 1563 and 1584–85 the privy council sought to limit the powers of the Crown should Elizabeth die or be assassinated in order to exclude Mary Queen of Scots from the succession. Burghley's contingency plans provided that, in the event of the queen's death, the privy council and parliament should not fail to act despite the lapse of their authority. He variously envisaged a 'Council of State', Great Council or Grand Council which would form a provisional government in the absence of a ruler and which would summon a parliament in its own name in order to adjudicate the claims of candidates for the succession. Not only was this aristocratic republicanism *par excellence*, Burghley's schemes suggest a procedure strikingly similar to the events of 1688–89 following the flight of James II. PRO, SP 12/28/20; SP 12/176/22, 28–30; Henry E. Huntington Library, San Marino, California, Ellesmere MS. 1192. P. Collinson, 'The Monarchical Republic of Queen Elizabeth I', *Bulletin of the John Rylands University Library of Manchester*, 69 (1987): 394–424. *Cf.* G. Townsend (ed.), *The Acts and Monuments of John Foxe* (8 vols.; London, 1843–49), vi, p. 68.

[34] Mary T. Crane, '"Video et Taceo": Elizabeth I and the Rhetoric of Counsel', *Studies in English Literature*, 28 (1988): 1–15.

[35] Holmes, 'The Last Tudor Great Councils', pp. 1–22. See also H. Miller, *Henry VIII and the English Nobility* (Oxford, 1986), pp. 102–32.

[36] Guy, *Tudor England*, pp. 310, 321–3, 456–7; see above, n. 32.

[37] Graves, *Elizabethan Parliaments, 1559–1601*, p. 45.

[38] J. E. Neale, *Elizabeth I and her Parliaments* (2 vols., 1953–57; reprinted 1969), ii, pp. 155–6.

axiomatic even in the privy council that counselling was a duty and not a right.[39]

Sir Thomas Smith's analysis of the Elizabethan parliament is received as standard. The relevant chapters of *De republica anglorum* treated parliament strictly in terms of its authority to legislate.[40] Smith amply endorsed parliament's representative character: 'every Englishman is intended to be there present, either in person or by procuration and attorneys'.[41] But his argument was shaped to prove that there could be no appeal against an act of parliament in a court of law. He did briefly allude to 'consultation' meaning deliberation and debate, but this was in the context of legislative procedure: the manner and form whereby bills were discussed, if necessary amended, and finally approved in each of the two Houses before their presentation to the ruler on the last day of the session for the royal assent.

A residual notion of *consilium* may have been envisaged when Smith likened parliament's legislative competence to that of the Roman *comitia*.[42] Yet the key to his interpretation was his view of parliament as the king's 'highest court' (or *curia*).[43] Despite the traditional formula which summoned peers to attend the 'great counsel' of parliament, the nature and functions of parliament were (in Smith's opinion) curial because parliament acted as the ruler's legislative instrument of government. Smith echoed *Fleta* that in parliament 'the king in council holds his court', and on this reading parliament was virtually an expression of the royal prerogative which summoned and dissolved it. For, if the 'high court of Parliament' was the king's *curia*, then the underlying assumptions were feudal, but not contractual. They derived from the feudal lord's right to impose suit of court upon his vassals, and in those circumstances the only kind of parliament that could be imagined was one in which those who attended performed the vassal's duty to counsel the lord in his *curia* when their presence was required.

Smith was a civil and not a common lawyer. It might be said that he lacked the common lawyer's urge to assimilate the metaphor of 'counsel' to schemes for limited and responsible government. But John Hooker was also trained in the civil law, and his *Order and Usage of the Keeping of a Parliament in England* (1572) stressed that the ruler summoned parliament to seek 'the advice, counsel and assistance of his whole realm' as well as to legislate.[44] Hooker enumerated the 'weighty and great causes' upon which the ruler 'of necessity ought to have

---

[39] The closest that Elizabeth came to acknowledging that MPs were 'counsellors' was in 1593, when she told the Commons that 'common knights and burgesses of the House . . . [were] councillors but during the parliament' as opposed to members of the privy council who were always counsellors. J. Loach, *Parliament Under the Tudors* (Oxford, 1991), p. 155.

[40] M. Dewar (ed.), *De Republica Anglorum by Sir Thomas Smith* (Cambridge, 1982), pp. 78–85, 89.

[41] *Ibid.*, p. 79.   [42] *Ibid.*   [43] *Ibid.*, pp. 78, 88–9.

[44] Snow (ed.), *Parliament in Elizabethan England*, pp. 145–7. Fifteen years later Hooker incorporated a version of the *Order and Usage* into the Irish volume of the enlarged edition of Holinshed's *Chronicles of England . . . Ireland . . . Scotland* (STC 13569).

the advice and counsel of all the estates of his Realm'.[45] Moreover, these 'weighty and great causes' were the baronial *negotia regni* by another name. In effect Hooker updated the list of 'great affairs' contained in the fourteenth-century *Modus tenendi parliamentum*, which he translated and printed under the title *The Old and Ancient Order of Keeping of the Parliament in England*. Yet he stamped his personal seal on the list when, in the context of the royal supremacy, he assigned to parliament the responsibility for religious reform in language resonant of the puritan campaign to purify the English Church.[46]

By 1604, when the Society of Antiquaries met formally to debate the power and antiquity of parliament, it seemed that a posse of common lawyers, antiquarians, and parliament men were citing the *Modus tenendi parliamentum* (often inadvertently and usually without acknowledgement) to argue that the *negotia regni* were properly concluded in parliament.[47] Defining the conceptual basis of parliament, Sir John Dodderidge declared: 'Now for the nature of a Parliament, it is *consilium*, and it is *curia*.'[48] Elsewhere Sir Edward Coke asserted: 'The King of England is armed with divers Councels, one whereof is called *Commune Concilium*, and that is the Court of Parliament.'[49] The lawyers and antiquarians in their discourse tended to suppress the term *negotia regni* in favour of such superficially neutral language as *grandia regni* or the 'public business of the commonwealth'.[50] But the 'feudal-baronial' resonance was embedded. Furthermore, the elementary topoi of *consilium* might quite unintentionally reinforce the rhetoric of parliamentary privilege. When Dodderidge remarked that there was nowhere a greater 'and yet a more free council than this in our parliament in England', his words were open to more than one interpretation.[51] Even Bacon defined parliament as 'the great Council of the King, the great Council of the Kingdom, to advise his Majesty of those things of weight and difficulty which concern both the King and the kingdom'.[52]

Dodderidge took the view that the *grandia regni* had been settled in parliament since the reign of Henry I, an opinion shared by Arthur Agarde.[53] Francis Tate cautioned that the term 'parliament' was not found before the reign of Edward I, but then invoked hermeneutics to argue that the 'general assent of the

---

[45] Snow (ed.), *Parliament in Elizabethan England*, pp. 145–6.   [46] *Ibid.*, pp. 146–7.
[47] Thomas Hearne (ed.), *A Collection of Curious Discourses written by Eminent Antiquaries upon Several Heads in our English Antiquities* (2 vols., 1771), i, pp. 281–309.
[48] *Ibid.*, i, p. 289.
[49] Sir Edward Coke, *The Institutes of the Laws of England* (1669–84), i, Bk. 2, ch. 10, sect. 164. Cited by M. A. Judson, *The Crisis of the Constitution. An Essay in Constitutional and Political Thought in England, 1603–1645* (New York, reprinted 1976), p. 70.
[50] Hearne (ed.), *Collection of Curious Discourses*, i, pp. 287, 291. The concept of 'public' business came to prominence in the debates on the Petition of Right when members of the Commons repeatedly claimed that the 'illegal' acts committed by Charles I's regime required a 'public' remedy. See R. C. Johnson, M. F. Keeler, M. J. Cole, and W. B. Bidwell (eds.), *Proceedings in Parliament 1628* (6 vols., New Haven, CT, 1977–83).
[51] Hearne (ed.), *Collection of Curious Discourses*, i, p. 281.
[52] J. Spedding, *The Letters and Life of Francis Bacon* (7 vols., 1861–74), vi, p. 38 (cited by Judson, *Crisis of the Constitution*, p. 70).
[53] Hearne (ed.), *Collection of Curious Discourses*, i, pp. 287–8, 298.

realm to make ordinances and laws' was termed interchangeably in Latin *consilium, curia,* or *parliamentum.*[54] This interpretation had first been advanced by William Lambarde, who wrote: 'The general Assembly in Parliament is termed in our old Writs, *Commune Consilium Regni Angliae,* the Common Councell of the Realm of England, called together by the King, for advice in matters concerning the whole Realm.'[55] For one antiquarian the role of parliament was such that members sat as 'sworn counsellors to their king'.[56] Soon it was a platitude to observe that there had been an assembly of the estates (if not a parliament by name) since the reign of Edward the Confessor, when the English had met in assemblies *per concilium* to discuss public affairs and to conclude such weighty matters as foreign policy or war and peace.[57]

It is by now apparent that this chapter is an essay in intellectual and not political history. In anticipation of charges of 'Whiggishness' and reductionism in my treatment of parliament I should clarify three points. First, that when discussing the metaphor of 'counsel' and exploring its resonances I am basing my analysis upon the recorded utterances of contemporaries and not attempting to judge the accuracy of their opinions as statements of historical fact. Second, it is integral to my argument that the political landscape before and after the accession of Charles I was different and that it was, specifically, the advent of adversarial politics in 1640–42 which sparked the outbreak of Civil War. Third, it should be remembered that there was a case *for* the Crown as well as against it. The case for the Crown was not that the king had *imperium* and that there was no room for *consilium,* but that there already was *consilium* and that it was the king's prerogative to choose between its voices.

Debate upon the nature and shape of English political institutions intensified under the early Stuarts. Yet the opinion that James I conceived 'divine right' consistently in terms of absolutism is outmoded. Despite *The Trew Law of Free Monarchies* and *Basilikon Doron,* James by 1610 had publicly propounded a thesis of 'a mixed polity created by kings' which if it did not pass unchallenged by the common lawyers, stood closer to the assumptions of late-Elizabethan political thought than to those of the 1630s.[58] Although James invoked theocratic language in a variety of contexts, notably in defence of his ecclesiastical supremacy, 'absolutist' political doctrine did not seriously impinge upon English administration before the publication of the 'Arminian' defences of Charles I's fiscal expedients in 1627, when it was claimed that taxation or

[54] *Ibid.,* pp. 300–1.
[55] W. Lambarde, *Archeion,* p. 102 (cited by Judson, *Crisis of the Constitution,* p. 70).
[56] Hearne (ed.), *Collection of Curious Discourses,* i, p. 309.
[57] J. G. A. Pocock, *The Ancient Constitution and the Feudal Law* (Cambridge, 1957), pp. 30–55.
[58] Paul Christianson, 'Royal and Parliamentary Voices on the Ancient Constitution, c. 1604–1621', in Linda Levy Peck (ed.), *The Mental World of the Jacobean Court* (Cambridge, 1991), pp. 71–95. See also G. Burgess, 'Common Law and Political Theory in Early Stuart England', *Political Science,* 40 (1988): 4–17.

'tribute' was due to kings from their subjects by the law of God, nature and nations.[59]

It is true that Buckingham, by the early 1620s, had subverted the privy council's authority; the Jacobean religious consensus was also dissolving.[60] Yet whereas James was cosmopolitan and urbane, Charles I was obsessive and inflexible. His court was dominated by an inner clique, he dispensed patronage on ideological grounds, and he diminished the traditional emphasis on bilateral communications with the provinces.[61] His exclusivity was particularly evident in religious policy, where he stressed the visibility and catholicity of the English Church and treated Calvinism as doctrinally and politically subversive. He believed he could impose his view of the Church on England and Scotland by proclamation, which in Calvinist eyes was idolatry. His relations with parliament proved counterproductive, and in 1629 he signalled his intention to rule in non-parliamentary ways. It is often remarked that Charles sought 'new counsels' in place of old; in reality he doubted the value of counsel itself. He questioned its purpose and necessity. He disliked criticism except in the realm of poetry.[62] Moreover, he mistrusted his privy councillors, whom he told as early as 1627 that 'the question was of obeying the King, not of counselling'.[63]

His Personal Rule was successful only while Charles remained at peace. Defeat in the Bishops' Wars placed him firmly on the spot. When the Short Parliament failed in the spring of 1640, the Covenanters forded the Tweed and routed the English. At this moment twelve illustrious peers, each excluded from the privy council, united to petition Charles to summon a new parliament where 'evils' might be redressed and the 'authors and counsellors' of them brought to trial.[64] The language of the petition seemed dutiful but was deceptive. As Clarendon hinted in his *History of the Rebellion*, several signatories were in collusion with the Scots to whom they insinuated: '[The] common interest [is] one, the End is all one: a free Parliament to try all Offenders, and to settle Religion and Liberty.'[65]

---

[59] R. Cust, *The Forced Loan and English Politics 1626–1628* (Oxford, 1987), pp. 62–7.

[60] T. Cogswell, *The Blessed Revolution: English Politics and the Coming of War, 1621–1624* (Cambridge, 1989); N. Tyacke, *Anti-Calvinists: the Rise of English Arminianism, c. 1590–1640* (Oxford, 1987).

[61] L. J. Reeve, *Charles I and the Road to Personal Rule* (Cambridge, 1989).

[62] K. Sharpe, *Criticism and Compliment: the Politics of Literature in the England of Charles I* (Cambridge, 1987), pp. 292–8.

[63] Cust, *The Forced Loan and English Politics*, p. 82. See also P. Donald, *An Uncounselled King: Charles I and the Scottish Troubles, 1637–1641* (Cambridge, 1990).

[64] S. R. Gardiner (ed.), *The Constitutional Documents of the Puritan Revolution, 1625–1660* (third revised edn; Oxford, 1906), pp. 134–6; J. S. A. Adamson, 'The English Civil War of 1640', *Platt's Chronicle* (June 1989), pp. 53–67.

[65] J. Oldmixon, *The History of England during the Reigns of the Royal House of Stuart* (1730), pp. 142–3; Edward Hyde, Earl of Clarendon, *The History of the Rebellion and Civil Wars in England* (new edn, 2 vols., Oxford, 1840), i, p. 63; P. Donald, 'New Light on the Anglo-Scottish Contacts of 1640', *Historical Research*, 62 (1989): 221–9; Donald, *An Uncounselled King*, pp. 246–7; Adamson, 'The English Civil War of 1640', pp. 54–6. See also *Calendar of State Papers and Manuscripts, Relating to English Affairs ... in the Archives and Collections of Venice* (38 vols.,

Charles's response was to revive the Great Council of peers, which he summoned to York in the hope of financing a fresh campaign without calling a parliament. But his opponents outmanoeuvred him. Oliver St John, who acted as legal counsel to four of the twelve peers, had revisited the sources of the baronial tradition.[66] Not unlike Starkey in his *Dialogue between Pole and Lupset*, he had investigated the nobility's 'authority' to act in an emergency.[67] As the Venetian ambassador reported, if the king did not summon a parliament, the peers would do so in their own name.[68] Hence Charles called the Long Parliament so that 'the counsel [for doing so] might not seem to arise from them who were resolved to give it'.[69] The threats of the opposition peers and their collusion with the Scots had established the rules by which politics would be conducted. Yet, despite the advent of adversarial politics, it was some eighteen months before the parliamentary propagandists couched their case so exclusively in one rhetorical form that the Crown became obliged *per contra* to couch its reply largely in another. It was not until June 1642 that both Houses finally agreed upon, and circulated, manifestos which reified the 'feudal-baronial' paradigm of 'counsel' as an uncompromising political ideology.

The Nineteen Propositions were the parliamentary manifesto.[70] They demanded that all existing appointments to the privy council and great offices of court and state should be rescinded and new appointments made only with parliament's approval. If posts chanced to fall vacant in the intervals between parliament, they might be filled by the assent of a majority of the privy council, but all appointments were subject to parliamentary confirmation. As to the reconstructed privy council, it was to be limited to between fifteen and twenty-five members sworn by an oath approved in parliament. Its functions would be to advise the king and vet all his public acts. Quite specifically 'no public act concerning the affairs of the kingdom' was to be considered valid unless warranted 'by the advice and consent' of a majority of the privy council 'attested under their hands'.

The language of these demands was unmistakable:

That the great affairs of the kingdom may not be concluded or transacted by the advice of private men, or by any unknown or unsworn councillors, but that such matters as concern the public, and are proper for the High Court of Parliament, which is your Majesty's great and supreme council, may be debated, resolved and transacted only in

---

1864–1947), xxv (1640–42), no. 112 (p. 79). My grateful thanks to Peter Donald for the reference to Oldmixon.

66 Conrad Russell, *The Causes of the English Civil War* (Oxford, 1990), p. 159; Adamson, 'The English Civil War of 1640', p. 58.

67 Russell, *Causes of the English Civil War*, p. 159; Adamson, 'The English Civil War of 1640', p. 58; Starkey, *Dialogue between Pole and Lupset*, pp. 155–6, 165.

68 *Calendar of State Papers . . . Venice*, xxv (1640–2), no. 109 (p. 77); Adamson, 'The English Civil War of 1640', p. 63.

69 Clarendon, *History of the Rebellion*, i, p. 66.

70 Gardiner (ed.), *Constitutional Documents of the Puritan Revolution*, pp. 249–54; see also W. H. Coates, A. S. Young, and V. F. Snow (eds.), *The Private Journals of the Long Parliament, 3 January to 5 March 1642* (New Haven, CT, 1982), pp. 543–50.

Parliament, and not elsewhere . . . and such other matters of state as are proper for your Majesty's Privy Council shall be debated and concluded by such of the nobility and others as shall, from time to time, be chosen for that place, by approbation of both Houses of Parliament.[71]

A few days later the Defence of the Militia Ordinance asserted:

The High Court of Parliament is not only a court of judicature, enabled by the laws to adjudge and determine the rights and liberties of the kingdom . . . it is likewise a council, to provide for the necessities, prevent the imminent dangers, and preserve the public peace and safety of the kingdom, and to declare the King's pleasure in those things as are requisite thereunto . . .[72]

These passages reveal the extent of the parliamentary debt to feudal-baronial vocabulary. The topoi of baronial rhetoric were that the 'great affairs' of the kingdom should be concluded by 'common counsel and assent'; that parliament was the king's 'great counsel'; that the king's (privy) councillors should be appointed in parliament and thereafter advise the king and vet all his public acts; and that councillors and ministers should be bound by oaths in parliament. In the summer of 1642 the reverberations were deafening, and in his published *Answer to the Nineteen Propositions* Charles I sharply protested that his opponents' utterances possessed 'a greater latitude of signification' than they ostensibly seemed to have, and that demands couched in such terms were tantamount to the deposition of kings.

When, therefore, Sir John Culpeper and Viscount Falkland prepared Charles's *Answer to the Nineteen Propositions*, it was largely to humanist-classical rhetoric that they appealed.[73] The relevant passage of the *Answer* declared:

We shall ever in these things, which are trusted wholly to us by the Law, not decline to hearken to the Advice of our Great Council, and shall choose to hear willingly the free debates of our Privy Council . . . but we will retain our Power, of admitting no more to any Council than the Nature of the Business requires, and of discoursing with whom we please, of what we please, and informing our Understanding by Debate with any Persons, who may be well able to inform and advise us in some Particulars . . . And though we shall . . . always weigh the Advices both of our Great and Privy Council, yet we shall also look upon their Advices as Advices, not as Commands or Impositions; upon them as our Counsellors, not as our Tutors and Guardians, and upon our self as their King, not as their Pupil or Ward.[74]

The king's position was emphatic. It was incumbent upon him to take counsel, but 'counselling' was a duty and not a right. He would listen willingly to the advice of his Privy Council, freely given. Neither would he decline to listen to his 'Great Council', whatever he meant by that term. As to parliament itself, the king was as much a part of it as the two Houses, and therefore he had

[71] Gardiner (ed.), *Constitutional Documents of the Puritan Revolution*, pp. 250–1.
[72] *Ibid.*, pp. 256–7.
[73] J. Rushworth (ed.), *Historical Collections* (8 vols., 1721), iv, pp. 725–35.   [74] *Ibid.*, p. 729.

the right to make answer freely to bills or other propositions. His answer could not be free unless he were permitted to take advice as his conscience dictated. Like Henry VIII, Charles flatly asserted his prerogative to choose his own councillors and to accept or reject their advice. It was his right to seek the advice of sworn or unsworn counsellors, to admit whomsoever he pleased to his counsels, and to determine the size and the agenda of his privy council. The *Answer to the Nineteen Propositions* made a permanent contribution to the theory of the 'mixed' constitution by conceding that the king was merely one of the three estates in parliament. But on the issue of counsel, Charles refused to budge. The 'newfangled' counsellors whom parliament proposed to approve and bind on oath to advise him and vet all his public acts were a blatant infringement of his regality.

From this impasse there was no retreat. Like Henry VIII and the leaders of the Pilgrimage of Grace, Charles I and his opponents were engaged in a dialogue of the deaf. Yet, whereas Henry VIII had retained the support of England's social leaders, Charles I's military élite were divided. No longer could the vocabulary of 'counsel' furnish a common fund of language for the orderly conduct of politics. The rise of adversarial politics in 1640–42 had caused the component elements of this rhetoric to disengage. The clash between the two conflicting ideologies was thereafter referred to the arbitrament of war.

My theme has been the rhetoric of 'counsel' and not 'the outbreak of the Civil War'. An account of the latter would have required a wide-ranging discussion of the Petition of Right, ship money, the Laudian canons of 1640, and parliament's insistence in the spring of 1642 that it should have control over the militia and of any expeditionary force raised to crush the Irish Rebellion of 1641. Nor is it my intention to suggest that the Civil War diminished the importance of consultation. It was in the public discourse that a significant change occurred. From the age of Fortescue until 1640 the ideal of 'good counsel' inspired a tradition which aimed to connect virtue and civic duty with political liberty. This tradition had a Stoic slant which did not pass unnoticed. In his *Utopia* Thomas More had offered a critique as well as an endorsement of it. His genius was his ability to debate both sides of the question, and through the voice of Hythlodaeus he gave examples to show that 'good counsel' was ignored by rulers while flattery and evil counsel were rewarded.[75] Again, the institutions of the Utopian commonwealth allotted only a minor role to 'counselling'. It was less the 'counsel' of senate and people which guaranteed the public good than a rule of life which mitigated the human element and thereby reduced the risks of evil and corruption. The values and institutions of Utopia *by themselves* defined the path to virtue.[76] More's pessimism echoed that of the Parisian conciliarist Jean

---

[75] E. Surtz and J. H. Hexter (eds.), *The Complete Works of St. Thomas More*, Vol. IV: *Utopia* (New Haven, CT, 1965; revised edn, reprinted 1979), pp. 86–102.
[76] *Ibid.*, pp. 122–84.

Gerson, who had attempted to close the loophole in conciliar theory by insisting that rulers must actually act upon their counsellors' advice.[77]

By contrast, the parliamentary campaign in the 1640s to achieve total domination of the king's counsels raised the spectre of bicameral parliamentary absolutism.[78] Whereas until 1641–42 the public discourse concentrated not on who should rule, but on how political institutions might best be organized to guard the state against tyranny, thereafter the question became 'Who was the rightful possessor of power?'

The new discourse was precipitated by the old, because the parliamentary campaign was founded on the premise that the king had been seduced by 'evil counsellors', had succumbed to incapacity, and that parliament in its role as the 'Great Council' must therefore act to secure the safety of the king and the kingdom. From this it was only a short step to the thesis that parliament (or more accurately the two Houses) was the supreme executive council whose ordinances were more obligatory than the personal acts or resolutions of the king. That was the thesis triggered by the clash over the militia, and thereafter the language of liberty and limited government was increasingly appropriated by 'constitutional royalists' and the 'country' opposition, and by the more moderate Levellers.[79]

Finally, the moment arrived at which the parliamentary attacks on royal prerogative were perceived as having become the prelude to more general attacks on subjects' liberties and property rights. The events of the Civil War and Interregnum precipitated a shift in the language of political thought whereby a lexicon of rights and interests was recognized as more relevant to the discussion of liberty and authority than the traditional vocabulary of 'counsel'. The leap could then be made to the distinctive paradigms of Hobbes and Harrington, which measured political liberty against the extent of individual rights and transmuted parliament into an assembly of freeholders' representatives. That transition was accomplished in the 1650s, whereupon the rhetoric of 'counsel' was redundant.

---

[77] J. H. Burns (ed.), *The Cambridge History of Medieval Political Thought, c. 350–c. 1450* (Cambridge, 1988), p. 502.
[78] M. Mendle, 'The Ship Money Case, *The Case of Shipmony*, and the Development of Henry Parker's Parliamentary Absolutism', *HJ*, 32 (1989): 513–36.
[79] *Ibid.*

Index

Lightning Source UK Ltd.
Milton Keynes UK
26 September 2009

144148UK00001B/75/A

9 780521 520140